From Wannsee to Storrs

A Perpetual Optimist's Journey

Curt Frederic Beck

1st Edition – March 31, 2018
ISBN 978-0-9891994-6-9

Cover Photos:

Home at Robert Strasse No. 9, Berlin-Wannsee
Mother in our window
Curt at 5 years old in grandfathers hired automobile
Lunch in our garden

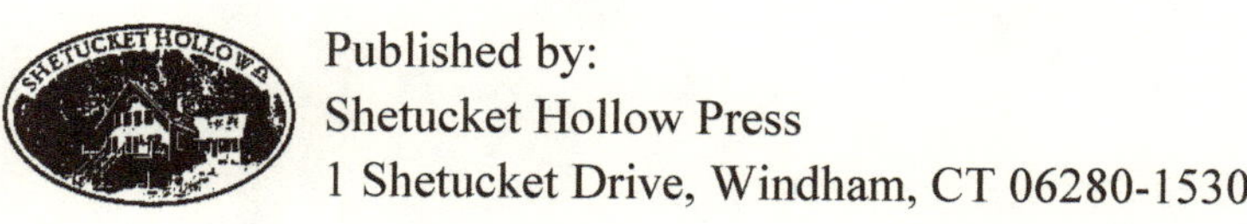

Published by:
Shetucket Hollow Press
1 Shetucket Drive, Windham, CT 06280-1530

Contents

Introduction

I grew up in a very peaceful, beautiful, interesting world. My large bedroom occupied almost half of the second floor of our modest but comfortable ivy overgrown house in Berlin-Wannsee. From my window I could check on what was going on outside. I enjoyed watching little chestnuts grow into tall trees much faster than I reached the height of grown-ups. I loved the school in Zehlendorf that I entered when I turned six. Taking the suburban train with my parents to Sächsische Strasse 73 where my grandparents lived in the center of Berlin, close to the Zoo and the classy Kurfürsten Damm was always a great event. Adolf Hitler closed this initial chapter of my life on January 30, 1933, when I was nine.

A few months later in September I found myself in Prague, Czechoslovakia, in an entirely new environment. It had taken us several months to get there because we had stopped in Marienbad to help us adjust to living in a different country. In Prague there was no big garden, just a little plot. I managed to plant a few flowers among big rocks that I had to dig up and move. There were 23 trolley lines in Prague, but no subway nor suburban trains. I managed to explore most of the new city by myself. Relocated, I created a new world that after a couple of years made me feel comfortable. I attended a French high school, adding French and Czech to the German, my mother and father spoke. I also learned to admire my new Czech neighbors with their different culture and interesting history.

Alas again this was not to last. At 14, I crossed the Atlantic, passed the Statue of Liberty, landed in Hoboken and discovered America. I had to learn my fourth language. Two years later, I ended up a freshman at Cornell in Ithaca, far above Cayuga's waters. It was a long bus ride from New York City. I was now not far from James Fennimore Cooper's Indian country that I had read about in Prague. In the thirties, distances had not yet shrunk and I felt that my previous life had occurred on a different planet.

At Cornell, I not only learned things others had decided were important for me to know but it also gave me an opportunity to reflect on my eventful journey from Wannsee to Ithaca, from a collapsing idyll to a happy hang-out, far from the approaching storm. Having watched the world around me unravel, I wanted to know why things went so wrong in the 1930s. That desire motivated my undergraduate and graduate education.

After becoming a U.S. citizen in August 1946, I was no longer an outsider; I could now participate in what was going on. For 45 years, I taught at UCONN. I hoped to develop an interest and some understanding among my students about world events, so that they would help the United States avoid the disasters of my childhood. I also sought to influence the direction of foreign policy. I tried to do that as a research analyst in the State Department in the early fifties. Realizing that political forces at home limit the actions taken by the U.S. government, I returned to Connecticut and got involved in local and state politics. I helped start the career of a very influential state legislator, my wife Audrey. I learned that politics could get complicated at every level, especially in Mansfield. I was not prepared for the intensity of conflicts at the University level. As I belatedly grasped what was going on, I started to enjoy some of it. It was possible to improve the quality of education and perhaps direct some students to improve our part of the world.

My garden and the outer world on two continents preoccupied me. A close-knit family held it all together. I took it for granted until the stress of finding a niche in the new world led to my father's untimely death in Little Rock, Arkansas. Ending up in Little Rock was further away from Plzeň, Czechoslovakia, then he possibly could have imagined when he was a youngster. Following my father's death at the age of 63, my 50 year old mother embarked on her own impressive career as a scholar, history professor and traveler. A year later I married Audrey an outstanding student in my class. Soon a son and daughter made it a family of four. Complications arose. Critical issues of divorce, remarriage and my daughter's mental illness forced me to add family and mental health issues to my preoccupation with local, national and world affairs.

Althea whom I married in1980 helped me deal with my daughter's illness. She also introduced me to America's Northwest, the region where she had spent her youth. Together we visited the places of her and my youth and then covered some of the rest of Europe, including countries that continue to create problems in our foreign policy. Unfortunately our life of adventure was cut short by Althea's fatal bout with cancer.

Introduction

In Mansfield, I live among trees, rocks, flowers and bushes that the deer love to devour in winter. Raking leaves, mowing the lawn and splitting wood reminds me of my early years in my Wannsee Garden of Eden. I share my Mansfield home, my new Eden, with Ina Ruth who brings me joy and happiness. At this late stage in my life, I felt compelled to explore and reexamine the many fascinating aspects of the journey. As I bring my story to a close I have the very uncomfortable feeling that some of the popular forces that enabled Hitler and Mussolini to dominate and destroy much of our civilization in the 1930's are stirring again. I hope that this is only a hiccup and not an earthquake.

Storrs, Connecticut
January 2018

I am very grateful for the help Cathy Cementina and Diana Perkins gave me in preparing my Memoir for publication.

Curt Beck

Part I - Growing Up

Chapter 1
Early Memories

Our modest house surrounded by a well kept lawn and fruit bearing bushes located in the Berlin suburb of Wannsee was my Garden of Eden. That is where I grew up and ran around protected by a fence that separated me from the world beyond. That is where grandparents Willy and Clara visited us regularly. It took them less than half an hour by train to get to our house from the center of Berlin, their home. Our house on Robertstrasse 9, was on a street dead ending on Wannsee Lake, a part of the much- traveled Havel waterway. I loved to walk to the lookout on the lake and watch the rowboats attached to a short pier bouncing gently in the mostly calm lake. Not very far away, across the bay, was a public beach, very busy on weekends, but otherwise a destination to which my mother promised to take me. A promise seldom kept. The beach was too noisy and crowded, she explained.

My father, not a very practical person, managed to mow our lawn occasionally with a hand-powered lawn mower. There were rows of bushes bearing my favorite berries: gooseberries, Johannisbeeren (red currants) and Brombeeren (blackberries). Strawberries were the easiest to pick, a habit I still continue to practice each June in my nineties.

Our ivy covered two-story wood constructed house had an open porch, my favorite entrance. That porch served as the center for our summer activities. There we ate our mid-day dinners during the five or six weeks in July and August, the only months the sun managed to warm us up in northern Europe.

My father, mother, our maid Trudy and I lived in this paradise for most of my first nine years. While I do not remember the beginning, I do recall the stories my parents told about events preceding my arrival in Wannsee. In the fall of 1922 Max[imilian], a scholar with a lot of free time encountered my future mother in the English Garden, a park bordering the University of Munich. She attended lectures at the University of Münich where she pretended to study medicine. Something about my mother appealed to him as he watched her sitting on a bench writing a letter. He patiently waited for her pen to run dry. He was disappointed as he told me that story that I did not share his excitement about waiting so long before finally accosting her. What took him so long to talk to her? After all, she was my mother. Big deal!

When he got back to his nearby apartment he immediately sat down and wrote a letter addressed to Ann which she kept and which I discovered among her possessions after her death in 2002. He wrote "Do not be angry if after such a short acquaintance I dare to ask you to be my companion this evening. I shall wait for you in front of your house at a quarter after seven. If you respond to my request, I shall consider this as proof of your self-confidence. Don't worry about the unconventional nature of our encounter. Some people get to know each other outside customary conventions. What do I want? Nothing else, than to get to know a young girl who is not below my level and who pleases me." While in the park she had apparently divulged her address.

My father loved to talk about his first encounter with my mother and her positive response. Less than a year later on April 17, 1923, he married her in Berlin where she had lived with her parents for more than twenty years. Nine and a half months later, on February 4, 1924, I emerged as a Berliner.

Whenever I interrupted my parents while they were busy doing something important and were not particularly interested in what I considered significant, they told the same story that had left a deep impression on them in their first idyllic year that they shared with me in Breitbrunn about an hour from Munich. There they had rented a small apartment in a house overlooking the Ammersee. My father was busy thinking deep thoughts about the nature and value of existence, the topic of his Ph.D. thesis. My mother entertained him and cared for me. In proper German fashion, I was fed at regular intervals in accordance with a strict schedule. I did not always abide by the schedule and voiced my displeasure at the top of my lungs. The landlord heard me and yelled through the wall, "Gehen sie zum Kind!" (Pay attention to your child)

Grandfather Willy was a practical person. Far away in Berlin he recognized there was a problem. My mother, his youngest daughter, was the first to have given him a grandchild. He wanted to make sure that grandchild would live a reasonably normal existence. Spending one's life admiring the Ammersee and writing down one's thoughts about Greek philosophers, visiting the Pinakothek, Munich's famous museum, meeting fellow University friends was fine, but primitive accommodations in a summer resort were not exactly what my grandfather had in mind for his only grandchild. As the major financial source of my parents' income, his "advice" to move to Berlin grew ever more insistent and sometime in the second year of my existence, we moved there.

How did they locate my Garden of Eden in Wannsee? Obviously, my mother had no problem returning to the city where she had grown up after attending universities in Berlin, Heidelberg and Munich, a normal routine for German students. She had studied medicine hoping to become a doctor. My father was the problem: His move from provincial Plzeň in Austria-Hungary to Munich in the kingdom of Bavaria in 1909, when he was 22 years old, was traumatic. It took him some time to grow roots in Bavaria. Eventually he succeeded and was reluctant to shift location again. Disdain by Bavarians and Austrians of Prussian culture contributed to his reluctance to move.

Grandfather Willy was a problem solver. He convinced my father that there were lakes and forests in Prussia, not far from Berlin. Wannsee was as attractive a lake as the Ammersee in Bavaria, a perfect location for contemplating the purpose of existence. Suburban trains connected it with the Kurfürsten Damm, the cultural center in Berlin. It would be easy to mix with intellectuals in Berlin. Hitler's failed Beerhall Putsch in November 1923 probably helped convince my father that Munich was not a particularly friendly environment in which to pursue his philosophical writings. My father was won over and agreed to move.

There was one major problem: Wannsee's charm and lack of development limited the availability of affordable housing. There were mansions and fancy villas, not exactly appropriate for a scholar like my father, and his young wife with no income. Grandfather Willy, first a banker in Braunschweig, then co-owner with his brother-in-law Norbert Levy of a metal processing company (*Montangeselschaft*) in Berlin knew someone who had lost his fortune in the 1923 monster inflation, but still owned a small comfortable house in Wannsee. He made the house available to us. I never learned who exactly owned the house. Grandfather handled this and other practical matters because my father, the philosopher, could not be bothered with mundane financial details. While I neither knew, cared, nor understood whether we owned or rented our house, I do remember being a little uncomfortable when adults discussed that a rich man, Schlesinger, owned the huge house across the street. Nobody ever comforted me that we owned our house. We just lived there. That was one small weed in my Garden of Eden.

It was also quite lonely, an only child, a typical German post-war condition. There were no playmates. Occasionally my mother would join another mother in the neighborhood who had a daughter roughly my age, and we would go to a nearby beach where Erika and I were permitted to wade in the ice-cold water. On one occasion, it was warm. I remember that day well. Take your clothes off! Our mothers suggested. Enjoy the sun and water! Only five at the time, Erika and I looked at each other in astonishment. Naked, we went into the water. All I carry away from that experience is a vague feeling of discovery and discomfort. We were lucky not to have encountered any snakes that might have lurked in my Garden of Eden.

***

My parents felt my boredom and tried to keep me busy. Let's go for a walk! The German *spaziergehen* implies much more. It is a task, albeit a pleasant one, but not an escape from work. By the time my memory clicks in, I must have been taken on all the possible walks in Wannsee and neighboring Nikolassee so many times that there was nothing exciting left to explore. My father wanted me to come along and see *Das Grosse Fenster*, the Big Window, his favorite spot in the Grűnewald, the large forest park that separated Wannsee from Berlin. I had to bring up the rear, as my mother and father happily marched through the woods, discussing this and that, occasionally pointing to some tree that had caught their special attention. Boring, I thought. If I had expressed that thought aloud, I would have gotten another lecture about the beauty of nature. Finally, we came to the destination: It was no different from the rest of the forest, except that from a hilly spot one could see the Havel, the river that connected the Wannsee with the Spree and other rivers in the Berlin region.

There was one walk I did like. After riding the bus to a stop not far from the *Glienicke* Bridge, near Potsdam, we walked some distance through a forest. This time there was a real destination: *Nikolskő*, a restaurant, which had wonderful deserts. From the restaurant's patio, one could see the Havel River. Closer was the Pfauen Insel, an island reached by a three-minute ferry ride. There the peacocks roamed freely, spreading their colorful plumage. That impressed me. Eating a strawberry tart and then chasing exotic peacocks, justified the long walk. I could not have imagined then, that revisiting this same area thirty five years later, patrol boats searching for freedom-seeking East Germans, had joined the peacocks as the main attraction.

I must have known that there was a mysterious and exciting world beyond Wannsee. Often my parents turned my care over to Trudy and left after an early evening meal for the Romanisches Kaffee near the Kurfürsten Damm and the Zoo, which was also the name of the suburban train station, to meet fellow ^pintellectuals, writers, artists, musicians. My mother told me decades later that initially my father went there alone, but as soon as I was older, she insisted on tagging along. I realized only much later that these Kaffee klatches played a significant role not only in my father's intellectual life but also in that of many Berliners in the Weimar Germany. Sometimes my father would park my mother at my grandparents who lived in Wilmersdorf on Sächsische Strasse #73, a couple of blocks from the Kurfürstendamm. Most of the time she participated. On many Sundays, the Kaffee friends were invited to our house in Wannsee and spirited conversations occurred on our porch which I remember trying to interrupt to get more attention.

I have mixed memories of my parents' frequent nightly absences. Perhaps I envied their fun, if that is, what it was. A stronger feeling was unhappiness to be left alone with Trudi, the maid, who took care of the house and me. She always wanted me to go to sleep early so that she could do her thing. I invented countless excuses to force her to read to me and otherwise entertain me. Once she tried to get even with me. If you want something, come help me take my bath. She gave me a brush and had me rub her back while sitting stark naked in the bathtub. That did it. I left her alone after that embarrassing punishment.

***

As long as I can remember, April 17 was a special day. It was my parents wedding anniversary. Each year we celebrated that day almost as much as my birthday and the birthdays of my parents. I subconsciously connected it with trees budding and shedding their winter barrenness. On that day, my parents appeared to me to be specially excited and talkative. This was many years before I started counting the months to discover that February 4, 1924, my birthday, was nine and a half months after they got married.

Flowers appeared in our house, not a common occurrence, since my parents did not indulge in buying cut flowers. Mostly we had to wait until the flowers in our garden were ready to be cut. In Berlin, this did not occur until May. In the evenings, on the 17th, my parents would entertain friends my mother had known going back to her school days. After going to bed, the noise level in the living room rose. As I got older, I speculated my parents and their friends must have reminisced about the wonderful years that made April 17, 1923, possible.

My father was thirteen and a half years older than my mother. This meant that my mother was much less sedentary and more active than my father. She played with me outdoors, while he told me stories and took me on walks. I was aware of the age difference. I was told this was a good thing: It takes years to earn a Ph.D. and only then, is one ready to marry and care for a child. I took that lesson to heart.

Even more important was the geographical divide my parents had to overcome before they could marry. My father after spending the first twenty years of his life in Plzeň, Bohemia, best known for its dark beer, had ventured forth to study in Munich, the seat of the King of Bavaria, a subservient but proud entity within the realm of the Kaiser's Reich. My mother, born in Braunschweig, had grown up in Berlin, the Prussian capital of Kaiser Wilhelm's German empire. I was told many stories of how reluctant my father had been to abandon Munich. Berlin did not meet his ideal as a center of civilization. My mother, on the other hand, considered Munich only a quaint place to visit and write home about. They compromised by starting their marriage in Breitbrunn, a small village on the scenic Ammersee in the foothills of the Bavarian Alps. It was probably there that I was conceived and after a detour to Berlin-Charlottenburg for birth in a modern hospital, spent the first year of my life absorbing the Bavarian environment.

That geographical divide affected me in my entire childhood. There was a never-ending discussion about North German versus Bohemian-Bavarian cooking. I benefited from all this: soups, vegetables and Königsberger Klops were Prussian and healthy. Knödel, Strudel and other desserts were Bohemian, they were delicious and therefore had to be avoided. If I enjoyed them too much, my mother was careful to discourage me from over-indulging. My father winked at me, silently egging me on.

The geographical divide also had cultural and religious aspects. While both sets of grandparents were Jewish, my maternal grandfather was a totally assimilated German Jew whose religion was limited to making financial contributions to his synagogue. He rarely attended religious services. My Plzeň grandfather not only belonged to his synagogue but attended it regularly. It was the center of his social life.

While my parents lived in the new liberated post-World War I intellectual world, they had not cut their ties to the past completely. They had a traditional marriage ceremony. This meant involving both sets of parents. Many decades after my father's death, my mother in her eighties, discussing her wedding, expressed her admiration for her father's ability to bridge the cultural divide that separated my paternal family's traditional Jewish traditions from her own secular upbringing. My mother's father invited my paternal father to Dresden, located between Berlin and Plzeň, to discuss the marriage. It was the first time my paternal grandfather had left his native Bohemia. To my parents' great surprise, the two grandfathers got along very well and quickly agreed on the religious format of the wedding. Apparently, both grandfathers had a common desire to get their children married and off their hands.

What about the wedding on the 17th? When I asked my mother about it, she answered, "the wedding went without a hitch and the Plzeň grandparents created no problem". Apparently, it went so well, that she seemed surprised that I even asked. The wedding formalized a relationship that had begun on that bench in the English Garden. When my parents had their silver wedding anniversary, I had my first regular job at UCONN's Fort Trumbull Branch and was able to afford a present: some fancy dining room ware that I mailed to them in Illinois where my father had one of his temporary faculty appointments, a far cry from the idyllic future contemplated in Munich or Berlin.

Two years later, on their 27th anniversary, I sent them my usual good wishes, this time from Storrs. They celebrated the anniversary in a temporary building of the start-up Central College in North Little Rock, Arkansas. I do not know whether my letter arrived in time. On April 20 in the evening, as my 63-year-old father was shaving, he had a fatal stroke.

***

My father dominated my Wannsee paradise. He was always at home, because that is where he wrote his books, articles and published his *Philosophische Hefte*. His room was on the ground floor at the opposite end of the house from mine on the second floor. He sat at his desk, thought and wrote. I learned at a very early age not to make any noise within his ear shot.

He spent every morning and most afternoons writing. I showed far less interest in his writings on philosophy than he would have liked. When I did ask what he was doing, he said that he was thinking about the purpose of life, its value, the soul and the nature of being. Those topics were not sufficiently tangible for me to comprehend. They failed to arouse my interest. Not until I was much older did I realize that not every youngster was privileged to have a father who tried to give correct answers to all questions. When he had no answer, he would point to a twenty six volume encyclopedia on the bottom shelf of his study. This was my preparation for life in academia.

When I was eleven a kid in my Prague school asked what my father's occupation was. I answered he was a philosopher. Next day the kid said his father told him that my father had to do something real because philosophy was just a degree. So what was my father really doing? I asked my father. Tell him that I spend my days lying on the couch and thinking deep thoughts. Laughter greeted this response the next day. It was not easy to be a philosopher's son.

Actually, my father did not spend much time on the couch. Very often, he went on walks in the woods, not far from our house, where he could think without being disturbed by the inevitable interruptions at home. His favored path he called the *Philosophenweg* (Philosopher's Trail). There he usually spent a couple of hours, and on his return, wrote down the ideas that had somehow occurred to him as he contemplated the pine trees.

In his forties, my father was not that sedentary. He sawed shelves for a bookcase that he fastened to the wall. This needed to be done. The books had piled up and required space. The shelves he built stretched from the floor to the ceiling on three walls of his study. He also mowed the lawn regularly, relying on the strength of his legs and arm muscles. In those days, lawn mowers were not machine driven. The age of horse drawn farm vehicles had barely passed. He was also practical. When the septic tank in the garden began to fail, he managed to lift up the cover. With a long-handled ladle, he scooped up unmentionable stuff and spread it on our vegetable garden as fertilizer. Voices from a large ugly building, the home of the *Ruderclub,* a rowing club situated between our house and the lake, yelled that the spreading odor was disgusting and urged my father to go to hell and take the smell with him.

All these practical activities were interludes from his preoccupation searching for answers to some fundamental issues concerning the nature and purpose of existence. He wrote about and argued with the writings of Heidegger, Husserl, Phänder and many contemporary and past German philosophers and their Greek, medieval and early modern predecessors. When the pages of his manuscript were a foot high, he would hand them to my mother who had the formidable task of transforming his great ideas from illegible handwriting into a typewritten manuscript that would enable others to comprehend his thoughts. That was not an easy task because my mother was not a professional typist. She had a typewriter that seemed huge when I was five or six years old. She had never taken any typing lessons and picked and pecked the letters on the machine on a hit or miss basis. She spent as much time erasing old errors as typing new ones. That is why it is very hard for me to understand how she could have typed countless articles, several books and an unlimited number of letters to important people on her typewriter.

His intensive preoccupation with writing was interrupted by frequent discussions with fellow intellectuals on weekday evenings at the Romanische Kaffee and other cafes along the centrally located Kurfürstendamm. On Sundays, philosophers, writers and artists came to our house in Wannsee. I was the only child present at those social occasions. My mother served food, carefully prepared by our maid. It was appreciated by all, including me. The adults always argued about this or that which was way beyond my scope of comprehension. That changed rather quickly: Beginning in 1930, I became aware of the growing intensity with which names like Hindenburg, Hitler, Gőring, Gőbbels, Schleicher, Nazis, Communists, were thrown around. It was then that I also felt that our hitherto carefree existence was rapidly being replaced by worries that others might hear what was being discussed. Voices were lowered and doors were closed. Once I overheard the adults talk about somebody having disappeared in *Nacht und Nebel*, [night and fog]. That was the first time I heard the word concentration camp. It was in the spring of 1933 and referred to a political detention camp near Berlin.

Among our frequent guests were some who aroused my interest and who stick in my memory because they paid special attention to me in spite of my young age. One, Flachsländer, an artist, who worked in the Ullstein publishing firm, presented me with a book that he had put together just for me It consisted of a modernistic collage of pictures cut out of newspapers. It typified the iconoclastic Weimar style, way ahead of the culture elsewhere. It would not at all be out of place in the U.S., seventy years later. Afra Geiger, a sculptor's daughter and fellow philosophy student from my father's days in Munich, fascinated me. Although she talked about topics that were beyond my horizon, she had a certain charm that helped me overcome our enormous difference in age and led her to give me some serious political advice. Afra fled to Holland before becoming a victim of the Holocaust. There was also Kohnke, a pianist and conductor, Mittenzweig, a journalist who according to my mother's recollection, had access to military circles. Then there was Herbert Marcuse, a fellow philosopher, whose articles my father published in the Philosphische Hefte. He lived in Freiburg but visited us occasionally. His wife Sophie (Wertheimer) was one of my mother's friends, going back to grammar school, where Sophie's sister was a schoolmate. Even back in the late twenties and early thirties, Herbert had strong controversial opinions, a harbinger of the role he was to play in the U.S. some thirty years later.

Only after leaving Berlin, did I learn that my father's work at home, his writings and his publishing the *Philosophische Hefte,* were intended to help him become a Philosophy Professor at a university in Germany. He had met the academic requirements, had excellent connections, but missed one essential prerequisite: German citizenship. That was not an easy quest. He had lived in Germany since 1909 and had applied for German citizenship after marrying my mother in 1923 but meeting German citizenship requirements was a complicated process. He dropped his quest after the 1930 election. The political center had lost its parliamentary majority, transforming German politics. The Nazis and Communists had gained the power to veto measures to deal with the Great Depression, thereby creating a political crisis. The possibility of Hitler taking control had become a real threat.

It was Grandfather Willy, who had enabled my father not to have to earn a salary and to live as an independent scholar. Grandfather Gustav was also a dependable source of financial support. Neither grandfather was particularly affected by the 1929 stock market collapse. That is true only if one ignores the fact that the stock market crash precipitated the Great Depression that caused the collapse of the Weimar Republic and enabled Hitler to gain control over Germany less than three years later. On the other hand, my father's failure to gain German citizenship and a professorship enabled us to depart before Hitler was able to hurt us. We had no stakes, the loss of which would have complicated our departure. As non-German citizens, Hitler did not prevent us from leaving Germany in 1933.

***

My mother, Anni Frank, came from an environment very different from that of my father. She was born on August 5, 1900 in Braunschweig, (Brunswick), grew up in Berlin the city that had only recently become the center of the newly united German Empire, quite a contrast from my father's Bohemia, a province of the declining and disintegrating Austro-Hungarian Empire. Grammarians had unified the German language, but dialects preserved regional differences and even words varied in their meaning. My mother's coat was a *Mantel*, but my father's, an *Űberrock*. January was *Januar* in Berlin, but *Jenner* in Plzeň. Having spent my first 9 years in Berlin, Hochdeutsch (High German), my mother's tongue, remained the language we spoke at home in Berlin and Prague.

Geographical origin and language were only the superficial aspects of a more fundamental cultural divide. Berliners liked precision, order, efficiency and valued procedures that were properly carried out. Their tongue and humor was sharp. They had no tolerance for sloppy behavior or poor performance. People in the Austrian provinces on the other hand, had a greater appreciation for beauty, art and food. They loved to talk and speculate. Being late was not a crime but a function of unavoidable circumstances.

Although both my father and mother had a 100% Jewish background, each reflected quite different cultures of the 18th and 19th centuries. This resulted in differences in behavior wider than the Prussian-Austrian divide. My mother had grown up not as a member of a distinct Jewish community but as an assimilated German, priding herself that her grandfather had served as a medical officer in the Prussian army that defeated France in 1870. Her mother's aunt was the wife of a distinguished professor at the University of Berlin who had achieved his position and considerable academic acclaim without having to abandon his status as a Jew. My mother considered herself a German whose religion happened to be Jewish, while some of her school friends were Lutheran. My father's upbringing in Bohemia on the other hand, automatically made him a member of a small distinct Jewish community in Plzeň. A further complication was the fact that in the half century preceding the First World War, Jews were a minority among the Czechs who in turn were a part of the Austro-Hungarian Empire, dominated by German speaking Austrians. While many Jews in the Czech lands wanted to become part of the general population, this was not easy because it required a decision whether to identify as a Czech or a Jew who spoke German and supported the Austrian overlords. This resulted in my mother considering herself a fully integrated German, while my father remained an outsider.

My mother obtained her *abitur*; having passed her final gymnasium examination that entitled her admission to the university shortly after the end of World War I. Germany was in turmoil. Old conventions and traditions were abandoned. While her two older sisters had conventional ambitions leading to a very active social life, my twenty-year old mother decided to become a university student and study medicine, following the example set by her grandfather. She moved into a male-dominated environment.

Her father's loss of his only male heir, his son Kurt, killed in *The War*, may also have been a factor encouraging my mother to seek a career as a physician.

Embarking on the study of medicine at the University of Berlin, forced my mother to move quickly from the vision of the doctor able to cure ailments and save lives to the reality of dissecting cadavers and getting her hands soiled by blood. Her enthusiasm quickly faded. Being an excellent student who understood how to study, did not help her handle a reality that she never had to confront in her privileged upbringing where maids took care of everything that was dirty in the kitchen and the bathroom. Her interest shifted to lectures that were only tangentially related to medicine and the details of the human body. She followed the typical German student pattern of moving from the University in Berlin to universities in Heidelberg and Munich where she met my father and terminated her academic career. Twenty years later, she resumed her studies on another continent.

My mother was lucky to have escaped some of the disasters the defeated Kaiser's Empire suffered. Revolutions, strikes, disorders, political murders, discontented veterans all upset the normally disciplined German order. As I became familiar with the history of the Weimar Republic, it surprised me that my mother rarely mentioned those events. There was however one aspect that was deeply imbedded in her mind: the breakdown of post-war health standards. Diseases were rampant as Germany suffered the consequences of defeat and malnutrition. The high standards of German hygiene had broken down. It affected her family. Her two sisters caught TB. My aunt Lise had a very serious case that forced her to spend years in a Swiss mountain sanatorium. My aunt Kate had a less severe case. It bothered me that my mother blamed her sisters' life styles for their falling prey to the disease. Of course, my mother knew better than to expose herself to such a scourge. Years later, my mother made sure I would not get too close to aunt Lise. The bacteria might still be there and travel from her mouth to mine, several yards away. Three decades after the acute phase of her illness, having survived German bombs in Manchester, England during World War II, aunt Lise visited us in Storrs and met Ronald, my three-year-old son. My mother took me aside warning me to protect Ronald from Lise's TB germs. After all, one never knows…

When I was old enough to distinguish roles played by adults, I thought of my mother as the one who made sure that the house was orderly and quiet so that my father was not disturbed while he wrote his articles and books. In a separate room, my mother sat at her big typewriter and methodically tackled piles of paper, converting them into manuscripts, which my father proceeded to correct, reorganize so much that my mother had to retype chapters and entire manuscripts several times. I took one look at all this and escaped into the kitchen where I spent a lot of time annoying our maid, untying her apron. Inevitably, the accompanying noise would attract my mother who would banish me to the garden.

In Berlin, and later in Prague, my mother never had a remunerated job, but it was she, who made all the arrangements to send the manuscripts to publishers. She arranged for the publication of my father's philosophical journal and corresponded with my father's fellow philosophers. My father and mother worked as a team without realizing it. It was only when they started to make plans to move to the United States that there were serious discussions about my mother having to find a job. Doing what? She was then 38 old and the idea of looking for a real job alarmed not only her and my father but also me. I would never have guessed that three years later she would become a research assistant at Yale, resume her university studies and, a decade later, earn a Ph.D. in the history of medicine. At the age of 50, she became a professor of history.

***

When I started to object to being called by my baby name Putzi, and insisted on my real name Kurt, my Grandfather Willy was very happy. It was the name of my uncle who had been seven years older than my mother, his youngest sister. At first, it did not particularly interest me that I was named after him. When his name was mentioned, it evoked a serious solemn mood that made an impression on me. When *The War* broke out in 1914, Kurt volunteered to serve in the Kaiser's army. He did not survive that War.

I was told that Uncle Kurt had shown exceptional promise at the University. He was only twenty years old when the War started. He promptly joined the Kaiser's army to defend the German Reich. He fought in the trenches on the Western Front for nearly four years until American soldiers, who had just arrived, overran his position near Reims, and killed him on July 13, 1918. I also was told that he did not become an officer because as a Jew, this was virtually impossible. He hardly ever was granted home leave, spending four years of his short life in open fields protected by piles of rocks, dirt and dead bodies. The constant noise of guns and exploding ammunition must have been unbearable.

Perhaps I felt that with my uncle, the owner of my name gone, it was logical for me to inherit it. I did not have to ask my mother many questions. She and everybody else in the family talked about him at the slightest provocation.

Exploring my mother's few personal papers after her death in 2002 I came across a printed commentary by Friedrich Munter on my uncle's life and achievements. While the commentary fills less than a page, it describes an amazingly thoughtful intellectual individual. Trained to become a chemist, he explored philosophy instead. He expressed himself in aphorisms that covered issues of the mind, emotion, and society. Two pages of his selected aphorisms and poems are attached to Munter's article. Since my uncle was barely twenty when he entered the trenches on the Western Front, he must have composed and written some very original ideas while fighting beside his comrades and killing the enemy. Some of his aphorisms:

Delusion is the light of the world.

Future is not the unseen, but that which has not yet been shaped.

I am part of the world, but my mind (soul) has no part of me.

Grandfather Willy often reminisced about Kurt, the oldest of his four children. *The War* was a frequently repeated topic of conversation. Aware at a very early age that my uncle was a fallen soldier, connected me to *That War*. My grandfather's secret hope that I might take the place of his son may have led him to encourage me, his only male progeny, to study chemistry. That is the science that I started out majoring in at Cornell. Unlike my uncle however, I did not escape into philosophy, but ended up in history. Her brother's orientation may also have been a factor attracting my mother to my father, a philosopher. My uncle Kurt occupies an important place in my mind.

More than half a century later, I happened to be on the Greek island of Crete. After visiting all the usual historical and scenic sites, I was intrigued by a memorial to the German soldiers who had died on the island in the 1941 attack and the subsequent occupation of Crete. A relatively small number of German parachutists had defeated a much larger force of British and Greek soldiers on an island with hills and valleys that should have been easily defended. The memorial did not dwell on Germany's military achievement. Instead, it highlighted the performance and individual sacrifices of the soldiers. The memorial referred to an association commemorating German veterans, including those who fought in World War I. That would include my own uncle. A shiver went down my spine.

My middle name is Friedrich (Frederic). When we visited my paternal grandfather Gustav in Plzeň, he called me Fritzi, the diminutive of Friedrich. When he did that, my mother cringed. She did not like that at all, but Grandpa Gustav insisted. That is how he had called my father's younger brother, my "other" uncle. Thus, I learned that I was named after not only one but two uncles who had been killed in *The War*. Uncle Fritz had served in the Austro-Hungarian army fighting the Russians in Galicia. He was killed shortly after arriving in 1915. I do not know exactly when. The Austrians did not keep as good records as the Prussians. Unlike my mother my father seldom mentioned his brother's service in *The War*. I knew that the Austria-Hungarian army was no match for that of the German Kaiser's military skills, long before I was taught modern European History. Kurt fought four endless years; Fritz lasted only a few months.

Only as I became older did the tragedies embodied in my name Kurt Friedrich, enter my conscience and connect me with the history of the Great War. Eventually it dawned on me that my grandparents placed their hopes in me as someone to renew hope for a better future. The War remained a topic that caused an embarrassing silence that even a six-year-old could not help notice. I remember asking, why I could not play with toy soldiers that I had seen in a shop window. My parents sternly responded, *War was not a game!* War games were a definite no-no. Not only was War bad because it terminated my uncles' lives, but also because it had destroyed my grandfather Willy's plans for enjoying the fruits of his earlier successful endeavors. My Wannsee garden was to protect me from the effects and memories of the *Great War*, Germany's disaster.

As I grew up, my avoidance of toy soldiers developed into discomfort with real soldiers and manifestations of excessive patriotism. The pictures of Hindenburg, Germany's World War hero, failed to evoke the enthusiasm of my fellow first graders. I had enough exciting topics that occupied me not to miss playing war with toy soldiers. My parents introduced me to the exciting world of Greek mythology and ancient Greek history. I respected Zeus, admired Poseidon, the god of the sea, and for some reason that I cannot recall, disliked Pallas Athena. Maybe she was too intellectual for me. When my parents read the Odyssey to me, I followed Ulysses all around the Mediterranean.

Having lost their brothers in World War I, my parents approached the possibility of my serving in World War II with considerable trepidation. I was the only male descendant of my two sets of grandparents. However, Hitler had to be defeated and I had to do my part. In June 1943, at the height of our preparations for liberating France, I reported for induction in New Haven, I was shocked that the army did not take me and classified me 4F because my blood pressure was too high. My parents pretended to sympathize with my disappointment but could barely cover up their sense of relief that I would be spared the fate of my uncles.

***

Bert, a friend whom I had known since his birth in Berlin, sent me an e-mail in 2009 that brought back memories. It was a picture of his smiling daughter and her husband standing among the dignitaries near the center of President Obama's Inauguration. While her husband was a key figure in Obama first term administration, it is his wife Carole, Bert's daughter, who lit a light reminding me of events of my childhood.

Carole in this picture looks just as I remember her grandmother Anni who had been my favored person in the adult world of Berlin-Wannsee. Anni was my mother's best friend going back to their first grade. They lived not far from each other, supported each other, when they felt bothered by their brothers and sisters, continued their friendship even after graduating from gymnasium [high school], both pioneering after World War I in medical school when women first emerged from the shadows. Back then, they pioneered as women competing as equals with their male counterparts. Anni continued her medical studies and obtained an ophthalmology MD. My mother was sidetracked in her studies by meeting my father and having me, but eventually got a Ph.D. in the History of Medicine. Of course, when I first remember Anni, none of this was relevant. The picture reminded me of Anni frequently visiting us in Wannsee.

When I was small enough to be carried by her in her arms, she lifted me up to help me get a better look at the pictures that my father had hung next to the stairway leading to my room. She stopped on each step and explained what the pictures were about. I do not remember what she said about pictures of Greek statutes, Dutch Winter scenes or Flights from Egypt, but I do remember how long it took to get to my room and how determined she was to arouse my interest in something to which I paid little attention. On her birthday, I wished her a long life. How long? I answered a hundred years. She died in 2000, three months short of the life span I had promised her.

When I was a little older, I recall her bringing a friend along. He had given her a ride in his sports car. Over the misgivings of my parents they took me on a long tour of areas near our home in Wannsee I had never seen. Her friend even let me sit next to him in the passenger seat where I helped him get us lost. A year later Anni had a new friend who also had a car. Even at my early age, I quickly realized this friend was special. Anni brought him to our house regularly and Arthur became my friend. He impressed me very much because he was one of the few adults in my parents' circle who did something that I considered useful and even important. He was a real doctor whose work was on his mind even when he spent Sunday afternoons at our house. When my school principal informed my parents that I had to stay home because I had a rash and coughed, and they diagnosed it as scarlet fever, Arthur almost immediately drove at least three quarters of an hour from his office in East Berlin's Neukölln to Wannsee, examined me, and promptly informed the school authorities that they were badly mistaken. I returned to school in a day. Shortly after that, I was invited to Anni and Arthur's wedding. It was the first wedding I ever attended. (The second one was my own, two decades later, which Anni attended). Bert was born a year later when my parents and I had already left Berlin. I remember clearly returning to Berlin on a short visit when Bert was two and playing with him in a sandbox not far from

Tempelhof, the airport that was to become famous years later as Berlin's lifeline to the West.

Hitler and the approach to the Second World War could not break our close relationship with Anni, Arthur and Bert. When Hitler first came to power, Arthur thought that his distinguished service in the Kaiser's army and his subsequent medical practice in Neukölln, Berlin's workers district, where he mostly treated those covered by the universal health care insurance system, created in 1882, would enable him to survive Nazi restrictions imposed on Jewish-run businesses and medical offices. Soon he realized his mistake and began to prepare to leave. In 1936, Anni and Arthur crossed the Atlantic and "explored" New York City. They wanted to find out what they had to do to re-establish a medical practice in an entirely different setting. In 1937 they finally left Berlin and settled in the Inwood section of Upper Manhattan. When my parents and I arrived a year later, Anni, Arthur and Bert were already established and were ready to help us find our way in the alien new environment. We moved into an apartment near Fort Tryon Park, within walking distance from their place. I still remember what Anni and Bert tried to teach me about our new environment: never touch a plant with a three-cornered leaf: that is poison ivy. It took me seven years to locate a patch, which I promptly tested with disastrous results.

Even though my parents spent only two years in New York and I went off to college, we remained in close touch with Anni and Arthur. I stopped in their guestroom whenever I visited the city. Arthur remained our primary physician. When a New Haven doctor examining me for the draft in 1943 declared me 4F, unfit to serve because of high blood pressure, suggested I see a doctor immediately, I visited Arthur, stayed in his guestroom where he took my blood pressure before breakfast and assured me I was perfectly O.K. I would reach old age. It turned out he was right of course.

Anni and Arthur made a special trip to Connecticut in 1949 when I told them that I was moving to Storrs to teach at UCONN. As I proudly showed them green meadows, a couple of ponds, a dozen brick buildings and many more temporary structures dating to World War II, Arthur could hardly restrain his Berlin humor and wanted to know where Storrs was. At least it was not Neuköln, I responded. 65 years later I might have given him a better response.

Arthur established a flourishing medical practice on 77th Street off Park Avenue. He was recognized as a leader among German refugee doctors. The Post War West German government had him verify medical aspects of claims brought by German Jewish survivors of the Nazi period. It was Arthur, who made me aware that I was entitled to $1,000 compensation for having my schooling interrupted in 1933. At his memorial service in 1973, he was recognized as a doctor with outstanding diagnostic skills. After his death, Anni continued to play a very important part of our lives. She remained in constant touch with my mother by phone and was the first to diagnose significant lapses in my mother's mental capacity. This was when they were both in their early nineties. Anni made sure that I would remember her after her departure: She presented me with a permanent subscription to T*he New Yorker* implemented by Bert. Each December I get a personalized Christmas note informing me of the gift subscription.

Bert became a Professor of French literature at Princeton. That is where I met his daughter Carole. She was much younger than her grandmother Anni was when she carried me up the stairs in Wannsee. After retiring from Princeton, Bert spent his time in Los Angeles and Paris. I saw him rarely. The Internet changed that. Bert used it to send me the latest crude Berlin-type jokes about politicians he disliked. Then suddenly there was a more personal e-mail: a biography of his son-in-law Timothy Geithner. As the 2008 financial crisis intensified, lo and behold, Bert's son in law made the front page of the *New York Times*. Bert's e-mails no longer had the Saturday Live tone, they had more of a Princeton flair. Berlin humor might embarrass a cabinet member whose every expression is carefully analyzed by the media. When Bert e-mailed me the picture of Anni's granddaughter Carole, it brought me back some eighty years. The resemblance was enough to give the past special meaning. Bert's son in law's signature is now on the Dollar bills I carry in my wallet.

***

In Berlin, the school year starts in April. Having skipped kindergarten, I could hardly wait to emerge from my beautiful but lonely paradise and join kids my own age and look at the world through my own eyes and not those of my parents and their many friends. My parents considered it necessary to prepare me for this major event by reassuring me that everything would be OK. The only thing that concerned me, was the size and content of the special colored paper cone that every German first grader is expected to bring to school on his first day. Mine was huge, filled with cookies and candies. It gave me confidence and impressed those kids whose festive cone did not measure up to mine.

The school was a considerable distance from our house in Wannsee. Since we lived less than a ten-minute walk from Nikolassee, I was assigned to a school in Zehlendorf that served Nikolassee and a number of adjoining suburbs. Most kids came from working class families living in multi-apartment suburban homes.

Getting to school was a challenge. There were no school buses. Children, regardless of age, had to get to school on their own. The first day, my mother accompanied me on a regular double-decker bus that stopped on Crown Princess Strasse (street), a major thoroughfare only one block from our house. After a twenty-minute ride, the bus stopped in Schlachtensee, two blocks from my school. That first day was the only time my mother had to chaperone me. I was six years old and perfectly able to climb aboard a bus and know when to get off. In the three years that I rode that double-decker, I had a problem only once, a real adventure. On a cold day in February, the roads were covered with ice. The bus driver lost control going down the hill as he approached the stop where I was standing. The bus moved sideways before the driver opened the door to let me in. The road had not been sanded and the driver was far more discombobulated than I was. On a hill in Nikolassee, a bit closer to the school, he repeated the same maneuver and gave up. He asked me to walk the rest of the way. Classes are never canceled in Berlin, regardless of weather conditions. I never took the bus on my way home. I walked all the way, taking shortcuts over meadows in less densely populated areas.

Dr. Bethge was the teacher who welcomed me on my first day. It was also the start of his teaching career. My parents told me that he took this job of teaching first graders, even though he had a Ph.D., because after the stock market crash in 1929 there were no other jobs available. Only when I was much older did that bit of information interest me. What mattered then was that Dr. Bethge immediately gained my confidence and made me, and probably everybody else, feel very comfortable. Dr. Bethge not only knew what he was teaching, but also enjoyed it. He gave each one of us equal attention. We all had to read and spell all our assignments. He obviously studied us closely and recognized that as an only child, I was not very well prepared to socialize with my fellow students. He maintained a very friendly classroom atmosphere. I do not recall any discipline problems. It helped the transition from my Wannsee Garden of Eden to the real world.

One day, after the regular classes were over, we were herded to another room for religious instruction. Naturally, I went with everybody else to the new location. As I entered, Dr. Bethge stopped me. You cannot go to this class, it teaches the Lutheran religion. You are of the Hebraic faith and your father has to send you to a class where they teach you the Hebraic religion. I was confused. Happy that I could go home one hour earlier than everybody else, but upset that I was no longer a fully integrated member of the class. My father found a religious teacher in Nikolassee who tried to teach me the Hebrew language. It was my first attempt to learn a foreign language. I had a few lessons and tried to decipher the Hebrew alphabet. I hoped to be able to impress my Plzeň grandfather as the youngest family participant at next the Passover service and read the question why this day was different from any other.

***

I do not remember how it all started. Maybe my parents reached the conclusion that at the age of eight I deserved something interesting and different. It was July: no school. Working on my plants in the garden was getting somewhat boring. Adventure books were O.K, but they were not the real thing. Sexier books were out of reach. Something had to be done, to keep me entertained. Even Nazi-sponsored street demonstrations were on hold. It was the summer of 1932.

We had traveled before. When I was very young, my parents must have taken me to Plzeň, Czechoslovakia, the home of his parents. I do not clearly recall those trips before I was six. However the trip in the summer of 1932 was memorable. I remember it from the very start: The taxi ride in the evening from my grandparents' home in Berlin to the impressive Anhalter railroad station was so smooth as if the city streets had a velvet cover. My grandfather bid us bon voyage as we climbed on board a sleeper coach where we were to spend the night on our way to Munich.

My mother, father and I shared a compartment with three bunk beds. Naturally, I occupied the one on top. That was the first time that I recall sleeping in the same room as my father. I discovered that he snored louder than the noise made by the wheels of the speeding train. The sun had risen before I awakened from a near-perfect rest as the conductor knocked at the door bringing me hot chocolate and a perfect roll with jam. Such luxury! There was hardly enough time to get dressed and washed in the tiny bathroom before the magic train arrived at our destination, Munich.

I do not recall the hotel in which we stayed in Munich. However, I do remember very well my father's excitement when we visited the philosophy professor who had supervised his Ph.D. thesis at the University in Munich. We visited him in his apartment. My father introduced me and I remember shaking the old man's hand. My father had completed his thesis 15 years earlier while World War I was still in full swing. As I look back on that visit, I think that my father must have hoped that I would follow his example, become a philosopher and get a Ph.D. I must have disappointed him because I pursued topics that were more down-to-earth.

After the short stop in Munich, our real vacation began. "Have we reached the Alps yet?" I kept asking, as I looked out the train window on the way to Garmisch-Partenkirchen. The mountains reached the clouds and I looked for the highest peak, the Zugspitze, Germany's tallest mountain. We stayed over in Garmisch-Partenkirchen, already then a very popular resort. It was much too popular and therefore my family had planned only a short stop. I do remember walking through a famous gorge, the Partnachklamm, where one could almost touch simultaneously the rocks on both sides of the gorge. Water rushed ferociously below the planks of the narrow walk.

Our next stop was up in the Alps, across the Austrian border, in Lermoos, a little mountain village. The train that took us there provided us with scenic views that impressed even an eight-year old. When the train stopped at a small village, I saw flames belching dark smoke through the windows of a building less than two hundred feet from the train station. It was exciting. What was even more interesting was the way the Austrians fought the fire. They pulled a very primitive looking fire fighting truck lacking an engine, in front of the burning building and with their own muscles pumped water into the windows. It seemed to work. Before we pulled out of the station, the smoke had diminished considerably. Watching the Austrians fight a fire made me realize that not everybody had modern equipment, something that I could not consider possible in Berlin.

In Lermoos, we switched to a postal bus. The bus brought us down from the Alpine ridge on the frontier to the bottom of the Inn valley. The serpentine road was an exciting introduction to driving in the mountains: the bus would approach a blind curve, not knowing what was ahead. The driver would blast his horn two or three times, scaring me, and hopefully alerting the oncoming driver that he better back into a safe spot, high above the river below. This experience stayed with me as a nightmare on many subsequent Alpine car trips as I wound my way down treacherous curves in Italy, Austria and Switzerland.

The bus delivered the mail and us safely in Imst. I observed then that the mail sacks that the driver delivered at the post offices on our way appeared not to be very heavy. In those days the driver seemed to transport far more passengers than letters. Alpine postal buses left a lasting favorable impression. However on more recent Alpine trips when some of them tailgated me, impatient with my reluctance to race around sharp curves, they scared me to death as I tried to avert my eyes from the precipices below.

From Imst we took another bus into the Pitztal. The road wound its way up the valley, passing tiny isolated villages. It made a pit stop, also of course delivering letters. Here I had an interesting experience. When I walked into the men's somewhat primitive toilet, with my father close behind, there was a man vomiting noisily, making quite a mess. I had never seen anybody suffering so much in public. When I asked my father for an explanation, he answered matter of fact, that guy drank too much. That is what happens to those, who drink too much alcohol! Watching this man in what was an Alpine paradise, made a lasting impression. I was afraid to drink lest I vomit like that man in the Pitztal. This memory kept me out of trouble in my college years. Not until I started teaching, did I forget my father's admonition and suffered the Alpine drinker's fate,

Fortunately it happened only once.

Our final destination was Mittelberg, the last stop in the Pitztal. There we could see glaciers reaching down to us, a few hundred feet below, at the little farmhouse where we stayed. My mother and I climbed up to reach Alpine huts on well-marked trails. Exciting panoramas greeted us. Grazing cows with bells around their fat necks had to be pushed out of our way. My father meanwhile sat in the sun near the house, read, thought and wrote. He repeated his favorite observation that the best way to appreciate a mountain was to look at it from below. After all, when you are on it, it is no longer above you and therefore it has lost its main attraction: a monument towering up there in the sky. Maybe that is where I learned that one could look at things from different perspectives.

The trip was a wonderful experience! It is strange, but I cannot recall anything about our return trip. The mountains remained in my memory for a long time.

Chapter 2
Swastikas

I had become aware of Adolf Hitler when I was six. The 1930 parliamentary election involved street demonstrations that my parents discouraged me from watching. That aroused my curiosity. Swastikas appeared on armbands. What is a swastika? Why do people in brown shirts wear them on their sleeves? After the election, normalcy did not return to the streets. Swastika flags started dangling from people's houses and swastika buttons were worn by people on their lapels.

In 1932, the streets became noisier. President von Hindenburg, a retired General and World War hero, a very old man from my 8-year old perspective, was running for re-election. Adolf Hitler sought to unseat him and mobilized his Brown Shirted SA [Sturm Abteilung] storm trooper street gangs to whip up popular support. Hindenburg prevailed, and my parents and all their friends heaved a big sigh of relief.

Adolf Hitler had transformed misfits who vented their anger as outsiders at the establishment into an instrument of his movement intending to instill fear in his opponents. Fortunately, in our suburban Wannsee neighborhood not many Brown-shirted troopers with their swastika armbands appeared on the streets. I managed to stay out of their sight. Acts of vandalism against Jewish shop owners did not occur in our somewhat fancy thinly populated suburb.

In Germany teachers stay with their students as the students advance to the next grade, Dr. Bethge advanced with me to the second grade. In a report card that year, he wrote that I possessed the confidence and friendship of my fellow students. Big deal, I thought. A short time later something unexpected happened. A swastika button appeared on the lapel of his jacket. That occurred during the contest for President in 1932, when Adolf Hitler, opposed President Hindenburg. Even though Hitler lost that contest Dr. Bethge became principal of our school. My parents who had been so happy about my school experience became concerned. They refrained talking to me about how the Nazis might influence my school, but I could not help becoming aware that there was a potential problem.

I remember a strange incident in1932. My physical education teacher, not Dr. Bethge, threw a climbing rope on the floor of the gymnasium and asked us what the shape of the rope looked like. We answered, it resembled the letter S. "And" ..., he continued. "A snake", one of us said. "Aha", his eyes lit up, and the teacher shouted, "like Schleicher" [slither in German]. Schleicher was the Chancellor of Germany at that critical time.

On January 30, 1933, I went ice-skating on a converted outdoor tennis court in Nikolassee. I had learned to skate and enjoyed the dance music that blasted from the loudspeaker. Suddenly the music was interrupted, and a voice announced, "President Hindenburg has appointed Adolf Hitler Reichskanzler (Chancellor) of Germany". There followed a moment of silence. The music resumed. Only 8 years old, yet I knew this was important. I took off my skates, raced home and told my parents. Since we had no radio, it was I, who was the bearer of the news, which would change all of our lives.

February 27, barely a month later, was another date to remember. In the basement of the building in which the German Parliament met, somebody ignited a fire that caused serious damage. The Nazis blamed the Communists for this and punished them by banishing them from Parliament, thereby consolidating Nazi control of the government.

The school year ended around Easter. The normal one-week vacation before the start of the spring semester was extended to give the authorities time to replace old textbooks with ideologically purified material. A few weeks later, another holiday: *The Burning of the Books*. Books written by Jews, Communists, *Degenerates* and others who threatened pure ("Nazi-Aryan") German Kultur, were ceremoniously destroyed in a gigantic bonfire in the center of Berlin. Our school assignment: Write an essay on the *Burning-of-the-Books Celebration*. When I got that assignment, I asked my father for advice. "Write about spring and what the day looked like". That is what I did: two pages about trees sprouting new leaves, the bright sunny day and festive street decorations. My teacher gave me a passing grade, liked my writing, but complained that I had not written anything about that day's festivities.

We had to learn the Nazi anthem, the *Horst Wessel* song. The first stanza refers to Nazis killed by "Reactionaries and

Communists" the second one gets more violent and goes after Jews and other enemies. Ever since, I have had some discomfort participating in mass singings of national anthems. Swastikas replaced the Black-Red-Gold German flags. The swastikas flew everywhere, on almost any day when something special took place. Swastikas also appeared on lapels, armbands, plastered on walls, in short, they transformed, i.e. ruined, the landscape.

***

In my garden in Wannsee at the edge of the big lawn beyond the raspberry, gooseberry and currant bushes there stood a huge poplar tree. It could be detected from a great distance. The year before, on a hot summer night, lightning had struck the poplar. The thunderous clap had scared me; I was only eight-years old then. It gave that part of the garden a special aura. Almost a year later, on a pleasantly warm afternoon late in May, Papi casually appeared on the lawn and joined me as I was watching my tiny chestnut plants emerge with their new greenery in my corner of the garden. Papi was usually busy writing or relaxing, so it was a rare event for him to join me in my garden.

We sauntered in the direction of the poplar tree. Apparently, he wanted to get away as far as possible from the house in order not to be overheard. He started a serious conversation. "We are going to move to Prague. You will have to learn Czech". I had been to Plzeň where my grandparents Gustav and Mathilde lived, and where Papi was born. They spoke German when we visited. "Why do I have to learn Czech? Do you speak Czech?" I asked my father, "Yes. Not well, but I do understand it". I was bothered by the idea of having to learn a foreign language. In third grade, I had finally become comfortable writing the required one-page essay that my teacher, Dr. Bethge, had praised as not only interesting but also well written. "Do I really have to learn Czech"? "Yes you do", Papi said. "When I was in school, we were taught in German because Bohemia was still part of the K and K [Kaiser und König, Emperor and King] Austro-Hungarian Empire and we spoke *kitchen Czech* with the maids. Now Bohemia is part of Czecho-slovakia and Czech is the official language".

The challenge of having to learn Czech preoccupied me. It took a few moments to consider the even bigger shock: "Do we have to leave our house and this garden?" Yes" "When? "In June as soon as school is over". I did not have to ask him why, I knew.

Our house in Wannsee was one block from the main highway that connected the center of Berlin with Potsdam, the residence of Kaiser Wilhelm who lost his throne when Germany was defeated in 1918. Shortly after becoming Chancellor, Hitler went on a ceremonial pilgrimage to Potsdam, symbol of the pre-war German Reich, to restore Germany's claim to world leadership. His procession moved noisily 100 feet from our house. Of course, my parents would not even consider letting me watch the procession. Thus, I missed my only chance of seeing Hitler with my own eyes.

So when Papi talked about leaving our house in Wannsee he did not have to tell me why. The Berlin where I had grown up and which I had loved, had changed and transformed itself so much, that my Berlin was no more. We did not leave Berlin. It had abandoned us.

***

On our way to Prague, in the summer of 1933, we spent two months in Marienbad. My father chose to stop in this famous spa to help my mother and me get used to living away from our land of birth. Although we were in neighboring Czechoslovakia, outside Hitler's domain, everyone spoke German, thus postponing the need for me to have to make the difficult transition to a new language. School in Prague did not start until September, giving my parents an excuse to spend our summer vacationing in a famous spa and learn to call it Marianské Lazňe. We pretended to be normal tourists, not refugees.

I missed Wannsee, especially my growing chestnut trees, picking strawberries that had not quite ripened before our departure and our occasional trips to the zoo, a ten-minute walk from my Berlin grandfather Willy's apartment in Berlin. The small hotel in which we stayed had a few attractions that helped me deal with the loss of my Wannsee garden: It was close to a small forest that I was permitted to explore all on my own, since my parents were busy getting adjusted to a new environment and were making plans for the approaching move to Prague. A local person befriended me, taught me how to pick mushrooms and helped me avoid poisonous ones. I informed my parents that I was an expert and knew that the best-looking mushrooms were the most dangerous ones. Papi liked my insight. Fortunately, I did not have to put my new knowledge to the test.

I also explored the spa itself, a long promenade where people relaxed, sipping the awful tasting liquid that made the spa so famous. To make the spring water palatable they sold Karlsbader Oblaten, special wafer-thin pastry. Visitors came from many countries to take a bath in the warm water that bubbled from the earth and supposedly contained ingredients that helped remedy and even cure illnesses affecting muscles and bones. Marienbad and its close-by sister spas, Karlsbad and Franzensbad had attracted visitors for more than a century and were especially popular with Jews from Central and Eastern Europe. Since my parents dismissed the alleged curative nature of the famous spring water I had no chance of testing the spa's claim to fame.

Bored promenading back and forth, one could always go on a *Spaziergang* or visit a restaurant overlooking the valley at the edge of a mountain meadow. These restaurants invariably had delicious deserts. The normal edicts against eating too many sweet tasting dishes were of course in abeyance on a vacation in a famous resort. Maybe leaving Berlin would turn out better than I had feared.

We followed the unfolding events as Hitler consolidated his power. Each step reduced our latent hopes that the exile would be brief and that we would soon be able to return to our Wannsee paradise. Even worse, there were indications that Nazi Germany had its admirers in Czechoslovakia, our country of refuge. I heard my parents talk about local Sudeten Germans, the German minority, who admired what Hitler was doing next door.

Worried that I would be bored promenading in the spa and eating at restaurants on long walks in the hills my father had to keep me busy. I was sent off to a small lake three times a week to learn swimming. The idea was great, but the water was frigid. I made only slow progress. I believe that I was the only nine-year old that a not particularly skilled instructor tried to teach in a very pedantic way. I learned the breaststroke, while imprisoned in a harness to prevent me from drowning.

To vary a diet of mushroom hunting and splashing aimlessly in the frigid lake, my father had me come along with him and my mother and have tea with a famous professor.

While establishing contact with German intellectuals living in exile my father had contacted Professor Theodor Lessing. He stayed at the Villa Edelweiss, a small hotel at the opposite end of Marienbad. His apartment had a balcony on the second floor. It was there that he entertained us. I did not have tea, but a wonderfully tasting cup of chocolate and pastry. That alone would have made the visit worthwhile. Professor Lessing had a beard that impressed me. He seemed to be interested in getting me involved in the discussion. We were about to go to Prague the following week and he had been there and told me all about the city and what to expect there. In short, he was a "nice old man" with whom a nine-year old could connect.

I was also interested in the discussion between him and my father. They covered the latest news that came from Nazi Germany and all the horrible things Hitler and his Nazis were doing. Lessing wrote articles that were published in the *Prager Tagblatt*. My father wanted advice on how he should go about getting his ideas into the paper as feuilletons, (0pEds). The *Prager Tagblatt* was the mainstream German newspaper in Czechoslovakia. It published articles informing readers in Prague about the threat presented by Hitler. That is why the Nazis lashed out at those Jewish refugees who, the Nazis claimed, spread lies about the "wonderful transformation" carried out by Adolf Hitler. My father and Professor Lessing were kindred souls and enjoyed their discussion, even a nine year old could figure that out. When we left the balcony and some of the uneaten cookies, the Professor shook my hand, auf Wiedersehen.

On September 1 in Prague, the front page of the *Prager Tagblatt,* displayed a picture of Professor Lessing surrounded by a black border. He had been assassinated on August 30 at 9:30 P.M. Two men had been seen running from the villa after shots were heard. The assassins had brought a ladder and shot him through the window, not more than a few feet from where we had had such a good conversation. The paper added that the two perpetrators had escaped across the nearby German frontier. It was later revealed that the two assassins had been in touch with Ernst Röhm, leader of the SA storm troopers. Only recently did I learn that Lessing had received threats that summer that he would be shot. When he entertained us on his balcony he was very composed and gave me not the slightest indication that he was aware of being one of Hitler's early targets. Apparently Marienbad was a little too close to Nazi Germany to provide us with sufficient peace of mind.

Chapter 3
Prague: A Temporary Exile?

When we left Marienbad on our way to Prague in late August 1933, school was about to start but we had to get settled first. My father had located a second floor apartment in a recently built two-story house that was situated at the modern outskirts of Prague, the centuries old city. Our new abode was surrounded by wheat fields stretching to the horizon. A highway, only a few hundred feet from our house, descended into the Šarka valley. The cultivated grain fields edged the Šarka valley: quite a contrast from my green lawn and the blue waves of the Wannsee.

While waiting for our furniture we stayed at the *Pension Šarka*, a small guesthouse located on a hill with an excellent view of the rural Bohemian countryside. On the day the furniture was to be delivered I reconnoitered the neighborhood, looking for our precious possessions. I located a horse-drawn wagon on a street not far from our apartment. The container it carried had German markings: It was easy to guess that it contained our Wannsee furniture. Two horses pulled the heavy load up the hill to our street, *Na Černém Vrchu* [On the Black Hill]. The load was too much for the horses and they balked. The driver took his whip and hit them mercilessly. They started to move again ever so slowly. To me it seemed that it took an eternity for the wagon to reach our house. Horses were still a necessary part of transportation in Prague; while in Berlin motorized trucks had replaced them before I was born.

Everything was different. My parents were shocked to discover that nobody on our street of recently built houses had a telephone. It took some time for telephone poles to be erected and for us to be reconnected with our friends. My parents let me choose the best of three large rooms. It had large windows on two sides that helped me observe what was going on in the fields and highway below. In the distance, the lights twinkled from far away villages. I could warn everybody when I noticed a storm approaching on the horizon. One summer a building was constructed next to ours. I watched the workers on the girders and worried that they might fall from their perilous perch. I was placed in charge of a small section of the garden behind the house. It was a poor substitute for the much larger garden left behind in Wannsee.

How about school? I did not yet know any Czech, so my parents hired a university student who, in order to earn a few Czech crowns, taught me enough words to converse in Czech, a Slavic language quite different from my German mother tongue. My parents enrolled me in a German school, a considerable distance from our apartment in Dejvice. It was a public school for German speaking children. To get there, I had to walk fifteen minutes to the trolley # 11 stop, ride on it for about half an hour, and then walk another ten minutes to reach the school in Holešovice, a not particularly attractive neighborhood. I was placed in fourth grade. Schoolwork required far less effort than in my school in Berlin. The only class challenging me was geography. We had to learn what each region, city and town in Czechoslovakia produced. I informed my parents that Czechoslovakia was really a huge country producing obviously more than any other in Europe. My parents were aghast, but were careful not to interfere with my rapidly developing Czechoslovak patriotism. I was shocked when I got my first report card. I got A's in everything except music and physical education. I knew I was not that good. I did not connect with my classmates. I probably did not fit in their group. They knew little about the Germany that I had left and could care less about a refugee from Hitler's Third Reich.

A year later I was ready to enter something comparable to our middle school. A Czech school was only a ten-minute walk from our apartment and my parents considered sending me there for my second year in Prague. A short distance further there was a brand new French Gymnase-Réal, an all-inclusive school combining grammar, middle and high school. It was operated jointly by the Czechoslovak and French governments to encourage close relations between these two allies that sought to prevent German aggression by forcing Germany to face the danger of a war on two fronts. After spending a year learning Czech, a language rediscovered by 19th century grammarians who got a kick creating pedantic rules including innumerable cases and declensions, the prospect of having to learn French, a third language, did not appeal to me. But when I visited the Gymnase Réal (Lycée) Français, I was very impressed by the brand new building, consisting of ultra-modern grammar school rooms surrounded by playing fields in a park-like environment, connected to the four-story Gymnase Réal. It was my first encounter with ultra-modern Bauhaus architecture. Only ten years old, I was captured by structures that were completely at odds with Prague's famous medieval castles, bridges and churches. I gave in and prepared myself for the task of tackling French.

I qualified for admission to a special 5th grade class that taught topics required for students to entering the French gymnasium, a middle and high school patterned on schools in France and taught by French teachers. Mademoiselle Besançon welcomed us on the first day of school in September with a big smile and a hearty *bonjour*. She told us in French that she knew only French and that is how we would communicate. She cheated a little and when we did not understand something, she would point to an object, use sign language or refer to pictures. This total immersion in a new language and culture worked amazingly well. Mademoiselle Besançon forced me to watch her so closely in order to understand her that I quickly developed a crush on her, even though I was only ten. Later I realized that it was not only Mademoiselle Besançon who attracted me, but also France, French culture, customs, literature and history.

Among the twenty kids in the preparatory class, there were Czechs, Germans, Eastern Europeans, one American boy, whose parents had returned to Prague as a result of the Great Depression and one girl from Great Britain. Most English-speaking people in Prague went to the English gymnasium [high school]. Since our class was so cosmopolitan, I was much more comfortable than in any of my previous schools. I had friends and even knocked the front tooth out of a fellow German refugee's mouth in a friendly, but unfortunate tussle. At the end of the school year, I passed the entrance examination into the Gymnase Réal.

My parents encouraged me to explore Prague. Initially they were my guides. That did not last long, since my father was primarily occupied with his philosophical writings and mingled with his fellow scholars. My mother did not feel very comfortable in a city where few people spoke a language she could understand, a feeling that stayed with her during our entire stay in Prague. In retrospect, I am embarrassed to admit that when I was eleven, twelve and even thirteen I passed by world famous Prague sites with hardly a second look. Some sites intrigued me: Charles Bridge over the Vltava [Moldau], the clock of the Town Hall with its figures going in a circle when the clock struck the hour, the Alchemists Alley on the Hradčany [Castle Hill]. What really attracted my interests was the trolley system. I made it my business to know the itinerary of each one of the 23 trolley lines. Perhaps, it was my father's poorly disguised embarrassment with his son's preoccupation with such a mundane transportation topic that egged me on in my pursuit. I had a map of Prague in my head, which prevented me from ever getting lost. Sixty years later, I had no trouble driving in Prague, even though by then there was a subway, somewhat confusing, but not erasing, my mental map of those ancient trolley lines.

Gradually the anxieties that had accompanied our departure from Nazi Germany, lessened as I regained some peace of mind in the French Gymnasium. The Czech and French governments jointly operated the school and we were encouraged to identify ourselves as Czech Francophiles. We had assemblies where French officials would give patriotic speeches. We would all sing the Marseillaise, the French national anthem. The French assured us of their undying support for Czechoslovakia, their favored Eastern European ally and partner in the Little Entente. We would then sing the Czech and Slovak anthems *Where is my Home* and *Thunder over the Tatra Mountains*. The French alliance was going to protect us from Hitler's threats. We were confident that France would stand up to Hitler and his swastika-wearing storm troopers. That was when I was eleven and in the first grade of my gymnasium. Unfortunately, my new sense of security was destined to be short lived.

***

I had known that our religion was Jewish, but that fact did not play a significant role in my upbringing. I remember very well the time that my maternal grandfather had arrived at our house and appeared dressed as Santa Claus next to our candle-lit Tannenbaum (Christmas tree). I must have been five or six years old and could no longer be fooled by grandpa. At Easter, I looked for colored eggs [and presents] in our garden where the Easter bunny had hidden them.

Being prevented from taking the regular class on religion in my Berlin grade school prevented me from feeling fully integrated. In my school, I was now no longer like everybody else. When on All Souls Day in November my class in Berlin went on an excursion, I was asked whether I wanted to come along. I answered: "of course". I did not want to miss the class excursion. We visited the cemetery at the local Lutheran Church. The sharp angles of the roof and tower gave the Church a very severe look that I still recall eight decades later.

After Hitler's appointment as Chancellor of Germany, not feeling like everybody else was no longer just my own concern, but a policy of the state. The fact that my great grandfather had served in the medical corps of the Prussian army in the 1860's and that my uncle had died for the Kaiser after fighting the French for four years in World War I was irrelevant. I was no longer considered German, but a racial impurity infecting the Aryan race. Fortunately, my father, born in Plzeñ had kept his Czechoslovak citizenship.

At the age of nine, I was anxious to integrate as quickly as possible into my new Prague community. There were major hurdles that I had to overcome. The apartment my parents had chosen was at the outer edge of the city. There were fields and villages in the distance. One could even walk into a scenic valley, the Šarka. But neighborhood kids my age? There were none, at least no one who talked German.

In the German grammar school in Holešovice, the kids there came from families that admired the Germany that I had left and had no sympathy for a Jewish refugee kid. That made me an unwanted outsider. At the Gymnase-Réal (Lycée) Français my fellow students were a mixed bag of Czechs, some German speaking Czechoslovaks, and children of foreigners residing in Prague. It was easy to fit in, at least during the five or six hours we spent in school. Since students came from all parts of Prague, there was little opportunity to socialize when classes were over.

It was a challenge to learn Czech as well as French, while talking German at home. On the street and in shops I communicated in Czech. In school, we were required to speak French. The French teachers considered their culture far superior to that of their old enemy, the Germans. Czech was interesting, but difficult to speak fluently. Anyhow, French was the language of culture and diplomacy. Czech teachers taught us their language, history and literature.

Being Jewish was obviously easier in Prague than in Berlin after Hitler's assumption of power. A somewhat disturbing

Jesus nailed to the Cross, bleeding badly, stared me in the face in my school's home room. The annual census of religious affiliation taken by the teacher revealed a great diversity among my fellow students: there were Catholics, Eastern Orthodox Catholics, Czech Hussites, a variety of Protestants, as well as Jews. Here I was not singled out: I was but one item in a rich religious stew. Perhaps most interesting was the fact that Czechoslovakia, a Catholic state, celebrated annually on July 6, the burning at the stake of Jan Hus in 1415 by order of the Pope and the Council of Constance. Czechoslovakia had a multicultural population that spoke several languages and shared a variety of religious beliefs. I felt at home.

***

Hitler's threat to violate the peace terms of the Treaty of Versailles that ended the Great War became clear almost immediately after Hitler was appointed Germany's Chancellor. Mussolini stopped Hitler from annexing Austria in 1934, after Nazi agents had shot Austria's Chancellor Dollfuss. Mussolini however quickly resumed his friendship with Hitler and embarked on his own conquest of Ethiopia in October 1935. France, England and the League of Nations failed to stop Mussolini. Hitler marched the German army into the Rhineland in violation of the Treaty of Versailles in March 1936. France let him get away with it. Four months later in July, Generalissimo Franco started a revolt against the Spanish government. In the ensuing civil war, Hitler and Mussolini supported Franco with air strikes and weapons. France and Great Britain failed to interrupt the flow of armaments to Franco's insurgent forces. Stalin and poorly organized foreign volunteer brigades were the only ones to support the Spanish Loyalists.

The failure of France and Great Britain to put a halt to Hitler and Mussolini's ever-increasing challenges to the world order, established by the victors of the First World War, rekindled my own sense of insecurity. After all, we lived in Czechoslovakia, a country that owed its existence to the victory of France, Great Britain and the United States in the Great War. The United States vanished from the scene in 1920 when it rejected the League of Nations and left Europe to its own destiny. Great Britain supported France with reservations. In Prague, we depended on France to protect us from Hitler. It was a bad omen that France began to manifest a growing lack of decisiveness while experiencing domestic political divisions. Reluctantly I began to question the kind words of friendship and support that the French officials who visited our school expressed on their frequent visits.

I do not recall why I always happened to turn on the radio when Hitler made a major speech. On March 7, 1936, he addressed the German Reichstag and announced that as he was speaking, German troops were marching into the Rhineland reoccupying the German territory they had agreed by treaty not to remilitarize. The sound of marching troops, military music, the *Horst Wessel* Nazi anthem and *Deutschland Über Alles,* [Germany above everything], blared over the airwaves. My parents shared my alarm. We thought France would surely do something. But there was no effective response.

I followed the news, reading the morning and afternoon papers before my parents could snatch them out of my hands. The visiting French officials at our gymnasium tried to reassure us that France stood solidly by our side. I followed the political contests that divided the French. I cheered when the Popular Front led by Socialists and supported by Communists won the May 1936 parliamentary elections. Led by Léon Blum, it strongly opposed Hitler's aggressive behavior. It was significant that Blum with his Jewish background became Prime Minister of France only thirty years after France's infamous Dreyfus affair.

There was another ray of hope. Our paper reported on the interesting 1936 presidential campaign in the United States. Franklin D. Roosevelt had made some critical comments about Nazi Germany. His opponent, Alfred Landon, seemed to avoid expressing any interest in what was going on in Europe. I was worried when a public opinion poll [something new to me] predicted that Landon would defeat Roosevelt. I waited nervously for the election outcome and was greatly relieved to see Roosevelt re-elected.

Developments in France and the United States restored some of my confidence that Hitler would be stopped. Instead, events all over the world continued to disturb and even frighten me. In 1936, Stalin escalated his campaign against Trotsky and other leaders of the Communist party by staging a series of Show Trials. At the same time, Stalin concluded an alliance with Czechoslovakia to protect us from an attack by Nazi Germany. Relations between Stalin and the French Popular Front government were also strengthened. This created a problem. How could I reconcile Stalin's execution of his erstwhile revolutionary allies and subsequent competitors, with his declared support for Czechoslovakia and France so necessary for our survival? I had no idea that I, and many others, would be stuck with this contradiction for a number of years.

In addition, there was the Spanish Civil War. I followed this conflict very closely because my Aunt Kate, her husband Hans and my only cousin Ruth lived in Barcelona. They had left Berlin and had hoped to settle in Spain, a country far enough from Hitler, to give them a sense of a safe haven. They had just settled there, when the Franco uprising upset their new life. Initially, we were optimistic in letters we exchanged, since the Loyalists held firm. The intensity of the battles worried us. Fortunately, Barcelona's proximity to France gave my aunt and cousin a potentially safe escape route to France. As Franco's forces advanced, Ruth and her parents left for Switzerland in 1938.

Other kids my age followed the fortunes of their favorite football [soccer] teams while I was preoccupied with the policies of my favorite countries opposing Hitler and Mussolini. Unfortunately my teams performed miserably. France did nothing to stop Hitler and Mussolini's support of Franco. Well, perhaps a tiny bit by making it possible for my cousin Ruth and her parents to reach the relative safety of Switzerland. Confidence in my French team suffered a nearly fatal blow when in March 1938, France became so deeply involved in an internal political crisis, that it was unable to lift a finger, nor shoulder a gun and certainly not frighten Hitler, thus permitting him to take Austria and threaten Czechoslovakia. We needed a more reliable friend to support us.

***

In Czechoslovakia we were not out of Hitler's reach as we had hoped. The prospect of a return to normalcy in our lives was elusive. As early as the summer of 1933, while in Marienbad, the local radio and newspapers kept us informed on Hitler's acts that stirred things up. There was the purge of his early cohorts. Some were accused of being homosexuals. I did not know what that was all about; but I assumed that it meant that anybody, whom Hitler did not like, was ordered shot. Then it hit closer to home when German Nazis murdered Professor Lessing one week after he talked with me because he had written anti-Nazi newspaper editorials. A year later, in July, Hitler's agents had tried to annex Austria by assassinating the Austrian Chancellor Dollfuss. Fortunately Italy's Mussolini mobilized his troops at the Brenner Pass, thereby forcing Hitler to delay his quest to annex Austria. Not far from Vienna in Prague, the assassination of Dollfuss was too close for comfort and made us nervous.

In subsequent summers we often spent some time in Marienbad. Located in a Sudeten-German part of Czechoslovakia, it was home to many Sudeten-Germans who admired Hitler. They were not allowed to wear swastikas and support the Nazis openly. They showed their sympathy for Hitler by wearing blue cornflowers in their lapels. Hitler was watching us. How could one feel comfortable under such circumstances?

As I grew older, I learned to appreciate the Czech environment into which Hitler had pushed us. I listened to Dvořák's symphonies and attended a performance of Smetana's *Bartered Bride*. I argued with my father who placed Handel, Bach, Beethoven, Mozart and Brahms on a musical level not reached by Czech composers. Listening to our primitive radio became my favorite habit after finishing my homework. While a concert was pleasant, far more exciting was locating short wave radio stations. I managed to locate *Schenectady* on my dial. The barely audible voice came all the way from America! Sometimes I managed to come across anti-Nazi broadcasts produced illegally by amateurs from secret locations. They hoped to start an anti-Hitler movement by stirring the airwaves. Unfortunately, a few honest comments shouted over the air were no match for the powerhouse that Hitler had constructed on the other side of the border.

Among the anti-Nazi airwave listening addicts were Nazi officials who were charged with purifying Germany's atmosphere and eliminating dangerous thoughts that might interfere with the Nazi version of events. These officials complained to the Czechoslovak government that they believed that some illegal radio broadcasts originated from somewhere near Prague. The Czech government said they would look into this. They reported back, that they could not find the source. A few days later, Prague newspapers reported the murder of a German refugee in a small village inn, not more than twenty miles from our apartment. German agents had driven around the countryside with their radio listening devices, locating the source in a village; zeroing in on a small inn. They sent a female agent into the hotel to order dinner. She noticed a German-speaking guest who kept to himself. She registered in the inn, took advantage of the refugee's loneliness, invited herself to his room and located the radio equipment. After spending the night, she reported the success of her mission to the Nazi team. They promptly killed and silenced the lonely anti-Nazi voice.

Hitler's voice became shriller and shriller. The *Anschluss*, the annexation of Austria, in the middle of March of 1938, was the last straw. We decided we had to leave in order to get beyond the range of Hitler's voice and weapons.

***

Shortly after Hitler's assumption of power in 1933, many anti-Nazis hoped that somehow or other Hitler's increasingly tight control over most aspects of German life could be terminated. If that happened, we could return and resume our previous life. Such a turn of events depended on a successful domestic revolt or on some action by a foreign country.

It became obvious however, that internal opponents had missed their opportunity. I overheard friends in Berlin and later in Prague talking in hushed tones about this or that acquaintance who had disappeared in *Nacht and Nebel* [night and fog] as they tried to escape political imprisonment for some anti-Nazi comment. The Nazis set up concentration camps for their political opponents. They staged the Reichstag fire on February 27, 1933, to justify outlawing first the Communist party and, then other real or potential opposition parties. On June 30, 1934, in the Great Blood Purge, on Hitler's order, even potentially unreliable members of his own Nazi party were peremptorily shot.

Foreign action was the only hope left to terminate Hitler's reign. One ray of hope appeared when Hitler's attempt to take over Austria in July 1934 failed. Ironically, it was his ideological kindred friend Mussolini who stopped him by moving Italian forces to the Austrian border at the Brenner Pass. No other foreign power helped Austria maintain its independence.

Again, on March 7, 1936, France and Great Britain lacked the guts to take action when Hitler sent his troops into the Rhineland in violation of the Treaty of Versailles that Germany had signed in 1919. That was an ominous sign that neither France nor Great Britain was willing to prevent Czechoslovakia from being taken over by Hitler

How about Hitler's main opponents, the Communists, and especially his nemesis in the East, Stalin? Stalin, in complete control of the Soviet Union after ousting Trotsky in December 1927, played a cagy role. Initially he ordered the German Communist party not to join the Social Democratic Party that had opposed Hitler in the election leading up to Hitler's appointment as Chancellor. Stalin had assumed that the contest between the Nazis and the center parties would divide Germany sufficiently to give Communists the chance to take over Germany. It was much too late before Stalin realized his colossal error of judgment. Only after Hitler had consolidated his power, did Stalin change course and turn on Hitler. He sponsored the Popular Front, an alliance of all parties opposed to Hitler. He also formed an alliance with Czechoslovakia in 1935, promising to help it, if was attacked by Hitler. Thus, Stalin became the most important opponent of Hitler who, we hoped, would help protect us.

When the Soviet Union became an ally of Czechoslovakia, I became curious about what communism was all about. My father explained that it meant dividing property equally. "That's great", I responded. My father then asked me, "how would you like to share your room, bicycle, garden with x, y and z", kids who were not exactly your friends." I agreed that was not a good idea. There were also stories in the paper about the terrible suffering that accompanied Stalin's collectivization drive in the Soviet Union.

At the time that Stalin carried out cruel domestic programs, he became increasingly important as one of the very few powerful leaders to stand up to Hitler in the mid-thirties. In Czechoslovakia, the ambivalent feeling about Stalin's Soviet Union was especially acute. One of the very few times that our French gymnasium class was taken to a theater to watch a movie as part of our class assignment, we saw a dramatic account of the Czech legion battling the Bolsheviks in Siberia in 1917/18. The Legion consisted of captured soldiers of the Austro-Hungarian army who had shifted sides and joined the Russians. Following the Bolshevik revolution in November 1917, the Czech soldiers were on their way out via the Far East to be shipped to the Western front. On the way, they fought the Bolsheviks. Naturally, the movie house resounded with our cheers when the Bolsheviks were pushed back or killed. On our return to school, we were led in a discussion of contemporary affairs. There we shifted gears and lauded the Soviet Union for standing up to Hitler and promising to protect us.

Stalin's offer of help gave us a certain degree of comfort. Relying on Soviet support came however with important caveats. The Soviet Union joined the League of Nations and organized the Popular Front, a coalition of left-wing parties that opposed the Nazis. Stalin intended to convince his critics that the U.S.S.R. no longer intended to go alone and operate exclusively through the Komintern [Communist International], the Stalin controlled Communist parties. On the other hand, there were those show trials!

Stalin shocked the world with news of domestic purges of almost all the original leaders of the Bolshevik revolution. Unlike Hitler's comparable Bloodbath, Stalin orchestrated his consolidation of power by first kicking Leon Trotsky out of the Soviet Union and out of Europe altogether and then by holding widely publicized trials in which Zinoviev, Kamenev and other former colleagues "confessed" that they had planned to oust Stalin and terminate the Soviet experiment. The public confessions were supposed to justify executions. Even more important, they became the cover for wholesale lower level political arrests and imprisonment that led to forced labor camps.

My worries about Hitler's next acts of aggression and the implications of Stalin's purges made it difficult for me to grow up with confidence in a happy future. When I was about to accept a German refugee kid's invitation for an afternoon game of ping-pong, my father warned me to be careful because the kid's father was a Communist. The kid beat me decisively. I guess I attributed my ping pong loss to the political views of his father. This was not the world that I had expected to enter. It was not the world of my dreams. It did not even resemble the stories I had read as a kid; the stories of the battle of Greek gods; romantic affairs among French courtesans and the stories of Scottish adventurers and explorers. It was a world where adults argued in my presence whether to believe

Trotsky or Stalin; trust the French or the Russians; place any hope that the British or the U.S. would recognize Hitler's ultimate plan to control the world. In retrospect, becoming aware of deep contradictions and fundamental conflicts in efforts to achieve political objectives and to implement ideals of justice and fairness at such an early age, directed my vocational goals and helped me understand and analyze international affairs.

***

While Hitler's threats were never far from my mind, they fortunately did not interfere with my rapidly intensifying interest in girls. I remember a long lasting crush on some female fellow class members of my French gymnasium, but these feelings were not reciprocated. One of my father's professional friends who lived within walking distance from our house had a son, Frank. We became good friends and discussed the exciting topic of girls. We had many such discussions on our ski vacation in December '37. He knew Lore who happened to ski with us. She was a great flirt. Unfortunately, Frank attracted her more than I, even though I was a year older than Frank. He and I invented a secret code in our letters, which we used to communicate news about Lore.

Luck had it that in the house next to his there lived Eva, another girl, just my age. The no longer used sandbox located between the two houses served as a perfect spot for discussing increasingly important topics of common interest, aims in life, and feelings for each other. Her parents were also thinking about leaving Prague. The uncertainty of our respective futures gave our daily encounters a dramatic edge. We had to make the most of the limited time. We could not imagine our more distant future.

June 1938 was warm enough to encourage us to go swimming in a public outdoor pool in a nearby valley about an hour's walking distance from our respective houses. Eva and I swam and fooled around. We chased each other up and down the terraced sun bathing areas above the pool. The adults followed us with their eyes. When they started to snicker and smile at our antics, I suddenly realized that my swimsuit failed to properly cover certain parts of my body. Eva egged me on and we had a marvelous time. On the way out of the valley, our discussion became very serious. We declared each other our love. Neither one of us knew what that really meant because it was the first time for both of us. We knew that soon we would part on our separate ways to an unknown future. We promised to write each other. And we did!

We had hoped and expected to meet soon again. After all, at fourteen we knew that there was much more than holding hands. The last time we saw each other in Prague in July 1938, I felt a strange unaccustomed attraction, a desire to be close, not just at that moment, but also in the future. I was the first to leave Prague and arrive in New York. She left for Bergen, Norway. That is where my letters went. Her letters reached me shortly after I had sent her a letter from New York with my new address. I seem to recall that her parents intended to come to the U.S. Time was running out and they managed instead to reach England. There, I addressed the letters to her in Shrewsbury, Shropshire. Addressing love letters to a place with such a name made the venture even more romantic. I enjoyed having my parents, and then my college friends, inquire about that mysterious person, the source of the thick envelops with interesting stamps and bearing notices that they had passed through censorship. Thus, we were made aware that the British government cared about our relationship. I do not recall the censor inhibiting our feelings for each other. Overseas mail took at least ten days. This meant that our letters crossed each other, sometimes leading to misunderstandings. Our love letters kept us going for almost six years until the war was nearly over. Eva's last letter announced her coming marriage to somebody in Shrewsbury.

I did not realize until later how much this romance had helped me get through the tribulations of adolescence unscathed. It protected me in my casual romantic college encounters. Whenever I became interested in a girl, I compared her in my mind to Eva who gradually evolved into the perfect partner beyond the reach of those around me. She was there in the letters counseling me to wait. When our romance was over, I had a clear signal that I finally could go ahead. The letters were also a perfect counterpoint to the dismal news from the several war fronts, especially in the first three years of the war. However bad the war news, the letters provided hope for a better future. Love may not have conquered everything, but it certainly made life more bearable.

Chapter 4
Time to Leave Europe

1938 was a very important year. Not only did I have my first girlfriend but my horizon expanded far beyond Prague, Berlin and the Austrian Tyrol to Switzerland and even further to Holland and eventually to the New World across the Atlantic Ocean.

That special year started early. A day after Christmas 1937 my friend Frank and I were sent off by our respective parents to a ski camp in mountains near the German border, the Riesengebirge [Krkonoše], where we were to learn to ski. We were about a dozen 11 to 14 year old boys and girls. During the day, counselors taught us to fall without breaking our bones and to avoid trees while schussing down the mountain trail. Before falling asleep, we discussed sex. It was fun.

The real world was never out of our minds. On the crest of the mountain range, we were within sight of Hitler's Reich and naturally, we at first imagined, and then actually saw, German border guards in threatening uniforms. It did not help that I received a note from my mother that she suddenly had to go to Berlin where my grandmother had succumbed to her kidney disease. Her death was another marker that put an end to the Berlin of my childhood.

Back at home in Prague, I was alone on February 12 in the evening and listened to the radio. Kurt Schuschnigg, the Chancellor of Austria, addressed his nation and news addicts like me. He reported excitedly what had happened earlier that day on his visit to Berchtesgaden, Adolf Hitler's mountain retreat. Hitler had requested him to agree to the annexation and incorporation of Austria by the German Reich. The term used was *Anschluss*. That meant that we in Czechoslovakia would be nearly completely encircled by Adolf Hitler's armed forces and swastika wearing storm troopers. Schuschnigg stated emotionally in his radio address that, now that he was safely back in Austria, he had scheduled a plebiscite to let the Austrian people themselves decide whether they wanted to join Germany or remain free. He stated where he stood: Rot-Weisz-Rot bis in den Tod [Red-White-Red until Death]. Those were the colors of the Austrian flag.

Before the people could vote, Hitler marched into Austria depriving Austrians the right to make their own decision. The invading Germans cast the decisive vote for the *Anschluss.* Hitler's move had a major impact on us: we were surrounded by Hitler's troops. The only question left was how much time we had to avoid the fate of Hitler's victims in his native Austria where popular anti-Semitic sentiment exceeded that in Germany. Refugees who had escaped by swimming across the Danube visited us in our safe living room in Prague and warned us what was in store for us. Czechoslovakia was next on Hitler's list.

We had to get as far away from Hitler as possible. America was our choice destination. Many of my parents' friends in Berlin and elsewhere in Germany had already arrived in the United States. The problem was that it was not so easy to enter that safe haven. The first step was a special Czechoslovak passport entitling travel beyond Europe. That was not difficult. We obtained it early in March. Then we had to obtain a visa permitting us to enter the U.S.; a one-way steamship ticket to cross the Atlantic; money to support us for at least a year in the U.S.; arrangements to ship our furniture across the Atlantic. Perhaps most important, I had to leave my friends behind. It meant abandoning the known past and embarking on an entirely new voyage to a different world.

While my father had abandoned his secure home once before when he was 22 years old, he was 51 now and set in his ways. He looked askance at the prospect of having to learn English. My mother was a more comfortable 38 and had learned English in school. She was willing to face new challenges. I had mixed feelings. On the one hand, I recognized the immediate threat that Hitler posed next door. After all I had followed with deep concern several instances of Hitler's murderous acts that had occurred close by. On the other hand, going to America did not seem very real to me. All the books that I had read about America had given me the impression that our destination was a land of adventurers, cowboys, Indians and outlaws. Could one live there a normal life? I had just reached the stage in my development where I had some really close friends I would have to abandon.

On March 13, the day of the Anschluss, the clock started ticking. To get a visa to enter the U.S., one needed an affidavit, a word that quickly occupied a dominant place in our vocabulary. An affidavit was a statement in which a U.S. citizen vouched for the fact that the immigrant would not become a burden to the U.S.

government, i.e. the person giving the affidavit promised to help support the immigrant financially. We had to locate a relative who had successfully established him/herself in the U.S. My father turned to his relatives in Plzeň. They referred him to Aunt Rosa in New York, the owner of an apparel company. Locating Aunt Rosa was only the first step. Communicating with somebody in the U.S. was not easy in 1938. Transatlantic mail went by ship. A letter would take a minimum of two weeks to be answered. We were lucky that the affidavit arrived May 29th, about two and a half months after the clock had started ticking.

The next day I skipped school and accompanied my parents to the American consulate on a street in the center of Prague, Na Přikopě [*On the Ditch*]. We were shocked to find the gate to the consulate locked. A sign in English and Czech explained that it was a holiday, Memorial Day. Since the world that I knew commemorated the Fallen War Heroes on November 11, we were made quickly aware that we were knocking on the doors of a different world. Disappointed, we returned the next day. Now the gate was open and we were ushered into a large room to wait for our chance to hand our application to the U.S. vice-consul. I was surprised that our fellow applicants appeared to come from small towns and villages and certainly were not dressed like we city folk.

I remember the American vice-consul as young with a friendly face. That surprised me. I had expected that the official guarding the entrance to the New World would be someone looking very important, certainly not friendly. The vice-consul found our papers in order. He promptly approved our application for a visa. Just one more question: Do you want to be considered a citizen of Germany or Czechoslovakia for the purpose of this visa application? We responded that we were of course citizens of Czechoslovakia. Think it over, he counseled us and explained: my father was born in Czechoslovakia and under U.S. law would be considered a Czech; mother and I were born in Germany and the U.S. could consider us German. U.S. policy was not to separate a family, it was therefore up to us to choose the national quota that we wanted our names to be placed on. Silence "If I enter your name on the Czech quota, there is a waiting list and your name may not come up for three years. The German quota list is shorter and your name may be reached in two and a half months". My father responded instantly:”for the purpose of getting permission to enter the U.S. we would not mind being German”. The vice-consul promised we would be informed about our quota admission date very soon. Indeed, a letter arrived a few days later informing us that we should present our passports to his office on August 12th, 1938, to obtain our official visa to enter the United States. In retrospect, my family owes an immense debt of gratitude to this American consular official who spared us the fate that befell to so many others, not as fortunate to have encountered an official with a heart.

***

As the summer progressed Hitler, as expected, shifted his propaganda and targeted Czechoslovakia. The Sudetenland, inhabited by the German-speaking minority of Bohemia and Moravia was Hitler’s next intended territorial acquisition. Nobody had stopped Hitler from annexing Austria. Would France carry out its commitment to protect Czechoslovakia from Hitler? Would Stalin who had signed a treaty to help Czechoslovakia? Would Hitler give us enough time to use our visa? On May 22nd, Czechoslovakia had placed its armed forces on a special alert because Germany carried out military maneuvers in Saxony, near the mountains where I had skied in December. Hitler was furious. He called the Czech action a provocation because he had no plans to attack Czechoslovakia in May. He did not say what he had scheduled for late September. On the hill behind our house in Dejvice, Czechoslovak armed forces deployed anti-aircraft guns. Light beams pierced the sky all night.

Were we safe until August 12? My mother was in touch with Grandpa Willy in Berlin. She asked him whether it was safe to stay in Prague. He suggested that we wait in Switzerland until we had our visas and could leave Europe. When my school year ended in June, our furniture and all our possessions were packed tightly into a container that would travel in the bowel of a ship to New York. Following Grandpa Willy’s advice we decided to spend July and early August in Kandersteg, a little village in Switzerland surrounded by the mountain peaks of the Bernese Alps, not far from the famous Jungfrau.

Getting there presented a problem. To travel to Switzerland from Prague required passing through Germany. My father, who had written and published many articles criticizing the Nazi regime, believed that he was not safe traveling in Germany. Crossing the German frontier was therefore not an option for him. The only alternative was to fly from Prague directly to Zurich staying out of reach of German officials. It had never occurred to us that my father would ever be on a plane. After all, he was still talking about his first train ride to Munich in 1909, a ride that had made him so sick that he had spent most of his time vomiting. For reasons I cannot recall, my mother and I felt less threatened and took the train. When German officials checked our passports at the German Swiss border, my heart pounded so much that I worried the German official would target me as an enemy of the Third Reich. Nothing happened and we reached Switzerland's safe haven. In Zürich, we met my father who surprised us by telling us how much he had enjoyed his flight. He did not get sick and even managed to look out of the plane's window.

After spending a couple of days exploring Zürich, we continued to Kandersteg in the heart of the Swiss Alps. We had rented a couple of rooms in a chalet. A short distance from us my aunt Käte, uncle Hans and, most important, my 7 year old cousin Ruth, the only close relative near my age, had rented another chalet. I had not seen Ruth since leaving Berlin when she was a baby. Spending a month with Käte and Ruth was exciting. After leaving Germany, they had spent a year in Belgium, decided that they were still too close to danger and moved to Spain. There they thought they would be safe: the Iberian Peninsula appeared to be beyond Hitler's reach. They settled in Barcelona, learned to speak Spanish, and Uncle Hans started a business to earn a living. General Francisco Franco, supported by Mussolini and Hitler, interrupted their plans by starting a civil war intending to overthrow the elected Spanish government.

From distant Prague, I had followed the course of the Spanish struggle, admired the valiant efforts by the Loyalists to stop Franco's advances, and watched newsreels of German fighters bombing northern Spain's Basque province. I was horrified by Britain and France's failure to lift a finger to stop Hitler's aerial attacks and Mussolini's provisions of arms. The Soviet Union was the only major power to help the Loyalists, mostly through the International Brigade. When it became clear that Franco could not be stopped, my aunt, uncle and cousin left Barcelona for

Switzerland. They had many stories to tell, but events were too recent for comfortable discussions. Instead, they worried about their next destination. Switzerland had given them only a short-term permit to stay. Their thoughts turned to South America. There they could use their newly acquired ability to speak Spanish. At least we knew where we were headed, unfortunately, they did not, and the clock was ticking. A year later, when we were already established in New York, Ruth and her parents sent us a postcard from the Panama Canal, on their way to Chile, their ultimate destination. I did not see my cousin again until half a century later.

Kandersteg reunited our family, but there was also a lighter side to our Swiss sojourn. We went on mountain trails far more impressive than the ones in the Austrian Alps. We explored and admired the stunningly situated Öschinensee, climbed up to the Gemmipass. There was a restaurant hut from which we could look down far below us onto the Rhone River. We took the train to Brig and the bus up to the Simplon Pass near the Italian border. There I swore at Mussolini, but he could not hear me. Seven years later, he was hung from a tree not too many miles away from the Swiss Alps. It had taken that long for my wish to be fulfilled.

A few days after August 1, the Swiss National Holiday, we said good-bye to Käte and her family. We stopped in Zürich, from where my father flew directly to Prague. My mother and I detoured for another good-bye. Crossing by train the German border we detoured to Constance on Lake Bodensee. There we met my grandpa Willy, who had taken the train from Berlin. We stayed in a fancy hotel overlooking the lake that separates Germany from Switzerland. In a nearby park, I saw for the first time a bench with a sign, “Not for Jews”. Naturally, I sat down and nothing happened. Maybe, because nobody saw me or knew, who and what I was.

My mother and I enjoyed my grandfather’s companionship for three days, which turned out to be our last time together. Not far from our hotel was a bridge that crosses the Rhine as it exits Lake Constance. On the other side was Kreuzlingen in Switzerland. We all walked to the border, which was adorned with Swastikas on one side and the Swiss White Cross on Red, on the other. At the arranged time my aunt Käte appeared on the Swiss side. Separated by only a few feet, Aunt Käte and Grandpa Willy exchanged greetings, their hopes for the future, some memories, questions, few answers, tender looks, good-byes. For a moment the officials who guarded the frontier and observed us, suspicious characters that we were, receded into the background, but did not disappear. That was the last time Grandfather Willy saw any of us. We went back to the hotel, said good-bye to Grandpa Willy. The train took us back to Prague without any incident.

***

Grandpa Willy had celebrated his 70th birthday on our lawn in Wannsee in 1933. He challenged me to kick the ball to the soccer goal line formed by two small trees: he scored as many goals as I did, even though he was 61 years older. He was in great shape. The occasion was even more amazing: it was January, but there was no snow on the ground.

I liked Grandpa Willy: He did not fool me when I was five, when he tried hard to impersonate Santa Claus as he emerged from behind all the candles that lit up our Christmas tree. Two years later I had immersed myself in Dr Doolittle's world of animals that lived close by and in remote places like the Canary Islands. Suddenly I started receiving postcards signed by those animals and on my seventh birthday I received a letter from Dr. Doolittle informing me that I had been awarded the "Star of Dr. Doolittle's Legion of Honor," a decoration that I was to wear proudly on my chest. The return address was somewhere near grandpa's house.

Only one week after we had celebrated grandpa's birthday, political events changed our world. Adolf Hitler was appointed Chancellor of Germany. In Prague we were separated from Grandpa Willy by a six-hour train ride. Our weekly get-togethers were no more. My mother and I visited him in Berlin perhaps once a year. After 1936, it became very difficult for Grandpa to get permission to travel abroad. We met only on special occasions. On one occasion when we were together in Marienbad, Czechoslovakia, and listened to Beethoven's Ninth Symphony broadcast from the Salzburg festival, he broke out in tears as the choir sang the Ode to Joy. It reminded us all of the Germany we had loved, that was no more.

Grandpa Willy considered the political changes a new challenge. A story that impressed me was his account of a trip to Switzerland in 1936 or 1937. Of course, nobody was permitted to take money out of Germany. As the train approached the German-

Swiss frontier, he went to the tiny toilet in his coach. He found a space where he deposited some German funds he had stashed away in his pocket. He went back to his seat, read a book and answered all the questions the frontier officials pestered him with. When the train started moving on Swiss soil, he immediately went to the toilet. After all, people over 60 have a special need for those facilities. He retrieved his intact treasure and deposited it in a Swiss bank account.

He helped my aunt Kate and her husband get established in Barcelona. When General Franco threatened that city, he helped them get to Switzerland and ultimately Chile. He encouraged my parents to put some distance between us and the Third Reich. His advice had always been on the mark. I wondered where he got his information. I learned later that he had "friends" dating to his business connections before retirement, who had dealt with materials used in armaments. One of his friends was in Japan's Berlin embassy. That friend informed him right after the annexation of Austria that Czechoslovakia's turn was next and advised him to get his daughter and family out of there as quickly as possible. He suggested that we wait in Switzerland until we had our U.S. visas.

In December 1937, my grandmother who had suffered for years from bone fractures and kidney failure died peacefully in Berlin. As long as she was alive, Grandpa Willy did not even consider leaving Germany. Now that he no longer had to worry about her and knew that Aunt Käte and my parents and I were on the way to a safer haven, he could start making plans for his own safety.

He lived with my aunt Lise, who was not in the best of health since her lungs had been permanently damaged by tuberculosis she had contracted in the turmoil after the First World War. Preparing aunt Lise and his departure was not easy. He had to give up and empty the house on Sächsische Strasse, where the family had lived since the early 1900's and where my mother and her siblings had grown up. Aunt Lise and he had to spend the summer of 1939 in a small rooming house preparing their possessions for sea transport to England and listing the content of all his carry-on baggage in triplicate. Officials had to approve every item, including soap, towels and handkerchiefs that Grandpa Willy and aunt Lise wanted to take with them. In a letter detailing all this before his departure, he wrote, “I had to pay a lot of money for that”. Finally, he mailed a postcard on a train in Holland, dated August 28, 1939, stating that he and aunt Lise had passed the Dutch frontier on their way to London. Free at last. In a letter, dated September 8, 1939, after their arrival, he explained why he was so late getting out, less than a week before Germany attacked Poland and the start of World War II. “I could not obtain my (exit permit) papers in spite of every effort…I was struggling for three months. Driven to despair and knowing exactly what was going on I succeeded at last, at the very last minute, to obtain admission to the top official and got our permits to leave. We went off immediately but could not get our heavy trunks and luggage. In this emergency we left everything behind.”

After a couple of days in London, where he was met by a cousin who had left earlier, he moved to 1 Mooreland Road, Didsbury, Manchester, to a house that had belonged to his sister’s family. He spent the remaining 8 years of his life there. We exchanged many letters. He had hoped that I would end up at Oxford. When I passed my Ph.D. oral exam at Harvard one year before his death, he was very pleased. He was even happier when I wrote him in the summer of 1947 that I had gotten a job teaching at the University of Connecticut. Before he died, he knew that at least one member of his family had a chance to live a normal life after surviving Adolf Hitler’s nightmare.

40 years later I managed to visit Manchester and look up his house. I asked a neighbor,” how come the surrounding houses all appeared to be more recently built than his?” “Did your grandfather not tell you that his house was the only one to escape a direct hit from Hitler’s air attacks?” He had never mentioned it. Other events had been more important

***

On August 12, 1938, my parents and I had our Czechoslovak passports stamped with the precious U.S. visa at the U.S. consulate in Prague. The passports also had a special entry entitling us to leave Europe. On the 17th, we went to the new Ruzině Airport near Prague. My friend Frank and his parents waved us good-bye. This was to be my first flight. We took a plane to Rotterdam in Holland, flying over Hitler's Germany.

When we arrived at the airport, they were loading the airplane, a small one by current standards. The airport official examined our passports, directed my parents and me to a special room where I was searched and then asked to undress completely. I was nervous because I was afraid the plane would not wait for me getting my cloths back on. "Where is your money?" the official asked. "I have fifty dollars". I answered. "That is impossible", he said, in not a very friendly manner. "How are you going to live in New York?" "Aunt Rosa sent us an affidavit that she would not let us become a burden to the government". I answered. We were allowed to take out only a ridiculously small amount of money. I learned much later that my father had met a Scottish Presbyterian clergyman to whom he gave two thousand dollars in Prague that this clergyman's U.S. counterpart would return to him in New York. When we finally boarded the plane, our fellow passengers were visibly relieved that the plane could finally take off. The plane rose quickly high enough to enable us to look down on the confining borders that Hitler had built around Czechoslovakia. I was 14 and a half when I left Czechoslovakia.

It was a very cloudy day, but in a few minutes, we penetrated the mass of fluffy cotton balls and emerged in the sun. It was all so simple! I started to relax and explored the content of the container attached to the seat in front of me. The flight attendant came over quickly thinking I needed help. She explained that if I felt sick, I could use that paper container to relieve my stomach pain. I replied that I was not sick, just very excited and that I had no intention of throwing up. Occasionally there was a break in the clouds. I tried to identify the part of Germany below us. Eventually the plane started its descent. I was about to get my first look at Western Europe. Holland looked different: Everything looked attractive; there were well-kept green farms, no hills that marred the level ground. We landed at the Rotterdam airport.

We had to wait two and a half weeks in Holland until the scheduled departure of the Holland-America ship Veendam. Holland was an exciting new world. One of my father's acquaintances had arranged for us to stay in Katwijk, a small resort on the coast. Breakfast in the Rotterdam hotel on our first day consisted of a great deal more than my customary continental breakfast. Instead of just rolls, jam and hot chocolate, there was a choice of fish, tropical fruit, eggs prepared in countless ways, a great variety of breads, baked goods and on and on. Then there was lunch, only a few hours later and equally plentiful. No wonder the Dutch looked better fed than we Central Europeans. The train from Rotterdam to Leiden came at frequent intervals seemed so modern and covered the admittedly short distance in record time. Then a single-car electric trolley took us over the dunes to Katwijk facing the North Sea.

That is where I had my first look at an ocean. Coming from landlocked Czechoslovakia, seeing with my own eyes what I had read about in Robert Louis Stevenson's novels. There was a beach of clean white sand, gently sloping into the waves. It stretched north and south as far as the eye could see. On the beach were countless cocoon looking chairs that intended to protect the scantily dressed sunbathers from the wind that relentlessly blasted cold air from the sea. One afternoon my mother and I walked for more than an hour in a southerly direction to a huge pier that stretched from an amusement park at least a hundred feet into the sea. It was Scheveningen, a suburb of The Hague. Another day somebody lent me a bicycle and I traveled on roads that were open only to bicycles. I visited The Hague and admired the park-like entrance and palace of the International Court of Justice. I was impressed. Maybe that is why five years later I took a course in international law at Cornell.

I was amazed that people behaved differently. As a fourteen year old, I enjoyed seeing many scantily dressed ladies on their beach chairs. My mother admonished me not to keep on looking. This would embarrass the targets of my interest. They did not seem to mind, so I kept on looking when my mother tried to divert my attention and pointed at some uninteresting seashells that I was supposed to investigate. I also had occasion to note that girls my age acted quite differently from the ones I had known in Prague. One afternoon, a family invited us to their vacation home. When the parents became involved in a political discussion, two sisters asked me to come to the other room where we could talk. It turned out that the only place to gab was in a bunk bed large enough for the three of us. It got very cozy.

All of this was only a way station. We had our U.S. visas and just paused briefly on the way to our destination. Even my parents, who were farsighted enough to realize that Czechoslovakia was not safe from Hitler, did not foresee that Holland would be devastated less than two years later. After all, Holland had managed to avoid the Kaiser's invasion in 1914 and, after abdicating in 1918, the Kaiser spent his exile in Holland. Coincidentally my mother's maiden name was Ann Frank, so Hitler's treatment of Holland was to have a special connotation in my mind.

***

On September 2, 1938, we said good bye to the friends we had met in Katwijk, took the trolley to Leiden, the train to Rotterdam and hailed a taxi to take us from the train station to the Holland-America Line pier where the Veendam was moored, waiting to take us to America. We could board any time after 6 P.M. The ship was scheduled to leave at one minute after midnight. As we approached the harbor, the road along the river was blocked. A huge crowd filled the street. The taxi driver, said, sorry that is as far as he could take us. There was to be a parade, we were on our own to locate our ship. I led the way, carrying our suitcases and used my newly acquired ability to communicate in Dutch, i.e. German, with a few words of English that I had just learned and some French, to ask where the Veendam was. I pointed at my passport, but somehow everybody understood what I wanted and directed us through the mass of humanity assembled for the parade to the waiting Veendam. We got on board, were shown our three bed cabin. It had a tiny porthole. I escaped from this prison as soon as I could to explore the deck. I asked what the multitude was waiting for. They were not just waiting to wave us good-bye: The Dutch Queen was celebrating the 50th anniversary of her reign, floating by with considerable pomp and circumstance after dark. From our choice location, we watched the Queen, music and fireworks. What a celebration! Then, ever so slowly, the Veendam started to move. We left all the light and noise behind us. What a send-off !!!

The Veendam started the transatlantic voyage quietly. The noise and lights of the evening's festivities faded away. One could hardly feel the engines. It's very late, let us all go to bed immediately, or else we shall miss breakfast, my father admonished me. I admit I was tired and fell asleep immediately. I did not sleep long. Considerable shaking woke me up. The Veendam had encountered the swells of the open sea as we reached the mouth of the Rhine and the ship made a sharp turn to the left to sail parallel to the coast. I peered through the porthole and saw nothing but open water. Our cabin faced the open sea. I was surprised how turbulent the waves were in the English Channel. For someone who had never been out to sea, this was not a good omen.

Daylight saw us floating along the French coast. After breakfast, our first meal on shipboard, we came closer to the coast and around lunch time anchored off the French port of Boulogne where a tugboat ferried additional passengers to our ship. Transferring passengers to come on board took considerable time. We were not in a hurry to leave Europe. It became obvious that the Veendam was not about to break any cross-Atlantic speed record. We were stuck on an ancient slow boat.

It was dark by the time we reached our next stop: Southampton on the southern coast of England. We stayed in the outer harbor waiting for a small boat to approach us with more passengers. Some considerably larger and more impressive liners were all lit up decorating the harbor. New images formed in my mind that, until a few weeks ago, had been limited to continental landscapes. The ship started to move again. We finally departed from Europe. Had we really left? I was surprised the next morning when land appeared on our left. I had thought that there was nothing between the southern coast of England and America. I had never heard of the Scilly Islands. They had semi-tropical vegetation. Why did Dr Doolittle's animals have to go all the way to the Canary Islands, if they could have stayed much closer to home here in the Scilly Islands?

Boredom set in on the third day. I joined the sailor who acted as a lookout on the bow of the ship. One has to remember that in those days there was no radar. Except for radio communication and steam engines, navigation did not differ that much from the days of Columbus. On some days, dense fog enveloped the ship and the ship's horn sounded every few seconds. I had heard the story of the Titanic's disaster that had occurred a quarter century earlier. I was looking for icebergs. Mostly the sea was calm; the calm before the hurricane, that was to hit the East Coast ten days after our arrival in America.

The Veendam took nine days to cross the Atlantic after leaving England. Crossing six time zones in nine days did not create jet lag, a term unknown then. Every other day the captain posted a note, asking us to set our clock back one hour. There were some kids my age among the refugees and we discussed what we had been told about American schools. I was pleased to learn that the school year in New York did not start until the third week of September. That was important: There was less to catch up. Food was another topic of conversation. Veendam's dinner menus offered few items that we were accustomed to eat. A new item that intrigued me and was to become a staple of my new

American diet was pistachio ice cream.

The day before we reached New York, I saw our ship heading straight for a stationary ship. At almost the last minute, the Veendam blew its horn and veered sharply to the left. We passed so close, that I was able to read the huge letters NANTUCKET LIGHT painted on the ship. It appeared that the captain must have been asleep at the wheel and shifted direction at the very last minute. Finally, something exciting had happened. I started to look for the coast of America, the continent that was to become my New World. Staring intently into the distance, I looked straight ahead, hoping to see land. It took several hours before there appeared a gray line on the Western horizon. New York? No, Long Island. It was getting dark. Lights twinkled in the distance.

After our last dinner on board ship, the engine slowed down. We entered New York's outer harbor. I looked for the Statue of Liberty. We anchored in the harbor to wait for daylight to land. There was a monument with twinkling lights. Was that the famed statue that was to welcome us on our arrival? It had a message in big letters: WRIGLEY CHEWING GUM. A discussion among us ensued: it was probably not the statue, just a gigantic advertisement. What a disappointment!

Early the next morning on September 13 a small boat approached us as we were sailing up the harbor. It delivered customs and immigration officials who promptly set up shop in the ship's Dining Room. We waited in line, had a cursory physical exam to keep those afflicted by contagious diseases from entering the United States. We had to show our passport with the treasured visa. Then the official asked an unexpected question: Do I want to change my name? That had never occurred to me. But, once asked, why not? The official had a friendly look, so I said, yes. Change my name from Kurt to Curt; that would appear more American. Instead of shocking my mother, she responded favorably. She informed me that her late brother who had fought four long years for the Kaiser had originally spelled his name with a C, but changed it to a K in World War I.

Having been admitted to the United States I was now able to pay attention to where we had landed. We were in Hoboken, on the New Jersey side of the Hudson. The famous skyscrapers were all on the opposite side. Coming down the gangplank, we were greeted by Aunt Rosa who had given us the affidavit enabling us to come to America. I do not remember how we recognized each other. My mother and I had never met her. My father must have been very young when he last saw her.

Rosa Kantor, the apparel company owner, led us to her car driven by a formally dressed chauffeur. Shortly after leaving the pier we entered a tunnel. I noticed *Holland* in big letters. This intrigued me: We had spent ten days crossing the Atlantic from Holland. Was this intended to remind us where we had come from?

My next observation was that for the first time in my life I saw a black person and I pointed to him. Aunt Rosa admonished me, telling me they were not called Neger (*negro)*, but *colored*. Furthermore, I was not to point. Next question: “Why do all those buildings have outside stairs?” “They are fire escapes,” she answered. New York close-up did not look as pretty as on the pictures that I had seen. Aunt Rosa deposited us soon on New York’s Upper West side, near Columbia University, probably relieved to get rid of this 14 year old who obviously did not fit into her world and who had demolished the romantic picture of her Plzeň childhood.

We had made it to America, our new home, far beyond Hitler’s reach!

Part II - Learning to Live in the New World

Chapter 5
Expectations and Reality

I first became interested in American politics in 1936 when I was twelve. I followed the contest between Franklin D. Roosevelt and Alfred M. Landon for president after Roosevelt's criticism of Hitler had caught my attention. A public opinion poll indicated that his re-election was threatened. That greatly worried me. I was relieved when FDR won by a landslide. A short time later some friends of my parents left for New York and wrote us that America was tolerable, suggesting we follow suit.

Leaving Europe and crossing the Atlantic to a New World, had been quite an experience. It was not just crossing a frontier and entering a country with people speaking a different language. It was a move that broke ties with the world that I knew and that I would have to abandon. In those days an ocean voyage took time: five days for the fastest ship. None of our acquaintances talked about returning to Europe. Crossing the Atlantic by plane was only a dream. Letters took a week. Transatlantic telephone calls were expensive and complicated. When we left Holland we left the world I knew and in which I had been comfortable for a destination that was unfamiliar and scary. It was not just an adventurous vacation, it was an irreversible move.

America had the well-deserved reputation as the preferred destination for Europeans who wanted, or had to leave their native country. I looked forward to joining all the other immigrants that made up America. In Prague, I had read many stories about America and knew the United States had problems. Earlier arrivals and their descendants had fought and destroyed Indians, the original inhabitants. Slavery had been legal long after it had been banished in Europe. It took Lincoln and a ferocious Civil War to outlaw slavery. I also learned that in the early 20th century there developed an antagonism to recent immigrants from Eastern Europe that had led to laws severely limiting "less desirable" immigrants. The 1924 immigration law had established immigration quotas intended to perpetuate the then existing ethnic population mix in the U.S.

Ten days on the Veendam had given me a lot of time to think and worry about what lay ahead. I traveled from my Wild West fantasies in my favorite adventure books to class lectures on Shakespeare's Macbeth at the George Washington High School on Amsterdam Avenue in upper Manhattan. In the spring I had conversed in Parisian French. Now in the fall everybody spoke English. I had to make friends with an entirely new set of kids and teachers in a school named after the first president of the U.S.

On our approach to New York, I worried about the future. I hoped that disgust with Hitler's crusade against Jews would trump past American prejudices about Central European refugees and that we might even be welcome. Watching the busy harbor from the Veendam's deck early in the morning on September 13, 1938, I was disappointed that the Statue of Liberty's torch was much smaller and less impressive than it had been featured in the books that I had read. It took some effort to note Miss Liberty's smile. Was her outstretched arm welcoming us? It took some time to find out.

Almost everything was different in America, even time. We had arranged to meet some friends on a bench in Morningside Park, a few blocks from Columbia University, on a Sunday afternoon at 1 P.M in September. We waited and waited. Our friends, also from Prague, were usually fifteen minutes late. They finally arrived at 2:10. When my father accused them of standing us up, they informed us that the clocks were set back that day to end daylight saving time. In America they save daylight in the summer!

Our first social encounter with American Society was not auspicious. Two weeks after welcoming us in Hoboken Aunt Rosa, the provider of the key that opened the door to our entry to the U.S., invited us for dinner. We took the subway and bus to get to her apartment on lower Park Avenue. A uniformed doorman opened the building's fancy entrance door and directed us to the elevator. Aunt Rosa's apartment was on an upper floor. It struck me as a very elegant place. I had not expected such luxury in our new country. Dinner was very formal. The fancy dishes did not meet the standards of my Central European taste buds. Grandmother in Plzeň had prepared much better tasting meals in her modest apartment. Aunt Rosa was surprised that the drink she offered, a bottle of Coca Cola, was new to me. She reassured me that in spite of its odd taste, it was safe. My father however looked worried as I swallowed this strangely colored drink.

I followed closely the table conversation. It quickly became obvious there was no meeting of minds. Sir Neville Chamberlain had just handed the Sudetenland to Adolf Hitler. Aunt Rosa agreed that that was too bad, but she did not get too excited about it, whereas my father wanted her to realize that was the end of the world, as far as we were concerned. "You got out, O.K?"Aunt Rosa remarked. My father wanted her to understand that many others were not so lucky and the U.S. should do something about that. It was my first encounter with the widespread feeling in America that the U.S. had no business intervening in the affairs of countries on the other side of the Atlantic. When my father and I praised President Franklin Delano Roosevelt for his handling of the Depression-caused crisis and his public warning about Adolf Hitler's threat to the existing world order, Aunt Rosa answered politely that she recognized that we probably had heard many good things about FDR, but she had problems with "that man in the White House". How could anybody not like the president of the country that had given us asylum from the horrors that were enveloping Central Europe? As a garment industry manufacturer, Rosa had to move her factory to Puerto Rico to escape Roosevelt's wage-and-hour laws intended to protect her employees. "That man in the White House has no right to deny me my rightful profits for the industry I built up." I recall only one other invitation to her place a year later. She made it clear to my father that we were on our own and that she had no inclination to support an intellectual whose views she did not share.

***

On October 1st, following our first location in a temporary small furnished apartment near Columbia University, we were able to move into an apartment overlooking the Hudson at 825 187th street. School did not start until the third week in September. The New World became real when my mother deposited me in the principal's office at the George Washington High School [GWHS], a twenty minute walk from our apartment. While only 14, I had enough course credits in foreign languages, science and history courses to qualify as a senior, except for English. Four semesters of English meant I would graduate in 1940, several months after my

16th birthday. I was given a mentor who was to help me find my way in this new world. The mentor was a refugee who had arrived a year earlier. I had no problem finding my way and after about half an hour I told my mentor I needed no further guidance. George Washington was much easier than my Prague French gymnasium. This meant I could quickly relax and begin to enjoy the New World.

GWHS differed from the school I had left in Prague two months earlier. It let me select the courses I wanted to take: an entirely new opportunity. No more Latin, no more ancient history. My father was shocked and dismayed when I rejected his advice. "Latin, Greek and ancient history were the foundation of knowledge required by a properly educated young man", my father said. "But this is America," I answered. It took me years to realize how right he had been.

The high school's name could not have been more American, yet most of my fellow students were recent refugees from Germany, Czechoslovakia and other Central European countries. Henry Kissinger was one of them. After all, GWHS served Washington Heights, Weimar Germany on the Hudson, in the thirties. My father asked me how many African Americans were in my school. The School's boundaries included the northern section of Harlem. I told him that I had noticed hardly any. He was shocked. "This is America which opposes Hitler's views about the superiority of the Aryan Race?" In 1937 he had attended an international conference in Paris at which U.S. scholars were fellow participants decrying Nazi pseudo-scientific racial theories. We began to realize that American practice did not match America's expressed principles.

Some of my fellow students, also relatively recent immigrants from parts of Europe beyond Hitler's immediate range, harbored thinly disguised resentment of all the attention showered on Jewish refugees from Germany and elsewhere in Europe. "You are a burden on the American economy", a Greek student probably echoing his father's opinion, told me several times. When I told him that our family consumed a lot of food and bought clothing that gave Americans jobs they might not otherwise have, he finally shut up.

Ten days after our arrival in New York it started to rain, school had started and my parents suggested I take an umbrella. I raised objections: walking to high school under an umbrella would make me look foolish. High school kids do not carry umbrellas, I told my parents. It became quickly obvious that weather in America was different. A severe hurricane targeted Eastern Connecticut and Rhode Island, giving New York a glancing blow. My umbrella, purchased in Prague, turned inside out. See, I told my parents, in America European umbrellas are useless. Under my breath I added, in America your advice is no longer relevant. Meanwhile our furniture was parked in a lift, as containers were named then, on a pier where it had been unloaded from a freighter. When we unpacked our furniture in our new apartment, we realized that the rain had leaked into the lift while it sat unprotected on the pier. It damaged our carefully packed furniture. Our books were soaked and my mother spent days trying to dry and save what was salvageable. The hurricane helped to further sever our remaining ties with Europe.

***

Berlin, Prague, Zurich, Amsterdam, paled in comparison with New York City. It was exciting to watch the huge transatlantic liners anchored at piers on the Hudson. The population of millions, speaking so many different languages and its congested traffic all made New York City an entirely new experience. Yet strangely enough, I found it easy to get around and feel comfortable as I explored my New World. Manhattan with its consecutively numbered streets and avenues fitted right into my geometry textbook that I had left behind in Prague. There just was no way of getting lost, except perhaps in lower Manhattan near Battery Park where the earliest immigrants had settled. Fellow refugee friends took us by ferry to the Statue of Liberty. I recall not particularly enjoying the narrow circular steps up the nose of Lady Liberty. Looking at the city from there did not impress me half as much as the city panorama visible from the ferry on our way back to the Battery.

There were however some disappointments. The Holland-America pier in Hoboken was far less elegant than the one in Rotterdam. The debarking passengers melted into a sea of humanity. Automobiles congested the streets. The buildings appeared ugly by Dutch or German standards. After emerging from the Holland tunnel the skyscrapers did not look the way they had on postcards. We were too close to get a proper perspective. Things began to look up at our temporary location near Columbia University where buildings were not so tall and trees.

I explored the New York subway system. For a nickel, I could travel almost anywhere. That was wonderful, except that I did not try too many destinations since most of my friends lived in upper Manhattan. I also explored exotic eating places, such as Horn and Hardard, where one dropped quarters in a slot and got a piece of apple pie. I went to my first Chinese restaurant and ordered chow mein and chop suey.

Our apartment in Washington Heights in the last building at the western end of 187th street faced the Palisades across the Hudson. The George Washington Bridge, visible from our living room window, challenged me to explore the park-like landscape on the other side of the river. It was possible for pedestrians to cross the West-side highway and gain access to the Bridge that looked so extremely impressive from our apartment window. I recall the walk across the bridge as not dangerous but quite long. Once in New Jersey, a well-maintained path bordered by trees and rocks encouraged us to descend to the park at the edge of the Hudson. That is where I first encountered an American innovation: picnic tables with attached benches. We walked north along the Hudson all the way to the pier where the Dyckman Street Ferry docked. We took it to return to Manhattan. One stop on the subway and we were back home.

Our apartment house was also a five-minute walk from Fort Tryon Park. That forested area near the top of Manhattan was one of the most impressive park areas that I had encountered up to then. It was well maintained and capped by the famous landmark, the Cloisters. The exceptionally well-restored Unicorn tapestries had been displayed only recently as if to celebrate our arrival. I enjoyed the otherworldly atmosphere of the cloisters, such a short distance from our new home. Washington Heights was a surprisingly pleasant and interesting destination and refuge from the Europe that had discarded us. No wonder that so many Central European refugees settled in Washington Heights in the mid-thirties.

And then, there were other parts of Manhattan that I could reach by subway. I explored Chinatown, the lower Eastside Jewish ghetto and Italian and Irish enclaves. On the way back by bus, we were impressed by mid-town Fifth Avenue, recently opened

Rockefeller Center and towering above the city and the whole world, the Empire State Building. I was warned to avoid Morningside Heights Park near Columbia University. It was alleged to be dangerous because the kids from Harlem might threaten me.

There were other boroughs beside Manhattan. In the spring of 1939, I visited Queens. My school got us season passes to the World's Fair. I took full advantage of that pass and spent many afternoons admiring the pavilions of competing countries that were about to go to war. The General Motors pavilion had the longest line. The exhibit was worth the wait. I loved to watch toy cars traveling on the yet-to-be-built Interstate highway system. These visits, some alone, some with friends, took my mind off the events in Europe, if only for an afternoon.

***

There were organizations in New York who cared about refugees and their children. I was lucky to have been picked by one that funded my stay at Camp Androscoggin in Maine for the summer of 1939. The intent was to make me aware that there was more to America than New York City with its hodgepodge of recent and some earlier immigrants who had spent several decades on this side of the Atlantic without ever venturing beyond Manhattan.

I had learned in my George Washington High School civics class that Maine held its presidential elections two months before the rest of the country and that the way the election went in Maine would predict the outcome in November. However in 1936, FDR lost in Maine, but carried 46 states. I looked forward to explore a state that had exhibited such odd behavior.

Camp instructions sent to my parents created considerable confusion. Where would we buy outdoor sleeping equipment for a canoe trip? What was a sleeping bag? Equipment to keep me dry when caught in a rainstorm on a hike lasting several days? Macy's answered most of my mother's concerns, but…

In the late afternoon on the last day of June, we went to Grand Central station and proceeded to a platform where a train consisting of at least ten coaches awaited us. Several hundred campers ranging from 10 to 16 and a dozen slightly older counselors boarded the assigned coaches. We waved good-bye to our mothers and fathers, entered an interminable dark tunnel and left New York City The entire train was exclusively ours and traveled non-stop. I was curious where we were going, what we were passing through and what cities I could brag about having seen from the train's window. We were probably in Connecticut when the sun sank below the horizon. I did not have a clue where we were. My fellow campers differed from the kids in my high school. They spoke English, not German. They talked about baseball and other sports about which I knew nothing. It dawned on me that I was about to get to know not just Maine but some real people from America. I climbed into the upper bunk and went to sleep.

The counselors woke us up as the sun rose. We had to get dressed in three minutes. The train stopped. The doors opened. We were expected to jump several feet onto the ground. There was no platform. There was no station. There were no houses, shacks or anything, but grass and trees. So this was the American wilderness that I had read about in Prague. Would the Indians appear from somewhere? After a very brief stop, the train left without us. We were all alone. We had been dropped off where the railroad bridge crossed a small river. After a fifteen minute wait we could hear a motorboat approaching. When it came around a curve the camp director rose to his full height, welcomed us with a bullhorn, and loaded us into the many canoes pulled by his motorboat.

The counselors were experienced canoeists and followed the motorboat on the river. We soon emerged from the wilderness and entered Lake Androscoggin, a huge body of water. In the middle of the lake there was an island, entirely occupied by Camp Androscoggin. We disembarked. Two campers and I were led to our summer home, the Aardvark cabin. All cabins were named after exotic animals that I had never heard of. That is where I spent my first summer in the United States.

Before unpacking and getting settled I had my first American-style breakfast. In New York my mother had prepared breakfasts consisting of orange juice, hard rolls, butter, jam and hot chocolate, just like in Berlin and Prague. I had enjoyed those breakfasts as long as I could remember. At Camp Androscoggin, we were served a large bowl of cereal, milk, eggs, bacon and toast. The kids at the breakfast table were incredulous when I admitted that I did not know what a cereal was and had never tasted that odd-looking stuff before. To this day, I still prefer my continental breakfast.

Survival at Androscoggin required total confidence in one's ability to swim and float in water for at least an hour, as well as paddling a canoe in calm and not so calm water. First, I had to pass a physical. A local doctor listened to my heart, frowned, listened again and said that it did not sound right. He called Arthur, my New York doctor, our family friend from Berlin, a recent arrival. Arthur reassured the Maine M.D. that there was absolutely nothing wrong with my heart and then asked to talk to me directly. He told me in a good Berlin accent, not to tell anybody, this local M.D. should go back to med school and study a little harder. I did not tell the local M.D. why I burst out laughing. Nor did I tell him that Arthur had not yet passed his New York test permitting him to practice in the U.S.

The high point of the Androscoggin experience was a five-day canoe and hiking trip. The camp truck deposited our group of seniors on the Chain of Ponds near the Canadian border. Before leaving us, the driver suggested that we cross the border and mail a postcard from Woburn, Quebec. As we crossed, an official asked us whether we were all Americans. No, I piped up. I am an immigrant. He smiled, that does not matter, you are all just going to Woburn, Yes, I answered. He waived us on. I was relieved that there was no problem getting back. When my parents received my card from Canada, they were not pleased. Did you not know that you might never have been able to get back?

The first night in a tent on the Chain of Ponds was quite an experience. We were targeted by a swarm of mosquitoes. Our mosquito nets helped, but the constant noise of the insects so close to their target kept me awake almost the entire night. After canoeing on the Chain of Ponds, we left the canoes. The camp truck transported them to the Forks on the Kennebec River. We had to track across forested hills from Eustis to the Forks. It was supposed to teach us self-reliance. It taught me how to survive a couple of hornet bites. The trip down the Kennebec involved a lot of effort because the river was sort of sluggish. The dam at Bingham marked the end of our adventure. I could now brag to my fellow high school kids that I had survived a week in the Maine wilderness and that New York was not like the rest of this large American continent. Maine was much more interesting.

Some campers left the third week of August. I left a week later. During that last week noises from the increasing crisis in Europe penetrated even the wilderness of Maine. A radio somewhere in the camp broadcast the news that Hitler's foreign minister, Ribbentrop had gone to Moscow and concluded a treaty with Molotov, his Russian counterpart. An attack on Poland was now inevitable. I was back in the real world.

***

And then there was the problem of earning a living in our new country. That had already come up in 1935 at dinner discussions in Prague when friends visited us who were planning to go to America. I also overheard my parents talking about friends, still domiciled in Germany, who spent the summer in New York to explore the possibility of starting new careers or resuming old ones in mid-life in an unfamiliar environment. Arthur, our doctor and long-time friend, contacted physicians in New York to determine what to take with him from his Berlin office. He also obtained information on requirements for a license to practice in New York. Another long time friend traveled across the U.S., exploring the possibilities of university connections in the West. He sent us postcards from the Grand Canyon: great scenery but no opportunities for earning a living. It was not easy for professionals in their forties and fifties to resume a life style in the United States that matched the one they had spent years developing in Germany. The fact that the United States was just emerging from the Great Depression compounded the task for refugees with a professional background. What greeted new arrivals was an America with WPA projects in New York and Steinbeck's *Grapes of Wrath* portraying a grim picture of survival of migrants from Oklahoma and other farmers displaced from parched farms in the West. It was an America with very limited job opportunities.

As a 14 year old kid I should not have been burdened with worries about how my family could earn a living. These were not normal times. While we had reached America, avoiding Hitler's tentacles, how was our family to resume a normal existence without a job? I was not told the details of my parents' finances, but I did know that my father's authoring books, articles and publishing *Die Philosophische Hefte* [Philosophical Journal] gave him considerable recognition among scholars, but hardly enough income to feed a family. In Berlin and Prague, both sets of grandparents had supported our quite comfortable life style. That ended when we left Europe.

Locating a job proved difficult. Not only was my father fifty-one on our arrival in New York, but he also knew no English. His Latin, Greek and German did not help him get a university position teaching philosophy. He also would have to start writing his articles in English. At least my mother knew the language. Her father's youth in Hanover with its English orientation, had left a permanent mark. While my mother had some academic training before getting married, she never had held a paying job. She typed all of my father's voluminous manuscripts: nobody else could have deciphered his handwriting. She prepared articles for publication and essentially managed the publication of the *Philosophische Hefte*. She enabled my father to communicate his ideas to a wider audience All of this was part of the marriage. When emigration to the U.S. became reality, it was clear to my parents that my mother would have to play a new role as the breadwinner of the family. But how?

Since she had helped my father publish his books, a Prague friend suggested, why not learn bookbinding,. My mother explored this idea, went to some bookbinding instruction sessions, but her enthusiasm waned quickly. She had difficulties passing a thread through the eye of a needle, usually leaving such detailed work to our maid. This posed another problem: How could we lead a normal life without a maid? Who would do the cooking, cleaning and everything else that my mother never had to bother with? We were assured that would not be a problem since modern American households required far less practical work.

Where was the money to get started in New York? My grandfathers were happy to help us. The problem was how to transfer funds from Prague to the United States. I was never told the details, but was able to figure out the basics. Among my father's many friends there was a Scottish minister who happened to be in Prague befriending scholars. He suggested that my father contribute to the local Presbyterian Church in Prague and contact a Presbyterian representative in New York who would transfer to my father his Prague contribution. That is how it was done. There was another angle to this story: My father, mother and I joined the

Presbyterian Church in Washington Heights and I remained a Presbyterian for several decades.

The amount, not much more than a few thousand dollars enabled my parents to rent our apartment in Washington Heights and to live frugally for two years. There were also some organizations that helped refugees get settled. My parents wanted to make sure that nothing would interfere with completing my high school education. Having reached the conclusion that there were too many other intellectual refugees in New York City and very few academic positions, my parents decided to try their luck elsewhere. After I graduated from George Washington High School in 1940 my parents moved to New Haven where my father became a visiting scholar at the Yale philosophy department. The compensation was minimal but it was his introduction to an American academic career. At the same time my mother got a research assistantship. That assistantship turned out to be the start of a distinguished 35-year academic career. My parents located an inexpensive one-room apartment on Whitney Avenue. It met their need after my departure to Ithaca in upstate New York.

Chapter 6
Cornell University

While New York City with its skyline, subways, movie houses were exciting it lost its luster after two years. The smile of the Statue of Liberty was no longer sufficient to cheer me up and feel particularly attracted to Manhattan, the island the Dutch had purchased from the Indians at a bargain price. It was not until I moved out of New York City to Cornell in New York's Finger Lakes region that I discovered the real America where I felt much more comfortable and welcome. There I was among students who, like me, had grown up in many different places with a common objective, to be properly prepared to face the challenges of a rapidly changing world.

My going to college was never a question. It was assumed that I would follow in my parents' footsteps: After all they had met at the University of Munich, my mother an itinerant student and my father with his recently earned Ph.D. He could not cut the umbilical cord connecting him with the University until my arrival forced him to leave the comfort of a university. He always took it for granted that his only son would attend a university as soon as I was ready. My grandfather Willy, an anglophile, mentioned Oxford when I had barely learned to read. Now I was in America. Oxford was too far away and obviously an unrealistic destination. So what does one do about getting a university degree in the United States? We did not have a clue.

I started applying to colleges as a high school senior, one year after arriving in the U.S. 15 years old, no car, nor any money, made visiting colleges an impossible task. Somewhere I picked up college brochures. Dartmouth appealed to me because it mentioned that it was in ski country, near the mountains, not that far from Lake Androscoggin in Maine, where I had spent the previous summer. I promptly applied and was invited for an interview with a Dartmouth alumnus in his Manhattan office. I was prepared to impress him with my academic achievements: knowledge of history, German, French and math. He was not interested in such nerdy topics. He questioned me about baseball, football, social skills and other things that were "really important". My answers confirmed his impression that I was one of those maladjusted refugee kids who probably should never have been permitted to land here, and who certainly did not fit into his alma mater. That was my first and only college application interview.

I was lucky that high school seniors in New York had to take Regents examinations in several subjects. Top scores automatically qualified for admission to Cornell University. The courses in my French Lycé Gymnase in Prague had enabled me to get nearly perfect scores in most subjects except English. That opened the gate to Cornell. I had no idea where Ithaca was, nor what Cornell looked like. I had however read articles about Cornell's reputation for research in science and agriculture.

Since we had no car and no money to spare, I traveled by bus. My mother accompanied me to the Greyhound bus terminal in midtown Manhattan and bought me a one-way ticket to Ithaca. I checked my one suitcase that included all my belongings, waved good-bye and off I went. I was 16 and now on my own.

After the bus crossed New Jersey and Pennsylvania we re-entered New York State. It seemed to take forever before we reached the Finger-Lakes region and arrived in Ithaca, on Cayuga Lake. From there I made it to Algonquin Lodge, my new home. How could I go to college with no money? I had done reasonably well at George Washington high school, graduating among the top 2%. At commencement I was called to the front to receive a reward for excellence in math and science. While my score on the New York Regents exam guaranteed entrance into Cornell; it was not sufficient to cover tuition. My parents had asked some of their friends for help. Their response: *In America you work your way through college*. Since I was only 16, when I graduated, why not take a year off and earn some money? Over this issue, my parents parted with some of their friends. I was not told about all this until later. Not surprisingly, my parents' Presbyterian friends again came to the rescue. I joined a cooperative at Cornell that provided housing in return for a couple of hours a week keeping the house livable. Nearby was another cooperative that provided breakfast and dinner. I became the chief washer of pots and pans, a skill I never forgot. I waited on girls in a sorority to cover lunch. I also earned some extra income by cleaning laboratory equipment in a Home Economics classroom. After the first semester, I no longer had to pay tuition. A

University scholarship and later a N.Y. Regents scholarship took care of that. I was glad not to be a burden to my parents.

Algonquin Lodge was a two-story house operating as a cooperative facility for students who took the responsibility of maintaining it. We had to put in one or two hours a week cleaning it, in lieu of rent. That was not a hard task: I cannot even remember what my specific responsibilities were. I do remember that we had regular monthly meetings where we discussed issues affecting the operations of the Coop. We had an advisor, a graduate student, Mr. Kok, who counseled us when necessary. It was never necessary, because we managed to resolve any disputes peacefully. We adopted *Roberts Rules of Order* as our guidelines after being requested to familiarize ourselves with them. That experience came in very handy at Mansfield Town Meetings twenty years later.

Three or four of us shared small rooms where we each had a desk and space for no more than twelve books. I was one of the first to arrive and picked a desk near a window facing the comforting greenery of a generally quiet cemetery. When I opened my window, I could hear the chimes from the Cornell Library tower.

Jack Robbins occupied the desk next to mine. He turned out to be an even more serious student than I. He was a chemistry major preparing himself to study medicine. He came from Yonkers, not far from where we had lived in Washington Heights. His family had emigrated from Odessa in Tsarist Russia. Having his desk next to mine helped me tremendously. Whenever I was tempted to interrupt my assigned readings, my eyes turned to Jack who casually remarked, let's have a cup of coffee and work for no more than another hour. Three hours later, I finished my task, while Jack remarked that he was almost done. When I had to hand in a twenty-page term paper at eight o'clock the next morning, I shivered at two o'clock A.M., way past my normal bedtime. Jack reassured me by saying that I would feel much better at 4 A.M. and could go to bed after my morning classes were done. I could not have managed without his support.

Jack's serious study habits, combined with a brilliant mind paid off in his getting top grades in what were generally considered very difficult courses. I was therefore shocked that he was not among the first batch of applicants admitted to Cornell Medical School. When the second batch of applicants with lower grades than

Jack got their acceptance letters, I encouraged him to go to his faculty advisor and ask what the matter was. Jack told me that his problem was that as a Jewish applicant there was a quota. In America, they discriminate? I thought I had left that behind. After Jack talked to his advisor, he came back beaming. With Jack in his office, his advisor called the professor in charge of med school admissions in New York City. Jack overheard expletives, and accusations, threats and finally a return to calm dialogue. After hanging up, Jack's advisor told him, the acceptance letter would be in the mail and Jack would get it the next morning via special delivery. This episode left a permanent impression. There was a wide gap in America between stated ideals and ugly realities. Jack completed his medical education at Cornell Med School and ultimately became a distinguished endocrinologist at the National Institutes of Health (NIH). He was mentioned favorably in a recent book by Harold Varmus, a former NIH director.

There were about half a dozen Algonquinites who were in the College of Arts and Sciences or Engineering, and came from New York City or other large population centers. The other two dozen had farming backgrounds, studied agriculture and came from up-state New York. That mattered a few months into the fall semester, when FDR ran for his third term. When I was depressed by the nasty comments made about my idol, the President, McIntyre from New Jersey consoled me: We Irish are going to knock the ... out them god d..m Republicans. You'll see! This was the first presidential election in the U.S. that I watched. I did not know what to expect. Of course McIntyre was correct. As we listened to the returns, McIntyre assured me that when the Irish votes came in, it was over. I was greatly disturbed by one up-state New Yorker who was livid, when it became clear that FDR would be re-elected to a third term. "Someone should shoot that bastard", he yelled. Watching the 1940 presidential election among up-state New Yorkers was quite an experience, an excellent but trying introduction to American politics.

Algonquin Lodge had no kitchen, only a hot plate where I occasionally prepared a cheese sandwich. A short distance from Algonquin, there was another cooperative, Cayuga Lodge. It had a kitchen, a student chef and served breakfast and dinner. If you worked in the kitchen, your meals were free. As the most recent arrival and probably the youngest, I was assigned the choice job of cleaning the dirtiest and biggest pots. I learned the technique, developed short cuts and enjoyed my meals, especially breakfasts which came without having to work in the kitchen.

What about lunch? I managed to serve lunches in a nearby fraternity. That is where I got to know my first person of African descent. A middle-aged black lady was the person in charge of the kitchen in the fancy fraternity. She quickly realized my ignorance about important social aspects of life at Cornell and imparted her extensive knowledge. I still remember her and her great insight. As an outsider, she seemed an incredibly astute observer.

Later, I had a job serving lunch at a sorority. That was not very enjoyable because those girls, some of whom my classmates, enjoyed reading from risqué letters, as I poured water in their glasses and dropped salad dressing on their fingers. They got a big kick embarrassing me. They obviously considered me a nerd.

It was at Cornell that I started making friends with real Americans. My experiences were challenging at times, but mostly interesting and satisfying. After my first two years in the U.S. it was only in Ithaca, that I felt I had a new home that could replace Prague, the place of my adolescence.

***

In Prague when I was 13 my father asked me what I wanted to do when I grow up. I did not have a clue, except that I did not want to be a philosopher. I did not want to spend my day sitting at a desk or walking in the woods while preoccupied with abstract issues. That was not a way of making money. Furthermore, a philosopher's answer to important questions appeared to have little to do with what I considered interesting and important. Grandfather Willy had made subtle suggestions by giving me books on topics that he hoped would lead me somewhere. Some dealt with chemistry; others covered conflicts involving the Basques in Spain and Indonesian opponents of Dutch colonialism, long before such little known nations made headlines. Such topics had held his interest. Might they possibly interest his grandson? Just before leaving Prague, I asked my father for which occupation I should prepare myself, if I wanted to earn money doing what I enjoyed then, namely following world events. "Study political economy", he suggested.

When I came to George Washington High School, I detoured to math and physics and chemistry. The sciences were taught by teachers who obviously enjoyed what they were doing. History on the other hand, was taught by teachers who would have preferred playing volleyball. Books popularizing great advances in science authored by Paul de Kruif, led me to express interest in chemistry. Being awarded the George Washington High School prize in science and mathematics also helped move me in this direction. Grandfather Willy must have been happy when my mother wrote to him and bragged about my performance, except that by then he undoubtedly was preoccupied with the damage caused by German bombs falling near his house in Manchester, England.

Shortly after arriving and settling down at Algonquin Lodge, we freshmen had to register for classes. I walked up the hill to the scenic main campus, past the Library tower where a student playing the carillon serenaded us freshmen with lively dance music, and entered the huge Field house where everybody lined up in front of tables organized by subjects. Nobody had warned me that a strategy was required to get the courses that you wanted by lining up at the tables offering the most important and popular ones as early as possible. The math course that I needed was full. A faculty advisor suggested that I take that course in my sophomore year; after all, I had done well in high school, so I would get by with what I knew.

I did get into the introductory chemistry course. I liked it, except that it was at 8 am, forcing me to race up the hill past the library tower in order to get a seat within hearing distance of professor Laubengayer. Professors did not use microphones in those days. Experiments he demonstrated on the table next to his lectern, registered only as finger movements accompanied by his words. I mostly looked at the gigantic table of 92 elements adorning the front of the lecture hall. We had a laboratory session where we were to get a hands-on experience with the topics covered in the lectures. What I do remember from the chem. lab was my neighbor, Ruth. We were seated in alphabetical order and I considered myself extremely fortunate in having one of the very few female chemistry students in such close proximity. Soon we started dating. Our conversations had nothing to do with chemistry. After discussing at great length the possibility of going beyond holding hands, we argued incessantly about foreign policy where we differed in our view of what Stalin was up to. That interfered with going beyond holding hands.

Chemistry majors had to take a course in physics. That is where my delay in taking math turned out to be critical. My high school algebra was not sufficient to help me answer key questions. I lacked calculus. In one quiz, I received a D+, my lowest grade ever. I remember crossing one of the gorges edging the campus on the famous swinging bridge and just for a moment, I thought of recent incidents where distraught freshmen had chosen the easy way out. My way out was to switch majors and return to what had interested me already as a kid in Prague: world affairs and what could be done to undo the mess that Hitler, Mussolini and others had gotten us into.

My decision to abandon chemistry and move to history was also influenced by my taking a modern history course with Professor Cornelius DeKiewit, who had grown up in South Africa and had arrived in the United States only a few years before I took his course. He stressed that if one was to understand what and why people did certain things in the past, one had to study more than names and dates. One had to visualize the environment in which past leaders operated. For instance, at the time of the Congress of Vienna in 1815, there were no trains. He had us figure out how long and how difficult it was for the British Prime Minister to travel from London to Vienna by a horse-drawn coach. Obviously, the British leader could not just turn around and travel back to London if he did not like the way the negotiations were going. He had to stay until the powers could work out a settlement. DeKiewit added that given that situation, proper entertainment was essential to keep everybody from going nuts. On a more personal level, he described the environment in which he grew up, and how it affected his subsequent attitudes. He was much closer to nature than we were, here in Ithaca: He recalls the noise that rain made on the tin roofs that covered houses in South Africa. He also taught us how to express our opinions while at the same time retaining an objective approach to the events that we were discussing. He was an exciting professor who helped me understand the events that I had observed and studied. He was not the only professor in history who attracted me to major in the social sciences. There were many other outstanding historians at Cornell at that time. That made my decision to major in history very easy and inevitable.

***

The Battle of Britain dominated the news when I entered as a freshman in September 1940. In June that year, Hitler had conquered France and driven the British out to sea. Chamberlain's policy of appeasement had collapsed and Winston Churchill was finally charged to pick up the pieces. Britain was now the target. In this terrible situation, there was one ray of hope: Churchill's voice. Hitler had met his match. He faced someone whom he could not intimidate with his rhetoric, nor threaten with his tanks. Now the task was to build a force that would give credence to Churchill's determination to derail Hitler's plans to dominate Europe and leave a legacy that would last a thousand years.

I was emotionally involved in the daily reports of Hitler's military moves. I hoped that he would not only be stopped, but that Czechoslovakia would be liberated as soon as possible and that the world from which I had escaped in 1938 would reemerge from its nightmare. Perhaps some of my schoolmates and other friends that I had left behind would reappear. I was especially concerned about Grandfather Willy in Manchester, England. In spite of the bombs that rained on Britain his letters were upbeat.

Most of my fellow Algonquin Lodge buddies paid minimum attention to the War. I attributed their disinterest to their New York upstate distaste for New York City and all those foreigners there who were not fully Americanized. They hated FDR and feared that he would get us into a war. Yes, there was some sympathy for the poor Londoners who had to suffer through nightly bomb attacks, and yes, they liked Churchill, the tough guy. Talk about being drafted intensified. The prospect of being called up and away from their up-state communities and farms aroused interest in how the War was going.

One Sunday afternoon on December 7, 1941, a few of us were gathered in the Algonquin living room listening to the New York Symphony's Sunday Concert on the local radio station. Suddenly the broadcast was interrupted. An announcer stated that Japanese planes had attacked our fleet at Pearl Harbor killing many sailors. Because of the time difference, it was morning in Hawaii and we had been informed of the attack shortly after it happened. When my initial shock wore off, I felt relieved: now the United States would join the effort to defeat Hitler and his Axis partners, Japan and Italy.

Next day FDR addressed Congress. *December 7, 1941, would forever be remembered as a Day of Infamy, the day that Japan attacked an America at peace*. I was immensely reassured when FDR immediately connected Japan's attack with Hitler's and Mussolini's conquest of Europe and their dreams of controlling the entire globe. He asked Congress to declare war not only on Japan but also on Germany and Italy. Thus ended the interminable debate on whether America should remain neutral or join in the defense of humanity against Adolf Hitler.

The shock of the attack wore off quickly at Cornell. I do not recall missing any classes on Monday, December 8. The timing of Pearl Harbor definitely affected my academic orientation and the acquisition of knowledge that was to serve me the rest of my life. Fortunately, I had shifted my major to history by then. Current events were relevant in most of my courses and my professors found it nearly impossible not to comment on the impact that the War would have on our lives.

Discussions shifted to the post-War world and America's position in it. Our interest intensified in happenings on Germany's Eastern front where Stalin's counter offensive was in full swing just at the time that the Japanese attacked us at Pearl Harbor. What an unexpected situation: Our new ally, the Soviet Union, had forced Hitler's army to retreat, the first defeat the Wehrmacht had suffered, at the very same time that we lost a significant part of our Pacific fleet! In class, our attention shifted from the 1815 Congress of Vienna to the 1919 Paris Peace Conference and to the expected conference that was sure to follow victory in this vastly expanded global conflict. It was all so exciting. My freshman chemistry and physics courses paled by comparison. The Day of Infamy ushered in days of excitement for me at Cornell.

Two months after Pearl Harbor I turned 18. On June 30, 1942, I registered for the draft. I was given number 11,875. On December 24, 1942, the day before Christmas, I was informed, "after considering your status as an alien, the Army found that you are, if otherwise qualified, to be acceptable for training and service in the armed services of the United States". I requested, and was granted, a deferment to complete my final semester in the spring of 1943. I do not recall any one from our Algonquin Lodge leaving for the War until 1943.

All along, I had been determined to complete my degree before being inducted. Taking advantage of my mother tongue, I obtained course credits in German literature, simply taking final exams without enrolling in the course. I also enrolled for a full load of courses during the summer of 1942. Thus, I managed to skip my junior year and became a senior at 18.

The War affected the courses I took. By the fall of 1942, a number of courses that I had planned to take had lost their professors who had joined the government in Washington as intelligence experts in the State Department and the OSS, the newly created Office of Strategic Services, forerunner of the CIA. Among professors not migrating to Washington was a scholar of Chinese history and culture whose enthusiasm for his subject opened my mind to an entirely new field of interest.

Thinking ahead, it occurred to me that acquiring the ability to speak and translate Russian might qualify me for military service involving liaison with our wartime allies. I enrolled in an intensive Russian language course taught by Professor Malamut, of Russian-Jewish background. Since I knew Czech, learning Russian was easy and even fun. The Cyrillic alphabet was another story, especially since Malamut gave us exactly 24 hours to memorize all the letters of that alphabet.

The 1943 Commencement was overshadowed by everybody's concern with what was lying ahead. I remember my mother traveling all the way from New Haven by bus to attend my graduation. The brief moment when she saw me and my fellow graduating seniors rise in the big hall to accept our degree was one ray of hope in an otherwise turbulent world.

***

Back in New Haven, I received the notice to Report for Induction at 7:30 a.m. on June 21, 1943, at the Orange Street Armory. I remember getting there early. I had gotten rid of almost everything that I would not need in the army and said good-bye to my parents who pretended not to be worried about the coming uncertainties. I expected the physical exam at the Armory to be a perfunctory exercise of formalities requiring patience. By 9 a.m. I would be off to war.

When I entered the Armory, I was one of at least three hundred men who had to report that day, all of them looking prepared to invade Normandy. Long lines formed. Papers were presented to be glanced at. Orders were given. New lines led to areas where local doctors gave each draftee a thorough medical examination to determine his fitness to serve. We had to get undressed en masse. After three hours it was my turn. The doctor listened to my heart and took my blood pressure. He asked me a couple of questions. I got nervous and impatient as he took my blood pressure again and listened to my heart intently. Finally, he ordered me to lie down on a couch behind a curtain and rest. After the doctor re-emerged fifteen minutes later to take my blood pressure the third time, he told me that it was obvious that I was not medically fit to serve in the army. Moreover, he appeared to be worried about my survival as a civilian. He counseled me to see my personal physician immediately, if I had one.

Before leaving the Armory, I had to join another line where those who were rejected by the army were officially certified unfit to serve and given the designation 4F. It was a surprisingly long line of more than 50 men my age. They showed no obvious sign of physical impairment. As a consolation, the official who handed me my official 4F designation informed me that it would be reviewed in a couple of years and I would have a chance to serve then, if my health had improved and they needed me.

When I returned home, my parents did not share my extreme disappointment. They did call Arthur, our long-time Berlin family friend and doctor. He asked me to visit him at his home at the top of Manhattan to check the condition of my health. I took the train to New York to stay at his apartment. He looked at me and thought I would survive long enough for him to give me an examination later. At seven the next morning, he knocked at the door, took out his stethoscope, took my blood pressure and laughed. "Normal", he said, "just as I thought". His diagnosis: "When you waited in line in the Armory, you got impatient and nervous. Solution: Relax." I trusted his judgment; he had always analyzed my childhood ills correctly. He had spent his younger years in the Kaiser's army on the Russian front in World War I. where he had learned a lot about surviving real and imagined illnesses. I was relieved to be declared physically OK only a couple of days after the New Haven MD had given his negative opinion about my future. "When can I ask for a re-examination so that I can join our armed forces?" Arthur and my parents suggested that I wait a while. They obviously hoped that the War would be over before the army would be interested in me again.

I was confronted unexpectedly with the task of re-examining my plans for the immediate future. Fortunately our professors at Cornell had suggested that we apply to graduate schools for admission while they still had us freshly in their mind and could write meaningful recommendations, even though the war might interrupt our studies for a number of years. I had applied and been accepted by the Fletcher School of Law and Diplomacy at Tufts upon my return from the war. When I informed Fletcher that I was ready to start in September '43, they were delighted. They needed students badly to keep the place running. Most of the other applicants probably were busy preparing to land in Normandy.

***

Fletcher School classes were scheduled to start in the middle of September. What was I to do in the meantime? Almost everybody I had known at Cornell was off to war. It seemed to me unpatriotic to engage in normal peacetime activities, such as going to camp and be a counselor or do some other job unrelated to the war effort. Why not return to Cornell and take a special Russian Area Studies Program? I had heard about this program before I had graduated. One of my favorite history professors, Philip Mosely, had been involved in setting up the program. Its purpose was to prepare Americans for the expected post-war task of working out a relationship with our potentially difficult wartime ally. I promptly enrolled and a few days later traveled back to Ithaca.

This time I went to Ithaca by train. Shortly after leaving Penn station, I discovered a bunch of students who not only shared my destination, Ithaca, but who were also going to attend the Russian Area program. After it got dark outside and boredom set in, the group broke out in song. They sang Russian folk songs and wartime tunes. It was fun. As the evening wore on, it dawned on me that this particular group acted like an organized band. Could it be, that they were real Communists and not just American students interested in finding out something about our Soviet ally? After worrying about spending my summer with a disciplined group of ideologues, I settled back and decided to enjoy the not-so-spontaneous musical performance.

The Russian Area program turned out to be a valuable experience introducing me to Russian history, culture, especially modern music by Prokofiev and Shostakovich. Soviet economic and political accomplishments were carefully examined and criticized. All except one professor insisted on a critical, analytical scholarly approach.

In addition to my Communist train companions, I met several very interesting characters. One was a Harvard student from Alabama with an intriguing southern drawl. Years later, he became the editor of the liberal New York newspaper *PM.* Another student from New York city whom I dated a couple of times that summer turned out to play a major role at the *New Yorker*, ultimately publishing a book about her extra-marital relationship with that magazine's long-term editor. My Communist train companions preferred to stay in the background, enjoying each other's companionship.

One afternoon, a U.S. officer in military uniform, attending the Russian Area program in preparation for encounters with our wartime ally, asked the Harvard student with the heavy southern drawl and me, with my German accent, to join him for coffee at the local joint. This was a rather unusual invitation. After some casual chit chat, he got down to business and told us that he had noticed from our comments in class that we were independently minded thinkers and were not part of the New York group of party-line Communists. He respected the opinions that we expressed in class. The officer continued that he wanted to warn us, so that we would not get into trouble. "Trouble?" We both asked. "Yes", he said."The FBI was making lists of Communists to protect us from a potential threat." "Even while Stalin's Soviet Union was our wartime ally?" "That does not make any difference, as far as the FBI was concerned". "How can we stay out of the FBI's clutches?" "That is very simple. It does not matter what you think or what topics you discuss with your friends. What does matter is that you must not get your name on a list"."A list? How are we to avoid that?" "Never subscribe to a Communist newspaper, a Soviet publication or sign your name when you attend a function sponsored by the Soviet Union or the American Communist party or any group allied with the Communist party." We both thought this advice was obvious, but thanked the officer for his concern with our future. Little did I know how crucial and relevant this casual encounter turned out to be in the McCarthy era, a decade later.

Chapter 7
Preparing for a Career in International Relations

When I contemplated what to do after graduating from Cornell, the War had reached a turning point. The prospect of a world at peace shifted attention to postwar plans. A career in international relations seemed an attractive possibility. The Fletcher School of Law and Diplomacy, administered by Tufts with the cooperation of Harvard University, located in Medford, a suburb of Boston, seemed to meet my objective. Established in 1934 it was intended to help create a better understanding of international relations in the hope that improved knowledge of world affairs would prepare future leaders for an active role in the world and counteract America's inclination to pursue isolationist policies

A distinguished faculty made Fletcher especially attractive. While the war encouraged some of the best-known professors to contribute their expertise to our war effort in Washington, part-time professors, such as the diplomatic historian Helmreich from Bowdoin in Maine and the economist Samuelson from MIT, were hired to fill the void. I hoped Fletcher would prepare me for a career in the Foreign Service or some related intelligence work.

In 1943 the prospect of victory was clearly in sight. Ten years after Hitler had assumed control of Germany and promised that the Third Reich would last for a thousand years, the German army suffered a decisive defeat in the Battle of Stalingrad. Hitler's last Russian offensive in that summer was halted before it could gain momentum. From now on Stalin's forces were on a steady course to Berlin, only halting to let stragglers catch up since they were inadequately motorized. The outcome on the Eastern Front was no longer in doubt. Interest shifted to the likely problems of a liberated Eastern Europe. Would the pre-war countries and their governments be resurrected, or would Stalin impose his imprint on countries his forces had liberated/conquered?

1943 was also the year when the power relationship between The United States and the Soviet Union shifted significantly. While Stalin had driven the Germans out of the Ukraine and approached Eastern Poland, American forces had postponed the liberation of Western Europe and concentrated instead on North Africa and southern Italy. The Japanese forces in the Pacific had been placed on the defensive but the Japanese home islands were not yet within reach. The discussion turned increasingly to the topic of the post-war balance between the U.S. and Great Britain vs. the Soviet Union. Stalin had now a much stronger hand than when the contest had started. All of these developments added a great deal of excitement to topics covered in every course and seminar. Instead of listening to professors patiently and methodically explaining the nature of world conflicts to our inter-war generation, we were now in the grandstand of a vast world arena watching our professors help us focus on a changing diplomatic landscape They attempted to explain why this or that was happening and prognosticated about where things were going and how we might influence the world in which we were about to operate.

Yet, I recall concentrating on topics that were not in the headlines. Perhaps I was attracted by the relative calm of reconnoitering obscure aspects of the past in the Balkans and the Near East, especially Turkey and Egypt. Professor Halford Hoskins, Dean of the Fletcher School, had written a book on 18th and 19th century routes to India that crossed Egypt from the Mediterranean to the Red Sea before the Suez Canal was opened in 1869. While probably one of the least exciting books I had ever read, it covered nevertheless a topic that explained much of what happened more recently. Professor Helmreich also helped me a great deal in understanding the Turkish Empire's treatment of its diverse religious and ethnic people.

The exciting news from the many fronts in Europe, North Africa, the Pacific as well as the stimulating seminar lectures and discussions, were only a part of what made my stay at Fletcher an extraordinary experience. The members of the class of '44 consisted of about twenty diverse students ranging from a Chinese Canadian who ardently advocated an independent nationalist China, a Panamanian who in spite of stunted growth enjoyed playing the role of the Latin charmer, an immigrant of Polish aristocratic background, a number of enthusiastic supporters of FDR's New Deal and a few "typical" Americans. They all coalesced into a very congenial group. This group interacted and enjoyed an exciting social life.

Having completed my undergraduate education in three years, I arrived at the Fletcher School at the age of 19, probably the youngest member of the class of '44. The absence of a normal contingent of able-bodied males was a great boost in my need to mature socially. The class included many extremely bright female students who not only had serious professional goals, but who also aroused some of my non-intellectual interests. I was ready for new experiences. It certainly was not a normal year. That made my stay at Fletcher special in many unexpected ways

Five years had passed since my last date with Eva, the first girl I had fallen in love with. We had continued to exchange intimate letters several times a month, in spite of wartime postal censorship delays. We both matured in increasingly different environments. Eventually the ardor of love faded and the dreams for our common future disappeared. I was ready for the opportunity to make new friends at Fletcher.

I soon realized that dating at Fletcher was more sophisticated and hence more expensive than it had been at Cornell. Ithaca's attractions were no match for those in Boston. At Cornell a date involved picking up Ruth at her dormitory; walking half an hour downtown to the movies, returning to the campus; arguing about world events; holding hands, exploring; theoretically of course, the possibility of a more intimate show of affection, only to be brought back to reality by the 11 o'clock curfew, which was rigidly enforced by some supervising dormitory witch.

Fletcher located in a suburb with no venues for social activities necessitated a trip to Boston. During the war nobody at Fletcher had a car. It took about half an hour by bus and subway (tube) to get to Boston from Medford. The next step was to locate the right restaurant to feed my date. Luck would have it that on one of my first Boston adventures my partner chose lobster, the most expensive item on the menu. Not only did I have to learn how to crack and disembowel an extremely ugly creature, more importantly, I had to figure out how to finance the rest of my activities that month.

There were other memorable dining adventures. Paul, our ardent Chinese nationalist, arranged for most of our group to eat a real Chinese dinner at a restaurant in Boston's Chinatown. He conferred with the chef in Chinese and arranged a very special menu. Then he taught us how to mix the various delicacies. We could not help overhear a loud discussion when Paul disappeared in the kitchen. He informed us later that the chef was from southern China and did not fully comprehend what Paul was trying to tell him in his best Mandarin. A few years later, I learned that Paul "returned" to mainland China and became foreign minister Chou En Lai's advisor on American affairs. Eventually, he was placed in charge of issuing visas in Canada to U.S. citizens who wanted to enter mainland China which we did not recognize until the '70s.

As Christmas approached, I became aware that Meg, an ardent New Dealer from Pittsburgh, appeared to pay me more than casual attention. At a social gathering in early December, she suggested that I improve my dancing skills (I had none). She was planning to dance with me at the Christmas Party. A whisky sour or two helped me overcome my fear and embarrassment of stepping on her toes. Thus fortified, I asked her for a turn. Dean Hoskins' wife, watching us from the sideline, noticed that Meg and I obviously had a good time. As the music stopped Meg, noticing that the Dean's wife was watching us and appeared sort of bored, suggested that I take the distinguished lady to the floor for a dance. Having by now gained excessive confidence in my newly acquired dancing skill, I danced with the Dean's wife not once, but several times. During intermission when the crowd settled down and we tried to recharge our batteries, the Dean came over and asked me whether I would be so kind to take his wife home to their house, a five minute walk from the party. He explained that his wife was tired and wanted to go home, while he of course had to remain until the end. I sobered up instantly as I left the hall and accompanied my distinguished dancing partner to the Dean's residence. I bade her good night as the servant opened the door. It did not even occur to me that I should have said, yes, when she asked me whether I wanted to come in for a while. Later I was told of rumors that the Dean preferred the company of the Fletcher librarian. I did not return to the party that night. Next day Meg gave me a very dirty look. Her well-laid plan had collapsed. Not until February did our conversations resume.

Almost half a century before unconventional sexual behavior aroused widespread public discussion in the '90s, the odd behavior of one of the relatively few male members of our class aroused my curiosity. Because some maintenance work in my regular dormitory room, I was assigned to a large bedroom that I had to share with Ed. Ed had been drafted, but had a serious accident terminating his military career prematurely. One day, while learning how to throw a grenade, he apparently spent too much time analyzing the process and was reluctant to let go. As a result, the grenade exploded in his right hand, causing him to lose two fingers. This terrible accident was especially painful to Ed because he had considered becoming an Episcopalian priest, a vocation requiring the use of his outstretched hands with five fingers to conduct religious services. A career in international relations was his fallback position.

On a Friday afternoon, Ed informed me that he wanted to go downtown and visit a bar. I was too busy preparing myself for an exam to keep him company. That did not bother him at all. "After all, there are lots of people there," he informed me. Ed was not back, when I went to bed. That meant that I could sleep with the window closed. He always insisted that they be left open even when it was below freezing outside. "Cold air is essential for your health", he often repeated. When I woke up the next morning, there were two people in his bed. A guy emerged, got dressed in a hurry, mumbled something, and disappeared. Ed, still half asleep, explained that this poor guy was too far from home and so he had offered him a place to rest his weary bones. It did not bother Ed at all that this explanation made little sense to me.

***

My increasing interest in Meg did not interrupt my academic pursuits. I was fascinated by the 19th century diplomatic contests over Suez and the Bosporus. France, Great Britain, Russia and Germany had such a wonderful time making the most of the waning Ottoman Empire, "the sick man of Europe". I wrote a 30-page paper on Persia/Iran, at the edge of this contested area. That is where I first learned about aspects of a nationalist revival in Iran following the end of World War I. The Kurds sought their own independence, thereby instilling fear and conflicts with the countries in which they lived: Iran, Iraq, Syria and Turkey. My research gave me far less trouble than the task of typing my first manuscript. At night, I sequestered myself in an empty classroom and laboriously pecked at the portable typewriter that my mother had turned over to me. Occasionally Meg and other students cheered me up and diverted my attention from the problems of the Middle East.

I spent a lot of time at Fletcher working in the library. This covered some of my living expenses. I assisted the librarian by accessing and shelving books. I learned to cope with the confusion between shelving books by the old Dewey decimal and the newer Library of Congress systems. Initially I had the impression that there was no particular reason why this relatively small library used two conflicting systems of arranging books on the shelves. When the school year was over, I came to realize that there had been a somewhat sinister plot causing my bewilderment. Two separate filing systems made it simple for Dean Hoskins to transfer the Library of Congress marked books from the Fletcher library to the newly established School of Advanced International Studies, SAIS.

Summer arrived early in 1944. We had some unusually warm days late in February and again in March. A comfortable outdoor environment helped Meg and me restart our relationship. We no longer needed dancing lessons as an excuse. We could explore the outdoors in the less developed forested areas of Medford to gain some privacy. We discussed the possibility of a serious and possibly lasting relationship. There were some problems. Meg was a couple of years older and anxious to start a family. She did not want to waste time. Because my parents had no real income, I was committed to complete my education and get a permanent job before raising a family. These differences did not interfere with our growingly close relationship at Fletcher.

I did not let my deepening involvement with Meg that spring interfere with my studies, nor with following with intense interest the changes swirling around our world.

We explored fancy restaurants in Boston's Back Bay overlooking the Charles and we also visited the many historical sites in the Greater Boston area. Meg took me along to a High Episcopalian Church in the Back Bay section where I was forced to kneel and pray, but the music was inspiring. When school was over Meg stopped in New Haven on her way to Pittsburgh and met my parents. The next day, June 6, 1944, when our troops landed in Normandy, Meg and I spent the day exploring the Sleeping Giant Park, not far from New Haven. I really enjoyed my year with Meg at Fletcher.

Sometime in the spring semester, we learned that Dean Hoskins had convinced some trustees who handled the affairs of the Fletcher School to move the school to Washington, D.C. and give it a new name, School of Advanced International Studies, SAIS. He had argued that since many Fletcher School professors had moved to Washington to help the war effort, it was only logical for the school to follow and give them an opportunity to resume teaching their seminars on a part-time basis when not engaged in critical activities, such as attending the San Francisco Conference that created the United Nations.

It had been no secret that relations between Dean Hoskins and Leonard Carmichael, the President of Tufts University, were chilly at best. Obviously, Carmichael refused to lose a significant part of his University. Dean Hoskins took measures to strengthen his own hands. He created a special foundation supported by influential members of the Boston establishment who favored a more interventionist foreign policy. A key member of this group was Christian Herter who was to become Secretary of State in the fifties. It was this foundation which had books classified by the Library of Congress marking system.

Dean Hoskins had his professors, his Foundation and his boxes of books. Now all he needed was a building and students. The Foundation acquired a building at 1906 Florida Avenue, a bloc from Connecticut Avenue, in the still fashionable part of Northwest Washington. The two lower floors had classrooms, offices, a dining room, while the upper two floors had individual rooms for male and female students on separate floors. One day Dean Hoskins approached me and offered me a scholarship to attend SAIS in its opening year. I had my M.A. and did not really want to get a Ph.D. or other advanced degree from a brand new untested school. But I had always wanted to go to Washington, the seat of power, so why not? I accepted.

How did Tufts University react to Dean Hoskins theft of the Fletcher School? Initially there was some confusion, but the decision was reached to appoint a new Dean and resume teaching, as if there had only been a temporary disturbance. There was no major disruption. In 1952, President Carmichael also left Tufts and followed Hoskins to Washington where he was to head the Smithsonian.

***

The opening of the School of Advanced International Studies was delayed a month.

That meant finding a job for the summer and early fall of 1944. The New Haven YMCA was looking for counselors at its Camp Hazen in Chester, CT. I had spent a summer there in 1941 as counselor. This time I was given the responsibility of entertaining and supervising the older campers, now that the administrators considered me mature enough to be trusted overseeing rambunctious high school kids on vacation.

Everything went well until the day that I boasted that I was immune from catching poison ivy. I had lived in the U.S. for six years and had never been bothered. I jumped right into a pile covered by the weed. The verdict was in instantly. It was impossible not to scratch the itch that quickly covered me from head to toe; I had invaded the ivy only clad in my bathing trunk. I was considered too sick to stay in camp and had to go home to recover.

After recovering in New Haven I decided to look for a job in Washington until the start of classes at SAIS. Some Fletcher alumni informed me of a vacancy in an apartment that they leased from a friendly older lady. Its location near the Washington Zoo gave me easy access to public transportation all over the city.

Getting a temporary, or any more permanent job, was a more difficult task. My lack of citizenship closed almost all doors to employment. I had missed getting my citizenship when my parents were naturalized in 1943. No longer a minor, I had to go through the naturalization process on my own. If I had gotten into the army, that would have speeded up the naturalization process. Moving my residence slowed it down. It took me therefore a couple of extra years to gain my citizenship. Shortly after getting to Washington I went to the U.S. Employment Office and filled out my job qualifications, including my knowledge of Russian and Czech. I received an official postcard asking me to report for a job translating Russian into English at the Soviet Purchasing Agency located near the apartment where I was staying. As I entered the building, I was referred by the receptionist to a small office where an official started by asking me where I was born. When I answered, Berlin, he unceremoniously showed me the door.

Finally, my job search took a positive turn: I was very pleased and somewhat amazed that the one place where I could find a job as a non-citizen was as an employee of the U.S. Congress. That turned out to be easy. One of the Fletcher students got in touch with her Congressman who gave me a reference. Thus equipped, I reported to the mailroom of the U.S. House of Representatives and was immediately put to work in a factory-like environment. My job: stuffing several thousand flyers into envelopes addressed to a Mississippi Congressman's constituents.

I looked around the large room where I had been assigned to work. There were several dozen workers, mostly middle aged women, stuffing, sealing, sorting sheets of paper into envelopes, going through their motions automatically, barely glancing at what their fingers were doing, exchanging at the top of their voices the latest gossip. One of the ladies near my position, asked her neighbor on the other side, "Who is this guy?" It sounded more like, "What the hell is this guy doing here?" I responded, "killing time" That satisfied them and they returned to their excited observations about this guy, or that guy, cheating on some girl. Meanwhile I tried to read the printed stuff the Congressman was mailing to the voters in his district. It was obvious that I did not keep up with my fellow workers. In the time that it took them to process 100 letters, I did about 25. I tried to concentrate and doubled my output, but still lagged far behind my neighbors. The woman in the row behind me could not help noticing my inability to keep up with the rest. She gave me some crucial advice on where to place the envelopes, how to arrange the items on my desk and where to move my hand; things that I never was taught in school or college. By lunchtime, I was doing better. Nevertheless, I had lost confidence in my ability to do this mechanical work for a month, a week or even just a single day. I called up Meg who had a job in the White House Annex, answering letters written to the President. She comforted me, instilling enough confidence in my bruised ego, to enable me to return to my job after lunch. I kept at it for six weeks until SAIS opened.

I even managed to enjoy the experience. We ate breakfast and lunch in a cafeteria located in the basement of the Capitol. While it was not fancy, it gave me an opportunity to overhear casual discussions by Congressmen gulping down coffee and a quick breakfast on their way to work upstairs. I will never forget overhearing two Republican Congressmen. They were furious with FDR, who the previous evening, had given one of his memorable campaign speeches making fun of Republicans who had attacked him for taking his dog Fala along on his plane. "That was not funny! That was disgraceful", the Southern Congressmen shouted for all to hear. My short stay in the basements of the buildings surrounding the Capitol brought my Cornell University lectures on the U.S. government to life.

Many of my Fletcher friends had obtained interesting entry-level jobs at federal agencies, ranging from the White House public relations office, to the State Department and budget handling agencies. Bonded by Fletcher, they jointly rented a large apartment. Meg was part of the group and then moved to a smaller apartment that gave us greater privacy. In many respects, Washington started out like Fletcher Year 2.

***

SAIS began with a curriculum and professors closely following the Fletcher model. I was fortunate to get a chance to take a course in Diplomacy with Professor Hajo Holborn whose reputation had drawn me to Fletcher in the first place, but who had left for Washington before my arrival in Medford. Hajo Holborn had distinguished himself in Germany as a scholar before 1933 and had immigrated to the United States because he opposed Hitler from the start. He could have stayed since Jewish ancestors made up an insignificant part of his heritage as defined by Hitler's racial laws. .

At Fletcher we had looked at world affairs from a scholarly perspective. We concentrated on the causes of contemporary conflicts and evaluated possible solutions. In Washington our professors conducted a seminar or lecture early in the morning before making policy decisions in their office. It was obvious that their attention was focused on the current issues they had to resolve later in meetings with top officials. This enabled us to watch history from a very close perspective. We tried not to lose our objectivity even though the real world, while exciting, was often not pleasant.

We also had important public figures come to lunch and share their ideas with us. Congressman Fulbright discussed his proposal for what was to become the scholarship grants bearing his name. The Ambassador of Thailand thanked us for America's support in the face of Japan's occupation and presented his country's plans for the post-war world. When post-war plans moved to the center of the stage, they preoccupied our professors, especially when some of them were about to participate in the San Francisco conference that created the United Nations. The preceding Dumbarton Oaks conference had taken place only a ten-minute walk across the park from our school.

Our location in Northwest Washington, while requiring a lengthy trolley ride, gave us access to the Library of Congress. As useful as Harvard's Widener Library it had the advantage of close proximity to the political center of power, the Capitol.

As the war in Europe neared its end, following the failure of Hitler's final offensive in Belgium around Christmas 1944, I had to confront again my own future. I considered applying for a job at the Office of Strategic Services, OSS, precursor of the CIA. I went for an interview in a building not far from the State Department. I was surprised to meet Herbert Marcuse, a Berlin friend of my parents and the acting head of the Eastern European section of the State Department's Office of Intelligence Research. Apparently, refugees were of some use in our planning the future of post-war Europe. Germany's surrender however terminated my job application.

On April 12th, we heard the announcement of Roosevelt's death. It hit us in the stomach. He had died in Warm Springs, Georgia. Like Eleanor, we had witnessed his final departure from afar. After racing to Georgia Eleanor accompanied the body to Washington, the seat of his power. Roosevelt was barely laid to rest when his nemesis, Adolf Hitler, recognizing at last that his grandiose plans for controlling the world had been thwarted, committed suicide to avoid capture. In about two weeks, the war in Europe would be over. So was my year at SAIS. Now I could no longer procrastinate. I had to decide what to do next. Professor Hajo Holborn suggested that I get my Ph.D. at Harvard and supported my application there. I was accepted.

Where was I to spend the summer until the start of the fall semester? My parents had left New Haven in September 1944 and had moved to Chambersburg, Pennsylvania, where my father had a one-year visiting professorship at Wilson College, filling the position of a faculty member on leave. My mother commuted regularly from there by train to the University of Pennsylvania in Philadelphia. There she resumed her academic studies that she had interrupted 21 years earlier. I did not consider Chambersburg a "home" to spend the summer after classes were over at SAIS. I decided instead to keep my room at SAIS until moving to Cambridge in September.

My social life had taken a significant turn. When it became clear that I would continue to spend the next several years working on my Ph.D., Meg and I parted ways. I was not ready to assume the responsibilities of a husband. Our parting on a warm day in the spring, at the end of a spirited discussion, sitting on a bench in a small park in downtown Washington, was dramatic, final, but friendly. Less than a year later, Meg married Tad, my Polish debate partner, a fellow Fletcher alumnus.

***

The War was over when I arrived in Cambridge early in September 1945. A month earlier on August 5th, I had visited my parents in Chambersburg, Pa, to celebrate my mother's 45th birthday. The next day we were amazed to hear about the first atomic bomb exploding over Hiroshima. Japan's official surrender followed in less than two weeks. The return to post-war normalcy was slow. For me that was mostly irrelevant. I was about to enter, my own post-war world.

I found a room at 14 Shepard Street, a twenty-minute walk from Harvard Square and close to the Radcliff dormitory quadrangle. My landlord was a kind older man who made his living renting rooms in his narrow three-story house to law school and other graduate students. Mine was on the top floor. This was the first time that I did not live in a college dormitory, an important step on the road to independence.

It took me very little time to fall in love with the Harvard campus and the Harvard Square neighborhood. Exploring bookstores, eating establishments, getting lost browsing through books, occupied much of my waking hours. And yes, there were the lectures and seminars. Having received credit for my graduate studies at Fletcher and SAIS reduced the requirements for a Harvard PH.D in Government. However I could no longer avoid taking courses in economics and political philosophy. They were so well taught that those subjects that I had avoided for many years, suddenly turned into fascinating fields to explore. The economics course was divided into two equal segments, each taught by a distinguished professor. They had opposite points of view; the Keynesian who believed in the government's responsibility to help the economy and the followers of Hayek who totally disagreed. It was up to us to reach our own conclusion.

Professor Charles McIlvaine taught a course on the history of political philosophy. To do this he had come out of retirement, filling a void left when some professors had joined the war effort in Washington. The lectures, open to advanced undergraduates and graduate students, were so popular that Professor McIlvayne delivered them in a large hall where it was difficult to find an empty seat. The professor reached every student without a loudspeaker, communicating directly by focusing on each one of us and chuckling with amusement when we showed our obvious collective ignorance as he carefully pronounced the name of an obscure medieval monk. He excitedly discussed that monk's arguments with another equally obscure monk. That led to some very profound observation on the necessity to limit the powers of a ruler.

There was another professor whose seminar I am not likely ever to forget. When Hajo Holborn at SAIS learned that I had been accepted at Harvard, he suggested that I not miss the chance of taking a seminar with Professor Heinrich Brüning, a predecessor of Hitler who was chancellor from 1930 to 32. Brüning's failure to resolve the economic and political crisis ushered in Hitler's reign a year later. Brüning had been chancellor when I started first grade in Berlin. Now a little more than a dozen years later, I was going to be in a small seminar room hearing this important man talk about what had been going on at the highest level of the Weimar Republic. I was very excited when I signed up for the seminar. Why such a small seminar room? There were only five or six other graduate students. It took little time to discover why. The word had gotten around that this was a seminar to avoid. Brüning was not only the most boring professor I had the misfortune of listening to, but he also suffered from a compulsive desire to justify his colossal failure to preserve the Weimar Republic. He claimed it was not he, who should he held responsible for the hell into which Germany plunged. It was France and Great Britain as well as everybody else, who did not forgive Germany's reparations. They were responsible. One lecture could have covered all his possible arguments. But we had to listen to the same arguments for an entire semester. I must admit that I learned something very important: If in a democracy, voters fail to elect intelligent leaders possessing sufficient judgment to handle critical situations, it can have disastrous consequences.

With two years of Fletcher and SAIS behind me, I assumed I would have no problems fitting into the Harvard Graduate school environment. I quickly found out that Harvard was special. Many of my new acquaintances appeared to come from a somewhat different world. They were, or pretended to be, very sophisticated. My seven years in the United States was a tiny fraction of their and their ancestors' presence in America. The vocabulary they used in seminar discussions included words, such as the constantly repeated *oxymoron* I had never heard before. I kept telling myself, learning to speak Harvard English can't be any more difficult than all the other tongues I had to learn. Multiculturalism was to reach Harvard only years after my departure.

Among the many interesting fellow graduate students in McIlwayne's course on the history of political theory there was a slightly older student sitting in a chair not far from mine who one day tapped me on the shoulder and asked, whether I would like to join him for some tea. Nobody had ever asked me out for tea before. My response was something like, "how about coffee and cake instead?" David and I had a pleasant discussion about the course and his earlier career in the Foreign Service. He informed me that he lived in one of the undergraduate Harvard College units where graduate students help maintain law and order, in return for free rent. "Come over and read the Sunday *New York Times* in my place, you won't have to carry it twenty blocks to your room." It took me at least a month before I became aware that mentioning my various girl friends, past and present, froze his customary charming smile into a painfully polite expression. I never asked, I never told, and it took me a heck of a lot of time before I understood what this was all about. After all, I was preoccupied with finding someone of the opposite sex.

I also learned very quickly that there was a wide gap between Harvard undergraduates and graduate students. We graduate students were of course "more mature and full of useful knowledge" but we lacked something intangible, class. There was little danger that we would mix with undergraduates, a fact that the administration took advantage of in using us to proctor final examinations. We not only spotted the occasional undergraduate who cheated; but we had few qualms about working with the exam supervisor who controlled activities from his high perch in the Armory. In those days, there was no honor system for Harvard undergraduates. Some of those we caught cheating came from distinguished families. Monitoring final exams was an easy way to supplement our meager finances.

By the end of the spring semester, I had completed my course requirements for the Ph.D. degree. I met my foreign language requirements by walking into the Government Department chair's office prepared to translate a passage from a German book. When Professor Merle Fainsod asked me whether I had brought a book along I answered in the negative. He picked one from his shelf. He had some fun witnessing me struggle rendering a typically convoluted German sociological study into comprehensible English. After a while, he remarked that I seemed to be familiar with German words, but had some trouble conveying their philosophical meaning. So much for impressing the department chairman! Nevertheless, I returned a week later to pass my French language exam. Again, he pulled a book from his shelf. I was able to translate the passage into English without hesitation. That intrigued Professor Fainsod. "Were you not born in Berlin?" "Yes" I responded. "How come translating French is so much easier for you?" An interesting conversation followed on the difference of thinking in French vs. German. We also got into Russian, which was his major area of research. Apparently, I had convinced him that foreign languages would not present a significant obstacle in doing my thesis research.

The foreign language requirement out of the way, there was one more obstacle before I could start my thesis: I had to pass the oral general Ph.D. exam. I decided to do a lot of reading during the summer and take the exam in early October 1946. Maybe getting away from all the diversions of Harvard Square, might not be such a bad idea. I accepted my parents' invitation to do my reading at their place in Champaign, Illinois, where they had rented a house while my father had a one-year visiting professorship at the University of Illinois. My mother was enrolled in her own Ph.D. program, the history of science and medicine. A never openly admitted competition, between my mother and me developed: who would first get a Ph.D.

Champaign was my introduction to the Midwest. I explored the neighborhood and tried to understand what distinguished it from the East Coast America that had become my home. I also had to take a three-day trip to the U.S. Middle District of Pennsylvania Court in Wilkes-Barre, where my citizenship application process finally reached a conclusion on August 5, 1946. Eight years had passed since my arrival in Hoboken, New Jersey. Why Wilkes-Barre? The residence for my application had been transferred from New Haven to Chambersburg when my father taught at Wilson College in 1944. My parents official residence remained in Pennsylvania long enough for me not to have to suffer another delay. Wilkes-Barre was the location of the Federal Court covering Chambersburg. It was inconvenient and quite an interruption in my preparations for the Ph.D. orals. I had to change trains at least three times to get from central Illinois to central Pennsylvania. However, it was worth it! Now I finally was a U.S. citizen (Naturalization # 6359940) with all that it implied. I will never forget the ceremony when the Judge welcomed us as newly minted Americans. That is also why I am aghast at Trump and those Americans who rail against immigrants and seek to make admission to full citizenship ever more difficult.

Several more weeks of reading followed. That summer I read many interesting books, hoping that this or that particular book would help me answer questions asked by one of the four or five distinguished professors on my committee. When I returned to Cambridge I grew somewhat anxious. On the morning of the examination I had a headache that I attributed to nervousness. The headache disappeared the moment I entered the examination room where a half dozen distinguished faculty members sat around the table and proceeded to have fun asking me all kinds of questions, some of which I had not expected. It did not take me long to realize that a relatively recent addition to the Harvard Government Department used my examination to show his colleagues that he had a brilliant mind. He used it to torture me by forcing me to contradict myself. He pursued a relentless line of questioning. What was Justice? I sensed just in time where the argument was going and to the relief of the other members of the committee I answered that I knew that the questioner was trying to box me into a corner and gave logical reasons why I did not want to go there. Everybody smiled and relaxed. Shortly after that moment, the chair asked me to leave the room while the committee discussed my performance. It did not take very long before a smiling face came out of the room and asked me to come back in. I was officially informed that I had passed my oral Ph.D. examination.

As I walked back to my apartment full of joy, I noticed that my morning's headache had returned with a vengeance. Apparently, it had nothing to do with my excitement. I also realized that I had a fever and proceeded to the University infirmary where a young doctor excitedly told me that I had all the symptoms of mononucleosis. I vaguely remembered that I had heard that disease mentioned as a recently discovered infection, also known as the "kissing disease" because it was transmitted orally, and found mostly among younger people. Naturally I immediately tried to recall whom I had lately kissed. My search was not very productive because in the weeks leading up to the oral exam I had put romance on the back burner. The doctor was not the least interested in my efforts to recall my recent romances. He talked excitedly about how happy he was that I had come to his office. He was doing research on that disease and immediately took blood and other tests that confirmed his diagnosis. He sent me straight to the University infirmary where I became his guinea pig. He pumped me full with penicillin, then a still relatively new anti-biotic drug. That treatment did not shorten my hospital stay.

My bout with mononucleosis delayed celebrating my Ph.D. oral exam success. I had planned to join my Fletcher friends in Washington for a couple of days of fun. When I finally made it to Washington, October was almost over and other events pushed the exam into the background. My friends were preoccupied with the growing political battles that had replaced America's wartime bipartisanship. I realized that my serious pursuit of an academic career had created a growing gap separating me from their concerns with the real issues the nation faced.

I was confronted by a similar encounter with political reality upon my return to Cambridge. Barbara, a senior at Radcliff, and I had become good friends. Her mother, an old-fashioned 1930ies labor organizer, encouraged our relationship by lending Barbara her car. I renewed my lapsed driver's license and drove Barbara to Walden Pond. As the November election approached, she was shocked to hear that I had not registered to vote. Never mind, that I had been preoccupied with my preparations for the Ph.D. orals. I was made to feel like a criminal for not being able to vote for John F. Kennedy, then campaigning for a seat in Congress representing Cambridge. Actually, I did not share her enthusiasm. I connected the young Kennedy with his father who as FDR's ambassador in London had played a somewhat ambivalent role. He had said too many nice things about Hitler's Germany. That was all water over the dam Barbara quoted her mother as saying. The 1946 election was the only one in which I did not cast my vote.

***

I was very lucky to have chosen Professor Rupert Emerson as my thesis advisor. While he had written books on colonialism in the Far East, his knowledge and interest also covered the Near East and Europe. He was a Harvard professor who unlike some of his peers was not condescending in his conversation with a lowly graduate student. I titled my initial thesis proposal: *How can a small country maintain its independence in a world of big powers?* Instead of suggesting, that this topic was too broad, ambitious and difficult to treat in a scholarly manner, Professor Emerson gave me a short deadline for submitting a synopsis of my proposal. It did not take me long to realize that a thesis was not the proper venue to resolve the rising postwar problem; assuring the independence of small countries in a world dominated by super powers, the United States and the Soviet Union. I scaled down my proposal to just one small country. Having done research on Iran at the Fletcher School, I picked that country. I decided to explore Iran, a weak country in the post-war era with however a proud past as the Persian Empire that had somehow succeeded in retaining its independence sandwiched between the Russian and British empires.

Professor Emerson after reading the first two chapters remarked that they were interesting but subtly raised the question about my knowledge of Farsi, the Persian language. A great deal was written about Iran in German, French and Russian, I responded. Emerson scratched his head and said, "don't you know Czech, German and Russian, languages that would facilitate your research if you were to pick Czechoslovakia as an example of a small country trying to maintain its independence?" "That would be too simple; after all I grew up there," I responded."I thought a thesis should involve a difficult topic." He burst out laughing, "A thesis involves making a scholarly contribution about something you do know, explore thoroughly and provide an original analysis of facts that you have discovered". Very sound advice!

I had received a graduate school scholarship for the 1946/47 academic year, specifically to enable me to devote my energy to working on my thesis. Sometime in January 1947 it downed on me that, even though I had not progressed very far I would have to start looking for a job to start my academic career that fall. After spending 6 ½ years in undergraduate and graduate studies, getting a teaching position required shifting gears. When I mentioned that I was looking for a job, Professor Emerson reprimanded me for not mentioning this to him before Christmas. The Political Science Association had just concluded its annual meeting during the Christmas vacation. At that conference contacts were made leading to academic appointments. Having missed that opportunity, I would have to go through a conventional employment seeking channel: the Harvard Graduate School Employment Office.

I went there and told them that I was looking for a university teaching job not far from Cambridge. I provided them information about my interests, academic record and the type of position I sought. I was told that introductory teaching positions would start with annual salaries in the $2,500 to $2,800 range. Locating a position in the Northeast turned out to be much harder than I had anticipated. The Northeast was dominated by the Ivy League: Harvard, Yale, Princeton, as well as smaller prestigious colleges like Amherst and Williams. I discovered quickly the prestigious colleges were reluctant to consider a prospective faculty member who had only recently arrived in the United States. Even though my parents and I had joined the Presbyterian Church in upper Manhattan, I was considered a German Jewish refugee, only grudgingly accepted by the not so open arms of Miss Liberty. At job interviews, I had expected to discuss world affairs, politics, and cultural topics, Instead I was sidetracked by detailed questions about my views on baseball and other sports that did not particularly interest me. The interviewers were more concerned about my fitting into the campus social milieu than in my academic competence.

My naiveté was partially at fault. I had followed my father's strong advice and concentrated entirely on getting a Ph.D. degree, which I assumed would automatically open the door to a rewarding academic career. I realized only later that while a Ph.D. degree was an essential perquisite, there were many other equally important factors helping or hindering landing a job in the immediate post-war academic world. Some obstacles were of my own making: I limited my search to New England and New York. I had no car and planned to continue my thesis research at Harvard's Widener Library. I had not anticipated that several universities way out West were the first to show some interest. Going to Utah or New Mexico was however something I did not even consider.

In a few days I was notified that there was a job opening at the University of Connecticut. Since state universities in the immediate post World War II era were only a recent addition to the trove of well known academic institutions in New England my initial reaction was lukewarm. The employment office reminded me that I had expressed an interest in a location not far from Boston. The University of Connecticut met that requirement.

George McReynolds, chair of the UCONN Department of Government and International Relations, traveled to Cambridge to interview me. We connected almost immediately. He was not only interested but positively excited by my European background; which he believed would enliven my lectures on international relations. His objective, he told me, was to invigorate the teaching of world affairs to help the post-war generation of students be better prepared for the inevitable crises the United States would face in the intensifying confrontation with Stalin's Soviet Union. As a member of the History department in Storrs before joining the U.S. armed forces and serving in the Pacific Theater of Operations, he had personally faced the consequences of Japan's attack on Pearl Harbor. On his return to UCONN he was asked to chair the newly created Department of Government and International Relations, consisting of faculty members previously members of the History Department.

My conversation with George McReynolds at the Harvard Employment Office was brief but extremely friendly and led to an immediate job offer. He suggested that I come and see the place myself before accepting the offer. Even without a car, getting to Storrs from Boston was simple in those days. There was a direct train from Boston's South station to Hartford via Thompson and Willimantic. I was picked up at the Willimantic train station by

Professor Linnevold, a junior member of the Department. He drove me to Storrs where I met other members of the Department, the Dean of Arts and Sciences and the chair of the History Department.

At lunch I learned how President Jorgensen had transformed UCONN from a small academic hideout into a state university modeled on long established public universities in the Midwest. It had shifted its emphasis from agricultural studies to the liberal arts and sciences and eventually graduate studies leading to the award of PhD's. After the war the University benefitted from the G.I. Bill which enabled returning World War II veterans to get a college education and resulted in rapidly expanding enrollments.

After digesting all this information at lunch I accepted the offer to become an instructor in the Department of Government and International relations. Apparently I fitted into George McReynolds plan to expand course offerings in international diplomacy. That was the start of my teaching career. Unfortunately George McReynolds ceased his role as my guide in academia much too soon. In 1951 he became Dean of the College of Arts and Sciences, a position he held for barely three years before succumbing to cancer in 1954. I think of him not only as a chairman and colleague with whom it was easy to work with but also as someone with whom I shared the hope of improving the post-war world, thus avoiding a repetition of policies that had led to the rise of Hitler and the Second World War.

After accepting the job offer there was a further question. Did I want to teach on the main campus at Storrs or at the Fort Trumbull branch in New London? Salary was a little better there and I would have the opportunity to transfer to the Storrs campus later. It was obvious to me that teaching in Storrs required a car, whereas New London was on the main line between Boston, New York and the rest of the civilized world. I chose Fort Trumbull, sight unseen. George McReynolds immediately drove me down to New London, introduced me to the Director of the Fort Trumbull Branch and my job search was over. I took the train in New London back to Boston, intent on finishing my thesis as quickly as possible, since McReynolds had made it quite clear that my future at UCONN depended on my completing my PhD thesis.

Working on my thesis in my Widener Library cubicle, surrounded by a wide range of interesting books, isolated from the outer world, did not prepare me for my new life at Fort Trumbull. There I fell in love with the view of Long Island Sound from my window. A lighthouse blinked at night. Submarines and other ships passed by frequently. On a very clear day, I could see Long Island shimmering on the horizon; quite a diversion from concentrating on research and teaching.

Teaching was also a bigger challenge than I had expected. I faced large classes of G.I. students who were my age or older and possessed a great deal of self-confidence. After all, they had won the War. Their knowledge of international relations was however usually limited to their own very recent encounters with armed enemies in Europe, the Far East, in the air or on the oceans. Many held strong opinions on issues they had encountered serving their country. I had to read two hundred exam essays in which they expressed all kinds of ideas, some brilliant, some not. This turned into a nightmare. My colleagues urged me to shift from reading and grading essay exams to counting the number of correct answers in multiple-choice exams. That would save a lot of time! Correct. However, making up multiple-choice exams was quite a challenge. I had to invent answers that could possibly be true. Only one, however, was closest to the target. That was not easy and took an awful lot of time. I recall sitting at my desk at 4 A.M. inventing answers when my mind started to travel into a world of dreams. As I awoke, I looked out the window. The beam from the lighthouse brought me back to the real world. I called it quits, even though the multiple-choice exam had only 20 questions. The students' initial joy about such a short exam turned to noisy rumbling, as they tried to pick the right answer among the intentionally confusing choices I had invented.

It became obvious that my planned concentration on my thesis had to take a backseat to teaching. There were other distractions. Fort Trumbull faculty members lived in comfortable rooms in a college type dormitory. We were in our twenties or thirties. While our student body was exclusively male, the faculty had a significant number of female instructors. This led to a far more active social life than I had been accustomed to at Harvard. We explored the restaurants on Bank Street in New London, played bridge, had dates and during the summer explored the further reaches of Ocean Beach.

My teaching responsibilities were not the only diversions from progressing on my thesis. The topic of the thesis presented me with new problems. The subject that I had focused on started to show some life. Czechoslovakia, my example of a small country maintaining its independence in a world of super powers, entered center stage in the post-war arena. I had to refocus my inquiry. Edvard Beneš, the pre-war president of Czechoslovakia and the restorer of its independence, was a strong advocate of cooperation between Czechoslovakia and the West as well as the Soviet Union.

Since he had for a long time directed Czechoslovakia's foreign policy, I decided to center my thesis on his ideas, plans and implementer of policies. Beneš had written a great deal, and had been at or near the helm of Czechoslovakia ever since World War I. He was therefore the logical focus of my inquiry. Professor Emerson heaved a big sigh of relief when I told him that I had chosen a more realistic title for my thesis: *Can Communism and Democracy Coexist; Edvard Beneš's Answer.*

That however did not solve all my problems. Czech Communists with the encouragement of Josef Stalin ruined Beneš's effort to create an independent state that could serve as a link between East and West. Before I could complete my thesis, the Communists implemented a take-over at the end of February 1948. Czechoslovakia's foreign minister Jan Masaryk, the son of Czechoslovakia's first president and a close friend of Beneš, jumped or was pushed from the balcony of the Foreign Ministry and died. A few months later Beneš, terribly disappointed, died a broken man. Current events kept on interfering with my thesis and forced me to change the answer to my question. Obviously, Communism and Democracy had serious troubles coexisting. As a result, I had to analyze the tortuous path that Beneš had traveled in his vain effort to secure Czechoslovakia's independence. My enthusiasm for my chosen topic took a big hit, delaying its completion.

George McReynolds inquired occasionally how my thesis was progressing. On its completion depended my moving to the main Storrs campus. I had to inform him that the thesis would take me an extra year. This meant that he had to wait an extra year before transferring me to Storrs in 1949. I spent the summer of 1948 in a frantic attempt to make significant progress. There was less swimming at Ocean Beach, less bridge playing and fewer dates.

Since the Cold War and developments in Czechoslovakia were headline news, working on my thesis became an essential part of my life. When the summer was over, I was able to send Professor Emerson several chapters, which he liked. As the 1948/49 academic year progressed, I realized that there was no way for me to complete a final draft by March '49, the deadline for getting the Ph.D. in 1949. At least I could blame Stalin for delaying me in getting my degree. McReynolds was sufficiently satisfied with my progress and accepted my promise to finish everything by March 1950.

In preparation for my transfer to rural Storrs, I acquired my first car, a 1938 Ford.

A Waterbury friend of a Fort Trumbull colleague sold me his ten-year old car for $370. The date was February 28, 1949. Next morning when I had to get the car registered and my driver's license updated the first major snow fall of the season made it difficult to locate the car in the faculty parking lot, since several inches of snow covered everything. After shoveling a lot of snow I managed to drive very carefully and slowly to the Motor Vehicle Department office in downtown New London. The weather made me the only customer. The official asked me how I managed to get there. She was very impressed and asked me no further questions, handed me all necessary papers, and urged me to get back home as soon as possible.

The car liberated me. I was no longer tied to Fort Trumbull. As it got warmer in April, I explored all roads that led to beaches between Old Saybrook and Watch Hill, R.I. I ventured even further, all the way to Washington, visiting my Fletcher friends, able to offer them rides. Fortunately, I managed to control my newly discovered freedom and return to the typewriter. Chapters started following each other at shorter intervals and the end appeared in sight. The remaining obstacles were time-consuming but manageable.

In September 1949, I moved to the main campus. The peaceful view of Long Island Sound faded into memory. I rented a comfortable second story room at the Avery's in a recently-built house on Moulton Road in Storrs. Located just beyond Horse Barn Hill it was only a short ride to my office. The Avery's downstairs had a young child. The mother informed me that they expected no noise that would disturb their treasured peace. Her father, Dan Graf, who had an influential position at the University, lived down the road. All this sounded great, the perfect environment to concentrate on my thesis. I had left behind the dormitory-like setting, where I had been surrounded by young male and female instructors. I was no longer tempted to socialize excessively and play bridge. There were no excuses for not working on my thesis.

There were however other diversions. I had two neighbors on the second floor of the house. One was a state building inspector who oversaw new campus construction. The other was a student who happened to be the son of the boss of a major construction company that built new highways. The inspector and the construction company son had heated discussions about why no project ever got done properly. They exchanged views on the honest and dishonest practices of construction companies. The discussions fascinated me. I participated as a very curious bystander. The issues they discussed emerged later as major newspaper stories and remained topical until the recent past.

State construction controversies had however nothing to do with my thesis. Fortunately, I realized that these Moulton Road conversations, while extremely interesting, endangered meeting my thesis deadline. Listening to all this was however a welcome diversion, since the Cold War was getting tiresome and the future of Czechoslovakia bleak.

Reluctantly, I shifted the location of my work in the evening to my South Campus office in the temporary building that housed the Government and History Departments, a short drive from Moulton Road. After the late afternoon stragglers left the building, I had the whole place to myself. This enabled me to concentrate on my primary task.

I left the door open and typed away furiously. It had taken me three years to type fifty pages. Once in my South Campus office, the pace accelerated. It took me only a couple of weeks to finish several chapters and I began to contemplate the real prospect of completing the project by early spring. I usually left the office around 11 P.M. since I had to teach a class at 8 A.M the next day. As I got closer to the finish line, I got more and more excited and stayed later. One night, well past midnight, I suddenly heard a loud noise. Somebody had entered the building and an older man in his fifties or early sixties poked his head into my office and curtly asked what I was doing there at this hour. He obviously was the night watchman, swinging his keys, ready to inform me that I had better be somewhere else at this time of the night. "What are you doing?" he asked. Writing my thesis", I answered. His demeanor changed and we started talking.

It took only a few minutes for us to realize we both had a Czech connection. Eleven years earlier, I had left Czechoslovakia and crossed the Atlantic, not realizing that Storrs would be my ultimate destination. His parents had left a small town in Bohemia decades earlier before the First World War and ultimately settled in Gurleyville, in the valley east of the University. A family member still owned the Grist Mill that has since been acquired by Joshua's Trust and is at present operated as a museum. "Do you know the Storrs Postmaster across the street?" he asked. "Enough to say hello", I answered. "He is a nephew of mine, a member of the Duda family". I told him that what I was working on, dealt with the policies and ideas of Edvard Beneš, Czechoslovakia's president, who had died shortly after the Communist take-over in 1948.

Our conversation continued long enough to delay significantly, his checking the rest of the campus buildings and slowed the completion of the chapter I was working on. After our first encounter on that memorable night, he stopped regularly at my door. In some strange way, his visits comforted me. They did not divert me from my work, quite the contrary. They connected my academic pursuit with real people. After all, the Czechs who had left Bohemia had come from villages not far from the one in which Beneš had spent his early years.

A few days after Duda's visit I located former Governor Wilbur Cross' autobiography, *Connecticut Yankee* in my bookcase. I turned to the reminiscences of his youth in Gurleyville and found a reference to recent Bohemian immigrants (p.57) who had bought the silk and gristmills from earlier settlers. I also noted the very Czech name, Novotny, of a secretary, working in a university department in a neighboring building. There were many Czech names on mailboxes in Bolton, Willington, Ashford, as well as in Mansfield. The name Zizka in particular, intrigued me. Žižka, as spelled in Czech, is the name of the warrior who led Bohemian religious fighters against the Austrian emperor in the 15th century. Here I was in Storrs, writing about contemporary Czechoslovak problems, in an environment that reminded me of the one that I thought I had abandoned forever less than a dozen years earlier. Mr. Duda's midnight visit had brought it all back.

In spite of these interruptions, I was able to send a draft to Professor Emerson shortly after the New Year. He approved it, but suggested I find an American born colleague to read the thesis and eliminate my German phrases and sentence structure. I asked Max Thatcher, my Department colleague who had also moved from Fort Trumbull to Storrs, to do me this favor. He did an excellent job, but forever afterward teased my use of certain German phrases. After he finished translating my thesis into acceptable English, I found an extremely competent faculty wife who typed my thesis, following the official Harvard rules for submitting the final draft. At the end of March 1950, I drove to Cambridge to deliver the finished product in person and on time. I passed the so-called Defense of the Thesis examination easily. In June, I got my degree, completing a very important phase of my life.

***

On April 20, 1950, just after getting up, George McReynolds reached me on my landlord's telephone (I had no phone of my own) to tell me I had to call my mother in Little Rock, Arkansas. It was urgent. I called and got the terrible news that my father had suffered a stroke the night before while shaving. He had passed away in a hospital early in the morning. She asked me to come right away. After teaching my scheduled 8 o'clock class I excused myself from the remaining classes that day. At McReynold's suggestion, I went to a bank manager in Willimantic and got a loan to cover the price of a roundtrip airplane ticket to Little Rock. I drove to Bradley airport which in those days consisted of a small building. After a short flight to LaGuardia, I transferred to a direct flight to Memphis, with a stop in North Carolina. Finally, on a regional airline, I reached Little Rock. It had taken 24 hours for my mother to have her son, the only member of her family, join her in grieving for our terrible loss.

The final years of my father's journey had been difficult. After getting some appointments as a visiting scholar with minimal pay in New York and at Yale, he started his westward journey. He spent two years at Wilson College, Chambersburg, PA, replacing a professor on leave, moved on to the University of Illinois in Champaign, Illinois, stayed there long enough for my mother to complete her course work for a Ph.D. in History, spent a year at Rockford College, Illinois, again replacing a professor on leave. The constant search for a permanent position had serious consequences. In 1947, he wrote a letter to Arthur, our Doctor friend in New York, expressing very dark thoughts about his future. Arthur was sufficiently concerned to visit me in person and relay his opinion that there was a limit to my father's eternal optimism. I had just started on my first job and was earning a salary. The implied question: Could I not help my father financially? I told Arthur what I was earning at Fort Trumbull. He dropped the subject.

Going over correspondence that my mother had closely guarded until her death in 2002, I learned how depressed my parents had become in their futile search for a permanent academic position. They wrote increasingly desperate letters to fellow philosophers at U.S. colleges and universities and applied for grants from a variety of agencies supporting scholarly research. My father attended annual meetings of the Association of Philosophy professors and wrote numerous articles on issues of interest to a larger audience. They covered topics ranging from racism, psychology, religion to the danger of not paying attention to key political issues. They were published in professional journals and well received. His request for financial support however depended on his getting a regular academic position. This was an insurmountable barrier since not until his mid-fifties, close to retirement age, did he master English well enough to give lectures that students could understand.

Despite their constant worries, my mother made great strides in an effort to finish her Ph.D. thesis in record time. They now could look for a college where they both could teach. My mother, 13 years younger than my father, had a better chance of landing a job. Her Ph.D. advisor at the University of Illinois urged her to shave a couple of years off her real age, and pretend that she was in her early forties, not yet approaching 50.

In 1948, 10 years after arriving in the U.S., just as my mother completed her Ph.D. requirements, my parents were both offered teaching positions at Central College, a small college in North Little Rock, Arkansas. It was funded by a religious organization and housed in an abandoned World War II facility. It tried to meet the demands of returning GI's for a college education. My parents hoped the teaching appointments in Arkansas would finally improve their financial situation.

They were happy to have found a permanent position. They did not mind the primitive living conditions in their abandoned World War II military cottage. They explored their new environment, as close to the storied Wild West, as they could ever have imagined in their wildest dreams. My mother learned to drive and bought a car to enable them to explore Little Rock and state parks in central Arkansas. They got to know their fellow faculty members and developed new friendships. When I visited them in the late summer of 1949, I could not help notice their different mood. For the first time since they had left New Haven, their basic optimism had returned.

Alas, this was not to last. Central College was conceived by dreamers. They lacked the know-how to operate a small academic institution. They knew how to entice faculty and students, but not how to raise money. This resulted in delayed salary payments and eventually in doubts whether the checks would arrive at all. My parents' brief respite from having to worry about the future was over. My mother played a role in helping to organize the faculty and present their case to the administration. Just when this crisis reached the boiling point, my father, preparing himself for the next day's lecture, started to shave in the bathroom and collapsed. He had suffered a fatal stroke. My mother got help immediately and he was brought to a nearby Catholic hospital. She spent a horrible night there with my unconscious father, fending off the efforts of the nurses to have my father receive the Last Rites. My mother was convinced that my father's intense worry about the future precipitated the stroke. My father was only 63 years old. Three days earlier, my parents had just celebrated their 27th wedding anniversary.

My mother and I were not really prepared to make all the arrangements for a funeral. The friends that my parents had made at the College were extremely helpful. The whole college participated in the funeral ceremonies. My father was buried in a cemetery in Little Rock, the final stop on his journey from Plzeň to the New World.

My father's funeral was given considerable publicity in the local press. One consequence was the college administration's effort to pay overdue salaries. My mother had however made up her mind to leave Central College and look for a new job. George McReynolds told me that I could take at least a week off from my teaching schedule to

help my mother. After the funeral, I drove her to the University of Arkansas in Fayetteville. She talked with members of the History Department. There were no openings. On our return to Little Rock, we explored the Ozarks. I developed a real interest in that part of America. After finishing the spring semester in Storrs, I arranged to help my mother move to Storrs. She drove her car to Knoxville Tennessee, where I met her and helped her drive to Connecticut.

Part III - Growing Roots in Storrs

Chapter 8
Audrey

Arriving in Storrs in September 1949 changed my life. My new more normal university environment facilitated interesting and somewhat unexpected encounters with members of the opposite sex. It helped that I had gained a few years on my students and while male students still dominated the scene, there were female students who entered the competition for grades, jobs and the instructor's attention.

Audrey was such a student. She was in my introductory government course that I taught in Rostov, a temporary South campus classroom building named after the city on the Russian front. A decade later, the E. O. Smith High School would be built on the spot where Rostov had been located and where my most important romance was about to start.

I had asked my students to write a paper on a topic pertaining to the governance of their hometown. Most papers were not particularly exciting though they contained reasonably accurate information. Late one night, having read at least 30 papers, I stumbled on one that stood out. This particular student informed me that his/her town did not fit the standard pattern that I had described in my lecture on local governments. Not merely was Norwalk's government differently structured, but its politics was also weird. There were independent fire department districts, water districts, etc. etc. The student saw no way of fitting Norwalk into the formal framework that I had described in my lecture. I sprinkled the paper with question and exclamation marks and comments. When I returned the paper to the class, I was curious to find out who this interesting student was. A smiling, but determined young woman from the back of the room picked it up and almost immediately tried to set me straight on the comments that I had written. She also questioned why I had not given her an A, but an A-. I informed her that I only rarely gave any grade better than an A-. Her smile barely hid her obvious intention to help me improve my grading practice, at least in her case. Before the semester was over, I realized that indeed she was an excellent student and deserved an A. She informed me that she majored in business. I suggested that she might consider majoring in government. She took my advice.

A few weeks later in April, when I received my mother's emergency phone call telling me of my father's death, it was Audrey working the night shift at the University telephone exchange, who had channeled my mother's call to George McReynolds, my chairman, making sure that I, her professor, would be instantly informed.

Upon my return from my father's funeral in Arkansas Audrey expressed her condolences. She then directed my attention to Norwalk, her home town, and especially the town's Rowayton section, her parents' home, the location of fishing and sailing piers. She informed me that she was a sea scout and had learned to sail. When she learned that I was only experienced with canoes floating on calm inland lakes, she immediately invited me to join her sailing on Long Island Sound. She would teach me how to handle a boat in calm and rough waters. I suppose this was her expression of gratitude for getting an A.

We arranged a date a few weeks later and I drove to Rowayton, where I was to meet her at a pier. Her Sea Scout coach had loaned her a sailboat. It was a warm, humid day in early July. In a role reversal in which she assumed the role of a teacher, Audrey proceeded to identify and name every item on the sailboat. Fortunately she did not quiz me to check my ability to retain all that information. I did however learn to duck quickly when the sailboat changed direction. The beam narrowly missed my head. We loosened the rope. The boat gently left the pier. We were on our way to the open waters of the Sound. There was one problem: no wind. The sailboat had no auxiliary motor. Audrey, a great optimist, as I was to discover, firmly believed that breezes in the Sound would soon replace the calm waters. There are always breezes there. We were however in an inlet, well protected from the strong currents of air that dominate oceans and even Long Island Sound. Well, we started rowing. Soon a motorboat carrying a couple of Coastguardsmen passed us. They immediately recognized Audrey. Apparently everybody knew her. They shouted and asked us whether we wanted to be towed into the Sound. Off we flew, quickly catching the breezes of the open Sound. We thanked the Coastguard.

Our destination: an island in sight of the shore. Audrey informed me that nobody lived there. We secured the boat at an abandoned old pier and Audrey led me through dense vegetation to a meadow overlooking the Sound with the Connecticut coastline in sight. The meadow bordered on an abandoned house. In her role as a sea scout, she had explored this island. Audrey was proud to show it to me. We settled down and enjoyed the lunch that we had brought. The romantic mood that enveloped us was interrupted by the distant yet ominous sound of thunder. Lightning struck targets on the far away shore and sheets of rain moved in our direction. Not even the magic of our new relationship could protect us from the approaching storm. We found refuge in a shelter connected to the empty house. By now, it was afternoon and we had planned to be back in Rowayton by 5 p.m. That is the time that Audrey had told her parents to expect her home on dry land. While the rain had nearly stopped, lightning continued to flash over the distant coastline. The storm appeared stationary. Our talk shifted from romance to the important question whether a solitary sailboat sticking out on the open sea was a likely lightning target. Neither of us knew the answer.

A new consideration entered our conversation. If we did not get back to land before dark, would Audrey's parents be sufficiently alarmed to ask the police to search for us? What would appear in the papers next day: UCONN professor and his freshman student lost/found on Long Island Sound? Never mind the potential of being hit by lightning. We agreed, appearing on the *Norwalk Hour* front page would be more deadly. We rushed to the boat, cast off the island, raised the sails, and driven by strong blows from the receding storm, gathered speed. In this critical situation, Audrey demonstrated that she indeed was an experienced sailor and managed to steer our boat directly to the shore. Instead of returning to the pier, we arrived at a nearby beach, closer to her home. As we approached, we quickly realized that our concerns had been realistic: In spite of the bad weather, a crowd of at least twenty was assembled. Some emergency personnel surrounded her parents. When it became clear that our expedition had suffered no losses, the assembly dwindled and Audrey introduced me to her parents. Quite an exciting first date!

After Audrey returned to the campus in September, our courtship did not only continue but proceeded in a clearly defined direction: marriage. Since my mother and Audrey's parents were well aware of the serious nature of our relationship, we both felt we had nothing to hide and were comfortable about our increasing intimacy. A few days after Audrey settled in her dorm, we decided to go mountain climbing in New Hampshire. I picked the closest one, Mount Monadnock, which in its solitary location succeeds in giving climbers who reach the top, the illusion they have accomplished something unique: they have an almost unlimited view of southern New Hampshire and northern Massachusetts. We, however, had so much to talk about that we hardly paid attention to the wide world far below.

We were both aware of the major differences in our respective backgrounds. Her father, Gilbert W. Phillips, was a worker in a hat-making factory in Brooklyn, New York, where Audrey was born in 1931. During the Great Depression of the 1930's his job moved to Connecticut. There her parents found a cheap house in Rowayton, a part of Norwalk. The father worked diligently and never lost his job for any significant length of time and therefore they managed to scrape by, even in the worst years of the Depression. While he worked hard, he never said very much and I could not recall Audrey attributing any significant opinions to him. Since he traced his ancestry back to immigrants arriving in the New World a few decades after the Pilgrims, Audrey considered her father's taciturnity a Yankee heritage.

Her mother, Mary E.B. Riley Phillips had a different background. A strong personality, she talked and expressed opinions on almost any topic. Once we visited Audrey's maternal grandfather in a retirement home on Roosevelt Island in New York City. Although infirm and quite old, he had not lost his Irish brogue and expressed himself forcefully. Audrey and her mother carried the Irish genes in their veins. It certainly helped Audrey express herself effectively. Mary's mother had also German and French forbears to which Audrey attributed her mother's stubbornness on every controversial issue. Coming from a Catholic background, Audrey's mother surprised me by her frequent vehement denunciation of the Catholic Church. Given the negative opinions expressed by her parents on religion, politics and many other topics,

I was impressed that Audrey found her way toward a positive optimistic view of the world around her.

Her mother's personality also helped prepare Audrey for her legislative career. While her taciturn Yankee father watched quietly, her mother would readily engage anyone in a lively argument. Audrey's maternal Irish grandfather certainly bore some responsibility for that. Audrey's diverse ancestry, ranging from those who had crossed the Atlantic shortly after the Mayflower to Irish, Welch, German and French immigrants of the 19th century, enabled her later to feel comfortable with almost any one of her constituents and fellow legislators.

Her mother stayed home until Audrey and her younger brother Gilbert both were in school. At that point she took a job to help feed the family. Audrey's school teachers were impressed by her outstanding performance in every course except home economics. They guided her into unfamiliar territory like former Connecticut Senator Hiram Bingham's fascination with Peru's Incan city of Machu Picchu. Her training as a sea scout enabled her to dream about a world beyond the Rowayton shoreline that she knew too well. A woman in an upscale household, who employed Audrey as a baby sitter, introduced her to the *Christian Science Monitor* and its worldwide news coverage.

She spoke enthusiastically about her school experience. I soon realized why Audrey stressed that her grade in home economics did not match her performance in her other subjects. She usually mentioned it when I asked her to sow on buttons on my shirt. She preferred to get deeply involved reading important literary works.

As an outstanding high school graduate, Audrey considered continuing her education and go to college. There was however a problem: how to pay for that. She also wondered which college and on what field of study to concentrate. With hardly any practical advice from home and good wishes, but little assistance, from teachers and friends, it was entirely up to Audrey to make all the right decisions. Only eighteen when graduating from high school, she decided to take a year off and work as an operator at the Norwalk telephone exchange in order to save enough money to cover at least one year of college.

As a long distance operator who connected some famous people in Fairfield County with numbers all over the United States and even abroad she managed to talk to well-known individuals from Darien and Greenwich who had dialed the long distance operator. She made the most of this opportunity. She regaled me with the comments that Claire Booth Luce had exchanged with her while she connected her to some important person in another state. Working a year upon graduating from high school had enabled Audrey to save enough money to cover her first year at UCONN. There she sought to gain all types of information and knowledge to help her answer the many questions that had intrigued her for so many years.

She had been successful at her job because she was good at multi-tasking, taking half a dozen calls at almost the same time and never missing the correct connection. When she had a part time job at the UCONN telephone exchange, she showed me how she managed to simultaneously conduct a serious conversation with me, while connecting people from all over the campus with people elsewhere. She earned and saved enough money in her year at the telephone company and in her part-time job at the UCONN telephone exchange to cover the cost of her two years at UCONN before we got married. She also saved enough to help her parents buy a used car that she did not drive because she did not have a driver's license. Her savings even paid partially for our honeymoon.

And then there was the question which college to attend. She first considered a State Teachers College. In the immediate post-war era, it was generally assumed that a woman planning a career would choose to be a teacher. Western State Teachers College in Danbury would have been the logical choice. Her job at the telephone company gave her time to think and raise her sights. Why not go to the rapidly expanding UCONN main campus and become a business major?

Once in Storrs her interest in business waned. Courses in the social sciences and the humanities attracted her and she switched to the College of Liberal Arts and Science in her sophomore year and decided to major in Government and International Relations. I would like to think that it was after she took my course. Once we started dating seriously, I raised the question whether it might not seem more appropriate for me not to be her major advisor. It might appear to some that romance could possibly interfere with my evaluating her academic performance objectively. Why not major in economics? Unlike many of her fellow female students at that time, she enjoyed her courses in that department very much. Female students avoided it, maybe because it was too nerdy.

That decision proved to be fateful. Economic issues almost immediately fascinated her. Her enthusiasm came to the attention of senior members of the Department, especially Professor Phil Taylor who played a significant role advising state and national officials on fundamental economic policy issues. Professor Joel Dirlam introduced her to John Maynard Keynes' economic philosophy. Professor Thorkelson reinforced her support for labor union philosophy. Her decision to major in economics helped my future wife and legislator to become an expert on state finances and a leading advocate of a state income tax.

When Audrey entered UCONN, she immediately joined the Debate Club. She wanted not merely to understand what was going on in the world, and especially in her immediate environment, but also to do something about social and economic conditions she thought were wrong. To do this she had to convince others. Learning to debate would help her. Not many freshmen were as enthusiastic as she was to master arguments pro and con on the major issues of the day. Two decades later, she applied those skills to demolish the arguments of fellow legislators who lacked her debating effectiveness.

Audrey's interests went beyond politics and economics. She loved Professor Robert Stallman's approach to literature and kept regaling me with the quaintest reinterpretations of what I had thought were obvious meanings of statements made by well-known authors I had read in college. We spent a summer traveling with Moby Dick. She even sent letters to the *New York Times Book Review Section* with comments based on her interest in literature aroused by Stallman's lectures. She graduated Phi Beta Kappa and was asked to become a teaching assistant and work for a master's degree. Audrey would have had to overcome some practical obstacles to get a PhD in order to become a regular faculty member. A PhD in economics had to be earned at a University other than UCONN, such as Yale. Yale required at least two semesters in residence in New Haven. Ronald and Meredith were not old enough to be abandoned by their mother for a week or more at their age.

1951 was a special year in our lives. Our wonderful romantic dates encouraged us to discuss the ultimate goal of getting married Before tying the knot we had to deal with issues stemming from Audrey's residence in an undergraduate dorm. Female students had to be back in their dorms on weekdays by 11 o'clock. This posed a problem when we attended a concert performance at the Bushnell in Hartford. I had to ask my recently married colleague Max Thatcher to invite Audrey to stay overnight at their rented house because I would not have been able to get her back to her dorm on time. After a few months, we had explored almost all the possible hideouts in Storrs and environs where we could spend an uninterrupted hour together. We got tired of having to worry about intruders. This and similar difficulties facing the unmarried couple of instructor and student encouraged us to set an early date for our wedding enabling us to lead a less complicated and more satisfying life.

We wanted to make sure that Audrey could get her bachelor degree before we would have the responsibility of caring for a progeny. She decided to take courses at the end of her sophomore year in the summer and some extra courses in her junior year. It enabled her to meet most of her graduation requirements in three years making it possible for us to get married a year after our first date on that romantic island in Long Island Sound.

On August 4, 1951, when Summer School was over, Audrey and I tied the knot in the Parish House Annex of the Storrs Congregational Church. The main building was not available: it was being renovated. We had a wedding reception at my mother's and my Mansfield Apartment which we had subleased during the summer. Many of our several dozen friends in Storrs, as well as Audrey's family and relatives made this day an unforgettable experience. The weather was perfect and much of the celebration, as well as a lot of noise, occurred on the lawn behind the apartment.

While the guests continued to enjoy the food, drinks, conversation in a very relaxed atmosphere, Audrey and I bade our good-byes and started on our honeymoon. We had no specific plans and just wanted to explore the coast of Maine and visit Quebec. In the pre-modern Interstate Highway age, this was quite an ambitious project. It was late in the afternoon when we had to drive through the city of Boston to reach our first night stop, a run-of-the-mill motel near the coast, not too great a distance from Maine. We were exhausted and ended up in a room that lacked any hint of luxury one would expect to enjoy on the first night of marriage. Fortunately we were both so exhausted from that day's activities that we fell asleep, in spite of the noise outside our window. What a way to start of our married life!

Next morning we reached the coast of Maine and drove to Pemaquid Point at the tip of one of the many narrow peninsulas that jut into the stormy Atlantic. There we found an attractive house overlooking the rocks below and the turbulent waves beyond. It turned out to be a charming small inn with a genuine flavor of coastal Maine. Audrey looked at the inlet and started saying something about there being an excellent breeze for a great sail. I looked at the rocks and stated that I did not want to end our new life prematurely by getting smashed against those rocks. We ended up on a bath towel on a huge rock under the sun, without a cloud in the sky. That was the real start of our honeymoon!

A couple of days later, we drove north to Quebec City. There were churches and museums, but we had been spoiled by admiring nature at the coast of Maine. We were both nature lovers, Audrey loved adventures on a sailboat and I enjoyed walking on the trails in the Alps and the mountains of New England. On our return, we passed through New Hampshire stopping on the shore of Lake Winnipesaukee long enough for me to tell Audrey all about my summer there in 1940. Back in Connecticut we made a quick trip to Audrey's parents in Rowayton and New York City.

We received a telephone call there from my mother informing us that the faculty member who's Mansfield Apartment we had sublet during the summer had requested us to vacate it immediately because the University administration had found out that he had illegally leased it to my mother during the summer. She had been able to sublet the apartment in the recently built Mansfield Apartments for the summers of 1950 and 1951 while the occupant spent his summer in Chicago working on his graduate degree. In those days, Mansfield apartment tenants were not permitted to sublet apartments because University apartments were very much in demand by the rapidly expanding faculty. We had been requested to hide our presence as much as possible, so that the University administration would not discover our illegal presence in somebody else's apartment. Our very happy but noisy wedding reception had revealed our presence. The University officials were not amused.

Kicked out of my Berlin--Wannsee paradise and then the hoped-for refuge in Prague, crossing the Atlantic, residing briefly in New York City, Ithaca, Boston, Washington and Cambridge, created a longing for stability. My lack of a permanent home was aggravated by my parents' wanderings. While I had not left the East Coast, they had moved steadily west, never staying more than a year or two in one place, finally reaching Arkansas. Even in Storrs, I had been continuously on the move. There was the nine months stay on Moulton Road. Following my father's unexpected death I had to find a place for my mother. We moved to 109 Standish Road on Coventry Lake which Mr. Standish rented to us, while he spent the fall, winter and spring in Florida. That owner was very generous and surprised us in January with a crate of freshly picked grapefruit. Upon his return from Florida, my mother and I had spent the summer in the sub-rented Mansfield Apartment. All these moves intensified our search for a stable residence as a newly married couple.

After my mother got her notice to leave the rented Mansfield Apartment, she located a small apartment on Storrs Heights that was owned by the mother-in-law of my chairman George McReynolds. Audrey and I, low on the University's housing waiting list, were offered a tiny apartment on Oil Can Row. The somewhat disparaging name was quite appropriate because the temporary structures dating from World War II, had oilcans facing the road. They provided fuel for the stoves that heated the small apartment. The heat was not sufficient to protect inhabitants from the flow of frigid air passing through the cracks in the flimsily constructed apartment walls. The only advantage living there was that it took only a three-minute walk to my 8 o'clock class. It certainly was not a pleasant place to start our married life.

While residing on Oil Can Row obviously was to be temporary, we firmly intended to make Storrs our permanent home. Oil Can Row did however help me make the decision to ask for a leave of absence from the University easier. I accepted the offer of a job as a State Department intelligence analyst with the prospect of a better living arrangement.

Chapter 9
Washington Calls

Shortly after our wedding, I received an unexpected inquiry about a possible job in the U.S Department of State. Stephen Fisher-Galati, a pre-WW II immigrant from Rumania, and fellow Harvard graduate, contacted me in October 1951 and asked me whether I was interested in doing research on Czechoslovakia as an intelligence analyst. I had met Stephen in 1946 while working on my thesis at Harvard at the time that. Communist consolidation of power in Czechoslovakia approached a climax. I expressed an interest in the offer. I had always wanted to work in the State Department and play a role, ever so small, in influencing foreign policy. Teaching and explaining foreign policy was fine, but helping shape it, would be more exciting. My low salary at UCONN also helped me decide to take the offer seriously.

It took only a few months for me to receive a formal offer. I had to overcome a major obstacle: the State Department required ten years of citizenship as a hiring qualification. I had been a citizen only a little over five years. Stephen informed me that the Department badly needed experts with my knowledge of the Czech language and, more importantly, recent Czech politics, and they would therefore make an exception in my case. It turned out that he was well informed. In April 1952, the Department asked me to start my job as an analyst in the Division of Research on the Soviet Union and Eastern Europe (DRS) as soon as my UCONN teaching responsibilities were over. I asked UCONN for a one-year leave of absence and was assured that it would not affect my tenure track position.

A complication arose: In April, returning from an exploratory trip to Washington, Audrey suffered from a bout of morning sickness and realized that she was pregnant. Our second year of marriage would be quite exciting! As soon as I finished grading exams in May 1952, we left Oil Can Row and moved to a comfortable apartment in Alexandria, Virginia, across the Potomac from the State Department.

Washington was far more interesting and exciting than Storrs. However the political atmosphere was deteriorating: Truman had had enough and was not running for re-election. Eisenhower was the candidate of the Republican Party. The attacks by Senator McCarthy on “Communists” in the government, especially in the State Department, intensified. My boss the Secretary of State Dean Acheson had to reassure McCarthy, the Congress and the country that there were no “card carrying” Communists, nor Soviet sympathizers in the State Department. This was obviously not a very auspicious time to join that Department!

One evening, shortly before leaving Storrs my close friend Harry Marks, a member of the History Department, asked me to come to his apartment after he had learned that I was going to work in Washington. Instead of regaling me with his customary jokes, he had an unusually serious expression as we met. There was something very important he had to tell me. Since I was going to work for the State Department, he had to warn me that Manny [Margolis}, a colleague of mine in the Department of Government and International Relations, was a Communist. “That is nonsense,” I replied. “Manny was very critical of our getting involved in the North Korean conflict, but that did not necessarily make him a Communist.” “There is more to it”. Harry repeated that he knew that Manny was a member of the Party. “How do you know?” I asked. “Just take my word for it”. This encounter disturbed me. I told Audrey about this rather unpleasant discussion. We agreed not to discuss this with anybody and I ascribed the episode to the politically charged atmosphere.

When I arrived in Washington, my concerns about faculty affairs at UCONN were pushed to the back of a very busy agenda. I was learning to live in Alexandria, my first experience in a southern state; struggling with commuters crossing the Potomac; working in the outdated State Department Annex that lacked air conditioning and had housed the Office of Strategic Services during World War II; and of course finding a parking space. I quickly learned essential tricks of saving time to get to my job. By arriving at 8:50 instead of 8:30, I could park “legally” within a three-minute walk from my office. By then, crossing the Potomac took less time, the traffic having thinned out. Imagine my surprise one morning to find a couple of early tourists who looked very familiar, waiting for me to pass so that they could cross the lanes circling the Lincoln Memorial. “Harry,” I yelled, stopping the car. “What are you doing here?” Harry, accompanied by his wife, was caught by surprise. He responded without hesitation that he was going to testify before the House Un-American Activities committee. Regaining his composure, he quickly added, “Please, do not tell anybody at Storrs about meeting us here”. Apparently I could not leave Storrs behind.

Learning the routine of an intelligence analyst involved a significant shift from lecturing and talking to students. I had to get used to not discussing anything that dealt with the topics that preoccupied me the whole day at the office. That was not an easy task. Audrey helped me a great deal by making sure that my office life and our own preoccupations were kept strictly apart. While we talked about office politics, she did not ask me to tell her what was going on in Eastern Europe and what we were doing about it.

My task at DRS was to analyze the political goings on in Czechoslovakia and to alert our government about any possible impact their political decisions might have on us or our allies. It was exciting to read and analyze the power plays within the Communist regimes that Stalin sought to control completely. Shortly after starting working in the State Department, Czechoslovakia moved to the center stage of the Cold War. A purge of the Czechoslovak Communist Party leadership reached its climax in October 1952 with a political purge trial that I had to analyze and explain. That was quite a challenge. It turned out to be one of Stalin’s last important acts before his death the following March.

It was only a few months after starting my job that I had the task of covering one of the Stalin era’s most preposterous spectacles of judicial assassination. Publicized trials were Stalin’s preferred means of getting rid of erstwhile Party leaders whose services were no longer needed. What made the November Slánský trial especially noteworthy was that it took place in a country with a genuine democratic tradition whose pre-war leaders had tried to establish a working relationship during and after the Second World War with Stalin’s Soviet Union. The Trial also shocked many of us by its openly Anti-Semitic character. In words that could have been uttered by Hitler’s Party agents the accused were identified as Jews and accused of being involved in ”international Zionist imperialistic plots against Czechoslovakia”. Following a pattern set in Stalin’s pre-War Moscow trials, all the accused “confessed” they had indeed conducted all the criminal activities as charged. A few days later most of the accused were executed. A few were given life sentences.

They served time in prison until the political winds shifted and opened their prison gate.

In 2009, 57 years after the trial, someone approached me at a meeting of the Society for the History of Czechoslovak Jews in New York and mentioned that she had heard that I had written an article on the Slánský Trial. She was wondering whether I might be interested in a DVD, she had made about the Trial. I assured her I was interested. After purchasing a DVD player and connecting it to my flat screen TV, the Slánský Trial with all its horror was resurrected in my living room. My new Czech acquaintance, a generation younger, did an incredible job interviewing sons, widows, and other relatives of those who had suffered and died because of Stalin's political crimes. I was transported back to my desk in the Old State Department Annex. I plan to watch the DVD several more times to reacquaint myself with that part of the past. No wonder that the dark side of the past continues to occupy an important part of my memory.

***

Audrey and I quickly settled down in our small but comfortable apartment on Commonwealth Avenue in Alexandria. Audrey had learned to cope with the discomfort of her morning sickness. This enabled her to enroll in a summer course at George Washington University to earn enough credits to complete the requirements for the bachelor's degree at UCONN the following May.

Our routine was interrupted when I came down with a bad throat infection and fever that forced me to use up two of my very few sick days I had earned in the first months at the State Department. Two weeks later, I woke up with a stomachache. I hoped the ache would disappear and not interfere with my busy work schedule. After all, Audrey's morning discomfort usually went away hours before lunch. Why should not my bellyache disappear likewise? I drove to the State Department, sat at my desk and tried to concentrate on the latest news from Prague. The ache got worse. I visited the nurse in the building. She gave me some pills to help me recover. At lunchtime, I could not even contemplate looking at food and went back to the nurse. She told me to go home and see my doctor immediately. Since we were recent arrivals in Alexandria, I knew only a general practitioner whom I had visited a few weeks earlier for my sore throat. Fortunately, my car was parked close to the State Department and the drive to Alexandria normally took only 20 minutes. I managed to be stuck almost the entire trip behind a CIA courier on his special easily identifiable three-wheel motorbike. I did not have enough energy to overtake him. When I finally made it to the doctor's office, I felt worse and worse, as I waited impatiently for the doctor to examine me. After many questions about my general health, my job and other trivial matters, he finally started tapping various parts of my body. Suddenly he tapped forcefully on a certain spot to which I responded with a scream that I am sure could be heard in the waiting room. The doctor was delighted. "I thought so, you have an infected appendix. It has to be operated right away!" He instructed me to go straight home, go to bed, eat absolutely nothing, drink some water, if thirsty, and have Audrey bring me to the hospital at 6 A.M the next morning. "Which hospital?" I asked. " Alexandria Hospital, of course! It is a few blocks from my office in the center of the city."

The operation went smoothly. When I woke up several hours later in a room right above the entrance to the emergency room, the sirens of frequently arriving ambulances brought me back to the real world, before dozing off again. An intern asked me how I felt. "Much better," I responded. He explained that he had assisted my doctor in the operation. "Your appendectomy was really exciting", he informed me. "The appendix was about to burst and that would have been the end. It was more exciting than the operations we watched in med school. You were lucky!" He did not seem to mind that I did not share his joy and excitement about my close call. I asked what his accent was. "I am Turkish and will go back to Ankara to practice medicine as soon as I complete my residency and internship requirements. " He wanted to know what I did. I told him that I worked in the State Department and dealt with Eastern Europe. His expression changed. Had he known about my foreign policy job before the operation, would he have been as intent on helping my doctor complete the operation successfully?

An older federal government employee shared my hospital room. He asked me who my surgeon was. I told him that I had no surgeon, just a general practitioner. He was shocked. He was even more shocked when I told him that it had not even occurred to me that one needs a surgeon to remove an appendix. When I asked my doctor later how many operations he had performed, he answered, "may be a dozen, and yours was an excellent experience."

I recovered quickly and managed to get back to my desk in the State Department in a week. On my return, my colleagues teased me mercilessly and suggested that my appendectomy was simply the result of my trying to compete with Audrey's pregnancy. She got all the attention and therefore I stuffed my belly with rotten food, instructed the nurse to give me the wrong pills and managed to alert a Turk who nearly killed me. Meantime I had neglected reporting the latest crazy acts of the Czech Communists who were about to start one of Stalin's notorious show trials.

Three months passed, the Czech Communist trials now received top attention. Some top officials were even interested in reading my reports. Audrey was scheduled to complete the pregnancy around Thanksgiving. In those days, one rarely knew the sex or delivery date of the baby with any degree of accuracy. We had zeroed in on Thanksgiving because I would have four days off from work and time to concentrate on Audrey and the baby. Thanksgiving came: great turkey, no baby. Friday evening, one week later, Audrey and I, tired of waiting, went to see a French movie in downtown Washington. I do not recall the movie's name, except that we both enjoyed in very much. When it was over, I became aware that Audrey, acting strangely, did not get up from her seat. The theater emptied rapidly. "What is the matter?" I asked. She responded that she suddenly got soaking wet. The water bag had broken, as we were informed later. We realized that we had not paid enough attention to the birthing process and had to do a lot of catching up.

We left the theater feeling somewhat guilty about having ruined one of their comfortable seats and drove back to our apartment in Alexandria. We decided to call Audrey's doctor and inform him that something was going on. Audrey had felt a new unfamiliar pain as we had driven back from the movie. By now, it was midnight. I suddenly remembered a notice in the paper that at midnight that day an extra digit would be added to telephones in the Washington area and people were therefore asked to avoid calling at midnight. Audrey felt another pain and we decided that our emergency justified not paying attention to the wishes of the telephone company. I looked at my watch; it was exactly midnight, so I used the extra digit: it worked. The only question the doctor wanted to know was the frequency of the pain. Just then, it happened again. He asked me to drive Audrey right away to Georgetown hospital, back across the Potomac in the District of Columbia.

Driving on the Virginia side of the Potomac, on the nearly deserted parkway, Audrey felt a particularly strong pain just as the gigantic Pentagon complex came into view. Watching Audrey's partially pained, partially excited and happy face with the Pentagon in the mirror, made this trip to the hospital an even more exciting occasion. A short time later, we arrived at the hospital. This was our first sight of Georgetown hospital. I knew it was a Catholic institution but was not quite prepared for the gigantic cross that greeted us as we entered the vestibule, nor all the nuns who ran the hospital. Audrey was quickly assigned a room and it was politely suggested that my presence was not needed or to put it more bluntly, I was a nuisance and should really go back home and get some sleep. The Doctor would call me in the morning with the news. I said good-bye to Audrey, wished her no pain and the nuns got me out of there in a hurry. Driving back home was lonely: I missed Audrey and all the excitement.

It is hard for me to admit this, but I slept soundly without nightmares. The telephone ringing at 6 A.M. woke me up. Audrey's Doctor wished me a good morning and informed me that I was now the father of a young boy whom I could see as soon as I wanted. Audrey needed a little more time to recover from her sedation, but would be O.K. by the time I got there.

I got dressed, shaved, skipped breakfast and rushed back to Washington as quickly as possible. Since it was Saturday morning, traffic was light. It was exceptionally cold for the Washington area. The Pentagon looked much less impressive than at night as I passed it in the morning sun. A smiling nun led me to Audrey's room. Audrey had fully regained her customary cheerful look. "Where is it?" I asked. The nurse brought me to a nearby glass enclosed area filled with little cribs containing tiny babies. "Which one?" I asked the nurse. "That is pretty obvious" she responded smirking, as she disappeared through a door to enter the newborn baby display area. I had about one minute by myself locating Ronald among the half dozen new arrivals. They were mostly asleep, only occasionally moving their arms a little. There was one, who managed to lift up his head and express his desire for some attention. “Could that be Ronald?” The nurse entered the enclosed area, pointed at the one who apparently knew he was to be introduced to his father. A few minutes later Audrey, Ronald and I were together in one room and a new phase in our life began.

***

While we were busy trying to figure out the ins and outs of the November 1952 Slánský trial with its strong anti-Semitic overtone, our attention shifted to Moscow where another Stalin-engineered spectacle was revealed: the alleged Doctors Plot with a similar anti-Semitic aspect reflecting Stalin’s frame of mind shortly before his death on March 5, 1953. Meanwhile events closer to home caught our attention. We had our own domestic troublemaker, Senator Joseph McCarthy. The Senator was in the news constantly with vitriolic attacks on Communists or *Commy-Sympathizers* who, he alleged, had infiltrated the Truman administration.

Secretary of State Dean Acheson had played a key role in developing our policy of containing Stalin’s plans for potential expansion, yet he and his Department were singled out for attack by McCarthy. Shortly after Dean Acheson had looked each one of us in the eye, shaken our hands to thank us for our contribution and to bid us good-bye in his office, his Republican successor, John Foster Dulles, addressed us at an outdoor rally in frigid January weather and demanded our positive loyalty. We had to prove it! It soon became clear he meant it. We were requested not only *to be loyal*, but also *to demonstrate our loyalty*. In practice, this meant that our intelligence division dealing with the Soviet Union and Eastern Europe lost valuable colleagues whose loyalty was questioned.

The purge that friends of Senator McCarthy carried out in our Division of Research for the Soviet Union and Eastern Europe [DRS] affected Kathleen Q who normally worked at the desk next to mine. One day she was not there. After she was absent a few days I asked Dick Tims, our immediate boss, whether she was sick. He evaded a direct answer. My suspicions intensified a few days later, when we were told that there was “a little problem” with her security clearance. Kathleen was kept from entering the State Department and was exiled to do her work in the Library of Congress. This surprised us since she was one of the few in our section who was not of Eastern European origin. Kathleen had traveled to Czechoslovakia in 1948 as part of her post college interest in Eastern Europe. While spending a semester there, she had met many students and some had become her friends. Her Czechoslovak experience led the State Department to hire her. When she lost her security clearance, she re-lived her exciting stay in Prague searching her memory for any acquaintance in Prague who might have been a Communist known to American authorities. Half a year later, a State Department security official casually informed her that it had all been a mistake. While on her way to Prague, she had stopped in London and had attended a lecture organized by the Fabian Society. That had aroused suspicions. When State Department security established that she had attended only one lecture and was not a member of that "leftist society" she regained her security clearance and returned to her desk. Kathleen's unpleasant exile from our Division was apparently the result of a nasty elevator argument over a boyfriend between her and an employee in another part of the building. Her rival had access to a McCarthy supporter and settled her argument with Kathleen by impugning her loyalty.

Kathleen was only one of a number of DRS analysts who had their security clearance questioned. In another case, an individual who had subscribed to a Soviet newspaper to improve his Russian in line with a suggestion from his University of California professor, was led from his desk and asked to surrender his clearance while we watched with considerable alarm. This also was cleared up eventually. Such incidents left permanent scars not only on those directly affected, but also on the rest of us. It did however help us gain a better sense of the mood affecting people in the Soviet orbit.

One afternoon in the spring of 1953, I was asked to meet a personnel official and clarify something in my own personnel record. Given the general atmosphere, I was concerned when the official started out by asking me whether I had ever worked for a foreign government. "Of course not", I replied. "Have you ever worked for an embassy of a foreign country"? "Of course not" "Have you ever worked for, or applied to work for a foreign government, an embassy or a purchasing agency of a foreign country"? Suddenly a light flickered in the recesses of my brain.

"Are you possibly referring to my responding to a job referral at the Soviet Purchasing Agency in Washington during the War in September 1944"? "Tell me about it," he replied. "While waiting for the School of Advanced International Studies to open its doors in October, I was looking for a temporary job. I went to the official US Employment Agency and cited my knowledge of Russian. I received a postcard from the US Employment Agency telling me to report to a certain address that turned out to be the Soviet Purchasing Agency" I answered. "So what happened", the official asked. "I did not get beyond the Soviet official to whom the receptionist referred me", I replied. "The Soviet official asked where I was born, since I was not yet a U.S. citizen. I told him, Berlin, Germany. He showed me the door." The State Department Security officer appeared relieved. He did however reprimand me for not having mentioned this in my State Department job application. "That had never even crossed my mind", I responded." After all, I went to the Soviet Purchasing Agency at the request of a U.S. government agency". I have often wondered how my ten-minute visit to the Soviet Purchasing Agency ever entered the official records. Maybe the receptionist at the Soviet Purchasing Agency worked for U.S. intelligence.

Charlie Tait was the third and most experienced and knowledgeable member of the contingent responsible for analyzing developments in Czechoslovakia. We got to know each other in the office, as well as socially. Audrey and I met his wife Kate and were impressed by her personality and her interesting background. She was the daughter of Bertrand Russell and Dora Grace, Russell's third wife. Dora Grace's father was a British Peer. One week end in March 1953 Charlie's mother-in-law made national news. Dora Grace, representing the Women's International Democratic Federation, was granted a temporary visitor's visa to attend the United Nations as an official Non-Government Observer. Her visit was limited to a seventy-block area of Manhattan, stretching from 28th street to 97th street between 8th avenue and the East River. This gave her access to the United Nations. The restrictions were imposed because the Federation was considered a Communist front organization.

Kate and Charlie wanted to get together with Kate's mother. They arranged to meet within the specified seventy-block section of

Manhattan. None of us could understand how Charlie got away with "fraternizing" with an officially designated Communist sympathizer without any of McCarthy's agents citing this episode as proof that the State Department was crawling with Communists and Communist sympathizers. Maybe they feared Lord Russell's sardonic wrath. This was very funny, we thought, except that it was also a reflection of how much the Cold War had undermined America's judgment, common sense and confidence in our underlying values. While my loyalty was never questioned, that of too many of my co-workers was. To lose friends, even for a relatively short period, was disconcerting and ultimately led to my decision to return to UCONN in September 1953.

In spite of all the unpleasant turbulence surrounding our work in the Research Division of the State Department I did enjoy my work there. It clearly was connected with my Ph.D. thesis research, updating and relating the ideas and goals of Edvard Beneš to the real world that marked the Cold War in Eastern Europe. Having access to daily events in Prague through local newspaper accounts, statements by key officials, accounts of the purge trials and observations by bystanders gave me a realistic account of post-war Czechoslovakia that quickly destroyed any illusions I might have had from my academic perch at Harvard. It raised also a serious concern about U.S. foreign policy. While I was pleased to have been given a relatively responsible job when not yet 30 years old, and while I enjoyed the multicultural environment in our Eastern European Research Division, it disturbed me that there were so few experts of a non-foreign origin dealing with an area playing a vital role in the Cold War. This was not only related to a failure to emphasize teaching and research in non-English speaking parts of the world, but also to America's underlying desire to escape from unpleasant realities in "distant parts of the globe". The few members of our division speaking without a Slavic, Hungarian, Albanian or Romanian accent seemed out of place. No wonder some of them became McCarthy targets.

Later that spring, I traveled to Storrs for a short visit to discuss details concerning my resuming teaching in September. I stayed two nights with a member of the history department. The news of my visit had spread and I was asked by a faculty member whom I had not met before, whether I could appear in two hours before the

Committee of Five. That committee was appointed to recommend how to handle a faculty member alleged to have been a Communist Party member. Given such short notice, I agreed reluctantly and interrupted my brief respite from watching the activities of Communist governments..

The Committee of Five immediately raised the topic that Harry had confronted me with a year earlier. Could I tell the committee whether Manny [Emanuel Margolis] was a Communist? I told the committee, this question really puts me in a very strange position. My job in the State Department was to analyze the power struggle and resulting trials and execution of Communist Party leaders in Czechoslovakia as well as Communist power struggles in the other Soviet satellites. While I knew something about Communist activities in Eastern Europe, I was not qualified to assess a colleague's alleged Communist Party membership on this side of the Atlantic. I knew Manny as a colleague who obviously disagreed with some aspects of our foreign policy. I had no idea, nor did I suspect his being a Communist Party member. I told the committee that the FBI probably had such records. "If the University administration was so concerned about this issue, why not give the FBI a ring?" I asked, and added that as long as Manny covered topics in his classroom in a professional academic manner, possible Party membership was hardly relevant. After all, he was not sending people to jail or sentencing them to death, as the Communists that I was observing in Czechoslovakia, were doing. The Committee had quite a laugh and I felt that I had possibly defused the situation. Following the Committee of Five hearing, Manny quietly left UCONN at the end of the term, took a law degree at Yale and had a very successful career practicing law for many years. Eventually he headed the Connecticut's Civil Liberties Union. An Op Ed article signed by him recently appeared in the *Hartford Courant*.

Bruce M. Stave in his *Red Brick in the Land of Steady Habits*, an account of the history of the University of Connecticut, discusses the impact of McCarthyism on the university, pp.73-82. Governor Lodge, 1951-1955, sent a list of alleged Communist faculty members to UCONN President Jorgensen with the request they be fired. The Governor upset his fellow Republicans, President Jorgensen and especially Provost Al Waugh, by injecting himself in matters that were rightfully within the University's exclusive jurisdiction. The University would handle it by turning the investigation over to faculty committees charged with the responsibility of examining accusations affecting the conduct of faculty members. In contrast to many other universities, the UCONN administration managed to protect the faculty from excessive outside interference during the McCarthy era.

Upon my return to the University in September, the turmoil in Czechoslovakia had calmed considerably. The hunt for Communists in academia also had lessened and it became possible again to pursue academic interests in a less charged atmosphere.

Chapter 10
Back in Storrs

Audrey had completed her requirements for her bachelor's degree in economics at UCONN by taking two courses at George Washington University. Her graduation was scheduled in May 1953, several months before our departure from Washington. We joked that she had gotten her MA (become a mother) before getting her B.A. We traveled to Storrs, stopping in Rowayton to pick up her parents for the graduation ceremony. Quite unexpectedly, the chair of the economics department, after congratulating Audrey, asked her whether she would be willing to become a paid teaching assistant while taking courses for an MA in economics. We looked at each other, nodding our heads, and Audrey said, of course. Her salary, added to mine, would almost match what I had made at the State Department. There was only one major obstacle: Would it be possible to coordinate our teaching schedules so that our not-yet-a-year old Ronald would always have one of us guard him at home? No problem, the chair responded. He had just become Dean of Arts and Sciences and would make sure that our schedules were coordinated. This offer to Audrey to teach sealed our decision to return to Storrs.

Immediate problems had to be resolved. Housing: Oil Can Row no longer met the needs of our family that now included Ronald. He was a very active boy, who needed space for his building blocks, his railroad tracks and his other projects. We were lucky to be able to rent a house on Storrs Heights, from a faculty member who was scheduled to go to India on a project to help an extremely backward rural area in Bihar province introduce modern agricultural methods.

There was also the task of coordinating tight schedules without neglecting a very active Ronald. Storrs Heights, only a ten-minute walk from the campus, made it possible for Audrey to return from teaching a 10 o'clock class and ten minutes later, for me to teach an 11 o'clock class. Most of the time, we tried to arrange for a more sensible interval. We had only one car and that forced us to plan our activities with tight precision. In 1953, we set a precedent with husband and wife caring for a son while both held full-time jobs. It took decades for a two wage earner family to become a common practice.

Our schedules were well coordinated. On Mondays, Wednesdays and Fridays, I gave two lectures in political science in the morning and Audrey took graduate seminars in the afternoon. On Tuesdays and Thursdays Audrey taught sections of the Introductory Economics course and I gave a graduate seminar.. One or both of us ate lunch with Ronald and played with him in the afternoon. Occasionally there were crises. One of us had to go to Hartford and the other had to combine course preparations with watching Ronald in his explorations in our rented house. He found a means of opening the not that tightly closed door to the basement, encountered the laws of gravity, rolled down the steps and lying on the basement floor announcing his feat with alarming screams. When Audrey in a state of panic called the doctor, his only comment was that the fact that Ronald screamed indicated a safe arrival. The bump on his head would quickly disappear. It did.

And then there was the morning when Audrey got deeply involved in a discussion with students at the end of her class Finally she looked at her watch and realized that she had been expected home five minutes earlier. She got in the car, revved the engine but failed to release the emergency brake. She stepped on the regular brake after passing South Eagleville Road on 195, the brakes locked and the car stopped instantly, toppling over and ending up on its side. Waiting for her arrival in front of our house on Storrs Heights I heard sirens and had a premonition that this commotion might explain Audrey's failure to appear on time. With Ronald in my arms, I raced to the accident scene and saw Audrey inspecting the damage suffered by the car. Audrey obviously was not hurt and supervised putting the car back into its upright position. After releasing the emergency brake, the car drove perfectly well and I made my class. Audrey accompanied Ronald back to the house and had lunch.

Sharing parental responsibilities and work schedules created some long-term consequences that affected my academic progress and promotion. I had my hands full teaching several hundred students, helping at home and becoming deeply involved in the activities of Ronald whose rapid development was extremely interesting and exciting to watch. All of this limited the time and energy that I was expected to devote to research and publication. I had some articles published that dealt with my work in the State Department, but there was much more that I had intended to accomplish. Another equally relevant factor responsible for not publishing more in the 1950's was my disappointment with the depressing situation in Communist Czechoslovakia, my principal area of interest.

After spending two years in the rented house on Storrs Heights, we were able to move into one of the Mansfield Apartments opposite the Storrs Grammar School at the edge of the campus. This greatly facilitated access to our respective University offices and classrooms. That location also insured easy access to school for Ronald and later for Meredith. Ronald and Meredith became involved in pre-school activities, and the regular school system enabling us to become a normal Storrs University family.

***

Ronald and Meredith, three years younger than her brother, were model children, whose development was exciting, a pleasure to watch. I always remember Ronald uttering the first word that I could understand. He was eleven months old. We were driving on a pre-interstate highway near Baltimore. Ronald was standing in his portable crib in the back of the car. In 1953 no seat belts were required. While I was talking to Audrey, maneuvering through heavy traffic, I heard the usual noise from the crib. Suddenly I thought I heard a question. It sounded like, "What's that?" Could my little boy have asked me a question? My eyes had to be fixed on the oncoming traffic, so I could not look back to see what was going on. So I responded, "That is a truck". Five seconds later, I heard Ronald repeat his question with a slightly different intonation and Audrey turned around to see what was going on in back. She informed me that Ronald pointed his finger at different trucks as he repeated the question. Audrey twisted her head trying to keep up the conversation with Ronald. Apparently, he had succeeded in establishing verbal communication with us. His vocabulary expanded rapidly, since "what's that?" turned into a magic wand that enabled him to get our full attention whenever he wanted.

Our Mansfield apartment had seemed quite large when we first moved in. Audrey and I had the comfortable bedroom upstairs, while Ronald occupied the smaller one. When Meredith arrived, we exchanged rooms. Audrey and I squeezed into Ronald's erstwhile small bedroom while Ronald and Meredith inherited our larger one. Even that large room soon limited Ronald's railroad lines and his building block construction projects. As Meredith started to move around, her space requirements collided with those of her brother. They gave us no trouble. They challenged us primarily by their fascination with new and, of course, interesting toys. The top floor of G Fox in Hartford had an extensive array of items they were interested in. They always needed an additional new one.

Somehow, they managed to respect each other's needs without their parents' interference. Once they got into the habit of having Audrey or me reading stories to them, our time for research, course preparation and correcting exams shrank significantly. I must confess that the adventures of Babar were far more exciting than reading the 45th essay in the test I had given to my students in the introductory international relations course. Our time was also taxed by the need for one of us to chauffeur Ronald and then Meredith to their numerous activities that went far beyond pre-school, kindergarten transportation. They led very active social lives that involved them in activities parents considered essential for developing skills they would need as adults. Fortunately, our Mansfield apartment was a children's paradise. If you did not like the kid next door, there was another one, two or three doors down, that you could play with. You could also cross South Eagleville road and enjoy running around in the Storrs Grammar School playground. Of course, we gave our kids strict instructions to cross the road carefully while one of us guarded their safe passage. Our neighbor's child was hit by a car while crossing the road. That made all of us nervous as we watched conscientiously our kids from the kitchen window playing with hardly a care on their minds.

There was also the afternoon when Ronald's close friend Danny climbed a tree behind the apartments. He was five or six years old and very agile. When he had reached a branch at least ten feet higher than our two-story apartment building, one of the kids watching him climb must have become a little nervous and informed us about the potentially dangerous situation. We contacted Eleanor, his mother, who barely managed to control her fear when she saw her son on his journey to the very top. Gently she called him, asking whether this was not high enough and perhaps he might start on his return to earth. He did, and only when he was back in his mother's arms, did she show the terrible fear she had suffered. All of us parents, and probably most of the kids, were deeply affected by this experience. It did not surprise me that this same kid, fifty years later, gave a talk at CLIR about his two-year stint teaching in Iraq's Kurdistan province.

I do not recall when Meredith uttered her first word that we could understand. What I do remember was her fascination with books. She loved every storybook that one of us read to her and quickly taught herself to recognize the words that connected with the pictures. As soon as she entered school she read voraciously. In high school she became fascinated by Tolstoy's *War and Peace,* the voluminous story she spent reading while earning money babysitting our neighbors' slightly younger kids. She also loved to write her own stories. Communicating in English was not enough: she learned French and German with minimum effort. This enabled her to travel by herself to Quebec, Germany and England while still in high school, and all over Europe while in college.

I involved myself in Ronald and Meredith's activities in their school more than most fathers, participating, for instance, in PTA meetings and occasionally conferring with their teachers. My own school experience in three different countries made me realize that the way math was taught in Mansfield differed significantly from the way I had been taught. History differed even more and language teaching could not even be compared. I wanted to make sure that Ronald and Meredith would get as much out of their school experience as I had from mine.

There was a widespread concern in the late fifties and early sixties that our educational system had to be improved if we were to keep up with the Russians who had thumbed their noses at us by being first in space with their Sputnik. Everybody went to the darkened school playground at night, hoping to see Sputnik blink at us as it passed overhead. Our PTA was particularly agitated and pushed for reforms. We needed outstanding teachers. Every kid should be able to read exciting novels. Math had to be taught in a new, better way, etc. etc. Storrs was the ideal place for parents to get excited about their schools, because a significant percentage of the children came from faculty families. It bothered me that there were few fathers who participated in PTA discussions. I remember joining a regional committee that met a number of times to recommend state-wide educational reforms. As I look back on that period, I cannot help but experience a deep sense of frustration that our efforts were in vain and that each generation has to repeat the goal of improving the educational system encountered by their children.

As Ronald grew older, school was not his only interest. Audrey introduced him to the boy scouts. As a very active sea scout in her youth it had enabled her to expand the scope of her social activities. She believed that Ronald would enjoy and benefit from engaging in outdoor activities. She was right: Ronald loved exploring forest trails, tracing them on geodetic maps, camping overnight in tents and cabins and ultimately leading some of his fellow high school students on mountain trails in New England. I became the chauffeur who deposited his group of four or five fellow explorers on one trail crossing the highway, and then picking the group up a few days later at a different crossing. This occurred in all seasons, including during a major snowstorm in Vermont. I was more concerned about driving my car through snowdrifts and getting enough traction to reach the top than worrying about the safety and comfort of the alpine snowshoe hikers led by Ronald. My university friends who had entrusted their kids to my son's care occasionally asked me how the adventure was going. I smiled. "Great", I said. Of course, I was as concerned as they were. My confidence in Ronald was fully justified. Everybody always emerged from the woods on schedule.

Watching our kids grow and mature was a very satisfying experience. I learned almost as much as they did. The only drawback was that that it involved time and attention some of which diverted me from my scholarly and teaching responsibilities. One cannot do everything; at least that is what I said comforting myself.

***

Audrey and I had been married ten years before we able to consider building our own house and deepen our roots in Storrs. After leaving Wannsee, I had always stayed in rented places that were privately or university owned. The idea of being able to afford to buy property with a mortgage seemed remote. It was the son of one of my father's German philosopher friends, who on his visit to Storrs in 1954, was astonished that we had no plans to get a mortgage to build a house. When I told him that I did not want to go into debt and have a mortgage hanging over my head, he suggested that I had better Americanize my thinking. I did not point out to him that on my ridiculously low faculty salary we did not even have the down payment necessary to apply for a mortgage.

While investing in a house had seemed unrealistic and something to be relegated to the distant future, Audrey and I nonetheless had spent many hours driving along less traveled roads in Mansfield and neighboring towns, admiring beautiful vistas, hidden valleys, small lakes with only a few cabins. We imagined building our house there someday, when I earned the salary of a full professor. In the early 1960's faculty salaries improved and then there was a piece of luck. Arthur, our friend from Berlin, informed me that the West German government compensated those German refugees whose education had been interrupted by the Nazi regime. All I had to do was to give evidence to a German consul that I had left a German school because of my religion. As an addicted packrat that was very simple. I dug up my report card from my Berlin school that I had received in June 1933, as we were about to leave Berlin. The consul in Boston photographed my report card, confirmed that I was the guy whose report card he had before him and a few weeks later I got a check for $1,000. That check was the only compensation anybody in my family ever received from the German post War government. Apparently interrupting my education was more important than the Nazis ruining my father's life, making it very difficult for my mother to earn a living, or confiscating my Berlin grandfather's possessions when he had to leave Germany in 1939. There was and could not be any compensation for my grandfather Gustav's death in the Terezín concentration camp.

Just then, two faculty wives, interested in current international relations, who audited my course in diplomatic history, asked me whether Audrey and I might possibly be interested in one of the two remaining properties of the Dunham Pond Association that their husbands and another faculty member jointly owned and wanted to get rid of. The developers of Dunham Pond had subdivided the original property into twelve units and reduced the price significantly. We struck a deal and for $3,000 obtained a five-acre lot on the side of a steep hill with the right to swim in Dunham Pond, two hundred feet down the road. The compensation for my interrupted education made the purchase possible.

I lost no time exploring the first piece of American land I had ever owned. I located the boundary markers, identified possible locations for a house, explored access from the road, removed brushes, cut trees, said hallo to the many small animals who obviously resented my interference with their long established routine. After a 27-year interruption, I finally could resume digging up soil, cutting and planting trees, an outdoor life that I had missed ever since leaving Wannsee.

When it came to getting a house built, we were lucky to have many faculty friends who had planned and discussed moving from their Mansfield Apartment to their own house. Architectural designs, the performance of different contractors, pitfalls that had to be avoided, were frequent conversation topics. We were seeking something cheap, modern, good looking, efficient, not too small, not too fancy, in short, the perfect house. *Techbuilt* houses were houses that were factory built, transported in sections that could easily be assembled and carried in a huge truck. Several *Techbuilt* houses had recently enlivened the Storrs landscape, so why not add another one. Our decision was helped by the excellent reputation of the local contractor who had put up most of them. The moment we met Mr.Trepal, the contractor, we decided to go ahead and build a *Techbuilt*.

We discussed architectural specifics, necessary adjustments to locate the *Techbuilt* properly on a relatively steep hillside without interfering too much with the property's tall pine trees and the existing meadow. Trepal and I quickly established an excellent relationship. His parents had emigrated from Bohemia and we exchanged comments in Czech when in the proper mood. The price of constructing the house was estimated to cost over twenty thousand dollars. Of course, if I were to paint the house myself, I could save a couple thousand. I volunteered to do that since I could take some time off in the summer. In agreeing to do the house painting, I did not foresee that Trepal, my contractor, would become my boss and order me to do what <u>he</u> felt was best for me.

Once the plans were finalized, I went to the bank and had no problem getting a mortgage. I was amazed how simple every step turned out to be. Trepal had planned to start construction as soon as the ground was no longer frozen. On April 1st a bulldozer arrived and bulldozed a several hundred foot driveway carefully avoiding the tall pines. The ground on the house site was excavated, the foundation was poured and promptly one month later, the truck with the *Techbuilt* parts arrived from Boston and had to be pushed up the muddy driveway by a couple of bulldozers. The beams were unloaded and I got a call from Trepal, while in my office at the University, informing me that the living room beams had arrived and I had better apply the preservative while they were on the ground. He knew I was afraid of heights and preferred not to paint standing way up there near the top of the ladder. I informed him that my classes were not over yet. His response was something like," that's tough buddy, when my workers don't come in to do their job, I fire them. So?" I quickly assured him, I would start applying the preservative in a couple of hours. I did. I quickly learned that painting a house, even a modern one with fewer walls, was quite time consuming. Fortunately, there were intervals when the fresh preservative or paint had to dry and I could use that time to read the students' final exams. The late spring and summer of 1963, I spent multi-tasking, even though I had not yet learned to use that phrase.

The house was quickly assembled and I, together with Audrey, started to paint at a furious pace in order to enable us to move in as soon as possible. That day came in August 1963. There were still many details to be done before we could fully enjoy our entirely new environment. Membership in the Dunham Pond Association meant not merely a joint responsibility for maintaining a relatively extensive pristine acreage of meadows, forests and Dunham Pond, but also many new friends and especially life on, and in, the Pond whenever the weather permitted.

Chapter 11
Scholarly Pursuits in the Real World

Economic pressures diverted my concentrating primarily on scholarly research and compounded the task of having a normal home life while bringing up Ronald and Meredith. Meeting our social obligations and entertaining other young faculty families were an essential part of furthering our budding careers. Our lives were further complicated by worries about my mother's search for a permanent academic position in the nineteen fifties, the decade following the loss of my father who had been at the center of her life for 27 years. We helped her move to Washington, back to Storrs, to Detroit, Madison, South Dakota and finally back to Connecticut. In 1961 she bought a house in South Windsor, after her appointment to a permanent professorship at the University of Hartford. She managed not only to teach but also to engage in research dealing with the practice of medicine in East Africa. She published several books based on her research. She especially relished her role as grandmother and preparer of outstanding Sunday meals relying on her treasured north German and Austrian recipes.

When I was hired as a member of the Department of Government and International Relations the Department was in its formative phase. G. Lowell Field, who succeeded George McReynolds as department head, not only lacked his predecessor's interest in international relations, but also espoused a pseudo scientific mathematical approach to government that clashed with my historical perspective. I should have taken these differences more seriously and looked for a position elsewhere.

Having spent 1952-53 in Washington in the State Department with a ringside seat from which to watch the transition from the Truman administration to Eisenhower's, my taste for life in Washington had soured. It had not been pleasant to watch colleagues suffer from Senator McCarthy's attacks questioning their loyalty. Before returning to Storrs, I explored positions at other universities. Unfortunately, the only good offers came from universities out West. I had no desire to leave the Northeast. After a long conversation with my new boss, G. Lowell Field, I decided to stay at UCONN.

The offer made to Audrey to work on her MA degree in Economics and teach a section of the Introductory Economics course was a major reason for our staying in Storrs. The opportunity for both of us teaching topics that fascinated us while at the same time watching Ronald and Meredith grow made us very happy. There were however complications. The nepotism rules precluded Audrey from being considered for a permanent position, even if she had completed the requirements for a Ph.D. Yale was willing to admit her to their program. That would however have involved her spending an academic year in residence at Yale. Without the prospect of getting a permanent well paying position at UCONN we did not think it was worthwhile for Audrey to spend two semesters away from our kids in their most formative years. Another problem was that a key member of the Economics Department became Dean of the College of Arts and Sciences, my boss. In spite of all these difficulties, Audrey managed to be reappointed regularly for a dozen years. She loved helping large numbers of undergraduates understand the fundamentals of economics and was disappointed a decade later when a new Dean, an English Professor failed to reappoint her. As a result a year later she ran for the legislature. In a role reversal the dean, her former boss, now had to discuss his budgetary needs with her.

***

When I chose Czechoslovakia as the example of a small state's search for security for my scholarly research at Harvard, it reflected my familiarity with that country. I was however not prepared for Czechoslovakia becoming Stalin's favored target in the intensifying Cold War. Its location, in the direct path between Moscow and Berlin encouraged Stalin to focus on it. The emphasis in my Ph.D. thesis on strategies by Edward Beneš, the last democratic leader of Czechoslovakia, to insure the survival of his country changed from a scholarly analysis of an idealistic statesman's writings to a hot Cold War topic Before completing the thesis, Beneš died and Stalin's Communists took over his country. Beneš had been too optimistic about the possibility of his small democratic state managing to coexist with the Soviet Union at its doorstep. I suppose I should have thanked Stalin for his quick answer to my theoretical question, bringing me back to the real world and my thesis to a quick unhappy conclusion.

A few years later, as a State Department Intelligence Analyst, I examined the political operations of the Czechoslovak Communist regime at the height of Stalin's preoccupation with imagined threats to his regime. Dramatic purge trials provided me with new and unexpected research material. Obviously Czechoslovak politics turned out to be anything but a boring topic. There was a problem however. How does one draw the line between a scholarly inquiry and quick conclusions based on data that could not be confirmed? Current events need a long enough shelf life to gather enough dust to be re-examined with sufficient scholarly detachment and objectivity.

Ever interested in following events that were different and exciting, I embarked in 1963 on an African journey to observe the impact of the Cold War on newly independent West African states. This introduced me to an entirely new and very interesting political landscape. But again from a scholarly perspective it was too soon to reach sound conclusions.

My search and exploration of relevant and interesting scholarly goals was made more complicated by deep divisions within the fields of government and international diplomacy. My undergraduate and graduate degrees were awarded by Departments of Government. At the time when I was hired by the University of Connecticut, the newly created Department was called the *Department of Government and International Relations*. This reflected the interest caused by the Great Depression and World War II in examining the operations of governments and the conduct of international diplomacy. George McReynolds had centered his scholarly interest on U.S. diplomacy. Unfortunately, G. Lowell Field, his successor, was not satisfied with research based on the observation and analysis of unpredictable events. He looked for patterns of behavior that could be precisely analyzed and resolved using mathematical equations. Based on such an analysis, he assumed future conduct could be predicted and possibly controlled. He familiarized himself with sophisticated mathematical formulas and sought to transform the discipline based on historical analysis and observation of current government activities into one capable of predicting and possibly altering government policies by applying scientific methods. Political *Science* would create order out of chaos.

The department meeting in which adopting the name *Political Science* was on the agenda, was one of the most contentious I can recall. Those of us who wanted to stick with *Government and International Relations* were outvoted. Overtaken by wishful thinkers who believed they, and only they, had found the keys that would open the doors to a properly operating domestic and international order, we had to retreat into a so-called cubbyhole of obsolete ideas. My colleague Fred Kort even wrote a prominent article in which he presented a mathematical formula that he claimed could predict how the Supreme Court would decide future specific cases. The shift to *Political Science* occurred at most U.S. universities. Cornell and Harvard, the universities where I had received my degrees, did not follow the pseudo-scientific scholars of political affairs.

As interest in the nature and conduct of diplomacy that led to the two World Wars faded, my primary scholarly and teaching occupation lost its place in the Department of Political Science. Maybe I should have shifted to the History Department where international relations originally was located. If neglect of modern diplomacy had been limited to the University of Connecticut, this would have been merely an idiosyncratic occurrence in Connecticut's Quiet Corner. Our subsequent embroilment in Iraq and Afghanistan proved otherwise. Even among the leaders of our current foreign policy and intelligence establishment, there has been an incredible shortage of individuals familiar with events of the not too distant past. Past confrontations and conflicts continue to determine the conduct of current rulers and people are currently dealing with.

I have asked myself whether I do not bear some of the responsibility for the shortage of experts and the general public disinterest in events that occur just beyond our immediate horizon. Why did I not take the trouble to write a popular book about important crises in post war diplomacy? Why did I not excite the mostly very attentive students in my international diplomacy course so that more of them chose to pursue careers in intelligence agencies or the State Department? I was diverted by exciting events closer to home. Preoccupation with local politics may have been my version of escapism.

I enjoyed the opportunity to influence elections on the local level where I met candidates who eventually played a role on the state and national scene. Political activities in Hartford can be far more personally satisfying than developing theories about the motivation of Communist leaders in Eastern Europe. You can argue with Ella Grasso, the Governor of Connecticut, and have her explain why she so adamantly opposed the state income tax, but you can only speculate why Brezhnev, the Soviet leader, proceeded so aggressively against the democratic forces of the Prague Spring in 1968. To put it more bluntly, events close to home pushed my early scholarly pursuits to the backburner.

In the 1960s, the Viet Nam War started to inject a further diversion that interfered with my research. The anti-Viet Nam War protests on our campus and especially their intrusion into my classroom forced me to recognize how far I had traveled from my initial scholarly objective of examining the chances of less powerful states retaining their independence in the turbulent post World War 1 international order. My preoccupation with Hitler and all the damage he caused was topped by Viet Nam.

***

On May 1, 2009, Ina Ruth coaxed me to attend the Connecticut Repertory Theatre performance of HAIR, first performed on Broadway 41 years ago. The Harriet Jorgensen Theater was packed with excited students. The atmosphere was electric. While the play mourns a dead Viet Nam veteran, it highlights a tribe of hippies, draft opponents, flower people and idealists whose mission is to defy conventions. The high or low point of the performance, depending on one's own hang-ups, occurred at the end of the first act when the entire cast of several dozen actors wiggled out of their messy outfits and emerged entirely naked. That episode bothered me, but by far not as much as the atmosphere that had greeted us almost as soon as the curtain was raised and the hippies emerged on the stage. I was transported back to a day in the late fall of 1968.

For several years, opposition to our involvement in Viet Nam had grown, especially on college campuses because of the draft. Under popular UCONN President Homer Babbidge, Storrs had been spared challenges of authority. When Richard Nixon was elected president in 1968, campus tensions intensified. On our campus, the opponents of the war focused on companies engaged in producing items furthering the war effort who sought to recruit graduating seniors. The opponents vowed to stop interviews with manufacturers of war-making tools.

Sitting in my first floor office in Monteith shortly before lunch one day in November, I was alerted by unusual noises. Curious, I walked out of the building, crossed Whitney Road in the direction of the increasingly noisy disturbance. The nearby brown house on 7 Gilbert Road served as the office where interviews were scheduled. About two dozen students and a few faculty members surrounded that building, trying to embarrass any job seeker from applying for a war-related job. A particularly rambunctious protester noticed that somebody had left unattended a garbage pail in back of the brown house. He picked it up, emptied its contents and proceeded to bang the metal top against the can. The resulting noise cheered the protesters. Two or three campus guards retreated to the porch steps of the building and emerged with riot sticks. The protesters felt challenged. They started to throw objects at the campus police targets who shouted warnings that nobody could understand. I realized that I was watching an increasingly explosive confrontation and retreated to a relatively safe observation spot a few feet from Arjona. More and more objects were thrown by the increasingly rowdy protesters and returned by the angry campus police.

Suddenly, the campus assistant security director, using a bullhorn, read the Riot Act. Everybody was ordered to leave the scene and go back to his or her office or classroom.[1] Minutes later, a contingent of state troopers, dressed in riot gear, approached from Hillside Road and marched down Gilbert Road, looking straight ahead avoiding therioters' jeering faces. The Anti-Viet Nam war movement had become alive in front of my own eyes. It was quite a shock.

More shocks were to follow. My good long-term friend, David Ivry, a School of Business Professor, was close to President Babbidge and got me to join him when the anti-war protesters occupied Gulley Hall, the Administration's Office building. We tried to act as go-betweens, urging the students not to create too much of a mess in the President's and Provost's offices which they

---

[1] (Bruce Stave, *Red Brick in the Land of Steady Habits*, p.135)

used as sleepovers. It bothered me to recognize some of my best students among the unruly crowd.

My worst experience was attending a class discussion about "imperialist diplomacy" leading to our imbroglio in Viet Nam held in von der Mehden, a large "classroom" auditorium. Sitting inconspicuously in the back, I had to suffer through comments and harangues pretending to explain the historical events leading to the current international crisis. Some of my own students were among the mob that played soccer with the facts. Reality was kicked all over the field. I could not help blaming myself for not having succeeded instilling in my students enough respect for truth.

Finally, I took a stand. The anti-Viet Nam protesters declared a strike. Classes were to be canceled to send the message that students opposed the war. I was a supporter of labor unions. I sympathized with strikes that were intended to accomplish improvements in working conditions. Students striking for a cause that the faculty or the University administration had no power to influence, was an entirely different matter.

I was scheduled to teach a large class in the lecture hall on the first floor of Arjona and stated my intent of following my regular schedule. The entire corridor leading to the room's entrance was lined with students who held placards announcing the strike, urging their classmates to honor the strike. Some strikers smiled as I passed by, others called me a strikebreaker and worse. When I entered the large lecture hall, I was surprised that the first three or four rows were occupied. Attendance, while considerably below normal, was nonetheless quite respectable. I told my loyal student listeners that I would depart from my scheduled topic and discuss instead the issue of resorting to a strike as a means of influencing foreign policy. I reminded them that this was not a new issue. The followers of Karl Marx, organized as the Second International, tried to stop World War I in 1914, urging *Workers of the World Unite and Stop the War* by striking. It was of course an utter failure. As I brought the discussion up to the current situation, the door opened and a dozen protesters entered the lecture hall. I asked them as politely as I could what they wanted. Their answer was not very coherent and suddenly two or three of my students shouted, "We want to hear the lecture!" The intruders were apparently unprepared for such a response, and hesitated. Suddenly almost all of my students started shouting in unison, "Get out, we want Professor Beck's lecture!" Such loyalty shocked me and I had some difficulty controlling my emotions. I was even more shocked by the intruders departing quietly and peacefully.

It turned out that I was one of the very few professors who did not honor the strike and got away with it. The following Christmas, I got a Christmas card from one of my erstwhile Fort Trumbull colleagues who had become an English Professor at the University of Hawaii. He wrote that he had seen me standing up to the strikers on a public television program. Only then did I realize that a big box that one of the intruders held was a television camera. I had thought that the lettering, *Revolutionary Public TV*, was just another slogan displayed by the strikers.

HAIR rekindled stashed away memories of this critical episode. Student opponents of U.S. engagements in Iraq and Afghanistan, survivors of Spring Weekend Celebrations, all confronting a world with few jobs, screeching to see their friends completely naked, was too much. Fortunately, this time it was mostly on the stage.

Chapter 12
Introduction to Politics

I had followed Connecticut politics before 1953, but mostly as an interested spectator. At Fort Trumbull, some of my students had asked me to be faculty advisor for the International Relations club that they had organized. It quickly became clear that the club dealt not only with foreign policy issues but also with affairs closer to home. In October 1948 they invited Chester Bowles, the Democratic candidate for Governor, an outspoken liberal New Dealer, to address a student assembly in our large auditorium. As a lowly instructor I was surprised to be asked to sit on the platform next to the candidate for Governor of Connecticut. Official pictures commemorate that event. A few days later, I cast my first vote enthusiastically for Bowles. I was happy to be able to support someone as liberal as FDR. Chester Bowles won narrowly and Truman managed to confound the experts by defeating New York's Governor Dewey. Unfortunately Chester Bowles failed to be re-elected in 1950.

When the Fort Trumbull student activists moved to the main campus in Storrs, they organized a chapter of the Connecticut Young Democrats and again asked me to be their faculty advisor. Apparently, they had noticed and liked my liberal views. The town of Mansfield, on the other hand, was still solidly Republican. When I shifted my registration from New London to Mansfield in 1950 Mansfield's Town Clerk was very suspicious about a faculty member like me who might threaten the centuries old order. He administered the reading comprehension test required in order for me to exercise my rights as a full citizen and voter in his town. Picking an obscure paragraph in the Connecticut Statutes he asked me what the passage meant. As an instructor of government, I managed to handle his obstacle course without too much difficulty. He expected me to register in the Republican Party; after all, that is what one did in Mansfield. When I chose the Democratic Party he failed to hide his dismay.

As a registered Democrat, I started to attend the local Party caucuses that selected candidates. Soon I was asked to become a member of the Democratic Town Committee. Things got interesting and exciting. Someone criticized Thomas Dodd, then still a member of the House of Representatives and not yet a Senator, for his role on the House Un-American Activities Committee. It so happened, that Dodd's sister, Mrs. Dwyer, was a member of the Town Committee and did not like her brother being criticized. There were also some positive events. Abe Ribicoff, a rising politician in the Democratic Party, decided to take on Governor Lodge in 1954. He campaigned in every town, regardless of size. This was a departure from past Democratic practice. Abe Ribicoff appeared on a clear autumn day in Storrs and addressed a relatively small group of Mansfield voters. We were on a Democratic Town Committee member's lawn near the Town Hall on Spring Hill, watching cars pass us a few feet in front of us. This reminded me of my encounter, six years earlier, when Bowles, had addressed a much larger crowd at Fort Trumbull. Abe had to raise his voice as he competed with the traffic. He promised, if elected, to give priority to books and professors over bricks and mortar. What a contrast to the incumbent Governor Lodge who had done so little to support the University. Abe Ribicoff raised our hopes and expectations.

Abe Ribicoff was elected. His election upended many traditions. He was the first Jewish governor in the Land of Steady Habits. Unfortunately, his electoral success made him somewhat cocky and difficult to get along with. His relations with UCONN President Jorgensen quickly soured. They both possessed enormous egos. While Ribicoff started out by keeping his promise to pay attention to the needs of the University, he reversed the priorities he had cited on his campaign stop in Mansfield. New academic buildings, financed by State bonds, transformed the campus. Money for books and faculty salaries continued to fail to meet basic needs. After a while, Ribicoff and Jorgensen argued publicly, a situation that made life for the rest of us at the University difficult. This dispute was not resolved until both Jorgenson and Ribicoff gave up their respective positions in 1961. Jorgensen was kicked into retirement and Ribicoff went to Washington to serve in J.F. Kennedy's administration.

I had my own encounter with Governor Ribicoff. I had become active in the Tolland County Democratic Association that covered all the county's 13 towns, a neglected but significant part of the Second Congressional district. Each month we met in a different town. Association members were political activists somewhat idealistic to believe it was possible to resolve problems through discussions that might lead to grassroots action. The Association passed a resolution in the late fifties supporting an income tax to resolve Connecticut's increasingly difficult financial situation. I happened to be president of the Association at the time and was asked to bring our income tax resolution to the attention of Democratic Party chairman John Bailey and Governor Ribicoff. Bailey listened, was somewhat amused by Tolland County's unorthodox thinking and quickly shifted to other topics, wanting to find out what was going on in my neck of the woods. He probably was not surprised when ten years later Audrey, by then representing Mansfield in the state legislature, introduced an income tax bill. Abe Ribicoff, on the other hand, put on his frostiest appearance when I tried to raise the issue with him at a campaign appearance in Tolland County. He totally ignored me and sat expressionless a few feet from me on the platform. It was difficult to introduce someone to the audience, who before the meeting refused to exchange a single word, except perhaps a cold, "how do you do, Curt." Governor Ribicoff made it clear to me that we in Tolland County had better learn to behave ourselves and never again mention the income tax. However we misbehaved.

I also continued to serve as faculty advisor of the Young Democrats throughout the fifties. The Young Democrats were a statewide organization and held annual conventions where resolutions were passed, candidates running for office in Hartford were endorsed or, just as often, criticized. Membership was open to any Democrat up to the ripe old age of 40. My UCONN Young Democrats surprised me a couple of times by asking me to join their delegation to these conventions and speak on behalf of resolutions that they had voted to support. After all, a 30 plus old professor might carry more weight than a twenty one year old student. The resolutions they wanted me to push ranged from recognizing Communist China to tax reform and the creation of a UCONN medical school. Needless to say, when I had my turn to speak on these controversial issues, the room filled with much older state politicians whose task it was to squelch such unorthodox proposals before the broader public got wind of the fact that there were some Democrats with crazy ideas. In back of the room my students had a great time shouting their support, as they watched their professor caught in the resulting political crossfire.

***

Having witnessed McCarthyism in Washington influenced my activities upon my return to Storrs in 1953: I became deeply involved in politics. In the State Department we had been at the mercy of Senator McCarthy elected by voters in Wisconsin. I recognized the importance of electing more members of Congress and Senators able to stand up to McCarthy. At town and county Democratic Party meetings I met kindred spirits. It expanded significantly my circle of friends.

At a 1954 meeting of the Mansfield Democratic Town Committee Anna Rockel, a teacher in Mansfield's pre-World War II two-room schools and later in charge of periodicals at the UCONN Library suggested that I might enjoy attending a meeting of the Tolland County Democratic Association in Vernon. In the 1950ies and sixties, the Democratic Party still had county as well as town organizations. At a meeting in Vernon, I met Leo B. Flaherty Jr., about my age, who dominated the meeting. He regaled the group discussing actions at the State Democratic Convention that he had attended a few weeks earlier. Leo there had taken the place of Leo Flaherty Sr., his father, a respected doctor in Rockville whom the local Party had regularly sent to Democratic State Conventions in the past. With his politically helpful Irish name and his father's reputation, Leo Jr. had no problem getting the attention of John Bailey, the legendary leader of the Connecticut Democratic Party. Leo asked the State Convention to condemn Senator McCarthy for calling those who disagreed with him Communist agents. While Bailey shared Leo Flaherty's disgust of McCarthy, he felt there was no point getting the Connecticut Democratic Party involved in this controversy. Bailey's motto was to avoid unnecessary battles and concentrate on winning elections. Leo, on the other hand, considered McCarthyism a moral issue on which one had to take a stand. The State Convention agreed and the Connecticut Democratic Party became one of the first Party organizations to condemn McCarthyism. Leo with his Irish oratorical skill had a way of arousing his audience simply by using reason and logic to make his case. I was delighted to have found someone who not only shared my political views, but who had the courage to stand up to prevailing public prejudices and, most important, who was able to convert others to his often not particularly conventional views.

When we first met, Leo had a daytime job at Pratt and Whitney, while completing his law school degree and preparing for his bar examination. He started to practice law in his family's living room. His practice and reputation grew quickly, but he did not abandon his interest and active participation in politics. We met often and agreed on almost all major issues. When a few years later Governor Abe Ribicoff lacked the necessary funds to implement his ambitious projects to build up UCONN, expand our highway system, modernize our governmental structure, as well as many other projects, Leo Flaherty and I passed the resolution placing the Tolland County Democratic Association on record endorsing a state income tax. There is no question in my mind that Flaherty's commitment to basic principles helped me a great deal in surviving bruising political battles.

As Leo's legal practice expanded, while also being elected mayor of Rockville, his principled involvement in significant political controversies continued unabated. Leo and I ran afoul of Senator Tom Dodd, Chris Dodd's father. Tom Dodd referred to Leo and me at some public meeting as that "Commie" lawyer and his friend the UCONN professor. Leo called me up and asked whether I had heard being defamed in public. I had not. He informed me that he was not willing to let Tom Dodd get away with such a statement. He managed to arrange two meetings where Tom Dodd in person apologized separately to Leo and me.

A short time after his father's death, Chris Dodd started his own campaign for Connecticut's Second Congressional District seat. He made a special point of seeking me out at a Democratic Party social affair in Willimantic. Since I was a Mansfield delegate to the 1974 Congressional Convention and Audrey's husband I was worth being courted. I asked him why his father did not like professors, especially those who taught international relations. We had a fascinating discussion in which Chris explained his father, why he admired him, especially for his role at the Nürnberg Trials as well as issues where he differed with him. Chris converted me. I wanted to make sure that I had not gone bonkers so I called up Leo who was a congressional convention delegate from Vernon. I told him that I was considering voting for Chris. He responded that he had a similar discussion and intended to vote for Chris. He had about eight other delegates from Vernon who would follow his lead. I had three from Mansfield. The convention was narrowly divided. Leo and I were known liberals who were expected to vote for Doug Bennett, Dodd's rival. When Leo and I, as well as our delegates, cast our votes for Chris, our unexpected votes put Chris over the top. I miss Leo. He died a few years ago. He was a man of principle, excellent judgment and a courageous idealist. Joe Courtney, the Congressman currently representing Eastern Connecticut started his career as a lawyer in Flaherty's Vernon office.

***

Examining, analyzing and describing the politics of the Kremlin and Stalin's foreign policy had been fascinating but depressing. Khrushchev's revelations of Stalin's gruesome political machinations confirmed what we already knew. Petty rivalries and political shenanigans at the expense of the interests of most of the people in the Soviet sphere continued unabated. This was particularly true in Czechoslovakia. When I shifted my attention to politics closer to home in Mansfield, I discovered that politics in my backyard bore some resemblance to Eastern Europe plots. While we did not have show trials and executions, the political plots, reckless denunciations and attempts to violate rules in order to seize power bore an uncomfortable resemblance to those in Eastern Europe. Mansfield's political battles of the 1950's and sixties were disturbing but in a way, helped me understand the multitude of social factors affecting political behavior.

Almost immediately after becoming a member of the Mansfield Democratic Town Committee, I became aware that not all local Democrats were on the same page. There were Democrats who had lived in town a long time. They had been accustomed to playing the role of the permanent minority in a traditional Republican-dominated rural community. They were the descendents of Irish, Italian, French Canadian or other immigrants, who were looked down on by the descendents of earlier settlers. Then there were the Democrats, recently hired by UCONN in the late thirties when the University started its dramatic expansion and especially following the end of World War II with the arrival of GI Bill financed war veterans. Many of these newly arrived Democrats were admirers of Roosevelt's New Deal and enthusiastically supported liberal Democrats like Governor Chester Bowles. The Townies and Gownies differed not merely in their political views, but more importantly in their quite different social and cultural attitudes. This lack of consensus first manifested itself shortly after Mansfield elected Dan Graf First Selectman in 1955 as its first Democratic local top official.

I happen to have known Dan Graf practically from the moment I arrived in Storrs in 1949. The room I had rented on Moulton Road was in a house owned by his son in law. That was probably not an accident, since George McReynolds, the Department chairman who had recruited me lived a few houses further down the road and was glad to recommend to me a perfectly located place. It did not take me long to realize that Dan Graf was a very important practical person. The fall of 1949 was a dry season. Surface wells ran out of water. When ours did, I would never have noticed, except that Dan Graf was there with a big tank truck pumping clean water into our empty tank. No big deal, his son-in-law told me, after all Dan ran the University's Facilities Maintenance Division.

A few years later Dan retired from the University. Dan was not the type who could sit still, relax and enjoy life. In 1955, he decided to challenge the incumbent Republican First Selectman. He ran on the Democratic ticket. Old timers were appalled by the audacity of a Democrat challenging a Republican incumbent. After all, Mansfield was a Republican town. Dan won for two reasons. He promised to make the job of first selectman professional and give it his full attention and not continue the practice of running the town as a sideshow for his contracting business. The second reason was a rumor that the Republican incumbent had gotten involved in an affair with a young woman on the dirt road the town was paving. Even a part-time road contracting first selectman was not given the freedom to mix sex with work, especially in Mansfield.

Dan quickly won the town's approval for the professional manner in which he managed town affairs. Dirt roads were paved and better maintained, The Town Office Building on Spring Hill was expanded, updated and a vault was added: Mansfield entered the twentieth century. Dan was re-elected several times with overwhelming support. As a Democratic Town Committee member, I shared most of my fellow Town Committee members pride in having a practical Democrat in our midst who knew how to make traffic flow and keep Mansfield attractive, giving the rest of us the luxury of arguing about national and foreign policy issues. I had no idea that this state of bliss would be short-lived. Dan Graf got into a conflict with our local chicken farmer, also a Democrat.

Joe Gill, the chicken farmer, was from New Mexico but somehow found his way to Washington during World War II where he met and married a girl from Mansfield. Joe developed a modern rapidly expanding chicken business and was a leader of the statewide organization representing the interests of the poultry industry. Newly elected Governor Abe Ribicoff turned to him, so that a Democrat could run the Department of Agriculture. Joe, chair of the Mansfield Democratic Town Committee, through his new role as member of the Governor's cabinet, appeared to move Mansfield Democrats from the outer reaches of politics closer to the center stage. We quickly realized that if Joe wanted to keep his job it was more important for him to do the Governor's bidding than to transmit to the Governor the constant comments from Mansfield's forever concerned and complaining Democrats.

We, the University trouble-making professors, were slow to realize that our academic interests were no match for the far more easily manageable problems of chicken farmers. The growing tension soon took on the aspect of the more traditional town-gown conflict. We recognized the problem, but comforted ourselves believing that university types were more involved than the townies and therefore our attendance insured our dominance of local Democratic politics. That is until the evening of an important caucus, open to all enrolled Democrats. More than half the seats of the Town Hall were occupied by what Joe proudly informed us were "his Dirty Shirts" mobilized by his brother in law. Thus, he let us know that we academics were a minority. Now the Fight Was On.

The battle escalated when we voted not to send Joe Gill to the State Convention that was to re-nominate his boss, Governor Ribicoff. We also got involved in a verbal fight with the sister of U.S. Senator Thomas Dodd and battled for a place on the State Central Committee of the Democratic Party. Finally, and most important, Joe Gill's faction tried to replace Dan Graf as First Selectman of Mansfield. After Joe Gill's faction had gained control of the Town Committee, Dan Graf lost the endorsement of the Democratic Party. Dan was re-elected in 1961 on the Republican ticket and a specially created Mansfield Party that consisted largely of University Democrats. He won handily. There was widespread support for the professionally competent manner in which he administered the Town's government. Two years later Dan lost the endorsement of both the Democratic and Republican Parties. A petition signed by mostly University Democrats gave him a place on the ballot and he was re-elected. That infuriated a young Willimantic attorney, Charles Tarpinian. Charlie had been chosen by the town Democratic faction as their Town Committee chairman. He found a provision in the Rules of the State Democratic Party, which he believed entitled him to have legal citations issued to those Democrats who had signed the petition to put Dan Graf on the ballot, requesting them to show cause why their names should not be stricken from the Registry of Democratic Party Voters. This affected about 80 voters. We were shocked, a Party Purge in Mansfield!

Those of us who had received the legal citation requesting us to prove that we were loyal Democrats met in our new house on Dunham Pond Road that still lacked furniture and was therefore ideally suited to hold a large assembly of excited Mansfield residents. My friend, Leo Flaherty, came from Vernon and agreed to represent us in Court. Sometime later, Leo informed me that the Judge had not only dismissed Tarpinian's effort to kick us out of the Democratic Party, but had privately reprimanded him for his conduct before the Judge. Our success in standing up to Tarpinian was the end of a very important chapter in the changes that transformed the Mansfield political scene. President Kennedy's assassination, shortly after our dramatic success to remain Mansfield Democrats, united America in grief, but it failed to put an end the battle for control of the Mansfield Democratic Party.

***

While I was a very interested observer and critic of the turmoil that roiled Mansfield Democrats, Audrey decided to join me and also get involved. Maybe it was in her Irish genes and her mother's upbringing that gave Audrey the confidence not only to participate in the public debates but to quickly take a leading role. Interested in the wider world she wanted to change and improve it.

It soon became obvious that Audrey possessed political skills. When factional fights within the Mansfield Democratic Party had demoralized the Party, efforts were made to have orderly constructive meetings where the differences dividing mostly University Democrats from Town Democrats could be ironed out. As a very effective public speaker who did not talk over the heads of those not connected with the University, Audrey was chosen as the moderator of a well attended public meeting. Her ability to make people laugh at their many foibles won over the crowd. She enjoyed the experience and soon was appointed to the Finance Committee of the Town of Mansfield.

In 1967 a new Dean of the School of Arts and Sciences decided not to renew her appointment as an economics instructor, a position she had held on an annual basis for 14 years. That upset her very much. At first, she got a job at the Windham Regional Planning Agency where she developed a plan for the region's economic growth. The following year, when asked whether she would be willing to be a candidate to represent Mansfield in the state legislature, she said yes with considerable enthusiasm. It meant defeating the very popular incumbent Republican, Foster Richards. Mansfield had always been represented by a Republican. Many considered Audrey's candidacy an extremely difficult, if not impossible task, especially because the 1968 national Democratic ticket led by Senator Hubert Humphrey carried the burden of Lyndon B. Johnson's unpopular Viet Nam War.

Undaunted, Audrey embarked on her campaign. She decided to follow a very traditional strategy of "going door to door", a method many politicians like to brag about but rarely implement. She also had a pink bumper sticker *Audrey* that soon found its way on many cars in part because of its unusual coloring. Audrey realized quickly that going door to door in Mansfield would involve talking to several thousand households. Many people were not at home or were reluctant to greet a stranger. She left a signed copy of her flyer. A greater problem was to find enough time to talk and listen to those citizens who were home and were anxious to let Audrey know what bothered them. While she was prepared to discuss proposed legislative issues and taxes, most people were concerned about somebody else's garbage, a drainage basin, a road that should be paved, or torn up. It was a real learning experience, which Audrey enjoyed tremendously. Some problems residents discussed with Audrey worried her a great deal. Teachers who had retired a decade or longer told Audrey they could barely afford buying sufficient food for their meals. There were dogs that barked. Some dogs threatened her, but she managed to calm them down. When the campaign was over, she won. In 1968 she was the only Democratic newcomer to oust an incumbent Republican legislator in Connecticut. As a consequence of her talking with so many Mansfield residents with all sorts of problems Audrey felt she now had the responsibility to deal and possibly solve the problems they had discussed.

A freshman legislator usually spends the first term quietly, learning the ropes, making new acquaintances and avoids controversy. Not Audrey. She came to Hartford with an agenda, a mission and above all, excitement. She had had bigger ambitions than spending her life teaching freshmen the principles of economics. She wanted to help Connecticut legislative leaders straighten out the state's antiquated tax structure and apply modern economic principles to the operation of the state government. While her agenda may have had an unmistakable academic flavor, her working class origin, her contact with Mansfield voters and a decade of practical Mansfield politicking protected her from being dismissed in Hartford as one of those misty-eyed intellectuals.

Her first move was to figure out how the wheels of power operate in Hartford. It was obvious in the late sixties that long-term Democratic Party Chair John Bailey was the key person to know if one was interested in influencing legislative action. Audrey's number one priority therefore was not only to get acquainted with the Party Chair, but to gain his good will and influence him, if possible. Audrey's unexpected victory, in a year when Nixon helped Republicans in close races, obviously impressed Bailey. He was anxious to get to know what made that freshman legislator tick. Reporting on their initial encounters, she expressed to me her genuine surprise that this famous politician known for his toughness, was really a very nice and kind guy. The initial encounter presaged a constructive and beneficial relationship.

Everybody assumed that a woman legislator would want to concentrate on issues involving education and health issues. Audrey surprised her fellow legislators when she chose the Finance Committee as her first committee assignment. She quickly familiarized herself with the main task of that committee: financing those operations the budget committee was prepared to recommend to the Governor. Her approach was to apply the logic that if there is an agreed set of services that need to be funded, you locate the necessary resources, i.e. taxes, to balance the budget. She quickly was recognized as professionally very competent in her handling the enormous amount of detailed fiscal information required to fund state government operations. Until Audrey's membership on the legislature's finance committee, the committee simply rubber-stamped decisions reached by Bailey and professionals in the Governor's office. While Bailey was quite willing to have a professionally competent person help him control the state's budget process, he was concerned that Audrey might be tempted to challenge some well established policies: her belief that only an income tax could resolve Connecticut's perennial budget shortfall, was political suicide and therefore not possible. She served also on the State Development Committee, undoubtedly because of her experience on the Windham Regional Planning Agency. Only when Republican Governor Meskill ran the state did Audrey join the Education Committee.

Among the legislators whom Audrey befriended were two representatives from New Haven. One was intensely interested in gambling in Nevada and tried to convince Audrey how much fun that was. It amused her to see somebody immersed in such an unreal world. When Audrey regaled me with these stories of her Hartford experiences, we tried to understand and analyze such strange behavior. The whole subject took on a different character however when that neighbor of hers became a strong advocate of solving Connecticut's revenue crisis by authorizing a lottery, betting on dog tracks, thereby balancing the budget on poor people's backs and encouraging their unrealistic dreams of sudden wealth.

The other representative from New Haven was the exact opposite. Mary Griswold was the widow of the former president of Yale. She shared Audrey's concern about the need to balance Connecticut's budget honestly. One day they met in the Ladies Room, discussed the budget intensely, and jointly reached the decision to introduce a bill that would have Connecticut adopt an income tax. A friend of theirs, George Ritter from Hartford, happened to wait for them outside the Ladies Room and when Audrey and Mary finally emerged, he asked them what had kept them there so long. They laughed and informed him that they had decided to introduce a Beck-Griswold proposal for a state Income Tax. Ritter was enthusiastic:" Finally" he said, "somebody has guts". On the spot, he asked them whether they were willing to have him join them and add his name as a sponsor of a Connecticut Income Tax. Of course, they agreed. Another representative, Howard Klebanoff, joined them a short time later. It took over two decades before Connecticut adopted a state income tax. It was Governor Weicker, who accomplished that task in 1993. Earlier Governor Meskill had one passed, but it lasted only a very short time before being rescinded.

Audrey surprised her critics on the right by being very concerned that state bonds have a high rating. Since her knowledge on this and many other financial topics was mostly academic, she decided early in her Finance Committee work to find out what factors enter into bond rating decision-making. She traveled to New York City and had appointments at bond rating agencies where she tried to absorb all the relevant information on factors affecting a state's financial reputation. Armed with this information, her comments on the state budget were generally accepted as sound. She traveled to Boston to attend a meeting of the Boston Federal Reserve Bank. Upon her return, I had to listen to her excited reaction to a Federal Reserve Board decision to lower or raise the rate by half a point. She talked so much about it that even I slowly realized the importance of the issue. It was obvious that serving on the legislative Finance Committee was something that Audrey not only loved, but also took extremely seriously. No wonder, when elected to the State Senate in 1974, she became Chair. She was recognized as the legislature's authority on many fiscal issues that other legislators preferred to ignore.

From the very start of her legislative career, Audrey involved herself deeply with the Payments in Lieu of Taxes, PILOT, legislation, a state tax issue of special interest to Mansfield. The PILOT law was the brainchild of E. O. Smith, who had represented Mansfield in Hartford in the thirties and forties. It was intended to compensate the town of Mansfield for the large amount of property tax revenue it lost because of tax-exempt property owned by the state, i.e. the sites of the University of Connecticut and the Mansfield Training School. While the idea of the Pilot legislation was fine, from Audrey's perspective, the actual $ that the state paid the town was insufficient to cover the large state-owned property hole in Mansfield's tax revenue. She updated the Pilot compensation formula to better reflect the values of contemporary property tax assessments. The problem was that any revised realistic Pilot formula would significantly affect the state budget. In order to build up support for her PILOT proposal, Audrey had the brilliant, but not particularly original, idea to suggest that other towns with state property also benefit from the PILOT program. Party Chairman John Bailey was quickly won over. After all, Hartford with its State Capitol, its buildings housing government agencies, could certainly benefit from a new source of revenue. Other mostly Democratic towns would also be helped. The only trouble with Audrey's approach was that widening the scope of the PILOT program would have to cut back the actual amount given to each affected town. Nevertheless, Mansfield benefitted significantly from Audrey's revision of E .O. Smith's idea.

While tax and budget issues dominated her activities in the legislature, Audrey never forgot the many concerns her constituents had raised in her campaign. There were catch basins that had to be fixed, traffic lights to be installed where serious accidents had occurred on state roads, complaints that state agencies had not dealt properly with a constituent's problem. She discovered that the state highway department was delighted to encounter a legislator who located their regional office and spent real time with them discussing the possibility of logical improvements. Our supper discussions took on a surrealist tone when we explored the issue of how many accidental deaths on a state highway intersection justify a traffic light. Many Mansfield residents were amazed that some of their requests were dealt with and that a communications link with Hartford had been opened. It was therefore not much of a surprise when Audrey, up for re-election in 1970, ran unopposed. Many of her colleagues in Hartford were jealous.

Active for many years in the League of Women Voters, in UCONN faculty activities and in Mansfield politics, Audrey never felt discriminated as a woman. In Hartford, by contrast, she was only one among a very small number of female legislators. When asked, how she wanted her occupation to be officially listed, she responded, *legislator*, not *housewife*. This set an example, which many of her colleagues followed.

Women legislators had their own organization, the Order of Women Legislators, OWLS. The Owls had a small room where exclusively women could socialize. The male legislators by contrast had a special social and dining area on the top floor of the State Capitol where women were admitted only by invitation from a male legislator. Since all important discussions and negotiations took place in the all-male dining space, Audrey quickly managed to get herself a standing invitation from friendly male fellow legislators and participated in all negotiations that mattered to her. Somehow, she also managed to have the clause excluding women from the male dining room eliminated. The past practice of discrimination based on sex, appeared not only unfair but also ridiculous. Audrey became known as a breaker of traditional barriers.

Her reputation as a feminist traveled to Storrs where one of my colleagues, barely hiding his sarcasm, wanted to know what had made Audrey such a feminist. Most of my friends however considered her a path-breaker and a model of the new generation. Her activities in Hartford, raising the level of issues affecting women, happened to coincide with a growing national awareness that the role that women played in national affairs had lagged far behind changing social attitudes and principles of equality and fairness. Responding to Audrey's activities, I added a course on *Women in Politics* to my academic agenda. It went very well, except that women on campus raised the question almost immediately <u>why I was</u> conducting the course. Obviously, it should be taught by a woman. I pointed out that I was well qualified since it was my wife, Audrey, who best exemplified the woman in politics. The women on campus looked at each other and made it clear to me that I just did not get it. They managed to convince me in a relatively short time and I gave up the course.

Part IV - Traveling to Check on the Cold War

Chapter 13
My First Look at Post-War Eastern Europe

In the summer of 1960, I took advantage of the American Political Science Association's offer of a reduced airfare charter flight to Paris. The jet age had not yet arrived and the propeller driven plane took over twelve hours to reach Paris. While slow by current standards, it cut nine days from the time I had spent crossing the Atlantic in 1938. My intention was to spend eight weeks in Germany, Czechoslovakia and Austria and observe changes wrought by the Cold War. I was also interested in Yugoslavia's version of Communism. It was all part of my professional concern with the impact of Communism on Central and Eastern Europe.

I left Audrey in Storrs to enjoy her summer while providing full time entertainment for seven-year old Ronald and four-year old Meredith. It was the first time we were separated for more than a day. We tried to stay in touch by exchanging letters several times a week. This involved careful planning so that I could pick up her letters addressed *poste restante* before leaving a particular city on the way to my next stop.

I had never been to Paris even though I had attended the French gymnasium in Prague for four years and learned to speak French fluently. Three days there were just enough to stir my interest but not enough to become comfortable with the Louvre, the Sorbonne, the Palace de Versailles, the Eiffel Tower, the Bois de Boulogne, the many historical sites, restaurants and artist hangouts. Paris served as my entry point to my real destination: Europe on the far side of the Rhine.

I took an overnight train to Munich. It was not crowded: Munich was not a popular destination. As I left Paris at eight o'clock in the evening, I realized how much I had missed the glamour and excitement that surrounded European train stations. The names of the cities that we passed evoked memories of high school geography lessons. I dozed off as darkness descended on the landscape.

An increase in noise from the undercarriage of the coach aroused me. We must be on a bridge. The crossing took some time.

This must be the Rhine! The train slowed down and a few minutes later stopped at a station. I poked my head out of the window. The platform appeared deserted. Suddenly a voice came from the public address system. "*Achtung, Achtung! Sie sind jetzt in Kehl Grenze, Deutschland*" [Attention, attention, You are now in Kehl/Frontier, Germany] Goose pimples went up and down my spine. As the voice continued it informed the traveler where to change to a variety of destinations. Not a soul left the train to take advantage of the loudspeaker's vital information. After all, it was after midnight and nobody coming from Paris seemed to have the slightest intention of visiting the many destinations the voice recited, punctuated by several more *Achtungs*.

Twenty two years had passed since I had last stepped on German soil. A long time and yet the voice uttering *Achtung* in the middle of the night brought back memories. As the train left *Kehl Grenze*, memories of brown shirted storm troopers wearing swastika armbands appeared in my mind. As the train gained speed *Achtung, Achtung* faded away and I fell into a deep sleep. When I woke up, it was morning and the train pulled into Stuttgart. Industrious cleaning ladies spruced up the coach to prepare it for its destination to Munich. I could not understand their Swabian accent. It certainly did not sound like the German I remember from my youth. I was entering a Germany I had never known.

Several hours later we reached the impressive Munich train station, the same one my parents and I had passed through twenty eight years earlier on our 1932 vacation that had never left my memory. I was 8 years old then and my parents showed me the city where they had met, where my father had gotten his Ph.D. and had spent years exploring philosophical concepts and romancing. After finding a comfortable bed and breakfast inn a few blocks from the railroad station I located the *Englische Garden*, the park where my father first had accosted my mother. The park did not impress me, probably because I had expected a magical place, considering the stories my parents repeated so many times.

More important than the park was the beer hall, the *Bürgerbräuhaus.* It was there that Adolf Hitler had held forth in the early 1920s and from where in November 1923 he led a march to the center of town in the failed Putsch to seize power. I visited that Beer Hall. The long tables were there, hefty waitresses carried more than five huge steins in each hand, skillfully pushing each stein so that it landed right in front of the targeted customer. The place was noisy and I could imagine Hitler addressing World War I veterans, inciting them against Communists, Socialists, Frenchmen, Jews and any other group his beer drinking frustrated and easily stirred audience was ready to hate with glee as they called for more steins of beer. It took me no effort to imagine the spirit of those times.

Later that day I stopped at a small contemporary restaurant for some coffee and cake. While eating and reading the European edition of the *Herald Tribune,* I became aware that an older Bavarian lady at the next table kept looking at me. I said *Guten Tag*, in my best German. She asked me whether I was from America since I was reading the *Herald Tribune*. When I said yes, she wanted to know, why I spoke German without an accent. When I answered, I was born in Berlin and had left Germany in 1933, she said slowly that she was so sorry and started weeping. Her so deeply felt reaction moved me. Apparently there were Germans with the desire to atone for Germany's guilt. We sat at our separate tables deeply absorbed in our thoughts and memories of that not too distant past. As we parted, she wiped her eyes.

Two days later, I took a train to Czechoslovakia. The coach was quite cold, far less comfortable than the one that had taken me from Paris to Munich. It was a clear sign that we were on our way to Eastern Europe, a different world. When we reached Cheb (Eger) on the Czechoslovak border, our relatively modern German locomotive was uncoupled, gave us a final push and abandoned us. After waiting at least five minutes, a big locomotive came from the Czech frontier, belching dark brown smoke and gave our coach quite a jolt. Attached, it pulled us across the iron curtain. The *Achtungs* from Kehl were replaced by uniformed officials examining passports, especially my American one. Finally, they stamped my visa. I entered Czechoslovakia. What a difference 22 years had made! Then Hitler's Germany inflicted fear. Now it was Czechoslovakia, the land refuge in the 1930s that I had to fear.

***

In 1933 our first stop on the way to Prague had been Marienbad, Marianské Lazňe in Czech. I was then nine years old. Now, 27 years later, memories grabbed me and I decided to get off the train in the world famous spa. The spa was intact and people walked along the covered path filling their glass with foul tasting spring water full of special salts that were intended to cure you of the many illnesses that rob you of your youth and health. The special spring water and the columned walkway had not changed much since my earlier stay. Everything else had. Back then, there had been crowds of visitors, speaking German, Czech, Polish and other Eastern European languages. It was there that I had seen for the first time bearded Ultra-Orthodox eastern European Jews, their heads covered by big black hats. Marienbad then basked in its 19th century reputation as the summer resort for not only the affluent, but also the writers and poets who sought a break from their normal routine.

Now, in 1960, the spa served as a short summer respite from work for those trade union members who had properly performed their assigned tasks and whom the government deemed worthy of a reward. Hotels were designated to accommodate specially selected groups of workers. This left only a few hotels for foreigners like me. It would obviously have been easy for the authorities to keep track of me, if they had felt a need or desire to do so.

As a former political analyst of Communist Czechoslovakia in the State Department, I had some knowledge about practices used by the regime to handle foreigners. Perhaps I was a little too confident and lacked enough respect to have any fear. Relying on my childhood memories, I explored the spa, town, neighborhood, covering considerable distances. I was careful not to draw attention to myself. I did not ask for directions and avoided looking at maps.

Remembering a 1933 excursion, I located a path to a restaurant on a hill above the woods surrounding Marienbad. Protected by tall trees I sat down on a bench. A lady passing by greeted me. I responded in Czech. My accent gave me away and I quickly identified myself as an American. She talked freely about her job, vacation and concerns about the future. She wanted to know what was going on in the outside world. We talked for about ten minutes. I said that I was on my way to the restaurant only a few hundred feet further on the path and invited her for a cup of coffee. As we emerged from the trees below the restaurant, she hastily bade me good-bye, obviously not wanting to be seen conversing with a foreigner, especially an American who spoke Czech. After that incident, I was more careful and talked with strangers only in public places.

A short time later, I passed a small church in situated on a large meadow. Even though it was the middle of the week, voices chanting hymns emerged from the building. That struck me as quite interesting. Unless they were historically significant, churches in pre-war Czechoslovakia had few parishioners on weekdays. Soon the doors opened and a multitude filled the sidewalk and rapidly dispersed. So that is the way people in a tightly controlled society express their need for reflection, I opined.

Before leaving Marienbad, I went on a special pilgrimage to honor the memory of Professor Theodor Lessing, the German refugee writer who had published articles critical of Hitler's Nazi regime in the *Prager Tagblatt*. The Nazis had killed him one week after my father had taken me along to meet him. Twenty-seven years later, I located the hotel and balcony. There was a plaque with Theodor Lessing's name. It commemorated the tragic event. Now many decades later, it still hurts.

***

On July 4, 1960, after a 22-year absence, I returned to Prague. Richard Tims, my boss in the State Department in 1952 and now the acting head of the U.S. Embassy, invited me to the Ambassador's Residence for an Independence Day celebration. Before the War this residence had been owned by a wealthy Jewish family, the Petscheks,. Not in my wildest dreams when I was 14 years old, could I have imagined returning and spending my first evening in Prague celebrating America's National holiday in a fancy embassy residence.

While Prague appeared little changed, I did notice the imprint of the tumultuous forces that had overwhelmed the city. The train entered the familiar tunnel on its way to Prague's Main Railroad station. Not surprisingly, the station had suffered the loss of its pre-War name. It had been named Wilson Station commemorating President Woodrow Wilson who had helped Czechoslovakia gain its independence. The trolley cars and their routes were as I remembered them, except that the trains and road traffic had been shifted to the right lane due to Hitler's intent to make Czechoslovakia an integral part of the Third Reich. 21 years after Hitler's annexation many cars still had their driver seats on the wrong side. In contrast to Paris and Munich, Prague's cars reflected the pre-war era.

I stayed in the Ambassador Hotel on Wenceslas Square, the commercial heart of Prague. The hotel was considered expensive: $3.30 a night (!!) My room struck me as luxurious: it had two washbasins and a shower! Situated on the most important square, it gave me easy access to almost everything of interest.

Approaching the city from Wenceslas Square gave me a different perspective from my pre-War location in suburban Dejvice. The Town Hall with its famous clock was only a short walk from the hotel. When the clock strikes the hour, small doors near the top of the tower open and apostles appear one after the other, shaking their heads in an impressive procession that focuses the gaze of the multitude below. Two days after my arrival I waited as the bell sounded the hour. Just like 22 years earlier, I watched intently. The apostles never disappoint. This time the doors did not open. I waited a few minutes and was about to put my camera back into its case when the apostles finally emerged laughing at me (and all the other tourists), we fooled you foreign tourists! Apparently repairing the tower's machinery was not a top priority of the Communist regime.

After entering and admiring a fraction of the most important landmarks in the Old Town, I crossed the Vltava (Moldau) over the Charles Bridge with its many statutes and climbed the steps leading to the Cathedral and Hradčany Castle, the seat and symbol of Czech history, independence and governmental power. The President of the Republic lives and has his office there. In 1937 my parents had taken me there to sign the register when Czechoslovakia's liberator and first president, Thomas G. Masaryk, was laid to rest. Now uniformed soldiers guarded the approach to the seat of power. I carefully kept my distance.

A short walk from the Castle is the Foreign Ministry. I tried to locate the balcony from which Thomas Masaryk's son, Foreign Minister Jan Masaryk, jumped or was pushed to his death shortly after the Communists ousted the post-war coalition government in

1948. I tried not to let my emotions overwhelm me. Back in the thirties, I had fun exploring and admiring this part of the city's ancient past. Events since then created a completely different mood. My PhD thesis had centered on the efforts by Czechoslovakia's democratic leaders to coexist with Stalin's Soviet Union. Jan Masaryk's death was not only a tragedy that intensified the Cold War, but it had also forced me to revise many of the assumptions, on which my thesis was based. All alone, I stood in the square staring at the balcony.

There was another area in the vicinity of Hradčany castle to which my parents had taken me: The Alchemists alley. This was a charming narrow street with small houses built of stone. In Medieval times, artisans had worked there, attempting to create precious metals from inferior material. The dream to become rich is eternal. I remembered a cozy restaurant that interested me much more than my father's explanations about the work of alchemists. The street was still there but most of the houses were closed or under repair. I did not find the restaurant of my memory. Instead, there was a plaque commemorating Franz Kafka, the famous Jewish writer, who had done most of his writing in the first two decades of the 20th century. The plaque stated that this was where he had lived. What a surprise! According to a number of accounts of his life, I had located his parents and his home in the Old City near the Town Hall. Several years later, the plaque was gone. Was this a modern day alchemist's trick?

I followed the exhausting Hradčany tour with a quite different one the next day. Some distance from Hradčany, but on the same side of the river was a gigantic monument commemorating more recent history. Built on the side of a hill there were steps leading to a giant statue of Stalin. He stood there admiring the city. The trouble was that he looked sort of lonely. He faced a part of the city that lacks the monuments, churches and museums that local people and foreigners alike make an effort to see. The large area surrounding Stalin was mostly empty. I asked a lonely guard where I could get a picture postcard to send to my family. You have to take your own picture, he answered, pointing to my camera. I almost felt sorry for Stalin there almost forgotten. Several years later the monument was taken down and replaced by a non-political park. Hradčany has rejected its intruder and regained its role protecting the city and country.

***

The next day I explored the past. I was drawn to the Jewish Museum, situated near the old Jewish cemetery where trees grow among the piled up stones that commemorate the dead of three centuries. Space was at a premium and bodies lie buried on top of each other. Next to the cemetery is the Pinkas Synagogue. It had been restored after the War and on its whitewashed walls I was amazed to see the names of the 77,297 Jews from pre-war Czechoslovakia who, according to official German records, had been killed by Nazi Germany. How about grandfather Gustav?

When we said good-bye in 1938, we knew he would have a hard time. He was almost eighty-three. He and we hoped that whatever happened, the Nazis would not touch him because of his age. Furthermore, we were simply unable to take him along to the U.S. There was no money and no visa and how could he have withstood the rigors of crossing the Atlantic? As the war progressed and stories of the horrors of the Holocaust appeared, we feared the worst, but still hoped that he would have been spared the fate of the younger victims. After the liberation of Czechoslovakia in May 1945, my parents contacted agencies that searched for lost relatives. They soon were informed that my grandfather Gustav had died. We had also been told that he had been deported to Terezín, a stop on the way to Auschwitz.

I was mesmerized by the tiny letters giving names, dates of birth and death of the victims that stretched from wall to wall, from floor to ceiling. I quickly realized that they were arranged alphabetically by place of residence prior to deportation. I wound my way past other viewers until I located **Plzeň.** It took only a few seconds before my eyes focused on Gustav Beck, 9/6/1855-8/28/1942. There were also several other Becks' from Plzeň, uncles, aunts and cousins. I then located Prague and recognized names that might have been fellow students in my French Gymnase Real who had not escaped. I stood there, overcome by memories and thoughts about the horrible way in which grandfather Gustav's otherwise happy life had been nightmarishly terminated.

The travel literature mentioned that remnants of the ghetto that the Germans had established in Terezín served as a military base where some Czechoslovak troops were quartered, but that Terezín was open to the public. After locating grandfather on the wall in the Synagogue, it occurred to me that I might find out more by visiting the place where Hitler had sent him.

On my third day in Prague, after recovering from a night of nausea caused by the food I had eaten in the hotel restaurant, I took a bus, destination Ústí nad Labem (Aussig), that was scheduled to stop in Terezín. The trip took about an hour and a half. I got off the bus where the highway made a turn away from the Elbe River it had followed for some time. On one side were open fields, on the other, a large cemetery with carefully arranged rows of tombstones. A large sign proclaimed that the cemetery housed the Anti-Fascist Victims of the Third Reich. No reference to the fact that this was a place where there might be some Jewish victims deported by the German occupiers. Beyond the cemetery were the remnants of a relatively small wartime German concentration camp, housed on the grounds of the small fortress built by Empress Maria Theresa in the 18th century which served as a museum of the not too distant past, It was my first visit to a former concentration camp with its small bunks, inadequate hygienic facilities, etc. There was also a small souvenir shop. I looked in vain for references to the ghetto that had housed Grandfather Gustav.

Disappointed, I left the Nazi Concentration Camp gate with its sarcastic motto, *Arbeit Macht Frei* (Work Liberates) and my eyes fell on a small sign, *Krematorium* that pointed to the highway where the bus had deposited me. I retraced my steps, saw another sign, followed the highway for at least half a mile, another *Krematorium* sign now directed me to turn left and suddenly I found myself on a road that entered a row of barracks. That must be the Terezín ghetto.

Things now got a little complicated. Tanks and other military vehicles were lined up by the side of the road and uniformed soldiers were everywhere. I was obviously a foreigner with my camera slung over my shoulder. I knew that photographing military facilities was a major crime in Communist Czechoslovakia. My earlier work as a State Department Research Analyst following the trials and purges of so-called enemies of the Communist government had prepared me for an encounter with Czech Communist authorities. Some of my research was subsequently declassified and published. I assumed that my name might be on some list kept by the Czech government. I did not want to arouse any suspicion and become a desirable target. I approached the nearest Czech soldier, pretended that I did not speak Czech and pointed to a *Krematorium* sign and indicated, with the dumbest gestures I could think of, that I needed help to find the *Krematorium*. In his most disdainful manner he responded by pointing to the sign and said follow the sign. Go that way… At least he knew that I was not taking any pictures of the tanks. He joined a bunch of fellow soldiers and they broke out laughing.

After passing the barracks, I was again alone in front of a small building that had served as a tiny place of worship in the ghetto. After passing under a bridge, I came to a large meadow bordered by the *Krematorium*. I was all alone on the large field that had very few markers. The *Krematorium* was open. A caretaker sat at a primitive desk. I asked him whether by chance he had any idea whether my grandfather might be buried somewhere here? Just a minute, he said, opened a huge book and asked me for my grandfather's name. I also gave him the date of death that I had copied from the Pinkas Synagogue wall. He located Gustav Beck from Plzeň and told me that since he was among those who died relatively early, he was buried in a "small mass grave containing only 30 bodies", Grave #XVI/3928, very close to the *Krematorium*. He was buried before they started to pass the dead through ovens that are preserved in the building.

When I returned with Audrey, 13-year old Ronald and 10-year old Meredith six years later, to introduce them to the past, the Pinkas Synagogue was closed for renovations. The old man in the *Krematorium* was replaced by a young functionary who could not consult the big book of records because it had been moved to Prague.

In 1995, I learned a great deal more about my grandfather's final year. After the 1989 Velvet Revolution when Czechoslovakia emerged from forty years of tight dictatorial control, several volumes were published commemorating Terezín. The volumes contain precise German records of the trains and the names of all the "passengers" transported to Terezín. That is where I learned that Gustav Beck together with ten other Becks, probably all relatives, left the Plzeň railroad station on transport T (the 20th transport to take victims to Terezín) on January 26, 1942. Some pictures in the

Terezín Memorial volume show the passengers traipsing through the snow as they assembled for their last train ride. Transport T carried 604 Jews to their destination. Only 67 survived their incarceration. Two other trains, each carrying 1,000 Jews, had left on January 18 and 22. There were 12 more Becks on those earlier transports. My grandfather apparently had managed to take the last and least crowded transport. I am sure he must have known the destination.

I am now older than my grandfather was when he had to leave his home on that cold snowy January day, carrying his belongings. I have a better understanding how he must have felt about having to face the horrible circumstances facing him just at the point where most people can relax and contemplate past events of one's life. Since he was in excellent health the last time I had seen him in 1938, I can visualize him managing to get into the freight car and somehow praying that not all hope was lost. Gustav was steeped in his religion that had comforted him through earlier stressful situations.

His life in a somewhat bizarre way had come full circle. At the time of his early youth, centuries of official discrimination against Jews in Bohemia had ended. His father moved the family from the countryside to the city of Plzeň, where Jews were finally permitted to reside. His father's generation celebrated this milestone by helping build a large Synagogue. In 1998, I saw for the first time the plaque in the synagogue entrance citing my great grandfather and other members of the Beck family for their role in helping build a structure that to this day dominates the skyline in the heart of the city. Gustav spent his entire life in Plzeň, participating as a successful merchant fulfilling the dreams of his ancestors. At the very end, he was not only kicked out of the city, but also out of the modern world back into primitive hell.

***

Once I was settled in my hotel I sought to establish contact with Arnošt, the son of my mother's cousin, one of the only few relatives who had survived the holocaust. My mother learned of his and his sister Susi's survival after the war. They were the only survivors of a large family in Prague with whom I shared a common great-grandmother. Arnošt, Susi and I had attended the same French lycé in Prague. I exchanged letters with Susi after her return to

Prague from her concentration camp ordeal in the interval before the 1948 Communist coup. She informed me that she had a job in the government. Arnošt was a scientist and taught engineering. I found his name and address in the phone directory. His address had not changed. I had not been in touch with Arnošt since leaving Prague in 1938.

I was aware receiving a call from an American, especially one who had worked for the State Department, might endanger him. I decided not to use the hotel telephone, but a public telephone on the street. I dialed his number. His unmistakable voice answered. I gave my first name and talked in German. I had said no more than that I was in Prague when he yelled that this must be a mistake and slammed down the receiver. I was disappointed and decided not to try meeting him.

Several months later back in Connecticut, my mother informed me, that she had learned Arnošt had escaped from Czechoslovakia and reached London. Three and a half years later, on my return from my journey in Africa I stopped in London and called Arnošt. This time he answered and immediately invited me to stop by at his apartment. After he gave me an account of his life spent under incredibly dangerous circumstances during the War and in post-War Communist Czechoslovakia, I turned the conversation to that phone call in early July 1960." Do you remember by any chance receiving a phone call from me?" "Of course I do, do you realize that when I received that call I thought our well-laid plans to escape from Czechoslovakia had been revealed and were about to fail?"

Over the next hour, I learned how unwittingly I had almost ruined Arnošt's chance of resuming a normal life in the free world. He had found it increasingly difficult to do his teaching and research at a technical university in Prague under the watchful eyes and ears of the Communist regime. His wife Ruth and he decided to leave with their two very young children, without telling anybody about their rather complicated plan. Crossing the Iron Curtain legally was not an option. The Communist regime also made it difficult for their citizens to visit neighboring Communist countries. It was however, possible to join a group and go on a joint vacation tour. It made surveillance by the regime easier. Arnošt, his wife and two young children joined a dozen fellow tourists in their own cars, on a trip to

Warnemünde, a port on the East German coast of the Baltic Sea: a coveted destination for Czechs who lived in a landlocked country.

The plan of escape was simple but risky. A modern East German ferry crossed the Baltic to Gedser in Denmark. Citizens from Communist countries were permitted to breathe the fresh sea breezes and imagine a liberated existence. They were not permitted to disembark in Denmark. They had to stay on board and return to Warnemünde a few hours later. While the ferry was docked at the Danish pier Arnošt and Ruth positioned themselves near the railing. When they noted that officials were not watching them, they gave each other a signal, each taking one child in their arm and jumped overboard. The ferry being in Danish territorial waters, the East German ship officials could only yell and not shoot. Danish police rescued Arnošt and his family. They asked for and ultimately were granted asylum in England.

Arnošt and Ruth had planned their escape for quite some time. They could inform nobody, not even Susi. The Communist regime was bound to go after anybody whom they could implicate in the escape. Just a few days before the planned auto trip to the Baltic, Arnošt picks up his phone and a totally unexpected voice greets him. Obviously, somebody must be impersonating his cousin with whom he had not been in touch for 22 years. It scared the hell out of him. Should he give up the attempt to escape? There were fortunately no other signs of a suspicious nature, and so they went ahead with their plan.

Three years after Arnošt told me the story of his escape, I took my family on a trip to Europe to show them the places where I had spent my youth. We started in Denmark. The easiest way to get to Berlin in our rented car was by ferry to Warnemünde, get a short-term East German transit visa and drive on designated highways to West Berlin. It was not until we had boarded a surprisingly modern East German ferry at the Danish port of Gedser that I was reminded of Arnošt's escape story. We had been served an excellent dinner, marveled at the elegance of the dining room facilities and the polite treatment we received from the staff. I shuddered to think how completely different Arnošt's mood must have been when he took the ferry on his way to freedom.

On my 1963 encounter with Arnošt and Ruth in London, I spent an entire afternoon learning how they survived Auschwitz, ultimately re-emerging into the troubled post-war world. On May 15, 1942, the Nazi occupiers sent Arnošt, his sister Susi, his younger brother and his parents by rail to Terezín. After a relatively short stay in what the Germans considered their model Jewish ghetto the entire family was transported to Auschwitz. As the family approached the post where an SS officer separated prisoners who were sent to work camps from those destined for the gas chamber, Arnošt was shocked to recognize the doctor who told the SS officer who was fit to work and who was not. It was his doctor from Prague. Arnošt had the presence of mind to give no hint that he had ever seen him before. After the doctor had directed him into the slave labor line, he angrily ordered Arnošt to get rid of his glasses. "You don't need them here." Arnošt quickly realized that this advice saved his life because the Nazis considered people with glasses unfit to work in labor camps. His sister Susi was also sent to a labor camp where she met and befriended Ruth whom she introduced to Arnošt when they were liberated. Soon thereafter, they got married. The rest of the family perished in the gas chamber.

When liberated, Arnošt started on the track back to Prague. Some of his fellow liberated camp mates fell by the wayside, not being able to control their appetite after years of near starvation. Their stomachs simply could not digest the sudden surge of food. Seeing his fellow survivors succumb in this fashion deeply affected him. Even more shocking was his experience as he reached the family's summer home in Roztoky, not far from Prague. When the family was forced to leave in 1942, Arnošt's father had asked their neighbor to stay in it until their hoped return. When Arnošt and his sister appeared and rang the bell, the neighbor was in a state of shock. Instead of showing delight at their return, the neighbor was deeply upset. He did not intend to give up Reiser's family summer home. Arnošt left, disgusted. There was to be no return to a pre-Nazi normal existence.

***

After my nine days in Prague, I ventured to less familiar territory: Adventure was to take the place of nostalgia. In the light of my subsequent travels, I felt that it was strange that in my youth I had not ventured beyond Berlin, Western Bohemia, Bavaria, the Austrian Tyrol and a brief stop in Switzerland. I had never even visited Moravia and Slovakia, two of the four provinces that constituted the Czechoslovak Republic. This time I planned to expand my Central European horizon and explore Vienna and the Balkans, a region where key events mentioned in my European Diplomacy course had taken place.

The first stop was Brno (Brűnn), the provincial capital of Moravia. I stopped for two days to explore ancient well-preserved churches, museums with frightful dungeons, torture equipment dating back to earlier centuries with perhaps ironic relevance to more recent times. Next stop: Bratislava, capital of Slovakia, two hours from Brno. The train left exactly on time but was jammed. I had to squeeze into the corridor, let a fellow passenger use my large suitcase as her seat and sway from side to side as the train sped around curves, slowed and then sped up as it zipped by local stops. Just when I was tempted to reclaim the seat on my own suitcase, we reached our destination.

My modern hotel in Bratislava was only a block from the Danube that flowed in a narrowed channel, racing by at a remarkable speed. Tugboats pushing barges upriver, belching black smoke, barely moved. Meanwhile boats moving in the opposite direction, raced by with nary any effort, judging by their clean smoke stacks. The Danube entranced me. I had read about it and imagined it while listening to Strauss' Waltzes. The stories told by Viennese refugees who had fled from Hitler after the March 1938 Anschluss and had stopped by at our apartment in Prague took on a new meaning. How they managed to survive jumping into the frigid Danube and swim to freedom on the Czechoslovak shore!

On my second day, I went on a two-hour boat ride on the Danube. That was a mistake: the Danube of my fantasy evaporated. Suddenly the fabled blue Danube turned into a gushing muddy gray-brown stream. When we reached dense reeds where the river widens and where I detected a lonely stork, the boat turned around. On the way back I admired the panorama of Bratislava, a well-preserved city topped by a fortress burned in 1811, now in the process of restoration, ultimately to be open to the public.

I spent almost a week exploring the surprisingly well-preserved older part of Bratislava. Fruit and vegetable markets gave the place life and color. Museums surprised me by their collections of modern art. A first class orchestra played a top-notch open-air concert within a few feet of my hotel.

The local paper covered Raul Castro's extensive visit to Czechoslovakia. He bragged that the Cuban revolution would spread to the rest of Latin America. The objective of his visit, only a year and a half after his brother's seizure of power, was to obtain modern weapons to guard against the expected Bay of Pigs invasion nine months later.

While I had some problems communicating in Slovak, I was surprised to find my Czech was good enough for me understand almost everything people said. Reading was even less of a problem since Slovak is closely related to Czech.

My favorable impression of Slovakia was somewhat marred by the memory of Slovakia's role in World War II, when the Catholic Priest Hlinka's Party assumed control of a Hitler-sponsored satellite state and dutifully implemented Fascist policies. Even though Hlinka had died in 1938, he had laid the foundation for close wartime cooperation between Nazi Germany and Hitler's most obedient satellite in Eastern Europe. After the Communists seized control in Czechoslovakia, Slovak Communists played a leading role not only in Bratislava, but also in Prague. The charm of the city did not entirely erase this troubling past from my memory.

Vienna is about 40 miles up the Danube from Bratislava. I discovered that the one daily train connecting the two cities was not running for "technical reasons". The bridge crossing the river was under repair. This meant I had to backtrack to Břeclav, halfway to Brno, again standing in the corridor all the way. In Břeclav, I had to wait for an international train to Vienna. The journey that should have taken less than an hour lasted almost six hours. This was a good lesson about the impact of the "iron curtain".

The moment I arrived in my hotel in Vienna, I sat down to write Audrey the longest letter of my journey. I warned her it would be trite because everything I was going to write had been said before and "yet I have to say it because I haven't said it before. First, it feels so good to be back from behind the iron curtain; second, there may be a hell of a lot of things wrong with our system, but in spite of all its flaws it is superior because of one vital fact: we don't live in a police state." I recited a number of incidents describing how ordinary people I met on trains and elsewhere had dealt with the police, customs and other officials. On the train entering

Czechoslovakia from Germany a lady sitting next to me, fussed a great deal with her young son, pointing to the Czechoslovak flags and asked him, " Jirko, aren't they pretty"? Meanwhile the police officials thoroughly questioned her and other passengers carrying Czech passports. When the officials had departed and the train started moving, she asked," have all the frontier guards been through?" Then she rolled up Jirko's sleeves and there appeared one watch on each arm, not children's watch either. Everybody in the train compartment laughed, she pocketed the watches. My comment to Audrey: "Even the most elaborate police system can only be skin deep if it is imposed on a reluctant population."

***

In my youth Vienna had been a frequent topic of conversation. My father had considered Vienna as the place to settle, upon graduating from his gymnasium. He wanted to leave Plzeň for a more cosmopolitan environment. He never told me why Vienna failed to entice him sufficiently. After all Vienna was the home of Sigmund Freud. His interpretation of dreams and discussion of sex had fascinated me, perhaps because I noticed my father's discomfort when I asked him why sex was so important in Freud's writings. My father's interest in studying philosophy led him to the University of Munich instead.

A few years later, when I studied history in high school, Vienna, the capital of the Habsburg Empire, symbolized imperial Austrian oppression of Czechs and other people of Slavic nationality. It was not until the fall and dissolution of the Austro-Hungarian Empire in 1918 that modern Czech nationalists led by Thomas Masaryk managed to resurrect the 17th century kingdom of Bohemia and Moravia as the Czechoslovak Republic.

. Vienna had also been the city where Adolf Hitler had failed in his efforts to become an artist-painter. Vienna had Schönerer as mayor in the late 19th century, perhaps the most vituperative anti-Semitic demagogue. His speeches had influenced young Adolf. In the 1930's Austria's Chancellors Dollfuss and Schuschnigg had however impressed me as among the few leaders taking a firm stand against Hitler's attempts to control Europe. None of these political and historical considerations convinced my parents to visit a city so prominent and close to Prague. Instead we vacationed in the Tyrolean Alps, ate Viennese Sachertorten, listened to Strauss

Waltzes. Vienna remained a destination not chosen. I intended to correct that omission.

I stayed at the *Weisser Hahn* [White Cock], a small pleasant and cheap hotel, a fifteen-minute walk from the city center. Near the hotel, I saw a tablet commemorating the furthest reach of the Ottoman Turkish advance to the center of Europe in the 17th century. I looked around and tried to take a mental picture of this important historical spot. I did not succeed because the street had nothing that distinguished it from all the other streets in the neighborhood. After the Turks were stopped, they retreated to Hungary and a couple of centuries later to the lower Balkans. A few blocks brought me to the Ringstrasse, the avenue that circles the inner city. The Ringstrasse has monumental structures housing museums, government offices that reflected the splendor and wealth of the Habsburg Empire. I could not hide my resentment when I realized that it was here in Vienna that the resources and assets drained from the provinces were trophies to be enjoyed by the Habsburgs, the rulers of the Austro-Hungarian Empire.

Next, I explored the city's oldest and most impressive center. The St. Stefan Cathedral rises to its full grandeur from the tightly knit surrounding old houses encircling it. Bombed during the War, its famous bell had to be put back on one of the twin towers accessible by elevator. I was not there at the right time: I had missed the hours when the elevator lifted visitors to the top. There was an alternative: A tour of the Crypt. Visitors entered through a narrow passage way where one could admire the sturdy foundations that supported the huge ancient cathedral. Then behind enclosures there were thousands of bones of long departed Viennese inhabitants. Large areas were set aside for the victims of various medieval plagues. I was impressed by these huge storage facilities for the departed. That is a side of the Cathedral that I had not known existed. They buried saints, kings and emperors, but ordinary folks?

I spent a whole week in Vienna, there was so much to explore and admire! In spite of my anti-Habsburg frame of mind, I toured the monarch's residence and government offices, as well as the famous horse riding school in the center of the city. Far more interesting was Schönbrunn, the huge castle and park, some distance away in a royal suburb. Exploring this well-maintained castle gave meaning to that part of my lectures on early 19th century

Diplomacy that dealt with the Congress of Vienna. No wonder the Russian, British, Prussian royal guests and their ministerial underlings were perfectly willing to take their time redrawing the map of Europe, developing plans for maintaining the new world order they had created. After all, the place was perfectly suited to have lots of entertainment. The large halls were perfect for dances and performances. Why go home?

I had no foreboding that less than a year after my visit an entirely different diplomatic encounter would take place at Schönbrunn: Newly elected President Kennedy had a tète à tète there with Khrushchev. JFK had to explain away our failure of the April '61 Bay of Pigs invasion and Khrushchev could not help gloating and planning to develop a missile base in Cuba. A century and a half had transformed Schönbrunn: it had lost its ability to charm powerful rulers into constructive and happy peacemakers. The Soviet War Memorial, commemorating Austria's liberation by Soviet forces in 1945, was a symbol of modern Russia's reach to the heart of Europe. The monument was a standard example of Soviet artistry, given more meaning by the fact that Austria was a unique example of the withdrawal of Soviet occupation forces as a result of post-war East-West diplomatic negotiations.

There was a lighter side to my stay in Vienna. In the Kűnstlerhaus art gallery I was amazed by the erotic aspect of Indian art. Many of the paintings and sculptures might not have passed muster in the U.S. until a decade later. In Vienna, however Freud's home was just a few blocks away, so it was O.K. I ended my stay by having dinner at a wine-tasting restaurant in the Grinzing suburb. I resolved to bring along my family on my next visit. Vienna was worth re-visiting!

***

On to Yugoslavia. This is where the plot to assassinate Austria's Archduke was implemented, the fuse that ignited World War I. The only successful resistance movement to German domination in World War II developed in Yugoslavia's mountains. Most importantly, Tito who had led this wartime movement was the only Communist who got away with talking back to Joe Stalin, thereby managing to keep Joe out of Yugoslavia's internal affairs. He outlived Stalin several decades. It would take me two weeks to touch all parts of Tito's land with one crucial omission: Bosnia-Herzegovina.

Ljubljana, the capital of Slovenia in the north has a name that Austrians would have difficulty pronouncing, but otherwise resembles its northern neighbor in architecture, the look of its inhabitants and its over-all orderliness. Except for the Slavic language I felt I was still in Austria.

In Zagreb, the capital of Croatia, I began to sense a difference: I entered the Balkans. I was fortunate to meet local intellectuals at a dinner given by Olga Zhivkovitch, the American consul, who happened to have been a colleague of mine at the State Department. She had a Czech background that had helped cement our social relations. I had a lively and very interesting discussion with many of Olga's Yugoslav guests and was careful to avoid criticizing the Tito regime. It was her cook however who left a lasting impression. She asked me how I wanted my coffee, weak or strong. When I answered that I did not care, she insisted and I said, "O.K., make it strong". Olga gave me a certain look to warn me. I drank the cook's coffee specially brewed for me.

On my way home to the hotel I witnessed a local brawl that had spilled over from a bar onto the street. Within minutes police cars arrived with sirens piercing the otherwise peaceful main square. After the inebriated troublemakers were led off by the police, I dared to continue, happy that the police watched and protected me. I returned to my modern eight-story hotel and went to bed after midnight. I thought that I would fall asleep instantly after the busy activities of that day. By the time the clock struck two, I remembered the coffee episode. The cook's smile appeared in my mind. I tried to remember all the coffee stories people had told me, especially the one that the further south one travels in the Balkans, the darker and stronger the coffee. Then, suddenly I heard a cock crow. And then, another one. I realized the modern hotel was planted in the midst of a traditional farm with plenty of chickens. The chicken knew a new day was dawning. As I was thinking about going to the window and yelling to the cocks to shut up and let me sleep, I finally had my wish fulfilled and entered a peaceful landscape. Of course, my carefully planned exploration of Zagreb the next day started very late at noon.

The train ride from Zagreb to Belgrade takes five hours. While spoken Croatian and Serbian are very similar Slavic languages, one is written in our Roman script, the other in Cyrillic that resembles Russian. Furthermore, Croats are Roman Catholics and Serbs Orthodox Christians, a split that had occurred nearly a thousand years ago. I shared the train compartment with five other passengers who quickly realized that I was a foreigner. They were surprised that I understood most of what they were saying since my Czech and German facilitated the conversation. One passenger dominated the conversation. When I asked her what her occupation was, she proudly responded that she was a miner. She did not look to me like the kind of person who spends her time in a dark tunnel running a machine that grinds its way through rocks. Her face and hands were far too well maintained to show the effects of life spent in hell underground. After further questioning, it became clear that she was managing a mine operation and only occasionally explored the mine in person. It was clear that she wanted to let me know that in Tito land all people were equal and that managers were no different from ordinary workers. O.K., I got the point. Next, I asked her whether she was a Serb or a Croat. Raising her voice, "I am a Yugoslav!" She looked each fellow passenger in the eye and asked rhetorically, "Are we not all Yugoslavs and not Slovenes, Croats and Serbs?" Everybody nodded vigorously. I got that point also: national differences were dead in Tito land. At least, they were supposed to be forgotten.

For some reason, which I have difficulty remembering, Belgrade the modernized capital impressed me as the least interesting Yugoslav city. There was a nice large park overlooking the merger of the Sava River and the Danube, but the scene was overshadowed by massive ugly looking housing developments. The past that preoccupies modern Serbia is located in almost every Serb's brain but not in Belgrade's architecture. Walking at the edge of a large dark park in the evening, I was captivated by the music that originated in a restaurant nearby: The sound was unmistakably oriental, very different from Vienna's Waltzes or even Budapest's Gipsy bands. I knew I was moving closer to leftover legacies of the retreating Turks.

***

I finally realized a childhood dream: I boarded the Orient Express to make the eight-hour journey from Belgrade to Skopje, the capital of Macedonia. The famous, mysterious, adventurous train did not measure up to my expectations. The coaches were in a somewhat run-down condition. The passengers wore no fancy clothes. But the view from the window more than compensated for all that. There were impressive valleys and mountains, peasants dressed in traditional local costumes as we crossed famous battle areas in what later became Kosovo. Some of the passengers pointed out certain areas where they had spent the War fighting the Germans. In the dining car, I sat with a couple of German tourists who whispered and pointed furtively at locations where they had fought Tito's Communists. Imagining what went on in the minds of the Serbs in my train compartment and the Germans in the dining car as we passed areas where they had tried to kill each other a decade and a half ago, emphasized the Orient Express role connecting enormously diverse people and cultures. Originally intended to link Western Europe and the Ottoman Turkish Empire, it aroused enough curiosity to provide a romantic setting for vanishing criminals and murderers.

Skopje, the capital of Macedonia, was the southernmost point of my trip. Even though I spent less than 24 hours there, the place left me with an indelible impression: So close to ancient Greece and yet it made me feel very far away from the modern Europe where I had grown up. After getting settled in a hotel appropriately named Macedonia, I explored the neighborhood. The city was surrounded by mountains. I followed the signs to a restaurant on top of one of the nearby hills. It was to open after 8 P.M. Since it was only 5:30, I turned around, explored the town below. Climbing back up to the restaurant when it was getting darker and the lights beckoned at the top of the hill I found a table and ordered something on the menu that I did not have the remotest idea what it was. It turned out to be spicy and tasted very good. It had no unpleasant after effects. I relaxed, listened to the unfamiliar music and sought to imagine what was hidden behind the darkness of the surrounding mountains. At this point, a well dressed man in his thirties or forties asked whether he could join me. He was accompanied by a younger woman who did not appear to be his wife. I do not recall what language we used to engage in a very interesting conversation. It probably was a mixture of German, English, Czech-Serbian. The only language the girl used was poke and touch under the table. That did not make me particularly comfortable because it interfered with my conversation with her partner. It turned out that the guy was a well informed intellectual. He was very interested in what I could tell him about America. At some point in our conversation, I pointed at the darkness surrounding the bright lights of the city below and remarked how romantic it was for me to be here, so far from any place that I know. That remark upset him. Don't you know where you are? This is the center of civilization!! This is where Alexander the Great came from!! Here you are at the center of things and where you live is …he did not finish the sentence. This conversation made a deep impression, so deep that I forgot all the poke–and-touch operations under the table. As we walked down the hill, back to the city, my expert on the center of civilization taught me how to recognize the ethnicity of the people we encountered. Those with the extremely colorful outfits were Gypsies. Those with dark hats were Albanians, the others were Macedonians, or maybe the other way around. As I entered my hotel, I saw a big picture of Tito. I finally realized that the photos depicting Tito had changed significantly on my way from Slovenia in the north to Macedonia in the south: His skin had gotten darker, his hair had turned from nearly blond to black.

I had planned to take a plane from Macedonia to the Bay of Kotor, the southern- most section along Yugoslavia's Adriatic coast. Travel agents in Zagreb and Belgrade could not or would not let me buy a ticket or reserve a seat. It had to be done in Skopje, I was told. The morning after my adventure on the hill at the center of civilization, I ventured forth to the airline office in the city's center. I inquired at what time there would be an available flight to the Bay of Kotor. "There is a flight that will take off in half an hour and the bus to the airport is standing out here in front". There will not be another flight until three days later. "I have to get my bag from the hotel." I was told to hurry, they'll wait for me. I raced two blocks to the hotel, packed, checked out, dragged my bag back to the airline office, climbed into the bus. Off we went. The propellers rotated as we took our seats on the plane. Lift- off from the grass-covered runway took place not more than 40 minutes after my downtown airline office visit. Some things were quite efficient in Tito Land.

Barely settled in my window seat I became mesmerized by the mountainous landscape below our half-empty plane. Rocks, a few meadows, deep valleys: I finally understood why the province under our wings was called Montenegro, Black Mountain. An attractive flight attendant engaged me in a conversation, wanting to hear stories about America. She even invited me to the back of the plane. Reluctantly I stopped admiring the impressive mountain ranges. I suspected she was working for Tito's intelligence services, or maybe she was just flirting with an American. In any case, I was very careful not to fall into any trap. The flight soon came to an end on another grass-covered landing strip. What a difference from Skopje. The blue waters of the Bay of Kotor and the Adriatic were bordered by semi-tropical vegetation, a dramatic change from the mountains of Macedonia and Montenegro.

***

The plane had brought me to Tivat, the southernmost Yugoslav port on the Adriatic. Why Tivat? Getting so close to the forbidden and mysterious country of Albania intrigued me. However, there appeared to be little contact between Yugoslavia and Albania that I could detect. Political antagonisms trumped geographical proximity.

The bus to Hercegnovi introduced me to the Bay of Kotor, a semi-tropical paradise. Until then I had known only beaches on the North Atlantic and the North Sea. The southern part of the Adriatic opened the door to an entirely different world. The bus went on a small ferry that crossed the Bay. The water was green and dark blue. Except for what appeared to be a naval base, the coastline had few modern settlements. Ancient villages climbed up from the coast. I saw my first bougainvillea with its brilliant purple colored flowers and branches. There were also the leaves and flowers of many other plants that I had not seen before. After a two hour ride, the bus unloaded me at the Hotel Boka, a small hotel in Hercegnovi, a town I never knew existed. I decided to stay there for a couple of days because of its idyllic location. From my room on the second floor I admired a seascape with the outer edge of the Bay of Kotor in the distance. A large island, completely dark at night, separated the bay from the open Adriatic. Ships passed by occasionally. Waves hit the strand of the hotel. Directly below my window there was a restaurant set among low overhanging trees, where I had my breakfast and midday dinner. In the evening music and dancing under the stars lasted well into the night. The orchestra below played Italian music from across the Adriatic. I missed Audrey and resolved to show this idyllic part of Yugoslavia to her and my kids.

I had received no letters from Audrey for several days. Hercegnovi had not been on my itinerary. Dubrovnik, my next *Poste-Restante* address, is where I expected to pick up mail from home. Getting to Dubrovnik involved a two-hour bus ride. Assuming such a ride was no big deal, I decided to take the morning bus, explore Dubrovnik and return that evening. The bus ride started normally. I had a window seat, admired the seascapes and listened to the popular music that the driver had turned on as we started. The bus began to climb the curvy road hugging the mountain at the very edge of the sea. Some curves were so sharp that the bus driver had to maneuver his big vehicle back and forth to get around the rocky bulge protruding from the mountainside. To better concentrate, he turned the music off. He took a huge towel from the side of his seat and wiped off the sweat from his hands. The driver's intense concentration comforted me, but looking from my window at cliffs that dropped down several hundred feet to the sea where waves hit them with brutal force, scared the hell out of me. It seemed like an eternity before we reached Dubrovnik.

At the Post Office, Audrey's letter had not yet arrived. The day's outing was however not in vain: I spent it exploring Dubrovnik, a historic treasure of an earlier maritime trading age. I climbed the stairs to the top of a stone wall circling Dubrovnik that was built centuries ago to protect the harbor from invaders. There were spectacular views from those ramparts. Nearby were charming old stone structures. Ships and the sea were visible a little further away. Unfortunately, these ancient ramparts could not protect Dubrovnik, a part of Croatia, from modern guns used by Serbian forces three decades later. My return trip to Hercegnovi was easier to manage than the one in the morning. I chose a seat on the side facing the mountain so that I did not have to look down at the churning sea below us.

After relaxing a few days in Hercegnovi, my semi-tropical paradise interrupted only by a strong thunderstorm that did havoc with lights and other electric conveniences, I started my journey back north. The bus had no room left, so I shared a taxi with a Yugoslav tourist on my second trip to Dubrovnik. The taxi ride was far less dramatic than my ride on the bus, since I was closer to the ground and did not have to stare down the cliffs to the sea from an elevated bus seat. After spending the night at a modern hotel in Dubrovnik, I boarded a ferry early next morning that took me on a twenty-four hour voyage on the Adriatic Sea to Rijeka, my last stop in Yugoslavia.

I traveled first class and had a cabin. Since it was August, not excessively hot, and few clouds on the horizon, I tried to make myself comfortable on the open deck. I quickly realized that first class did not entitle me to a deckchair; it just identified me as a foreigner who had to be watched. Tired of leaning on the railing, I noticed that experienced local travelers located partially tarp-covered lifeboats as a useful flat area on which to relax and enjoy the sea breeze. I selected one not far from my cabin and made myself comfortable. The spot was not very far from the bridge where the captain stood steering the ship. I noticed the captain spotting my position but apparently not objecting to me making myself comfortable on the lifeboat. I quickly learned that on that ship once a particular location was physically occupied by a passenger, the spot belonged to that particular passenger. There was little give and take.

The other end of "my" lifeboat was occupied by a young woman who quickly identified herself as a secretary from Zagreb. We conversed in my usual Czech version of Croatian which she had no problem understanding. I had planned to spend that day catching up with my reading, not realizing that traveling along the Yugoslav coast would make this impossible. We had barely left Dubrovnik when scenic islands appeared in view. Some we just passed. We stopped at Korčula and Hvar where passengers disembarked or boarded our ship. At Hvar there was a big sign advertising its warm winter, promising money back if there was any January snow. The first lunch setting was announced. Somebody informed me that it was for foreign tourists: my turn to eat. The secretary from Zagreb stayed behind, protecting my location. I do not recall what I was served, but do recall it was not cheap. When I returned, the secretary had her turn at the ship's restaurant. In mid-afternoon, the boat stopped in Split, long enough to enable me to go on a twenty minute walk to visit the entrance to the cave at the ruins of Roman Emperor Diocletian's palace. Back on board ship, my lifeboat neighbor, the Zagreb secretary, suggested I skip the first call for dinner and eat with her and other Yugoslavs because the food is better and half the price they charge foreigners. That turned out to be excellent advice. They cheat foreigners, she remarked.

She sort of hinted she would not mind sharing my cabin since she will have to sleep in the open lifeboat. I informed her that I was a married person and that an older guy occupied the bed below mine in my cabin. Since he was a Yugoslav and acted as an important person, he was probably a Party functionary. The first argument did not seem to impress her, but the second convinced her. The aggressive nature of this secretary amazed me. The moment we got off the boat next morning in Rijeka (formerly known as Fiume), she raced into the arms of somebody, perhaps her latest boyfriend.

Rijeka, a port claimed by Italy, struck me as a dirty industrial city, not worth exploring. I took a train to Trieste, leaving Yugoslavia and Eastern Europe. My two weeks in Tito's land had made quite an impression. I had known that Yugoslavia was very diverse, but the reality of the cultural differences between the Slovenes in the north, the Macedonians in the south, the Montenegrins and Albanians in the southwestern mountains amazed me. It was obvious that Tito had done an incredible job of keeping this hodgepodge of Slavs together. I was therefore not particularly surprised that shortly after his death Titoland followed him to the grave.

***

Crossing the Italian border surprised me. I had expected a friendly welcome on my return to the West. Italian customs officials corrected that expectation. They were the least friendly I had encountered on the entire trip. I suspect that they operate on the assumption that travelers from Eastern Europe are smugglers bringing undeclared illegal items to Italy.

Italy was on my two months tour of Central and Eastern Europe because it was on the direct path between Yugoslavia's Adriatic coast and Munich, where I would complete circling Eastern Europe. I had grown up with many negative feelings about a country where fascism originated a decade before Hitler's coming to power in Germany. Mussolini's attack and conquest of Ethiopia made Emperor Haile Selassie one of my early heroes. His appearance at the League of Nations attacking Mussolini made him the first ruler who spoke to the world as a victim of Fascist aggression.

Italy was also the home of the Papacy, which had ordered the burning at the stake of Jan Hus on July 6, 1415, a day commemorated in Prague in my youth. Jan Hus, a revered Czech hero criticized corruption in the medieval Roman Catholic Church a century before Martin Luther and the Germans expressed similar ideas.

I had however also some positive feelings about Italy. Our walls in Berlin were covered with pictures of Italian painters that my father had tried hard to get me to appreciate. Italian operas could often be heard on our radio. In my history class in Prague we were told a lot about Mazzini's national movement to unify Italy. Even the Mafia had a positive connotation in Czech history because Czech nationalists admired the Sicilians who had successfully challenged Habsburg rulers, the oppressors of Bohemia. The most positive memory was recent: Mussolini had brought his troops to the Brenner Pass in the Tyrolean Alps in 1934, thereby delaying Hitler's quest to annex Austria by four years.

My first stop in Italy was Trieste, a port that had provided Austria-Hungary access to international shipping on the open sea. It had figured in countless stories of American immigrants departing from pre-World War Eastern Europe. It had been contested by Italy and Yugoslavia after Yugoslavia achieved its independence. I expected to arrive on a battlefield with Croats, Slovenes and Italians spitting at each other, fighting in bar rooms. I encountered nothing of the sort. Quite the contrary: a single neighborhood had churches serving Roman Catholics, Christian Orthodox and Protestants. Restaurants served a wide range of ethnic tastes. In short, Trieste turned out to be a cosmopolitan tourist attraction.

After a 2½-hour train ride, I arrived in Venice. Everybody had told me that I had to stop there and admire the canals, the architecture and museums. I was reluctant to interrupt my research-centered venture and turn American tourist. O.K.: just for a couple of days. Surprise! Venice was special. As I got off the train, I was surrounded by dozens of guides, porters, helpers who tried to grab my suitcase and spirit me to hotel X, Y, Z preferably by gondola. They were collectively appalled when I asked which hotel was closest to the train station. The attacking army disintegrated and one lonely guy muttered to follow him. I probably chose the least attractive hotel.

By the time I had placed my baggage in my room, it was late in the afternoon. I decided to explore Venice before dinner. San Marco was my destination. Getting from point A to point B was quite tricky. Bridges crossed canals but rarely where I needed them to follow my arbitrarily determined trajectory. After a while, I discovered arrows on ancient building walls pointing in the direction of San Marco. That simplified my exploration. I managed to climb the dozen or so steps each elevated bridge requires to permit boats to pass underneath. It was fun to cross more and more bridges. Suddenly the narrow alleys widened, fancier store windows appeared, I passed through a gate-like structure onto a very wide square and the waning rays of the setting sun lit up the profusion of colors of the palace at the eastern edge of San Marco Square. I could not believe what I saw. It was like a picture out of a storybook. "Is this real?" I pondered. I stood there completely overcome. Gradually the sunlight diminished and reality set in. "How about dinner?" I looked at the menu of several of the outdoor restaurants on San Marco Square. Even after converting the numerous digits of Italian Lire's into U.S. Dollars and Cents, the dinner prices struck me as beyond my means. I gave up on San Marco and ended up in a little charming restaurant. It had not taken me more than two hours at most to fall in love with Venice, a real magical place.

Next day I took a ferry ride on the Grand Canal, visiting several museums. I toured the Biennale Exhibit of Modern Art, a World's Fair of Modern Art. Thirty countries had pavilions in which they exhibited what each country wanted to brag about. I did not care for the exhibits of the leading powers: the Soviet Union, Great Britain and the U.S. Smaller countries, both East and West, had far more interesting art to show. I was most impressed by the pavilions of Denmark, Spain, Belgium, Czechoslovakia, Poland, Israel and Venezuela. It struck me as ironic to view an avant-garde 20th century art exhibit in a city that had changed little for five or six centuries. My stop in Venice added art appreciation to my trip's agenda.

Before leaving Venice, as I walked around the huge San Marco Square, a picture came to mind showing my grandfather Willy and my grandmother standing in that square feeding pigeons. It had been standing on my mother's desk. It was taken probably in 1932 when I was 8 years old. It was the last real vacation trip my grandparents had taken. When I looked at that picture I had always thought my grandparents had visited a fairy tale city. Now I was there! I did not follow their example: I did not feed the pigeons.

A postcard Grandfather Willy had sent me from the same trip influenced me in choosing my next and last stop in Italy: Bolzano in the South Tyrol. It showed peasant women with their hair covered by colorful kerchiefs picking grapes from bushes overloaded with gigantic bundles of juicy looking berries. Merano was written in big letters at the bottom. For a reason that I cannot recall, this postcard had left an indelible impression in my memory. Merano was only a short distance by bus from Bolzano and it was my destination the second day. There were many fancy hotels, but I could not locate that vineyard on the postcard.

Disappointed and back in Bolzano, I took an ordinary looking street trolley which transformed itself a short distance from the center of the city into a [cable] car and shifted from a horizontal position to an angular 45 degrees. I was lucky not to sit at the bottom part of the car and therefore was spared the privilege of staring at the point where the car took off on its journey into the clouds. That point of departure became smaller and smaller and the prospect of the car disengaging its rail contact and hurtling back .... In spite of my fear of heights, I became increasingly impressed by the terraced vineyards on both sides of the slowly climbing car. The terraces were kept incredibly well maintained and the berries on the bushes seemed ready to be picked and processed. Near the top, I got off the trolley, had lunch with a view of terraced vineyards rising to the top of the mountain and tiny villages in the valleys below. Ever since that experience, wines from Northern Italy have been my favorite.

Back down in the city, I admired the sidewalks that were protected from rain and snow by solid curved overhanging arches, permitting one to admire shop window displays in any kind of weather. Those shopping areas protecting shoppers from mountain storms predate our shopping malls by several generations. Although I am a very reluctant shopper, I could not resist the temptation to enter one and carry home hand-made plates that we still use half a century later on special occasions. One block around the corner was a street market where all types of fruit, vegetables, meat and other farm products were sold. Everything looked exceptionally fresh and attractive. It was one of the most inviting markets I had ever seen.

I had expected to encounter signs of friction between the German-speaking South Tyroleans and those Italians who had settled in the Alto Adige only after Italy annexed the area following World War I. Because Hitler needed Mussolini's good will, the German speaking South Tyrol was the only German inhabited area outside the Reich that Hitler did not annex. After World War II, the old conflict resurfaced in attacks by German South Tyrolean extremists who interrupted power lines that carried electricity into Italian areas. While I was in the region, there was peace and no apparent signs of the conflict that I had read about.

I left Italy via the Brenner Pass. That strategic entrance to Western Austria had been constantly in the news before I left for the U.S. in 1938. Now I finally crossed the Brenner Mountain Pass myself. I looked out of the train window. How boring!

***

After spending a day in Innsbruck, admiring Tyrolean folk art in store windows and a museum, I rode seven hours in a train from Munich to Bonn. I happened to share a compartment with a German father, mother and their two daughters, 8 and 10 years old. The father identified himself as an employee working in the state tax department. Our conversation became interesting when in answer to their inquiry, "how come you speak such good German if you are an American?" I told them that I was born In Berlin and left when Hitler took over in 1933. I asked him how he spent the war years. He answered that he fought on the Eastern Front. His wife interjected, "You did not volunteer, you were forced to fight there". "Yes," he answered, "I had no choice". It became clear almost immediately that the two girls suddenly paid a great deal attention to their father's account of his wartime activities as if they had never heard this before. I quickly realized that my question had opened a can of worms in this German family. The father and mother were busy explaining more and more details of their earlier life to their kids and it was obvious that there were contradictions which bothered the innocent little girls. On a small scale, I witnessed the problems confronting most Germans who had to explain to the younger post-war generation what they were doing during the Nazi period and why. I must admit that I got some satisfaction seeing the father squirm, I also felt sorry for the problems this discussion in the train created in that family's life.

I stopped in Bonn, at that time the capital of the West German government. I was more interested in Beethoven's birthplace, only part of it open. I did however visit the Bundeshaus [Parliament], and interviewed officials in the headquarters of the Social Democratic and Christian Democratic parties. Bonn struck me as a very provincial town, hardly the capital of a rapidly growing economic and political power.

I spent only a couple of hours in nearby Köln, admired the famous cathedral and, more important, bought a bottle of *Kölnisch Wasser* [*Eau de Cologne]* for Audrey. The train ride from Köln to Paris took seven and a half hours. We passed through towns and areas familiar from both World Wars. As we approached the French frontier, the three French couples who shared my compartment showed obvious signs of nervousness. The French border officials barely glanced at my passport but asked their own citizens many questions. The couples lit and extinguished several cigarettes and hardly said a word. As the train started rolling again, the French passengers broke the silence and burst out laughing, greatly relieved they had crossed back to their homeland unscathed. They were happy to tell me what they had gotten away with. Each couple had bought washing machines, kitchen and other household equipment in Germany at a much lower price than they would have had to pay in France. Their stuff was carried in the baggage car. They avoided paying an import duty. They excitedly informed me that the European Common Market, eliminating all duties, was scheduled to go into operation a year or so later and they could not wait and instead implemented the Common Market on their own.

After a day in Paris, I met my mother who had spent her two months in Scandinavia and Great Britain attending conferences and doing research for her book. The flight back to New York took 14½ hours. It was high time to end my longest absence from Audrey, Ronald and Meredith.

Returning to Storrs did not end the trip. The information that I had gathered entered my lectures, my writings and, more important, helped confirm some and change other opinions about conditions in Czechoslovakia and Yugoslavia. I felt that I had a much better and more accurate understanding of the Europe that I had left 22 years earlier. I was asked to show slides that I had taken on my trip to groups in Storrs. I was asked even to be interviewed on WGBH in Boston because I had mentioned somewhere that I was struck by the fact that churches in Communist Czechoslovakia were much better attended than I had remembered them from before 1938. My family had to watch my television appearance at a friend's home because we did not yet have our own set.

Chapter 14
Exploring Africa

1963 turned out to be a very busy year. Before I could fully settle in our new house on Dunham Pond Road, I was already involved in making rather complicated arrangements for a trip late in the fall to West Africa. I had picked West Africa as a region where I could study the latest manifestations of the conflict between the West and Soviet Bloc countries, especially Czechoslovakia. French and British West African colonies had gained their independence in 1958 and 1960 and the Cold War had quickly enveloped the African continent. I was bored, watching the changes in Eastern Europe proceed at a glacial pace. Why not shift to a new/old exciting area? I was scheduled to take a sabbatical and took that opportunity to visit an area stretching from Casablanca in Morocco to Lagos, Nigeria. A research travel grant helped.

I learned quickly that newly independent countries are very proud of their just acquired rights to grant travel entry visas to inquisitive foreign scholars. Even my Harvard connected travel agent in Cambridge, MA, could not speed up the process. The embassies in Washington waited until the last week to fill up my passport with full pages of artistically designed verbiage permitting me to enter their sovereign territory for no more than x number of days.

As a teenager, I had been fascinated by Stanley's successful search for Livingston and the source of the Nile. That was East and Central Africa and the Congo. West Africa on the other hand was much closer and easier to reach. Or, was it? I quickly realized that almost all travel to Africa in the 60's had to be routed through the capital of the newly independent countries' ex-colonial rulers. To get to French West Africa I took a detour to Paris. I crossed the Atlantic flying on my first jet engine-driven plane. A strike in France delayed our plane by about an hour. The delay was made up by the fact that the airport was deserted and no officials stopped us from getting to the bus to take me to my hotel in the center of Paris.

***

From Paris to Casablanca was a short three-hour hop. The plane started its descent when we were flying over the green fields of Andalusia in Spain. So much color in November was striking.

Casablanca was not far from the Mediterranean coast, yet the atmosphere was remarkably different. My impression at the time, conveyed to Audrey in my daily report: "As you step out of the plane, the tropical plants charm you at first until you notice that not only flowers, but also insects and people thrive in this lush atmosphere. Perhaps the briefest description would be this: a mixture of the beauties of a botanical garden with the smell of a zoological garden in which a social work documentary film is shown. You are shocked by the squalor you pass on the way downtown to the luxurious restaurants, remnants of colonialism, the broad avenues, the tall buildings, the tropical parks and modern gas stations."

I found my way to the Hotel de Noailles, a relatively modern hotel, and was surprised that my room had a radiator. Answering my questioning look, the hotel clerk informed me that it does get cold in Morocco in January. I acquired a taste for couscous, the favored local meal. Scared of a chaotic maelstrom of humanity, I avoided entering the local souk, the traditional market place. Eventually my curiosity got the best of me and I dove into the mass of humanity that tried to locate their favorite fruit, bread, vegetable, jewelry, and other items that I could not imagine anybody possibly buying.

A few feet further back where shops selling locally made rugs. Why not buy one for our just completed Dunham Pond house? I made up my mind very quickly to venture forth and make a major purchase, a most unusual decision for my normally miserly attitude. Implementing the decision turned out to be quite an adventurous learning experience. Upon entering the relatively large building, stacked with rolled up rugs and a few that hung from the ceiling, a friendly person emerged from some dark recess, addressed me in Arabic, French and ultimately what he considered English, and offered me a chair. Tea arrived in a minute and only then, "what kind of rug are you interested in?" "Not too large and not too expensive", I responded. An assistant emerged carrying half a dozen rolled up rugs. They were spread out in front of me, while I was offered more tea. Each rug was colorful, made anywhere between Constantinople, Rabat, possible even Afghanistan. While the assistant stretched out individual pieces of art, the salesman carefully studied my facially expressed reaction. How else would he have known, even before I had made up my mind, that there was one particular colorful rug that had really appealed to me? The other rugs were quickly rolled up and replaced with one I did not like at all. My instant response: "No, no, that one over here, not that other new one!!" "More tea, he asked?" Now the fun began. "How much?" I asked. "How much do you want to pay for it?" If I had been properly prepared for oriental bargaining, I might have said $5. Instead, I started with $50. He responded with $150. We ended up with $100. He took care of packaging and mailing and it arrived at Dunham Pond when promised. I wrote out a personal check, which did not bounce. Half a century later, I still have that rug.

The next day I took a one-hour bus ride to Rabat, the capital. That is where the king has his palace. Again, what interested me most was the exciting life in the local souk. The sights, the smells, the rising voices overwhelm ones senses. It was dark by the time I rode back to Casablanca. As I looked out of the bus window, I was struck that there were no signs of life anywhere. On my trip in the morning, we had passed through many small towns. Apparently, there was little access to electric power in these villages. It occurred to me that when darkness descends in rural areas in the developing world, there is not much to do in the evening, except sleep and procreate, hence the population problem.

Many women in Morocco were covered from head to toe with a dark colored garment, the burka, with two narrow holes over the eyes, permitting the wearer to see other human beings on the sidewalk. I was impressed by this show of religiously dictated modesty. On my second or third day, I noticed a sound coming from one of the burka covered women standing at the corner not far from my hotel. When I passed the corner again sometime later, I thought I heard l'amour, l'amour. How clever! In Paris they exposed as much of their leg as possible, whereas here in Casablanca they exposed only their eyes. The object however, was the same. Once I had reached that profound conclusion, I became intrigued by the question, how to tell one prostitute from another. Was that burka-clad lady on the corner always the same one? I decided to avoid the corner and cross the street on the opposite side. Again I heard, l'amour, l'amour. As I wrote in my letter to Audrey, my curiosity was purely of the academic pedantic type.

In the three days that I spent in Morocco, I also visited American officials at the U.S. embassy to learn something about Moroccan politics, the condition of their economy and their foreign policy. The impression I gained was that if Morocco had problems due to the wide gap between the few who are well off and the vast majority of impoverished citizens, the neighboring North African countries of Algeria and Mauritania are much worse off. A couple of days later I was to find out that compared to the countries south of the Sahara, Morocco was doing quite well.

***

I left Casablanca on a slower propeller driven Air Maroc, which took six hours to fly along Africa's coastline to Senegal. That turned out to be one of the most boring airplane rides I have ever taken. The plane flew at an altitude low enough for me to see clearly the coastline that stretched interminably from Casablanca, over a patch of Mauritania and finally northern Senegal. The coast was marked by a white line created by cresting waves that separated the blue-grey Atlantic from the light brown sand of the Sahara. There were occasional villages and a few boats but I probably missed noticing most of them. There was nothing for hours. The pilot enlivened the flight once by warning us that he was going to shift his engines and not to get scared by the unusual sound. I was scared because I waited in vain for the announced shift and when I did not hear anything nor any further announcement, I thought the pilot was unable to accomplish his intended maneuver. The plane however continued on its steady course. Finally, as daylight faded, the sand of the Sahara was replaced by some vegetation. The pilot began our landing approach and we arrived at the Dakar airport.

Elegantly dressed French speaking Senegalese ladies at the airport tourist office arranged a reservation at the hotel Clarice, their fourth choice, the others were full. They assured me it had air conditioning. My travel bag got pushed into a taxi. The friendly driver left the bright lights at the airport terminal entrance, drove around a big circle and then stopped suddenly on the opposite side, where many Senegalese were congregated, barely discernible in the darkness. I was somewhat uncomfortable in this entirely different environment within sight of brightly lit airport entrance. The driver lowered his window and addressed a waiting crowd. He was speaking in Wolof. "What is this all about?" I wanted to know. "I got to fill up the taxi," he answered. I quickly began to realize that my taxi served as a miniature bus. As the taxi bounced on the poorly paved road to the city center, I could clearly hear the crunching noise made by the car body scratching the wheel housing. I had arrived in sub-Saharan Africa.

The hotel was comfortable and I turned on the air conditioning the first night because the heat and humidity in mid-November got to me. I informed Audrey in my letter that a huge cockroach traveled across the page I was writing. I was bothered in Dakar, as I had been in Casablanca, by the obvious huge gap in living standards between the few beneficiaries of past colonial rule and the vast majority of Senegalese. Modern restaurants and hotels were almost exclusively the domain of foreigners. Independence had been achieved. The promise of an improved living standard for most Senegalese remained to be fulfilled. After interviewing several Senegalese as well as U.S. embassy officials, I spent my time exploring the city and especially the cliff drive overlooking the Atlantic. Restaurants served French delicacies, such as tète de boeuf (head of an ox). I refused to eat the eye that stared at me when the waiter placed it in front of me. "Is that what I ordered"?

A significant experience in my stay in Dakar was a boat ride to the island of Gorée, which had served as the place of detention for African slaves captured in the interior until the early 19th century. We were shown the cave-like structures in which the slaves were kept until ready to be shipped to North America. The place was spooky. Hardly any explanations: The clammy darkness, the big rocks, the decrepit wooden structures, all spoke for themselves. Topping the slave holding area was an impressive-looking French-built fortress, a symbol of past colonial power. I did not see any Senegalese tourists at this reminder of African denigration. A corpulent big American tourist from Georgia took countless pictures. His happy countenance led me to speculate that his grandparents were probably slave owners and that he filled in some missing details that would have interested his ancestors. I was much more impressed by another encounter on Gorée: An African lady who was delighted to hear me speak English. She was a visitor from British Sierra Leone and obviously not comfortable in French speaking Guinea. We had quite a conversation and I was struck by her having more in common with a white American than a French speaking African from next- door Guinea.

I had planned to meet a Senegalese active in organized labor who had been part of a group of African political activists that had been invited to visit UCONN sometime earlier that year. When he stood me up at my hotel, I decided to seek him out at his place of employment in the railroad yard behind Dakar's main railroad station. Locating him turned out to be quite an adventure. I asked for him and everybody recognized his name immediately, pointing me away from the platform to the railroad tracks sneaking away in an easterly direction, where I eventually found him in a medium sized shack from where he directed the not that complicated operations of the railroad line. Fortunately, none of the locomotives, which slowly maneuvered in the area, came close enough to frighten or hit me. It was a very exciting experience to cross countless railroad tracks actually used by puffing steam engines. We had a long conversation about his job, Senegalese politics, dissatisfaction with President Leopold Senghor and many other interesting topics. In retrospect, I was glad that my diverting him from his job had not caused any train collisions.

November 22 was my last day in Dakar. I had my main meal at a comfortable French restaurant, looking at the international edition of the *Herald Tribune*, while enjoying my food. I could not help noticing my waiter talking to the bar tender while listening to a radio above the counter. They kept turning their heads in my direction. My waiter finally came to my table and asked whether I was an American, pointing at my *Herald Tribune*. "Of course", I answered in my best French. "Your President has been shot!" "Don't joke!" I responded, "African and Asian presidents and leaders get killed, not my American president!" He marched back to the bar, talked with the bartender. Both of them returned to my table and the bartender asked me whether my paper did not say that Kennedy was scheduled to go to Dallas, Texas. They were right, it did. They informed me what they had heard. The shock slowly sank in. They said they were sorry to have to give me this bad news.

When I left the restaurant, I felt lost. I could not confirm, nor share this horrible news. I tried to overhear the news on the radios that blared from the shacks that lined the street near my hotel, but could not make out what was said. I took comfort from the fact that in less than 24 hours I would be in Conakry, Guinea where I was scheduled to stay with people from Storrs. At the Dakar airport next morning, I happened to see an officer wearing an American air force uniform striding to a gate. I stopped him and asked him whether it was true that President Kennedy had been shot. "Yes, of course," he answered. "I pledged allegiance to President Lyndon B Johnson last night" and off he went to a U.S. air force base in Senegal I had not known existed.

***

I had a ticket on the national Guinean airline to fly on a modern Soviet-built turbojet from Dakar to Conakry. The flight took a little over an hour. The landscape changed from moderate vegetation to dense impenetrable green bushes and trees. Compared to Dakar, Conakry looked like a village. When we stepped out of the plane onto the tarmac, the humid air overpowered me.

Fortunately, at this critical moment in history, I had arranged to stay with friends from Storrs, the Spaulding's, who spent a year teaching English to Guineans as part of a U.S. government effort to gain influence in a Cold War contested country. I could hardly wait to find out what had happened in Dallas and America's reaction. While I got additional information they had gathered from short wave radio stations, there were few hard facts and a lot of speculation. Was Castro's Cuba involved or perhaps agents from the Soviet Union? Listening to all this in a country ruled by Sékou Touré, a friend of the Soviet Union, made us somewhat nervous.

On my first or second day in Conakry, I met Herdeck, the American Chargé d'Affairs, who represented the U.S. in Guinea in the absence of Ambassador Loeb a New York friend of Averill Harriman. The Chargé happened to be of Czech parentage and we shared many common interests and clicked immediately. He wanted to know what I knew about the Czech Communist regime from my research at the State Department a decade earlier. I pumped him for data on Guinean politics. He quickly found some way in which I could be of some use to him. He had been invited by the Guinean government to attend some trade union celebration centering on President Sékou Touré. The United States was of course in mourning and therefore he had to decline attending any social function. How would it be if I took his place? A visiting professor does not have to follow diplomatic etiquette, he informed me. I said sure, I would love to help him out. “What about my informal attire?” He suggested I put on a tie.

I quickly changed my outfit. The ambassador’s chauffeur driven limousine picked me up at the Spaulding’s. Heads turned, and I was off to meet the President. Officials stuck their heads into the car and addressed me, *Monsieur le professeur*. In no time, my head swelled. Fortunately, my UCONN students were far away on another continent. I was introduced to the President and he extended to me official condolences for the loss of my President. I responded, ”I will convey these generous expressions of sorrow to my superior, the Chargé d’Affairs”. Following these formalities, I was led to a large round table, set aside for Americans. Dancers and singers appeared on the stage entertaining the President and the rest of us for several hours. Many dances and songs had revolutionary themes. One song enthusiastically praised Patrice Lumumba, the Congolese left-leaning nationalist leader who blamed the U.S. for everything that went wrong in the Congo. It was received with greater enthusiasm by the audience than the lower key song that mourned the loss of President Kennedy.

The female dancers would turn around and show us their behinds, waving their flimsy skirts at us. This was not a sign of disrespect, I was told, quite the contrary. Dancing on the floor of the large well- decorated hall made this a special occasion for me, introducing me to Guinean folk art and music. Several of my table female mates were young attractive Peace Corps volunteers who were asked by emissaries of the President to dance with him. I could not help overhear their conversation upon their return to the table. They barely had managed to avoid being squeezed by the President where their respective lower body parts met. Fortunately, they managed to handle the potentially embarrassing situation diplomatically. I learned a lot that evening about the operation of the government. When I made my report to the Chargé d’Affairs the next morning, he was not at all surprised. “This is normal around here”, he informed me.

On the day of J.F.K.’s funeral, we all assembled on the lawn of the Ambassador’s official residence, a tropical paradise. The waves of the Atlantic were within earshot. We listened to the Voice of America’s short wave radio coverage of the funeral procession as it wound its way through Washington D.C. The sound of the horse drawn hearse, the somber voice of the reporter mentioning the somewhat cold temperature made our tropical environment even more incongruous. As I contemplated this, I kept wondering how Audrey, Ronald and Meredith were coping, as they watched the funeral across the Ocean in Storrs.

The Chargé d'Affairs shared with me the many worries created by the assassination. He did not know how to fly the U.S. flag at half-mast since the pole extending from the front of the embassy building was just long enough to cover the length of the Stars and Stripes. He had the flag removed entirely and placed mourning decorations on the door. His Guinean staff assumed the United States would have a 30-day mourning period during which the embassy personnel would fast. I forgot how he explained to his cook that he and the embassy employees would of course not eat their usual "fancy meal", but they would have to be properly nourished. He also noted that in all the extensive training he had received before assuming a responsible embassy position, he could not remember ever receiving instructions on how to deal with this kind of emergency. One of his assistants lent him a black tie and dark suit that fortunately fitted him.

The conversation quickly turned to the subject of the new President. The staff was quite worried about Lyndon B. Johnson. They were careful to keep their specific fears to themselves. Their main complaint was that Johnson had shown no interest in foreign policy and probably knew little and looked at the world from a southern Texas perspective. They hoped he would not look at Africa as he would at Mexico and Latin America. By contrast, J.F.K. had taken a personal interest concerning the impact of the Cold War on Guinea. Guinea occupied a strategic position as a potential base for Soviet planes from which Latin America could be reached, thereby significantly expanding Soviet influence in America's backyard. Not only did J.F.K. read the dispatches sent by the Chargé d'Affairs to the State Department, but he wrote comments, asked questions that the Embassy was honored to answer as expeditiously as possible. In the light of these discussions in Conakry, I was not all surprised that Lyndon B. Johnson was ill prepared to resolve our involvement in Viet Nam.

While JFK's assassination dominated my stay in Conakry, I did manage to seek answers to some of the questions that had brought me to Guinea in the first place. I wanted to find out the extent of Soviet influence in that part of West Africa, the reaction of leading Guineans to the Soviet charm offensive and America's response. Having met President Sékou Touré and watched the singers and dancers praise African revolutionary leaders who had fought the European colonial powers in order to gain their independence it was obvious that Guinea considered the Soviet Union a friend of newly liberated Africa.

I met an influential Guinean official who invited the American Chargé d'Affairs and me to his home for dinner. The Chargé told me that this was his first invitation to a Guinean's own home. We were both impressed by the importance our host attached to our presence. He had invited his very large extended family and his wife had prepared an interesting menu consisting almost entirely of local delicacies. The host's brother had spent some time attending Charles University in Prague and looked at the world from the perspective of an East European. Our host on the other hand, had visited America and did not agree with his brother's views. Another brother was "the judge" in Guinea. A relative was a priest and another close relative was charged with setting up a modern phone system in the country. We spent five hours until well after midnight discussing and arguing about nearly all possible problems confronting the world. I carried away the impression that there was a genuine admiration for the U.S. during JFK's presidency.

We gave more economic aid to Guinea than to all the other former French colonies in West Africa combined. In contrast, Soviet aid, while forthcoming, was inaptly organized. Walking along a countryside road on the outskirts of Conakry I came across a long line of farm vehicles lined up by the side of the road with markings identifying their Soviet origin. Their function, i.e. milk tank, grain storage, etc. were marked on the vehicles in English, suggesting that some Soviet bureaucrat either did not know, or care, that Guinea had been a French colony and French was the official language. Perhaps it was for that reason that this particular Soviet gift was stored on a side road for two years where I noticed the rust the vehicles had gathered in the tropical humid environment.

While it was encouraging to witness the competition between the U.S. and the U.S.S.R. to gain influence in this newly independent West African country, I realized that the common people's well-being had hardly improved. Signs of poverty were everywhere and very few signs of economic development. I was amazed to learn the single largest foreign aid group operating in Guinea was a Chinese contingent. The Chinese had also been instrumental in getting a North Vietnamese road construction crew to work on an incomplete highway connecting Conakry with the airport that had been left unfinished by the French.

My American hosts, the Spaulding's, took me to an Anglican Church on Sunday where we and a couple from the British Embassy were the only whites in the entire 70-member congregation. A Guinean, educated in England with a degree from Oxford, conducted the service in English. His assistants kept up a running translation into French and Susu. The congregation was self-sustaining and lacked funds to maintain the building. The roof had a hole. The windows were broken. I spent part of the service fascinated by the antics of a monkey who peeped at me from a tree branch outside the broken window. I realized that I had managed to visit the old Africa so vividly portrayed in the picture books that I had read to Ronald and Meredith before they were ready for school.

At the Spaulding's I became aware of another significant problem facing Guinea: Ethnic conflicts that challenge the somewhat artificial unity of an independent state stuck with colonially created boundaries. The Spaulding's modern house had two floors. The street level had columns supporting the rest of the house and an entrance to the stairway. An employee lived in a little attached room near the stairway entrance. He was the guardian protecting the inhabitants upstairs and kept the grounds clean. He also maintained the stairway. Most foreigners had similar houses protected by guardians. Upstairs, the Spaulding's had a housekeeper who worked mainly in the kitchen, served food and kept the living area clean. On one occasion, the housekeeper dropped a plate while removing dishes from the dining room table. It was no big deal: she had simply tried to carry too many dishes all at once. As Bess Spaulding helped her straighten out the tiny mess, the guardian who had heard the dish fall raced upstairs and unleashed a stormy tirade attacking the housekeeper's incompetence. How did she dare break a dish! He asked Bess to fire the housekeeper immediately. When Bess finally succeeded calming the guardian and convinced him to return to his post downstairs, I learned the cause of this noisy conflict.

The guardian was a Fulani who spoke a different language from the housekeeper's Susu. The Fulani had been trying to convince Bess all along that she should hire a Fulani; they were much more reliable and more competent than those inferior Susu. Dropping the dish proved his point, he told her. Bess told the guardian that he had better get along with the housekeeper, or else. The conflict between Susus and Fulanis went beyond language differences. Susus had lived for a long time a settled life in the coastal region of Guinea, while the Fulani's were nomadic herders who ranged over a vast area at the southern edge of the Sahara desert stretching from the Atlantic coast to northern Nigeria. More recently, the borders of the newly independent states hampered their nomadic life and forced them to settle more or less permanently in a particular community. This led to conflicts with populations who had occupied the coastal regions for generations. There were also religious differences. The Fulani were mostly Moslems, while the Susu were Christians or held on to traditional indigenous beliefs. The French effort to impose French culture and language on all of Africa under their control collapsed with the end of colonialism. This permitted many diverse cultural traditions to reassert themselves including competition among tribes for employment opportunities.

I found the two weeks spent in Guinea extremely worthwhile. I had met so many interesting people and learned a great deal of new information. Nevertheless, it was time to get to the next stop on my ambitious journey.

***

Air Mali was the airline connecting Conakry and Bamako. I had never heard anything about this airline. It flew a Russian Ilyushin 14 propeller-driven plane with a thirty-passenger capacity. My anxiety was greatly reduced when I realized the pilot was a Czech. The pilot ran the engine on the tarmac for several minutes to check for any possible malfunction. There would be no place for an emergency landing between the two capitals. I also wondered how he communicated with the Susu or Mali speaking airport radio operators who presumably spoke French and might not understand his Czech version of French, or possibly English. The plane speeded up on the Conakry runway accompanied by a fire engine, just in case…

The flight turned out be a short one and very smooth. The dense vegetation near the coast soon gave way to browner looking sparser trees and ultimately shrub covered hills as we approached Bamako. I was horrified to see many fires on the hills. I learned later that Mali farmers burn the dry shrubs to create fields for planting. That made little sense to me because there was no sign of rain in the near future; we were in the midst of the dry season. Burning the brush would only further the expansion of the encroaching Sahara desert. After the pilot made a perfect landing, the plane stopped at the end of the runway, a considerable distance from the terminal. The pilot ran the engines through all kinds of tests before continuing to the terminal and letting us disembark. I thanked the pilot in Czech for the safe trip and we exchanged pleasantries. To my question why he stopped at the outer edge of the Bamako airport, he answered that he wanted to make sure everything worked before turning off the engines. What would he have done if he had found a problem? He would have taken off and flown right back to Conakry because he had fellow Czechs there who would have made necessary repairs. That would have meant that I would have had to stay on the plane and flown back to Conakry? Sure, you would have gotten back here to Bamako a couple of hours later.

A passenger who had sat next to me on the plane turned out to be a fellow American. The inscription on his eye- glass container had given him away as hailing from Washington, D.C. He told me that he was trying to trace his forebears who originated in West Africa. In America, his complexion was typically African-American. In West Africa, on the other hand, he was too light colored to be confused with any local citizen. Upon arriving at the Bamako airport, he turned to me for help to locate a hotel and act as a translator with the French-speaking officials. African-Americans may have roots in West Africa, but they have become much more a part of America than some believed until very recently. My fellow passenger obviously felt like a complete stranger in Mali. When he encountered me on the street the next day, he greeted me enthusiastically as a fellow American.

Its location at the edge of the Sahara Desert, gave Bamako a character quite distinct from Conakry's lush tropical appearance.

While the Niger River winds its way through the city, its water does not make up for the otherwise extremely dry atmosphere. On the road approaching a bridge crossing the Niger, I noticed two women carrying big bundles on the top of their heads. Their breasts were uncovered and they were engaged in a lively conversation. Suddenly they noticed me. I was the obvious foreigner, who examined the bridge and stared at the Niger. They focused their eyes on me. When I returned their stare, they acted in unison and pulled the shawls that had been resting on their shoulders right over their breasts. Then they continued over the bridge, staring at me, laughing and talking animatedly. After a couple of minutes, again in unison, they pulled their shawl back over their shoulder, liberating their breasts to be admired by the local citizens. What a difference from those ladies in Casablanca, who had let me look only at their eyes!

I had an interesting conversation with a local labor leader whom I had met on his visit to UCONN when he was part of a group invited by the University's Institute of Labor Relations. What I learned was the obvious fact that Mali lacked the strategic importance of Guinea and appeared to be a lesser target in the Cold War. This impression was confirmed by the discussions I had with U.S. diplomatic officials.

I did not have the opportunity to shake the hand of Modibo Keita, the President of Mali. I did however see him pass by in a motorcade on a city street. It had been announced that he was returning from an important tour of the country. That was a euphemistic way of saying that he had found it necessary to assert the central government's control over restless tribes in the vast northern part of the Mali Republic. His return to the capital was accompanied with considerable noise and parading military units. Bamako residents were encouraged to watch the leader's triumphant return. I joined them. No time for his arrival was announced. At every street corner along the parade route, there was a drummer, who beat his instrument at an eerily steady rhythm. Gradually the rhythm got faster. I noticed that the drummer followed the pace set by the drummers at the intersections from where the parade approached. The drummers were communicating to us, who were waiting, "Modibo Keita is on his way, he will be here shortly" ..."Here he is!" The drums were now deafening and the crowd applauded enthusiastically. Primitive musical instruments can serve a modern ruler as a means of communicating with, and controlling, the crowd.

Among the few hotel guests, I encountered a relatively young woman, who in response to my inquiry as to what she was doing in this remote part of Africa, informed me that she was on her way to an even more remote town, Timbuktu. "Was it to prove that this place of mystery really existed?" I asked. She informed me that she was an Israeli citizen working for ORT (Organization for Rehabilitation and Training) that had a program to aid people in developing countries, such as Mali.

Going to Bamako's main post office to mail my letters to Audrey and the kids opened my eyes to the impact of improved mass communications in a shrinking globe on people who have not been able to break the shackles of the past. In the square in front of the post office there were individuals sitting on folding chairs who were handed letters by their fellow citizens. I soon realized what was going on: People picked up letters they had received from their sons, daughters and other relatives who were working in Europe or studying in the U.S. and had the letters read to them by professional readers because they were illiterate. Only a small percentage of the local population had had an opportunity to go to school. Watching the emotions visible in the people's faces as they listened to their relatives' letters brought tears to my eyes.

***

After staying five days in Bamako, I took another flight with Air Mali, operated by two Czech pilots. I was impressed that the small little country of my youth played such a significant role in post-independence African air travel, transporting me from Conakry via Bamako to Abidjan, skirting the Sahara. I landed in the capital of the Ivory Coast. Originally, I had planned to stop in Ouagadougou, Upper Volta. Probably the name of the capital attracted me. Upon further reflection, and difficulties with airplane schedules, I decided to skip Upper Volta, which years later in 1984, abandoned its French colonial name and called itself Burkina Faso, after the name of its people.

Like Senegal, the Republic of the Ivory Coast had kept much of its former French colonial cultural character after gaining its independence. The area of Abidjan in which my hotel was situated was modern and reminded me of Paris with its avenues and parks. I was amazed at first by the city's modern appearance. I soon realized that my hotel was situated in the quarter where French colonists and elite Ivoirians had settled to enjoy a tropical paradise. After passing an invisible barrier, one was back in real Africa. The superficial elegance of the city was in large part due to the personality of the Republic's President, Houphouet-Boigny, leader of the West African independence movement, who had thoroughly familiarized himself with French politics and its culture.

I stayed in Abidjan for only two days. The Nigerian Airways plane that I was scheduled to take to Accra, Ghana, my next stop, did not honor my ticket. It had no seat left. Luckily, my Czechs came to the rescue. Air Guinea had a seat and the very short hop proved to be uneventful.

***

Ghana interested me because in 1957 its Prime Minister Kwame Nkrumah had emerged as the first African leader to force a colonial power, Great Britain, to grant independence to his people. Britain's willingness to grant India and Pakistan their independence in 1947 had started the independence ball rolling, but Nkrumah's powerful kick pushed the ball over the line. He took full advantage of the Cold War, managing to use friendship with the Soviet Union as a means of wringing concessions from the West. The United States and Great Britain were however intent on preventing the establishment of a major Soviet outpost in this strategically located part of Africa.

In my letter to Audrey from Accra, I noted that Accra was the only place in Africa where the anti-American tone expressed in the papers and on the radio was sufficiently strident to make me feel uncomfortable. I also noted the inscription on the Nkrumah monument placed in a central square: *Seek ye first the political kingdom and all the other things will be added unto it*. That about sums it up, I added.

Accra was the first place since leaving New York, where people spoke English, and drove on the wrong side of the road. The Ambassador Hotel had a certain air of elegance. It was situated near a park in which animals in enclosures amused tourists. It reminded me of the city's not very distant colonial past. More than any other place that I had visited, Accra reflected Europe's conflicting legacies: The colonists had called it the Gold Coast. Kwame Nkrumah, the liberator of his people, saw himself as a nationalist dictator who admired strong leaders like Mussolini and Stalin. Large squares were prepared to serve as parade grounds. Nkrumah who "had sought the political kingdom" could stand on a platform and savor his people's adulation. His dictatorship did not last very long. In 1966, he was ousted in a coup, while on a trip to Beijing. In the 21st century, Ghana changed sufficiently to permit a peaceful transition of power, an act that led President Obama select Ghana for a visit highlighting it as a model for other African countries. It struck me as quite a positive sign of hope in contrast to the depressingly totalitarian environment on my visit half a century earlier. The one bright spot that I had visited in Accra was the University of Ghana, some distance from the city. It has a nicely designed modern campus with an excellent library.

After my short two-day stay, I took a short flight on Nigerian Airways from Accra to Lagos, the easternmost West African city on my trip. The pilot was a Pole who apparently had served in the exile Polish armed forces in London during World War II. The contrast with the Czech pilots who had flown me from Dakar to Ghana could not have been greater. The propellers and jet engine started before the doors were closed; the plane quickly went on to the runway and before I had even buckled up, the plane lifted off the ground and reached its cruising altitude in a matter of three or four minutes. The pilot entered the passenger cabin and talked to everybody. I asked him who was piloting the plane while he entertained us. "My buddy" he answered, "he is quite competent. We'll beat the schedule", he promised. "Why was he in such a hurry", I asked him. "It's more fun to spend the evening in Lagos than here on the plane", was his instant answer. I was relieved when we disembarked at the relatively small airport in Lagos.

Compared to Accra, Lagos was much more crowded. Here chaos reigned. Quite a contrast from Ghana's police controlled order. There were different challenges: a dozen porters fought for the privilege and tip to carry my suitcase. A battle ensued over which taxi would be privileged to take me to my hotel. I took a bus instead. As a result, I made the mistake of picking a hotel closer to the airport and across the bridge from the center of Lagos.

When I woke up the next morning and looked out the window, I saw an open market that seemed to attract a huge crowd. The noise and the odor stemming from carved up animals spiked on hooks and dripping blood, while exotic, was not particularly appealing. The hotel's location introduced me to the "real" Nigeria. In order to get from the hotel to the city I had to cross a bridge and watch helplessly as my taxi driver maneuvered his car into positions where head-on collisions were avoided with only inches to spare. I quickly realized this was normal driving routine in Lagos. While there were a few houses reflecting the comfort and taste of Nigeria's erstwhile British colonial rulers, most of the city consisted of ramshackle buildings housing masses of people that created a slum-like atmosphere. In my letter to Audrey, I described Lagos as "the world's worst hellhole I have seen".

Since I visited Nigeria barely three years after the British terminated their colonial control, I laid the blame for Nigeria's chaotic conditions on its former colonial masters. I felt that the British lacked the will or ability to help the indigenous population improve their status. They certainly did not prepare Africa's largest center of population for the modern age. Subsequent tribal wars between Ibos, Yoruba, Hausa and Fulani, as well as the corruption surrounding Nigeria's oil industry, confirmed my impression. I had met and taught some outstanding Nigerian students at UCONN and had looked forward getting acquainted with their country. What a disappointment!

On the way to the airport, my bus driver and his friend conversed in a local version of English that was almost completely incomprehensible to me. Stuck behind a slow moving bus, the driver crossed the double line to pass the slowpoke. A police officer materialized instantly and requested my driver to show his license. Instead of writing out a ticket, a palaver ensued. I had been informed earlier on my trip that a discussion between Africans and European explorers had a distinctive character. It was dubbed a "palaver". By the time I arrived on the scene, palaver applied to arguments among Africans that continued without resolution. At first, I watched the palavering with considerable amusement. My driver continued to refuse showing his license to the officer, holding it before the officer's nose, but not letting him touch it. Apparently, it was a matter of principle. As the palavering continued with no early end in sight, my thoughts returned to reality: Precious time was passing and my plane's departure was getting closer. I joined the group of palaverers and casually informed the police officer that I was on my way to the U.S. and my plane was waiting for me at the airport. That opened up a whole new line of discussion. Did I like Nigeria? What was I doing in America? Slowly, but surely, I was able to move the discussion in the direction of us meeting the plane's schedule. Palavering lost its intensity, everybody patted each other on the back, I got back on the bus and we resumed our ride. I do not recall the driver getting a ticket, nor exchanging any money. As we continued our journey, the noisy, but friendly discussion between my driver and his friend continued as if it had never been interrupted.

I was scheduled to take a Nigerian Airways plane to Kano, in northern Nigeria. The plane was on a direct flight from Lagos to London, stopping in Kano and Rome. Checking in at Lagos airport turned out to be more complicated than at any other airport on my trip. They discovered that my suitcase was sort of heavy. Unfortunately, I did not catch on. I realized too late had I given the official some local currency that would have tipped the scale in my favor. When I stupidly asked what I had to do to get my suitcase on the plane, he started calculating what to charge me for the extra 12 pounds. That 1¼ hour flight was the only one where anybody was concerned about the weight of my bag.

I am glad that I stopped in Kano. It made me realize the diversity of Nigeria. We had left the tropical humidity of Lagos, situated on what used to be called the Slave Coast, and reached the much drier but still quite warm land closer to the Sahara. In my comfortable modern hotel, I could sleep without turning on the noisy air conditioner. I found the northern Nigerians, Hausa and Fulani, more dignified and more pleasant than the Southern Nigerians. It is amazing how quickly I developed all sorts of prejudices of my own.

I took a guided three-hour taxi tour of Kano and sites surrounding the city. I was shown a structure that looked like an Egyptian pyramid from the distance. I was at least fourteen hundred miles from Egypt. As the taxi got closer, it turned out to be ground nuts stacked in the shape of a pyramid. Then we came to a large tent that served as a home for a family, the taxi driver explained. I started to position my camera for a picture of a couple of kids standing at the tent entrance. My taxi driver warned me that I would have to pay the kids for the privilege of snapping their picture. As I pulled a couple of shillings out of my pocket to give the two little ones, the news spread and other family members joined. More and more appeared. Before I could snap my picture, at least 25 family members emerged from the tent and joined the group. On the one hand, I was happy to have been able to uncover some of the people my superficial observation might have missed. It helped me understand why Nigeria's first census revealed a significantly larger population than previous estimates. On the other hand, there was no way that I could possibly compensate all the people, young and old, who had emerged to get their shilling. I just did not have enough Nigerian coins. When I located some U.S. coins, the group got really excited. I beat a fast retreat to the taxi.

My taxi driver also showed me a mosque and suggested I climb up the tower to get a better view of Kano. "Can someone who is not a Moslem believer do this?" I asked. "Oh sure", he responded. I overcame my fear of heights and climbed up the narrow, somewhat dirty steps of the minaret to the spot from where several times a day, the people are called to pray.

My taxi driver was very proud to show me a museum and a place where they make indigo cloth. Before returning me to my hotel, he suggested an evening tour; after all, it was Christmas Eve. It did not take me long to realize that he did not have any religious services in mind. He wanted to introduce me to some girls he knows and he winked and pinched me in the leg, in case I did not understand what he had in mind. As politely as possible, I told him I was busy getting myself ready for my flight to Rome at midnight.

***

The plane from Kano to Rome took off after midnight and flew over the Sahara desert on its way to the Mediterranean coast of North Africa. It was the night before Christmas. Not surprisingly, the plane was nearly empty: the reindeer were traveling a route considerably further north. I was able to occupy three empty seats enabling me to stretch out and sleep soundly while the plane crossed the desert. When I woke up, we had reached the coast of Italy on our approach to Rome. What a privilege to arrive in Rome on Christmas Day when the Pope greets and blesses a multitude of worshippers who have traveled great distances. However my timing was a coincidence..

A British fellow passenger suggested I stay at the Tirreno, a small centrally located hotel in Rome. Getting there was simple. I was immediately struck by the gulf that separated the hardship of coping by most West Africans from Italians who, while not as prosperous as many other Europeans, appeared to live a life of near luxury by comparison. That bothered me. I wrote to Audrey, "I have become extremely pessimistic and cannot imagine how such a gulf can be overcome in our lifetime".

I spent what was left of Christmas Day exploring the most ancient city I had ever visited. Less than twenty-four hours had brought me from semi-tropical northern Nigeria to wintry Europe. While the layers covering the past were only slowly being removed in Nigeria, in Rome I could not walk more than a block without the ruins of the ancient Roman Empire staring me in the face. I started with the Coliseum, walked on the Appian Way, looked at some ancient catacombs and visited museums before collapsing in my hotel room. There simply was too much ancient history for me to absorb in one day. After another day of roaming in Rome and eating outstanding meals, I had enough and took off on my flight to London.

The flight to London, which I had expected to be the least complicated part of the entire journey, turned out not to be at all that simple. As soon as I got to the Rome airport, I learned that all planes from and to London, were either late or canceled because London was fogged in. We were placed on board a British airliner that originated in Athens. When we finally took off, the captain casually announced that the plane would land in Manchester if the fog had not lifted by the time we crossed the Channel. Of course, the fog stayed put and the pilot diverted us to Manchester. "Ground transportation would be arranged and a bus would take us to our destination: London"

I toyed with the idea of spending a day in Manchester and taking that opportunity to explore the city where my grandfather Willy had spent the last 8 years of his life. It was only 16 years since his death. However, I would have had to pay my own way to get to London if I failed to take the bus provided by the airline. I also was somewhat exhausted from my busy sightseeing in Rome. The visit to my grandfather's Manchester home would have to wait another several decades. I took the bus for what I thought would be a relatively short ride, after all Britain was a little island. After a couple of hours when we were still a considerable distance from our destination, I had to revise my perception of England. Britannia that ruled the waves was not that small.

The passenger who sat next to me on the bus asked whether it was O.K. to open the window a little bit. After all, it was so stuffy in here. I mumbled that I had just come from Africa and that it was cold outside. With a smile and a show of politeness, he overruled my objections. The cold air immediately irritated my throat and made me aware that a sore throat that I had first noticed in Nigeria had worsened considerably, probably because my body had not yet adjusted itself to the European Winter climate. The open bus window made me very uncomfortable. I decided to take on my neighbor, closed the window and gave him a very dirty look. After this incident, I calmed down and, looking out the window, began to wonder whether I was dreaming. Almost all the place names on the road signs were familiar towns in Connecticut. Not surprisingly the early settlers in New England must have been homesick and therefore chose the names of their English places of origin when tired of the names spoken by the native Indian inhabitants.

In London, I picked the Green Park Hotel, probably because I liked the sound of the address: Half Moon Street in Piccadilly. I chose well: Green Park was in the center of London, within walking distance of almost any place that I wanted to visit. The room and service, especially breakfast, matched that of any place I had stayed on my trip.

I wanted to get in touch with Arnošt, my mother's cousin whom I had tried to contact in Prague on my Eastern European trip in 1960. That attempted phone call had almost ruined his carefully laid plan to leave Communist Czechoslovakia. When I called him this time, he was delighted to answer immediately. He invited me to his place in the suburb where I had a wonderful evening with him and his wife Ruth discussing the past. When I complained about my sore throat, he called a doctor who would examine me in my hotel. I could have gone to a hospital and gotten free care under Britain's socialized medicine, Arnošt said. The private doctor's hotel visit would save time. He was right. The doctor came exactly when promised, diagnosed a strep throat and injected antibiotic medicine. He marveled at the fact that after spending two months in Africa, I had avoided serious infections of all sorts, only to get a strep infection on my return to Europe, the healthy continent.

Next day, Ruth took me to a museum. Afterward we sat at a café where she gave me a detailed account of how Arnošt and she managed to survive Hitler's concentration camps, their return to Prague and their experience in Czechoslovakia after the 1948 Communist take-over. It was perhaps the most emotional couple of hours of the entire trip.

After spending four days including New Year in London, I flew back to New York. I had left from Idlewild Airport, but on my return it had been renamed JFK. Audrey, Ronald and Meredith welcomed me home in Storrs a few hours later.

***

It took me some time to sort out the multitude of impressions gained traveling in a part of the world, new to me. I had approached Africa confidant that the shift from colonialism to independence would usher in a new, better era. Reality quickly brought me back to earth. Colonialism had left an enormous and burdensome legacy that the new leaders of populations whose expectations were changing significantly were unprepared to meet. Colonial boundaries reflected relationships among European rulers and not local historical, religious, tribal relationships. Nation building that had taken Europeans centuries to accomplish could not possibly be done by the newly independent African states in a short time frame.

Not only was there a legacy of neglected development and serious issues left unresolved by centuries of colonial rule, but independence also removed excuses by the new states to blame others for the failure to resolve countless local and regional problems. When the new state leaders realized it was their responsibility to meet the growing expectations of their people, they took the natural, but dangerous path of prioritizing the buildup of their own power base. After all, if you have so many new tasks, you need better tools to run a nation's affairs. These efforts by Africa's national leaders provoked intertribal conflicts and played into the hands of outside powers involved in the Cold War. Neither the United States, nor the Soviet Union were particularly well informed, nor really interested, in the problems Guinea, Mali,

Ghana or Nigeria faced. They just had to be kept out of the other's reach.

As I traveled from country to country, even my short stays opened my eyes and mind to the incredible tasks that lay ahead. It was not only a matter of building up modern infra-structures, but expanding educational facilities, introducing modern health facilities and above all, reducing the huge gap that separated the well-to-do few from the vast majority of their fellow citizens. Recognizing these difficulties, did not detract from my hopes for a new and better Africa. Quite the contrary, I realized that resolving Africa's problems, more difficult than I had expected, were even more urgent and had to be confronted.

Illustrations

World War I Victim
Uncle Kurt Frank

Grandmother and Grandfather Willy and Clare Frank

Mother
Anni Beck
Nee Frank
in her garden

Father Maximilian Beck

Curt and his growing chestnut trees

Curt on school outing

Mdme. Besançon Class

Grandma having tea on the balcony in Marienbad

In Holland waiting for our ship

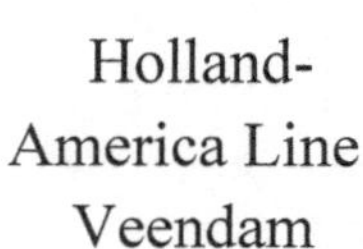

Holland-America Line Veendam

View from our New York City apartment

View of the Hudson from our window

Curt and Audrey Beck at our wedding

Audrey and daughter Meredith

Meredith and Ronald

Curt and Meredith

Part V - Great Expectations and Tragedies of the Seventies

Chapter 15
Turmoil in Academia and Hartford

My poking behind the Iron Curtain in Eastern Europe and gaining a perspective on the Cold War in West Africa helped me to lessen but certainly not eliminate my preoccupation with issues at UCONN. The faculty had suffered for a long time from incredibly low salaries, slow promotions and heavy course loads. As a result, complaints and unrest dominated academia in the fifties. UCONN had expanded dramatically after World War II with the return of our soldiers who with their GI benefits helped UCONN grow. An expansion inadequately funded by the state.

My worries increased when I realized that my optimistic expectations of leading an exciting constructive academic career by helping open the minds of post-Depression and post-World War II generation students to a world of new ideas and by publishing the results of my research were somewhat unrealistic. There were too many diversions to provide an atmosphere conducive to research. While UCONN had become a full-grown University that offered graduate degrees in a wide variety of fields in little more than a decade, it had become obvious that the underpinnings to make this transformation successful were weak.

UCONN President Jorgensen enjoyed seeing his campus physically expand. I often encountered him casting an admiring look at a new building under construction, inspecting the layout of a new sidewalk, arguing with an electrician about the installation of a fancy light post that gave the neighboring area a romantic appearance. To implement his vision of creating in New England a university modeled on a Mid-Western State University, Jorgensen spent much of his energy winning the support of the Governor and the legislature in Hartford. The prestigious private universities that had dominated public thinking in Connecticut and New England rendered the task of gaining public support especially challenging. He left the running of the university to Al Waugh who had been elevated to the position of Provost in 1950. Waugh, a very fair and well-disciplined individual, had an excellent sense of humor which he used to impress everybody on and off campus. However Jorgensen's and Waugh's relations with Governor Ribicoff were strained. In the absence of a top-notch women's basketball team we lacked the publicity capable of releasing an avalanche of public funds.

On a spring day in 1961 as the annual Spring Day Parade consisting of student floats slowly passed in front of the Mansfield Apartments. My faculty neighbors and I watched students perform their antics. Some of us instructors and assistant professors started talking about our salaries, large class sizes and delayed promotions. We compared our respective salaries and realized that with only minor exceptions we were all in the same boat. We expressed our frustrations. Our mood was in stark contrast to the hope expressed in the recently delivered inaugural address by President Kennedy. At the same time, Bob Stallman, a highly respected English professor published a letter revealing his own ridiculously low salary. The realization that I was not alone dramatically improved my mood.

The shift from individual to collective action with colleagues in all parts of the University was helped by an unexpected incident. *Campus,* the student newspaper, published each year the *Scampus* on April 1st. This was an opportunity to make fun and raise issues not appropriate even for a college newspaper. In the 1961 *Scampus*, Jorgensen became the butt of off-key humor. His name, although altered, was clearly recognizable. Parts of his lower body were verbally revealed. Perhaps it was not in good taste. Jorgensen was not amused. The student editor McGurk, was severely reprimanded and asked to leave UCONN. Many of us felt that the punishment vastly exceeded the crime and, more importantly, revealed Jorgensen's sense of self-importance, lack of humor and detachment from the University over which he presided.

Galvanized by our new sense of collective grievance several fellow junior faculty members signed a petition requesting the University to reverse the actions taken against McGurk. The circulation of the petition presented me and of course everybody else with the choice to go public and censure President Jorgensen or to continue to hide and hope for the best. I chose to sign my name.

The consequence of signing the petition surprised all of us. The news of the McGurk affair spread to the Connecticut press. None of the faculty who signed the petition suffered retribution. Instead, we were elated to learn that Jorgensen terminated his presidency and chose to retire.

Energized by our success, several of us decided to go further and involve ourselves directly in the budgetary process in Hartford. I joined several colleagues to meet legislators at the Capitol where we requested additional appropriations for faculty salaries. John Glynn, a friend and member of UCONN's Institute of Labor Relations, introduced us to a legislator from New Haven who was a labor union leader. When we told him what salaries we were receiving and asked his support for appropriations for salary raises, he was shocked that we were earning less than many of his union members. He asked us why it had taken us so long to ask the legislators for help. "How much do you need?" We asked him to give us a few minutes to translate our vague request for help into a specific amount that would be included in an appropriations bill

Our group of three or four faculty members adjourned to the spacious part of the Men's Room on the second floor of the State Capitol, scrounged for a couple of sheets of paper, frantically tried to estimate the size of the faculty, the average salary increase we considered appropriate and then engaged in old fashioned multiplications. We did not have a pocket calculator. We came out of the Men's Room and resumed our conversation with the friendly legislator giving him the $ amount of our request on a sheet of toilet paper. "Are you sure that is enough? Why not add another $100,000 to be on the safe side." We looked at each other and nodded our heads in astonished approval.

A few days later, we appeared at a legislative committee hearing to testify in support of the UCONN faculty salary increment included in a larger appropriations bill. A top official of the University with whom we exchanged furtive looks, watched us testify and then followed us and endorsed the bill. We were shocked but delighted. The bill passed and faculty salaries rose significantly. We all felt a sense of empowerment. It taught me to speak up for matters that really concerned me. Silence may be golden, but speaking up sometimes gets results.

Earlier in the fifties I had already expressed my interest in raising academic standards at the University in by participating in the Association of University Professors (AAUP) drive to strengthen the University Library's collection of books and magazines, which lead to my becoming AAUP president in 1965. From 1960 to 1980, I served as a College of Arts and Science representative on the University Senate. That is where we discussed crucial issues affecting almost all aspects of the University. Thus early in my career I had ceased being an observer and by-stander and chosen to be an active participant in the affairs of the University. This activism matched Audrey's rapid rise to prominence on the state political scene.

***

I had attended Democratic State Conventions before, but the one held in 1970 turned out to be much more exciting. A major political change was in the making and an almost entirely new state Democratic ticket had to be selected and nominated. Governor Dempsey, who had succeeded Abraham Ribicoff in 1961, and had been re-elected twice, chose to retire, necessitating the selection of a new slate of statewide candidates. Senator Tom Dodd had been censured by the U.S. Senate. He chose to run for another term as an independent candidate, precipitating a contest for a Democratic candidate to succeed him. Secretary of State, Ella Grasso, vacated her position and chose to run for a seat in the U.S. House of Representatives. In the past, in a situation of this sort, Democratic State Party Chairman, John Bailey, would conduct intense behind the scene negotiations with all contenders and present a carefully balanced ticket to the convention delegates for approval. Nineteen-seventy was, however, not a normal year. Discontent over Viet Nam spilled over to the convention delegates. There was also a growing dissatisfaction with delegates approving decisions reached behind closed doors. In short, as the convention assembled, it had a charged atmosphere.

A short time before, some of Audrey's political friends suggested that she run for the Secretary of State's position vacated by Ella Grasso. The state ticket needed someone from Eastern Connecticut and the Secretary of State's position had been filled since 1939, usually by a woman. Audrey seemed to fill the bill perfectly. She quickly warmed up to the suggestion and started building a base of support among convention delegates from Eastern Connecticut. After making considerable headway, she discovered she had two competitors from Eastern Connecticut who were prepared to challenged her drive for the nomination.

As the day of the convention approached, Audrey's quest for delegate support got entangled in the obviously more important battle for the nomination of a candidate for the U.S. Senate. Joseph Duffey, a liberal and critic of our involvement in Viet Nam, had gained the support of many delegates. Audrey sought Joe Duffey's endorsement thereby hoping to further her own candidacy. The evening before the vote, Audrey and I went to Duffey's headquarters at the Hilton Hotel to personally speak to him and gain his support. As we approached the room, many delegates were lined up waiting for an interview. Audrey's two opponents from Eastern Connecticut were there waiting in line. I noticed that Sam Gejdenson, one of my students, was the official doorkeeper who communicated with those inside to determine the order of admission. Sam recognizing me, smiled, and immediately let Audrey in to speak to Duffey. I could not help notice the fiery looks from Audrey's competitors as they waited, while Audrey marched into the room. Duffey promised Audrey his support.

The next day at the Bushnell Convention Hall, a town-by-town roll call for the Secretary of State nomination was called. The delegates had a choice of five candidates: Audrey and the other two candidates from Eastern Connecticut, Gloria Schaffer from the New Haven area, and a candidate from the Waterbury area, a friend of Party Chair John Bailey. As the roll call proceeded, it became apparent that no candidate attracted enough support to win a majority. Bailey ordered a recess to resolve the impasse. He asked each one of the contestants to meet jointly with him in a small room, behind the stage. Each candidate was requested to bring her campaign manager. Audrey asked me to accompany her. After managing the labyrinthine passages behind the stage to the hideaway, we found ourselves at the center of action where the real decisions were made. Most of those assembled were visibly awed, but not Audrey. While the other candidates whispered in the ear of their supporting managers, Audrey, having mentally added up all possible votes, recognized the need for a calculated compromise. She whispered in Bailey's ear, exchanged a meaningful glance with me, and was ready with her proposal, the moment Bailey asked the contestants to state their position.

She turned to Gloria Schaffer and offered to withdraw from the race promising to ask her own delegates to throw their support to Gloria. The candidate from Waterbury, who had been promised Bailey's support, was visibly taken aback because it had generally been assumed that, with no candidate a clear winner, Bailey would use his enormous influence to advance and assure her nomination. Audrey's decisive move put a quick end to what many had expected a contentious brawl in the secret crevasse behind the Bushnell stage. Bailey returned to the podium and asked the delegates to take their seat, the convention would resume. The delegates were surprised to see Audrey appear at the microphone to address the delegates. The noise quickly abated.

Audrey smiled broadly, as she surveyed the large hall. She obviously enjoyed this rare moment, when she had everybody's full attention. This was so much more fun than addressing a class of freshmen economics students. She thanked all her delegates for their support. She briefly summarized what she had hoped to accomplish as the Connecticut's next Secretary of State. Since she lacked the necessary votes to accomplish her goals, she wanted everyone to know that there was another candidate, who shared her objectives and whose judgment Audrey trusted. She asked her delegates and everybody else to throw their support behind Gloria. Audrey's brief speech was extremely well received. It certainly was a high point and a completely unexpected moment of the convention. Audrey's move sealed Gloria's nomination.

In November Audrey was re-elected to the Connecticut House of Representatives, having been endorsed by both the Mansfield Democratic and Republican parties. Gloria Schaffer was only one of the two Democratic candidates on the state ticket to win that year in which Governor Meskill and Senator Weicker carried the state for the Republican Party. Audrey's performance at the State Democratic convention had propelled her to a prominent spot on the Connecticut political stage.

When Audrey was first elected, my friend Sam Witryol greeted me as the Honorable Mr. Audrey Beck. What a silly joke, I thought. When another colleague asked if I could arrange to have him meet Audrey for lunch at the Faculty lunchroom, where he hoped to get state funding for a project that would help the University (and especially him) I started to become concerned about keeping our professional lives separate, but compatible. It got worse when a legislator of the opposite Party questioned the propriety of Audrey casting her vote on the University's budget. "Are you not voting on your own salary, since your husband teaches at UCONN and he provides your room and board?" Caught by surprise, Audrey offered to abstain voting on the University's budget. Most legislators broke out laughing. She thought that was a great joke until the story reached Storrs where her constituents pointed out that they voted for her to represent them and she had better not abstain from voting for UCONN's budget.

My role in the University Senate, where my active role preceded Audrey's prominence in Hartford, was made more difficult by many colleagues' exaggerated expectations that I could use pillow talk opportunities to further important University projects. We made every effort not to mingle University and legislative agendas. There were however situations where Audrey's familiarity with University affairs turned out to be very helpful. Several years later when Audrey had become chair of the Senate Finance Committee a particular incident is deeply edged in my memory. The Chair of the Legislature's Senate Appropriations Committee invited himself to our house after 10 P.M. to discuss with Audrey an item in the Appropriations bill pertaining to the University budget that did not make any sense to him. They sat at our dining room table and had pages of the budget appropriations bill spread out before them. When they came to the item that neither of them could fully understand, they yelled for me and asked me to explain what that particular program was all about. I was not sure either and suggested they call a top academic administrator who lived around the corner. In ten minutes he joined the two senators and the confusing program was discussed at length. The kitchen cabinet meeting adjourned shortly after midnight. Next morning in Hartford the Senate met and the two Chairs answered all possible questions leaving nobody in doubt about their competence on this and other issues.

***

Audrey assumed a leadership position in the House of Representatives after the 1972 elections in which the Democrats had lost control to the Republicans. She became an Assistant Minority Leader, a promotion that essentially confirmed the key role she had played for some time in developing legislative policy. It was however frustrating to operate in an environment dominated by Governor Meskill, a Republican, on the state level and Richard Nixon in Washington. Audrey hoped that the 1974 election would provide an opportunity to make a change, at least on the state level and hopefully also in the legislature. She decided to play a more important role and run for a seat in the State Senate.

In the late sixties, the State Senate had been redistricted. Mansfield and Willimantic joined towns in the state's northeastern corner to form the 29th district. A Republican, Louise Berry from Killingly, had captured a seat normally held by a Democrat in the 1972 election. When Audrey informed Chairman John Bailey that she was considering running against Louise Berry and recapturing the district, he pointed out that defeating a dynamic incumbent was a risky affair. After all, Audrey was already recognized as a leading member of the House of Representatives. Audrey answered that she preferred to be a leader among 36 senators to having a leading role in a crowd of 151 House members. Anyhow, she liked challenging incumbent Republicans.

She was not given much time to firm up her a decision. A casual comment to a friend reached the ears of one very interested in succeeding Audrey as Mansfield's voice in the legislature. Her long-time friend and erstwhile colleague in the UCONN Economics Department Dorothy Goodwin called us up and invited herself to our house for coffee. She had barely sat down, when she popped the question, "Audrey is it true that you are going to run for the Senate and give up your seat in the House?" Audrey hesitated. "I have to know", Dorothy continued, "I am interested in running for the seat. If I am a candidate, I have to let UCONN know tomorrow, that I plan to resign as Director of the Office of Institutional Research. They must find someone to take my place before the fall semester! Yes or no?" Audrey turned to me who was watching the drama from the far end of the room. We looked at each other for half a minute. I raised my shoulder indecisively. Finally, Audrey turned to Dorothy and said, "Dorothy, you forced me into it. Yes, I shall run for the Senate". After a brief good bye, Dorothy raced to her car, informed the University of her intent to resign and run for Audrey's not yet vacated warm seat.

When Audrey first considered running for the Senate, we spent an entire afternoon touring all the towns that made up the 29th district stretching from Mansfield and Windham in the west to Thompson, Putnam, Killingly, Sterling and Plainfield along the Rhode Island state line. That northeastern "Quiet Corner" was connected to our slightly more centrally located towns via Scotland and Canterbury. The task of getting to know the voters in such a diverse district seemed impossible at first glance. "Where do I start?" "Why not in Putnam," I responded, "I visited Congressman St. Onge in Putnam many times." "But he died in 1970" she retorted. Putnam is former Governor Dempsey's town. We discussed ancient history, noticed the differences in political culture. They had campaign posters all over the lawns, while we in Mansfield had passed ordinances strictly limiting political signs to several weeks before an election. There were many factories dating back to the 19th century. Most were on their last leg. There were hardly any up-to- date shopping centers. Instead, they gambled their hopes for the future on a dog track in Plainfield. How was Audrey going to learn all about the people, their problems, develop proposals for the future, all in the few months before the November election?

Audrey had to develop a plan. She started by contacting all the Democratic politicians and activists in the districts she or her friends knew. Then she picked one or two in each of the district's nine towns and appointed them as her campaign coordinator for that particular town. First, she sat down with them and asked them to tell her all about that town's politics and problems. Then she gave them the responsibility to keep her informed about everything that mattered. Most importantly, she requested them to let her know of any social, political, church or business event that she ought to attend. She was fortunate in having picked very helpful coordinators. Her Thompson coordinator suggested she attend a social in a church or veteran's hall where the ladies played a card game. When word got around that Audrey not only visited the well-attended affair, but also quickly learned a game she had never played before, gaining the participants' respect and admiration, her opponent was informed and also appeared. Unlike Audrey, the opponent was reluctant to participate in the game. Audrey attributed her electoral success in that town to that particular event.

Her campaign in the 29th district was a very constructive experience for Audrey because it helped broaden her understanding of the wide range of interests controlling people's lives in just one senatorial district. There was of course a flip side to Audrey's exploration of the "Quiet Corner": Her friends in Storrs, listening to her rapt account of the problems in Sterling or Moosup, started worrying about her forgetting essential concerns of the UCONN faculty. They need not have worried: she simply expanded her legislative agenda, pushing more bureaucratic buttons in Hartford.

Audrey enjoyed campaigning with Chris Dodd in his first run for Congress. As the son of the late Senator, Chris benefitted from name recognition. When Chris visited factories in the 29th senatorial district, he invited Audrey to join him. He opened the door for Audrey to contact textile and other workers she might otherwise have never met. There was however a problem: Chris and Audrey entered the factory floor together. As Chris greeted a worker here and there, he managed to cover twenty or thirty rows, while Audrey was stuck near the entrance, engaged in a discussion of great importance to both, the worker and Audrey. By the time she had advanced to the second or third row, Chris was at the exit, shouting, "AUD, where are you? Time to move on!"

There were also many others who helped. Betty Heiss, a faculty wife, not only advised her on campaign literature format, but also helped her drive. This was important, since Audrey's sense of geography did not quite measure up to her otherwise incredibly active mind. Betty helped connect the dots, enabling her to get from Thompson to Plainfield without ending up in Providence, Rhode Island. They did get sidetracked occasionally discovering interesting dining facilities, such as the Golden Lamb in Brooklyn. When I raised my eyebrows because that restaurant was not in the 29th district, I was invited to their favorite eatery and forgave them their detour. One of my graduate students, interested in politics, also gave Audrey invaluable assistance gaining a considerable amount of information in the process. Audrey won a decisive victory. Her campaign strategy had worked. She was ready to start a new chapter in her legislative career.

***

Audrey became a state senator in January 1975, the same month that Ella Grasso became Connecticut's first female governor.

Audrey's position as chair of the Senate's Finance Committee brought them in close contact, not necessarily without friction. Some of the reasons for conflict were inevitable and stemmed from the fact that the governor, in order to run the state, needs adequate funding financed by appropriate taxes she proposes, are then modified and approved by the Finance committee and finally the legislature. Audrey took her job as senate Finance committee chair very seriously. She was the first chair to set up an office in the attic of the State Capitol and staffed it with well-qualified UCONN graduate students. Audrey operating in her Spartan attic office was no match for the Governor in her comfortable office suite on the second floor with countless aides at her disposal. It did not take long for Audrey's office to be perceived as a fly that kept on buzzing and annoying Ella. Other more complex reasons were responsible for the difficult relationship that developed.

Ella and Audrey had a very similar educational and social background. Both came from working class families, Ella's was Italian, Audrey's family English, Irish and German. Both majored in economics and received Phi Beta Kappa rewards, Ella at Mount Holyoke and Audrey at UCONN. Both married educators: Ella's was a school principal. They may have read each other's mind so well that each knew the other could not be fooled. Ella obviously knew that Connecticut's persistent financial crisis required a radical solution: an income tax. Audrey knew that no governor could come out for an income tax and survive the ensuing political storm. When Audrey teased Ella by asking her publicly why she did not abolish the soldiers and sailors tax, something dating back to an ancient Connecticut law, Ella did not think that was funny at all and told her privately where she should go.

Audrey helped Ella in her 1974 and 1978 campaigns. She accompanied her on several state tours. Her staff selected Audrey in part because they knew she would not mince any words and tell the governor to change her wardrobe at a roadside motel because at the last stop a coffee cup got spilled on her blouse. On matters not involving state finances, the two got along like a pair of college friends. Ella invited both of us for breakfast to her newly finished house in Windsor Locks in 1978 to discuss whom she should pick as her lieutenant governor to succeed Robert Killian. We were surprised she picked William O'Neill. Her response, "well, what can I do, I need an Irishman".

In spite of this very close relationship, or, perhaps because of their friendship, they had a fallout that seriously affected state government. I cannot remember the particular cause, in part because Audrey herself was not certain what she had done or said that got Ella so mad at her. The episode started in February. The governor stopped all contact with Audrey. This meant there were no negotiations between the Executive branch and the legislative Finance Committee. When absolutely necessary, intermediaries showed up to deliver messages. On Audrey's birthday, August 6 at 6:30 AM the phone rang. I got out of bed and was shocked when the governor without fanfare asked to speak to Audrey. We thought she was going to wish her HAPPY Birthday. No, the governor apparently was not aware that this was Audrey's special day. She had chosen that day to make peace and approved several of Audrey's projects in Eastern Connecticut and wanted her to be at the Killingly airport at 11 AM to announce her approval of these projects. She also asked her to get somebody to drive her car from Killingly to Norwich because she was going to take Audrey with her on the helicopter. That was Audrey's first ride in a helicopter. She quickly realized that this was Ella's clever trick to take her along for the ride but prevent her from discussing anything of substance because the helicopter's engine made it impossible to conduct a meaningful conversation.

Chapter 16
The Kids Grow Up

Audrey's increasingly time-consuming involvement in local and state politics was helped by a stable and very comfortable life at home. We were extremely fortunate that both Ronald and Meredith were outstanding students. Occasionally I worried about their not being challenged sufficiently in all their courses, but never about their grades nor completing their homework.

Ronald wrote a short paper *Who am I, Why am I?* at the start of his senior year that I discovered many years later. His teacher wrote the comment "Well done, Ron" at the top of the page. The paper struck me as an incredibly mature philosophical discussion about existence. He was only 16 when he compared civilization to" a moving sidewalk, where he was walking on and on to an unknown goal …the sidewalk propelled only by those on it..I am in the middle of it…and want to find out what I am on, I want to see how I got here and whether I will get off; I want to see how I got here…whether I can change direction…I want to move forward-and I have help because everyone behind me is pushing and directing. And I find out only one sure thing: I am a person searching to find out who I am and why I am what I am. I know for sure that whatever threads of knowledge I pick up will help those in front of me. I can give them a push because they are headed in the same direction I am." My son's reflections reminded me of my father's ruminations, when slightly older he titled his Ph.D. thesis *Wesen und Wert* (Being and Value). No wonder Ronald had an easy path to Princeton.

While Ronald had to limit his extracurricular reading due to his extensive hiking, canoeing and snow shoeing adventures, Meredith used her baby-sitting jobs to read many classic novels as well as Tolstoy's *War and Peace* from cover to cover. She edited a literary journal at E. O. Smith High School. It should not have surprised us that when she applied to 13 colleges, she received only one rejection. She chose Harvard.

We could rely on the mature behavior of our kids. At a time when many families had to worry about wild parties and drugs, my biggest concern was to find time to drive Ronald and his group of fellow hikers to some distant trail crossing in Vermont in summer or winter and then locate them several days later to return them to

Storrs. I suspect that Ronald postponed getting his driver's license so that I had no choice but to act as his dependable chauffeur. Only once, when he had already graduated from Princeton, did he give us cause to worry. He and three of his friends crossed a lake in northern Canada and canoed the seldom-traveled Kaniapiskau River to Ungava Bay along the Arctic coast of Quebec. They failed to call us on the promised date to let us know they had arrived safely. Audrey was about to interrupt her campaign, when a message reached us that the Canadian Mounted Police had located them as they arrived belatedly at Fort Chimo, their destination. They had been delayed by wild rapids around which canoes had to be carried, snow had fallen earlier than expected, and the wind had blown in the wrong direction, slowing their progress across a big lake.

Meredith too engaged in activities that demonstrated her incredible self-reliance and curiosity to explore the world. Perhaps her wanderlust had been nurtured by our two trips to Central and Eastern Europe when she was ten and twelve. We had driven from Denmark to Italy and the second time from Vienna to the Balkans, the Alps and Switzerland, crossing the Iron Curtain to show our kids where I had grown up. I had wanted them to see my homes in Berlin, Prague and, perhaps most important, the Terezín concentration camp where my grandfather Gustav was forced to spend the last nine months of his life. While still in high school, she traveled on her own to Montreal, London and Hamburg. In college, she took a semester off to journey alone all the way from London to Athens. She stopped to see distant relatives in London and Prague and a friend of her grandmother in Holland. She managed to spend considerable time on the Orient Express without ever experiencing the type of episodes that had given a dangerous but romantic reputation to the journey of early 20th century travelers in the Balkans.

In 1973 our house became an empty nest: Audrey and I were left alone when both Ronald and Meredith attended college. At first we felt little change because they had always been self-reliant, hardly ever interfering with our activities. Just before Ronald had left for Princeton he introduced a new member into our household: Albatross. That name Ronald had given to a mid-sized black and white dog, which he and a girl friend had picked up in West Hartford. The dog needed a home. We never had any dogs or cats and perhaps as a last minute effort to correct such neglect, Ronald had phoned and asked whether he could introduce us to Albatross. "When?" I asked. "In half an hour" he responded. I hesitated. He offered to take care of him. It did not quite sink in that this was a meaningless offer since he obviously was not going to take Albatross to Princeton two weeks later when classes were to resume. It took me some time to understand that introducing the dog into our house was our kids' well-meant gesture to make sure we old parents would not be at a complete loss for companionship after their departure.

Initially Meredith helped me adjust to Albatross' need for some attention. She taught me how to trust him. Never having lived with a dog, I was somewhat scared initially. It did not take us much time to adjust to each other's habits. He tried to impress me with his ability to chase rabbits away from our meadow where they and other wild creatures had ruined my landscaping efforts. Occasionally he paraded in front our living room door with a rabbit in his jaw. He was pleased when I thanked him for a job well done. Once he accompanied our neighbor's kid to E.O Smith high school. That was the only time that I received a request to come to the principal's office to pick up a truant member of my family.

Ronald had done extremely well in high school and I had every expectation that attending Princeton would present him any challenges that he could not meet. While that turned out to be correct, I was not prepared for the quite distinct path his college career took. When I attended Cornell, I had been in the U.S. barely two years. I looked at my son's college experience through my nostalgic glasses of a classic European University, expecting him to absorb pearls of wisdom cast at excited and studious students by professors in the humanities and sciences. From my son however, I heard complaints about foreign professors and graduate students who had to write mathematical formulas on the blackboard because their English was incomprehensible.

Ronald ended up with a major in biology and geology. He chose as his senior thesis project *The Impact of Winter Climatic Variations on the Geographic Distribution of Vegetation on Mount Washington*. To do the necessary research for this project, Ronald camped out a couple of days in the coldest part of winter near the peak of Mount Washington. While his Princeton professor was impressed by the originality and courage of his endeavor, Audrey and I were worried about exposure to frostbites and worse on his way to graduation.

Ronald was much prouder of his achievement in a phase of college life about which I knew little. He and a friend had surreptitiously explored the UCONN Field House while in high school and had discovered a squash court that mostly stood unused. Somewhere they found the rules for the game and practiced enough for Ronald to compete at Princeton with students who had learned and practiced the game at prep schools. He became a member of the Princeton Squash team. In a crucial championship game with Harvard in his senior year, Ronald won the decisive seventh game, thereby adding to Princeton's sports reputation. My son never lost his love for squash. He participated in squash competitions and not only gained and maintained a ranked place, but to this day, operates a web site for those interested in squash.

After graduating, he got a job at ERCO, [Energy Resources Recovery Company] a small start-up environmental firm that tried to develop novel methods of resource recovery in the Greater Boston area. He developed many quite interesting research grant proposals dealing with environmental issues still relevant years later. He carried out studies that examined the impact of chemical emissions on water quality in Long Island Sound, dangers involving hot water emissions from nuclear power plants, groundwater problems resulting from enhanced oil recovery among others.

Ronald's job brought him back to New England, to the Greater Boston area, only an hour and a half from our home. He took advantage of the many academic institutions in the area to pursue his quest to excel in squash. He invited us to watch him smash the ball into the four walls of the cage-like court while he and his adversary were wiping the sweat off their faces. I watched many exciting games, where Ronald and his partners spent hours hitting a ball with intense fury and then enjoyed discussing their hits and misses. Ronald developed first rate playing skills.

Chapter 17
1977

A couple of years later, Ronald introduced us to Cathy, a co-worker at ERCO. It soon became clear that Cathy was more than just a friend. Plans were made for a wedding in Portland, Oregon, Cathy's hometown, on the West Coast.

The wedding was set for July 16, 1977. Audrey and I planned to take advantage of the wedding to explore the West coast from San Francisco to Portland. My mother was also invited and planned to fly directly to Portland. Meredith however had arranged to participate in an OXFAM scheduled trip to help a local project in Banjul, The Gambia, in West Africa. She left several days before we were scheduled to fly to San Francisco. On July 7 barely an hour before leaving our house to catch the limousine that would take us to the airport we received a phone call from OXFAM informing us that Meredith had suffered a psychotic episode in Banjul and was being flown back to New York. We were extremely worried and concerned. Instantly we had to make a decision to possibly change our plan to fly to San Francisco. Before reaching a decision, we needed more facts.

Eight months earlier, Meredith had phoned me from Harvard asking me to visit her because she had something important to tell me. I arranged to see her in Cambridge that same evening, assuming that she was going to inform me that something very embarrassing had happened that she did not divulge over the phone, like being pregnant. I picked a very comfortable and scenic restaurant in Boston overlooking the waterfront where we could discuss her concern. "Daddy" she asked, "would you be willing to pay for regular weekly sessions with a psychiatrist? Harvard Student Health Services recommended that I have these sessions and they chose a psychiatrist for me to see." I was greatly relieved that there was no pregnancy and this was only about permission to see a psychiatrist. There was a lot I had to learn!

Her subsequent academic year at Harvard proceeded normally. She performed well in her classes and never skipped a session with her psychiatrist. At that time therapy consisted of talk treatment. Meredith received no medication for schizophrenia, her illness. One can only speculate that if her illness had occurred two decades later, new medications would have prevented the illness from devastating her life. It is now known that early treatment of schizophrenia considerably ameliorates the course of the illness. Meredith had the unusual insight to self-diagnose herself and ask for help. If only the right help had then been available! I have since learned that patients with a severe mental illness should avoid exposure to stress. Unfortunately making the grade in college, especially at Harvard, is fraught with more than the normal amount of stress.

Before Meredith made the decision to spend the summer of 1977 in West Africa on an OXFAM project, I asked Meredith's psychiatrist whether Meredith would be able to handle such a project. She assured me that this would be O.K., probably because Meredith had a year earlier traveled all over Europe by herself. When the call came informing me that Meredith had a psychotic episode in Banjul and had to be brought back, my first move was to call her psychiatrist for advice. She had none and was just as shocked as I was about Meredith having suffered a psychotic episode. She had not expected such a development. My respect for her dropped considerably.

Since my mother was not scheduled to leave for the wedding in Portland for several days, I asked her to pick Meredith up at the JFK airport. We also had one of Audrey's assistants stay in our house during our attending Ronald's wedding. She offered to drive Meredith and my mother back to Storrs and then watch Meredith while she was recovering. After making all these arrangements in less than an hour, we left Storrs to fly to San Francisco on our way to the wedding. Meredith's critical condition was to overshadow our intended celebration of Ronald's wedding.

In the pre-cell phone age, flying to the West Coast meant cutting off direct contact with vital events affecting our family and relying instead on periodic after-the-fact telephone inquiries. I did not mind that we had scheduled only a two-day stay in San Francisco. I could not wipe from my mind the fear of the infamous earthquake that had destroyed the city some seven decades earlier. Taking the streetcar that climbed up the steep hill hardly matched the performance of the trolley that I had taken in Bolzano, Italy, climbing up a real mountain, flanked by vineyards. The Golden Gate and Bay Bridges were however quite impressive. We had a brief tour of Berkeley and visited one of my very few surviving relatives from Germany. On our way north, we stopped at a vineyard in Napa Valley and dutifully tasted a variety of vines. We admired the huge trees in the Redwoods Park and, Eureka, we reached the Pacific.

It was on our first stop in Oregon, at the Inn of the Beachcomber in Gold Beach at the mouth of the Rogue River, that we learned in a long, memorable conversation with my mother the latest news about Meredith. After picking her up at JFK airport, Meredith seemed to act relatively normally in our house. Audrey's assistant who also had been one of my political science interns, was very concerned the next day when she found Meredith standing in the kitchen as though in a trance. She consulted Sam, one of our neighbors who taught psychology. He suggested my mother take Meredith to Natchaug Hospital. She did, and Meredith was admitted for observation and treatment. I called the hospital, talked to a doctor, also to Meredith, telling her we would see her in a few days. I will always associate the Beachcomber at Gold Beach with my coming to realize the tragic turn that Meredith's life had taken.

As we made our way up the Oregon coast, the wild nature of the beaches impressed me. Huge tree trunks littered the beaches, pushed there by the Pacific, an ocean that struck me as having more powerful waves than the ones I was used to along the Atlantic coast. There were only a few towns along the Oregon coast spoiling nature. Logging, that was another matter. One could not help being either impressed, or annoyed, by the frequent encounters with huge trucks carrying heavy loads of large trees. This was all very new and interesting, but Meredith's illness hung over everything we experienced in Oregon. We were in a hurry to get to Portland, meet Cathy's parents and somehow get into the appropriate mood to enjoy Ronald's wedding.

***

We arrived in Portland a couple of days before the wedding. Hopefully this would give us enough time to emerge from the dark shadow that Meredith's misfortune had cast over our lives. The first day we attended a reception for out-of-town wedding guests at a fancy club. That was not exactly our cup of tea. It did not take us long to realize that our academic status was no match for Cathy's father's entrepreneurial business friends. A university president's six-digit salary was peanuts, a guest claimed, after all, he had just sent off a $100,000 check to the IRS to pay his stupid income tax a few weeks ago!

On the second day we shifted gears and chose to explore northwest America's wonders of nature. We were awed by Mount Hood's grandeur as we stopped at a charming resort nearby. We visited a dam on the Columbia River and watched salmon trying out the specially built bypass they were supposed to take to propagate upstream. The day ended with a Square Dance. None of the day's activities took our minds off the worries about Meredith and our concern that her brother's wedding might be affected by the stigma attached to a family where someone suffers from a severe mental illness. This, after all, was still the age when an individual suffering from a mental illness was removed from society and placed in an asylum so as not to disturb the rest of us "normal" people.

We spent the next day getting to know the bride's stepmother. Cathy's mother had died a few years earlier of cancer. We felt it unfortunate that Cathy appeared uncomfortable with Ann, her new mother, whom Audrey and I liked very much. Ann took us on a tour of the Japanese and Rose gardens in Portland's perfectly located park. She had played a major role in developing and cultivating the Japanese garden. That impressed us. After some further exploration of the city, we almost felt at home in Portland. The evening ended with a rehearsal of the wedding. Ronald prepared himself for the occasion by getting in a game of squash, his favorite occupation. His soaking wet hair from the after-game shower was a dead give-away.

The wedding proceeded without a glitch. It took us some time to adjust to the new reality that Ronald was no longer our young adventure-seeking boy but a college graduate earning his own salary and even a married man! Richard Rosen, who ran ERCO, the company in Cambridge that employed the newly married couple, hosted a post-wedding dinner. We bade Cathy and Ronald and all their Oregon relatives and friends, good-bye. If not for the tumultuous events in our lives that preceded the wedding, this would have been the perfect ending of a week of magic. We took off the next morning, flew back to the East coast and reached Storrs. We were in a hurry to see Meredith.

***

Back in Storrs, we rushed to Natchaug Hospital, ten minutes from our house. It was located in a brick building that I had passed a thousand times on our way to Willimantic without ever giving it more than a passing glance. Now it suddenly loomed large before our eyes as we entered with some trepidation. We were led to Meredith's room and found her looking well, but uncharacteristically subdued. We were careful to avoid mentioning her African trip. She assured us she was fine. Talking to her, reassured us somewhat.

Her doctor informed us she would have to stay in the hospital for an indefinite period to recover from her psychotic episode. After we asked him how soon she could resume her normal activities and return to Harvard to complete her senior year, he decided that it was we who needed help. He had us sit down in a conference room and started out by stressing that Meredith was really quite ill. He had us look at something she had jotted down on a piece of paper. "Does that look like her normal handwriting? Obviously not". He proceeded to explain how serious schizophrenia, her illness, was. There was, however, some light at the end of the extremely dark tunnel. About twenty years earlier it was realized that the drug Haldol that had been used for a different purpose had an unexpected effect on patients suffering from mental illnesses: it treated the "positive" aspects of the illness. The so-called "positive" aspect was the mentally ill patient's inability to control his/her violent temperamental outbursts. That had made it possible to begin the exodus from mental asylums in the 1960's. It would take several weeks to find out how a new patient, like Meredith, would react to Haldol. She might then resume some of her normal activities. Maybe there was some hope, we thought, as we went home.

After responding appropriately to her medication and treatment, Meredith was able to return home in August. Unfortunately, she had lost her drive and enthusiasm and spent most of her time resting in her room. Now we understood what the doctor had told us at Natchaug: Haldol had dealt with the "positive" symptoms of the illness, but not with the "negative" ones like depression. There was no remedy in the late 1970's to help patients suffering from schizophrenia resume an active constructive life. It would take a dozen more years to make available the first of a set of more effective drugs dealing not only with the "positive symptoms" but also the equally important "negative" aspects of schizophrenia.

We decided to have our own Storrs party celebrating Ronald and Cathy's wedding in late August. We held it outdoors at our house on Dunham Pond. Meredith was able to attend and participate. We hoped this would lift some of the dark clouds that had cast such an ominous shadow on the Portland festivities. When one of our neighbors pulled me aside and told me that I had better concern myself with Meredith's health because she seemed to be somewhat depressed, I could not help but inform my neighbor that her observation was not exactly a surprise to me.

Meredith spent the fall and spring semesters at home gradually regaining enough confidence to return to Harvard the following summer. She managed to pass successfully her courses and in the fall of 1978 resumed her regular senior year course schedule. We

celebrated her commencement in June 1979; two years after her illness had derailed her hopes and aspirations.

Meanwhile the newly wedded couple settled down in a house Cathy's father had bought for them in Carlisle, north of Boston. I divided my time between watching my son play squash and my daughter explain some exciting aspects of psychology, her major.

Chapter 18
Divorce

Audrey and I had been married twenty-five years when we had to face and deal constructively with Meredith's mental illness. We also had to adjust ourselves to living in our empty nest home. The negative atmosphere created by Watergate, Nixon's exit, and the dreadfully slow termination of our Viet Nam venture exasperated the overall negative environment of the 1970ies. We were slow to realize that all these developments affected our marriage. Our daily routine had changed and we were facing new challenges.

The novel experience of being an important legislator's husband had worn off. Audrey's election to the Senate concentrated almost all her attention on key issues of state governance, while my attention focused increasingly on university problems that worried me as a member of the University Senate. I gradually became aware that our daily lives were moving in separate orbits. Ronald remarked years later that his parents only talked about politics at dinner. In retrospect, I must agree with his observation. While we both had followed closely Ronald's and Meredith's continuing academic adventures there were few other topics that kept us together. As much as he tried Albatross could not quite fill the growing void.

My social life at the University had for years revolved around a lengthy noon-time walk with colleagues to the faculty club, a spirited discussion of the issues of the day, the latest gossip about administrative decisions, commiseration with each other's department member's research projects, in short, "very exciting topics". In the early seventies, the tone of our conversations changed. "Did you notice that most girls don't wear bras anymore?" one of my colleagues asked me, on the way to the faculty club. "How can you tell?" I responded. He told me to figure it out myself, or better yet, ask Audrey. I asked her, but it was obviously not an issue to match her interest in finding an appropriate way to balance the state's budget.

Changes in social attitudes also affected student faculty relationships. Some of my female students shifted from modestly approaching their professors to a much more aggressive line. A student in one of my introductory classes accosted me as I left the classroom on my way across the street to my office, and in a half serious tone of voice accused me of having insulted her in my lecture. Had I not talked about a big frog in a little pond? I admitted I might have used that expression, but why in the world would that

have insulted her? She answered "did I not know that in our commonly used lingo, *Frog* is used derogatorily to refer to a Frenchman? My mother is French, my name is Monique, so you see you insulted me, when you placed me in a little pond". I apologized and assured her I would keep frogs out of my class discussions in the future. Monique used this novel opening to invite herself into my office and tell me that she was one of those results of America's liberation of Paris in 1944 when her father, a U.S. soldier, captured the heart of a cheering Parisian young woman as Paris was liberated. Monique thought this was exciting and offered to tell me much more before leaving my office.

Even more interesting than the story of her own past, was what she told me about her current involvement in a somewhat shady aspect of Hartford's business community. She called herself an entrepreneur located in a well-known downtown office building providing entertainment for mature business leaders hungry for something special. She seemed to be also in touch with key men of the local Mafia. This intrigued me. There had been an unresolved case of a leading politician's disappearance in Audrey's senatorial district. The politician was somehow connected with the newly opened Dog Track in Plainfield. He had left a telephone message for Audrey in her Capitol office. Several hours later, when Audrey attempted to return it, there was no answer. The politician had gone to his summer cottage near the shore, where he was found dead. Audrey blamed herself for not responding faster. No sensible explanation ever appeared in print about the circumstances leading to the politician's end. Since Monique had mentioned a key Mafia leader in that part of New England, I thought she might help me shed some light on this case. I quickly realized my amateurish crime investigation strategy failed to reveal anything.

While Monique's approach was perhaps too aggressive, there were several other students at that time who sought to convert academic relationships into social ones. With a little effort and self control I managed to adjust to a milieu quite different from that which had prevailed in my first 25 years of teaching.

One day when Audrey and I drove back from some political event in Hartford it struck me that we had exchanged hardly a single word on the entire trip. I called that fact to her attention. It made us both wonder what was going on in our lives. Was it because our kids were now adults with their own lives and problems? Was it because the mental health problems Meredith confronted were outside our past expectations of what a normal happy middle age couple faces? Both Audrey and I took refuge in our very busy professional lives leaving little room for common activities. She was busier than ever trying to resolve the financial and tax problems of Connecticut, occasionally helping Ella Grasso, sometimes annoying the Governor. I was not only active in the University Senate, but also chaired the Mansfield Democratic Town Committee.

When we had planned our trip to San Francisco for the week before our son's wedding, I had hoped to turn that occasion into a belated celebration of our own wedding. The crisis that hit us created an environment that discouraged a celebratory mood. However, there was much more than that to deflate this attempt at restoring a happier close relationship.

A year after our return from the West Coast my life began to change. I started to look at my surroundings and friends in a different light. Feeling lonely, I looked for companionship. At least, that is what it seems to me in retrospect. Almost completely unexpectedly, a neighbor on Dunham Pond Road that I had known for many years attracted me enough for me to have to think seriously about what lay ahead. My neighbor Althea helped me by insisting that our relationship required us both to divorce our respective mates and restart our lives jointly. Neither her husband nor Audrey had the slightest inkling of the momentous decision we had made to start divorce proceedings. Somewhat naively, we believed that we would inform our spouses and then proceed normally on the new track that we had chosen, without any undue commotion or damage.

We were quickly brought back to reality. After Meredith had successfully graduated from Harvard and gotten her first job, I informed Audrey that I was thinking about a divorce. She did not react the way I had expected. She said hardly anything at all. A couple of days later, she complained of a terrible ringing in her ears that forced her to postpone her trip to the State Capitol. She had overdosed on aspirins. She claimed it was accidental. A couple of weeks passed. About a month later, coming home from my University office in the evening, Audrey's car was in the garage, but Audrey was not in the house. On my desk in my study was a thick envelop, containing a seven-page letter, addressed to me. I did not have to read beyond the second page to realize that it was a lengthy explanation of why she was planning to end her life. Meredith and I immediately started to search the house and neighborhood. It was twilight and flashlights did not help that much. It was Meredith, who ventured to the pier on Dunham Pond and discovered her mother lying there, overdosed with Extra-Strength Tylenol. Audrey had assumed that she would quickly lose consciousness and fall off the pier into the water and drown. We brought her to Windham Hospital where they helped her get rid of the Extra-Strength Tylenol. She recovered in time to go to work the next day.

Audrey's suicide attempt shook me up, forcing me to recognize that the path leading to a divorce would be far more complicated and fraught with unexpected problems that I had naively ignored. Audrey had always shown the public, her family and me, such a happy, positive face, full of laughter and cheer, that I had ignored another side. There had been occasions, early in our marriage, when instead of responding to some comment, Audrey would clam up and not say any word whatsoever for a considerable period. She would then continue the conversation as if nothing had happened. While such episodes occurred very infrequently as our relationship matured, her suicide attempt confronted me with the fact that I now had to deal with the other side of Audrey: serious depression, a state of mind facilitating her seeking shelter in her own chamber of refuge. In retrospect, it is obvious that my talk of a divorce had pushed her into a position where she saw no hope.

A few weeks before her attempt, the chair of the Connecticut Democratic Party had invited Audrey and me for lunch at a restaurant where Democratic Party affairs were always on the lunch menu. The purpose of the meeting was to discuss Audrey's possible candidacy for the Second Congressional District seat that Chris Dodd, the incumbent, was going to vacate as he planned to run for the U.S. Senate. Audrey knew then that I was planning to divorce her and the Chair knew. They wanted to know whether I was going to interfere with her possible candidacy. I assured them that obviously I would not. The discussion then got around to raising money for such a campaign. In my opinion, this was a much more difficult issue where, as a UCONN Professor I could be of little help. The lunch discussion confirmed my impression that Audrey's reputation and prominence in Hartford would help her get over the divorce. I was engaging in wishful thinking.

Less than a month after her Dunham Pond pier suicide attempt, Audrey tried it again. After finishing a lecture, my Political Science Department secretary informed me that I had a message to call the police. There I learned that Audrey had made another attempt, this time on our property in plain daylight. She had slashed her wrist while sitting on a blanket a considerable distance from the house. An early snowfall made Audrey so uncomfortable while waiting for the loss of blood to take effect that she changed her mind, walked back to the house and called our doctor. He called the fire department, which called the state police and transported her to St Francis Hospital in Hartford. When I got to her bedside, Governor Ella Grasso was sitting at her bedside; Ella gave me a dirty look and asked me what took me so long. I explained that I did not learn of what had happened until my class was over. The Governor however had been informed by the State Police the moment anything unusual happened to a legislator.

Audrey was treated in a psychiatric section of St. Francis with restricted access. Her psychiatrist informed me that he had prescribed a drug that would deal with her state of depression, but warned me it would take more than a week to become effective. He also had us both in to discuss what was wrong with our marriage. His role as a mediator turned out to be that of a silent third party observer who would turn his face first in Audrey's direction, then in mine, asking us each in turn to say whatever was on our minds. We told him nothing. His efforts were a total failure. I was shocked when nine months later he testified on Audrey's behalf at our divorce trial. That same psychiatrist chaired the State Board of Mental Health a few years later. When it happened that I was appointed to that Board, he failed to appear at the first meeting I attended. He promptly resigned. I never tried to find out whether that was a coincidence.

After staying less than a week at St. Francis, Audrey returned home. The medication had improved her mood. She informed me that there were at least a hundred different ways of ending one's life. She felt well enough now not to want to try any other method just yet. Instead, she was going to put up a fight in the coming divorce proceedings.

I contacted my long time political friend Leo Flaherty, the Vernon lawyer. After confirming the logic of my decision to seek a divorce and representing me in Court, he reconsidered because he remembered having represented Audrey a few years earlier in a speeding case where he got her off the hook. Reluctantly he felt it improper to represent me after helping her. He recommended another lawyer. It became quickly apparent that the best legal minds had been assembled by Audrey's Hartford friends. My lawyer told me that this was unfair. What normally would have been a routine case in the Rockville Court became a three-day affair with countless witnesses testifying on Audrey's behalf. A large audience of Audrey's Hartford friends tried to demolish me as they stared at me with contempt.

I had thought that passage of the no-fault divorce legislation a few years earlier was supposed to have simplified the process. I learned too late that no fault simply meant that you kept your shirt, but lost everything else. I had suggested that we divide the assets fairly. The judge granted the divorce and turned over the house into which I had put so much effort to Audrey and gave me a nominal compensation with the order to leave the house within a day. I got my study cleared and the books into the car when the locksmith came to change the locks. That is how my life with Audrey ended; a life that had been so full of promise, excitement and happiness. A few days after the Judge settled the divorce proceedings Althea and I got married on my mother's porch in South Windsor and a new chapter in our lives started.

***

Our children kept us informed and therefore distantly involved in the major activities of our respective ex-partners. Audrey and I met occasionally to discuss problems affecting Meredith, possible solutions and actions we had to take. Carrick, Althea's younger son, spent one semester of his senior year at our home and the other with his father. The next year his father and we helped Carrick start his academic career studying engineering at the University of Rochester. We were therefore not caught completely by surprise, when we learned that Audrey and Charles, Althea's ex-husband, had not only become close friends, but were planning to get married.

Their wedding was scheduled for Saturday, March 10, 1983. Carrick and his girlfriend had arrived earlier that week from Rochester. Ronald who had divorced Cathy and was on his way to Storrs, accompanied Ariela his soon-to-be wife. They had stopped in Rowayton to visit Audrey's parents. Althea's daughter Kate, accompanied by her husband and nearly two-year old son, were on their way. All family members and close friends were in various stages of preparation anticipating the important day. While Althea and I were not expected to participate we followed the preparations because Carrick and Meredith casually told us the latest news about the planned festivities. On Thursday, however, there were no exciting tidbits of gossip. Late Friday morning, Carrick casually informed us that Audrey had not been seen since leaving the State Capitol on Wednesday. "Were they looking for her?" I asked. "Of course" he answered. My thoughts immediately turned to Audrey's suicide attempts three and a half years earlier. Althea and I raised the question whether it was appropriate for me to get involved in any search. After all I was reasonably familiar with Audrey's mental process of choosing some special out of the way spot from where, all alone, she could leave this world.

A short time later, while on an errand, the news on my car radio mentioned not only that Audrey had disappeared, but that it was believed that her car with its telltale legislative license plates had been located on a dirt road. Her body was found nearby.

Charles' home was transformed from a wedding preparation headquarter to an assembly of grieving families. Everybody was there, except Althea and I. We felt that our presence would needlessly inject a thorny memory. It was however impossible for us not to get involved in the news accounts of Audrey's suicide. A reporter spent almost an hour interviewing me in my office. The first and only time that ever happened. Audrey's important role in the legislature, her close relationship with the Governor brought the tragedy to center stage. Flags were flown at half-mast and a Memorial Service was held at UCONN's Jorgensen auditorium.

Ronald gave a wonderful tribute to his mother, by far the most moving statement presented to a packed auditorium of mourners. Ronald's ability to rise to the occasion without any apparent difficulty was remarkable. Not only did he make sure that Audrey's life and contributions would be appropriately remembered, but he also took care of all essential tasks connected with the funeral, the estate and everything else few people of his age have to face. He established a UCONN student scholarship in her name.

As I learned details about Audrey's last known meeting with an old friend and the place where she was found two days later, it became obvious to me that our marriage and its dissolution still had weighed heavily on her mind. She was agitated when she had bidden good-bye to her friend Betty at the State Capitol. This worried Betty. Audrey ought to have been excited and in a positive mood about the coming wedding. Instead, the vestiges of past wounds overwhelmed her. Maybe she had stopped taking the medication that had helped her recover from her previous attacks of depression. She sought to get away from it all and drove to Mason Road in Willington an unpaved out-of-way dirt road less than a mile from where thirty-three years earlier she and I had dated and started our common lives. Apparently, she had driven there, parked her car some distance from the main highway, locked the car, leaving the keys inside, and walked a short distance into a wooded area, took some pills and waited for the end. By locking the car, she had made sure that unlike in her previous failed attempts she would not be able to change her mind. It is hard to understand that a full day passed before a passing motorist decided that it was somewhat strange that a car with a legislative license plate was left unattended on an unpaved road in the midst of nowhere. The motorist finally called the police. By then Audrey's fateful decision could not be reversed. The inscription marking her gravestone in the Storrs Cemetery:

Audrey Beck
Friend of Eastern Connecticut
Leader with Vision and Insight

Less than two months after Audrey's tragic suicide, Ronald became a father and I a grandfather. Nathan's birth on May 2, 1983, managed to lift our mood. At last, there was an occasion we could celebrate. It hurt that Audrey departed before meeting her grandson. If Nathan had arrived several months earlier, might this not have given her the boost she needed to face life's challenges?

***

Just about the time of Audrey's suicide in March 1983, I had to face another crisis. Flames became visible at an improperly connected segment in the stovepipe above my woodstove less than ten feet from the desk in my study next door. I called the Mansfield Fire Department, inquiring calmly whether closing the air intake would solve my problem. A brusque voice asked for my precise address and access. I had barely put down the phone receiver when I heard fire engine sirens and a fireman pulled the fiery logs out of the stove into a metal container. The flames in the pipe opening disappeared and a lecture on how to operate a woodstove began. The firemen realizing instantly the hopelessness of dealing with a UCONN Professor, shifted to Plan B and gave me the name and address of a professional chimney sweep couple whom I was instructed to call before even thinking about lighting a match to kindle a piece of paper, twig or log. Properly intimidated, I followed instructions.

The chimney sweep couple reflected the cultural-social revolution of the sixties and seventies. She was a feminist eager to prove that exploring a chimney should not be left to males and Santa Claus. He was a scholarly youth who wanted to show that replacing a stovepipe gave greater immediate satisfaction than having to explain mathematical equations about air circulation velocity and heat generation. I was taught all about maintaining a hot stove in a manner to avoid the buildup of creosote and how to identify logs that burn most efficiently. They also installed a stovepipe thermometer that helps me keep the stove at the proper temperature.

There is one other person who has helped me enjoy my woodstove. My chimney sweep couple had suggested that I make sure that my logs are neither too green, nor too wet, come from the right type of tree and are properly stacked. To keep me from rolling my eyes, they suggested someone who delivers wood. That person stopped delivering logs a decade ago. Now I have Mr. Kelly. Mr. Kelly is at least 30 years younger than I, but his deep Irish voice delivers advice I would not dare ignore. After dropping the load from his truck, he picks up individual logs and shows me crucial details. It seems as if he hates to part from the logs he has so lovingly split, loaded on his red truck, driven to the circle at the end of September Road and then carefully backed up the steep rise and dropped the load for me to stack and cover to protect them from rain and snow.

My woodstove is in the basement next to the room where I take refuge from watching TV. It is there that I write and read. It is not really a refuge because I am connected with the world through the internet. Paying attention to the stove, starting the fire, feeding and controlling it, gives me a sense of warmth and comfort. Occasionally the stove trumps the book I am reading. The flames are real; the words that I read depend on my brain to make sense. The flames talk to me. They tell me pay attention or they will either die down or get so hot that I had better put my flame resistant gloves on. As I stare at the flames, my memory brings back one of the first real discussions I had with my father when I was six or seven. “Why do things burn? What makes a flame?” My father, the philosopher who avoided math and science, covered himself by answering, “a chemical reaction.” “What is that?” He terminated the discussion by promising that I would get an answer to this difficult question later on in some advanced course in school. By the time I got to college I had lost interest in the question.

As I watch the fire, my thoughts turn to the burning logs. It is the logs, which connect me with nature. Trees overshadow our house. I pick up the branches a storm breaks from the tree trunks to lighten their load. Some of the bigger branches I manage to cut into pieces and split, adding them to the cords delivered by Mr. Kelly. When the flames devour the bark, for a second or so, I feel sorry for the suddenly naked stem totally exposed to the raging flames. The train of my thoughts quickly shifts as I watch the cords compete for rapid extinction. The temperature rises, I check the thermometer, the needle has not yet reached 500 degrees and I can return to my book and read another chapter. A perfect evening!

Part VI - A New Chapter in my Life

Chapter 19
Althea

Althea had a major impact on my life. She had lived in Storrs almost as long as I. Kate, her daughter, and Malcolm, her older son, were close in age to Ronald and Meredith. For more than a dozen years, both of our families were members of the Dunham Pond Association. We even shared the *Macbeck*, a rowboat incorporating our last names with a little assistance from Shakespeare. Our relations had always been casual and friendly but certainly not intimate until at first her and then my prior marriages hit difficult patches. We began to pay more attention to each other. We discovered we had very similar attitudes, experiences and expectations. It took us no time at all to enjoy each other's company as if we had always known each other. Our lives were joined and transformed. We shared common thoughts, wishes, idiosyncrasies, similar political views, loved classical music and regularly attended the productions of the Hartford Stage. Our mothers had lived ten time zones apart, her mother in Bremerton across the Bay from Seattle, Washington, and mine in Berlin, Germany, and yet our dates of birth were only four months apart.

We had a very informal wedding. On August 1 1980, the local Justice of the Peace married us on my mother's porch in South Windsor. Meredith and Malcolm, Althea's older son, attended. Ronald joined us later at a restaurant in Windsor. At the end of August we moved to a house on September Road that was built less than ten years before. Our common venture was about to start.

On our honeymoon, we explored Canada's Maritime Provinces. On the way to Nova Scotia, we visited Franklin Delano Roosevelt's Campobello Island summer home. Althea was as ardent a New Dealer as I. We shared similar political views on almost every conceivable issue. We were impressed by the simplicity of Roosevelt's childhood home that was later associated with his paralyzing polio attack.

The highlight of our trip was touring Cape Breton on the Cabot Trail. After spending a night at the Keltic Lodge on Ingonish Beach, and eating an excellent dinner, the fish that they served Althea caused her stomach to revolt. In spite of being nearly incapacitated for 24 hours Althea insisted we continue our journey. She managed to open her eyes when I stopped the car to show her incredibly scenic coastal vistas on the Cabot Trail.

We took the ferry to the western end of Prince Edward Island and drove to the other end. We were disappointed not to find any landscape comparable to the forests and mountains that dropped precipitously into the sea on Cape Breton. Not even the House of Green Gables made up for the Island's boring flat green meadows and occasional historic relics.

After returning from our ten-day escape from reality, we had to make final preparations to move into our new home on September Road. Althea returned to her desk in the University's Office of Institutional Research, where she had to tackle a number of reports with tight deadlines. I still had a couple of weeks to get ready for the fall semester. Arranging a mortgage, dealing with lawyers, bankers, and real estate agents seemed almost fun compared to the travails of the divorce trial the previous month. In retrospect, it was a very exciting and interesting summer. Not surprisingly, only a couple of my old friends at the university had the courage to ask me how my summer went. They approached me gingerly, reluctant to converse about my new status as the guy who had switched wives, but when they noted that I really had not changed that much, our relationships resumed and returned to their previous pattern.

Divorce and remarriage did however affect our children. Ronald in his third year with Cathy encountered difficulties in his own marriage. I ignored them. I was too deeply involved in my own situation. In retrospect, it is obvious that at a critical time in his own life I did not provide a stable background when that might have helped him. The impact on Meredith was more serious. Her psychiatrist recommended that she move out of our Dunham Pond home when informed that her parents' marriage was about to break up. Given Meredith's mental illness, starting her own independent life proved to be quite stressful and unfortunately contributed to the worsening of her illness. It turned out that Althea was able to deal with Meredith's illness more effectively than either Audrey or I. As her friend, not related by blood, she could observe and help her with greater objectivity. She encouraged me to inform myself about the most recent research on schizophrenia. We both became involved in the National Alliance for the Mentally Ill (NAMI), which helps relatives deal with individuals who suffer from a mental illness.

***

Althea wanted me to meet her sister, brother and mother. Just ordinary folks, she claimed. Quite an understatement! Her sister Shirley was born almost exactly a year after Althea. So close in age, they competed as they grew up. Althea considered Shirley the more attractive one. These ancient memories had not quite disappeared. While Althea completed her college education at the University of Washington Shirley met Jeff, a soldier on leave from his service in the Aleutian Islands. They got married and had a son several years before Althea got married to Charles, her first husband. Posted in Japan after the Japanese surrendered, Shirley's husband was attracted by the culture and people he encountered there and later in Korea. He became a Methodist minister and embarked on a long lasting career as a missionary. They lived in South Korea until Jeff retired in the nineteen-eighties and they settled in San Antonio, Texas. While Althea was married to Charles, she hardly ever saw Shirley. A few weeks before our marriage, Shirley got in touch with Althea, calling from New Haven where Jeff was attending a Korean language program at Yale while on leave from his Korean missionary work. Shirley suggested we meet for dinner in Westport. Reassured by a very pleasant dinner discussion, we had Jeff, the minister and religious authority, express supportive positive thoughts, thereby blessing our wedding. The family connection was restored.

Stuart, Althea's brother, was several years younger and lived near Seattle. I first heard his voice a couple of months after our marriage when, after introducing himself, he asked to speak to his sister because something terrible had just happened. I gave him Althea's office phone number. After only a few minutes, Althea gave me the horrible news: Stuart's 15-year old daughter, on her way home from high school, had taken a short cut through a small park, where she was attacked by a guy and killed. We were shocked. When we visited Stuart some time later, and saw the well-kept neighborhood in which this tragic crime had occurred. I was appalled that such a tragedy could have happened

Hilda, Althea's mother, was a very energetic and spry grandmother in her late seventies. She flew across the continent to see us shortly after our marriage. On a walk in our neighborhood, I learned that she had come to America when she was nearly the same age that I was when I had crossed the Atlantic. Hilda's father, who had worked on airplane designs shortly after the Wright brothers had launched their first plane, contracted a serious infection and died leaving his family in dire straits. At the urging of a Mormon relative, Hilda's mother took her family to Canada, crossed Canada by rail and settled in a small town in eastern British Columbia, just across from Idaho. There being no high school in her town, Hilda traveled by herself to Idaho where she stayed with distant relatives. In Idaho, she met her future husband who was on his way from the Midwest to Washington State, where his father worked in a Bremerton shipyard. Hilda and I shared our feelings and memories about crossing the Atlantic at a young age. She seemed pleased that someone was interested in these experiences of her youth that she could finally share with a fellow immigrant. Meeting Althea's family gave me a new perspective. Most of my friends and acquaintances were Easterners or Midwesterners. Althea's Northwest background intrigued me and we quickly resolved to travel to the state of Washington to let me savor firsthand the idyllic places of her youth. But first, we had to visit Germany and Eastern Europe where I introduced Althea to the land of my youth.

Althea's daughter Kate, who was close to my son Ronald's age, happened to get married the year before my divorce. That introduced me to Louisiana, a state with a charm all of its own. Her husband, Billy Amoss, was one of five brothers whose parents played a prominent role in New Orleans. I first met them at the wedding, which had an extremely scenic setting at *The Golden Lamb*, a restaurant-farm in nearby Brooklyn, Ct. Her father, who ran one of the few shipping companies then still operating in the U.S., rekindled my interest in transatlantic ocean crossings that dated back to my teenage years. Her mother explored customs and folktales spread by some of the older New Orleans residents, a city with its French-Cajun culture from the pre-Napoleonic era and Black Jazz .

Althea and I were quick to accept an invitation to visit our new in-laws and discovered a fascinating part of America. Hosted by a family with deep local roots enabled us to move quickly beyond the well-publicized Old City Quarter with its jazzy Mardi Gras carnival atmosphere and visit impressive mansion-style houses in park-like mini-gardens. We visited a modern museum showing not so ancient art, explored Cajun inhabited areas near the Mississippi estuary and looked at the somewhat neglected harbor. As one who had received his historical training in a French gymnasium in Prague, I felt sorry that Napoleon had to give up this priceless part of the New World. That was a long time ago.

Billy's parents also had a summer home in Pass Christian, Mississippi, a two minute walk from the Gulf coast. We spent an afternoon shucking clamshells and enjoying a maritime barbecue with the crash of the waves as musical accompaniment. Amidst this romantic backdrop, the conversation shifted to tales of past hurricanes that had brought the Gulf of Mexico to the family's first floor. Billy's brothers covered a wide range of interests. The eldest, editor of the *Times Picayune*, satisfied my curiosity about Louisiana politics, answering questions asked and those that were still hidden in the back of my brain. Another brother spent much of his time in Hong Kong. A younger one was racing horses and the youngest trained to become a doctor.

Billy was the only one of the Amoss brothers who had no clear objective when we first met him. His interest ranged from Russian music and history acquired at Yale to business. His father encouraged him to work in the family's shipping company. A year after their marriage Billy took Kate to Germany where he spent a year in Hamburg at the *Hapag Lloyd* Shipping Company, learning the essentials of contemporary Atlantic commerce. It is there that Kate awaited the birth of her first child.

Althea was anxious to see her first grandchild and comfort her daughter in an unaccustomed foreign environment as soon as possible. While the baby arrived on schedule, his schedule did not coincide with the University calendar: The spring semester had three more weeks to go. The problem was quickly resolved: Billy's mother spent the first week following her grandson's birth in Hamburg, Althea arrived one week later, and I completed the circle of grandson cheerleaders the third week after correcting final exams. Our visit turned out to be helpful in resolving a German-American culture conflict on how best to treat the mother at childbirth. Kate was imbued with a strong desire that the whole process be as natural as possible. Her German Doctor neither cared nor agreed, with the wishes of the mother and followed the latest rules and regulations about safe delivery. Three weeks after the event, I spent hours trying to convince Kate that her doctor was not some monster without feeling, but an MD who followed German medical regulations. After all, Germany was still the land of Law and *Ordnung* [order].

***

Saturday, August 3, 1991, Althea and I went to our favorite beach at Watch Hill, Rhode Island. Later that day we had a very relaxing time at a nearby restaurant. The food was excellent and the atmosphere transported us far away from our everyday concerns. When we got back to Storrs, it was nearly 11 PM. We were happy, tired, skipped the 11 o'clock news and went to bed and fell asleep almost instantly.

The phone next to my side of the bed must have rung several times before my brain noted the noise. Somehow, I managed to locate the receiver and asked, "Who the hell is disturbing me at this ungodly hour?" "This is captain so and so from the New York City police. Can I talk to Mrs. Beck?" I was by now completely irritated. Why in the world would a New York policeman call me after midnight. No one, with whom we were currently in touch, was in New York, as far as I knew. I asked the person on the line to stop making stupid jokes and let us sleep. Undistracted, the caller asked to speak to Mrs. Beck about her son Carrick. That changed everything. Carrick was indeed Althea's younger son. As far as we knew, he was in Boston. I turned the phone over to Althea who by now was awake.

From Althea's reaction, I guessed instantly that something terrible had happened. "Is he O.K.?" and then Althea stopped talking. I could hear a steady monotone from the receiver. Occasionally Althea would respond yes and no, and then be silent."The phone number of his father?" She gave it to the caller. The conversation stopped and she told me what she had just been told. "There was a terrible accident. Carrick had gone to New York to visit some college friends in Greenwich Village. He had fallen from the roof of the house of the friend with whom he stayed. He was fighting for his life in a hospital".

The phone rang again. A doctor in the hospital's emergency section called to inform Althea of Carrick's critical condition. "Should she come right now?" The doctor gave a somewhat negative response, Carrick was not conscious. A visit can wait until daytime. Charles, Carrick's father and Althea's former husband, called. The New York police had gotten in touch with him. He and Ruth, his wife, were considering driving to New York in half an hour. They would let us know when we should come.

After these phone calls, a completely unaccustomed feeling overpowered me. It felt as if an extremely heavy weight had dropped on me. I could hardly move. I could not think about anything. I felt helpless. Althea and I looked at each other and could not face the fact that Carrick who was always cheerful, busy, full of plans, happy in his job, socially very active, had just fallen from the roof of a three-story Greenwich Village house to his death. How could we get through this night and drive next morning to New York?

We stayed in bed. Every half hour or hour the phone would ring. Charles or Ruth would report their latest phone conversation with staff at the emergency room. Finally, at daybreak, they called after setting foot in the emergency room. Charles suggested that Althea not come. Carrick was in a condition that would hurt Althea's memory of her son.

How did this tragic event happen? Charles and Ruth talked at the hospital with Carrick's friends, the police and the hospital staff. Althea and I heard Carrick's friends repeat the same account of events a few days later. Carrick, a very active person, had decided to spend a weekend in New York with some of his Rochester University college pals. A decade had passed since his exciting college years in up-state New York. Apparently, he was bored with his usual social weekend activities, sailing in Boston harbor and dating a very interesting girlfriend from Idaho. Carrick and three or four of his college pals spent Saturday afternoon playing ball on the street near the friend's house who had invited him. A passing stranger offered Carrick and his friends some cheap drug. This reminded the group of their college days. They did not give it a second thought and swallowed whatever they had been sold. Nobody except Carrick had a significant reaction. Either Carrick, not accustomed to drugs since college, or having been given a more potent portion, reacted instantly. His friends realized this almost immediately and managed to get him into the front door of the friend's house. Obviously completely confused and not familiar with this place, he behaved as if it were in his own apartment house in Boston. He raced to the top floor and opened the door, thinking it was the door to his Boston roof top apartment. Instead, he was out on the roof in Greenwich Village. He teetered at the edge overlooking the street below. Before his friends could catch him, he fell several stories onto the street pavement below.

Chapter 20
Traveling with Althea: A Widening Horizon

In the 1970's I had focused on Connecticut politics and University affairs, in the 1980's Althea helped me broaden the scope of my inquisitive interests. While the growing families of Ronald and Althea's Malcolm and Kate never ceased to concern us, Meredith's illness always required our attention without interrupting our travel plans. Althea shared my interest in exploring the wider world with our own eyes.

Our visit to Kate's giving birth to her son Philip gave us the opportunity to explore Hamburg. I had never visited Hamburg before and was delighted to have this chance to see a city that my mother had often talked about when I was young. Many of her cousins on her father's side had their homes there before the Holocaust. None had survived as far as I know. Armed with a cousin's old postcard, address and picture, I located the house. It looked almost exactly as it did on the postcard. On my return I informed my then eighty-one year old mother that I had located the house of her cousin. She was amazed.

Traveling in northern East Germany gave me an opportunity to show Althea the Berlin of my early years. On our way there I was unable to locate the house on Inselpromenade 8 in Braunschweig (Brunswick), where my mother was born and where she had spent the first six years of her childhood. She had given me the address. Apparently Braunschweig had changed considerably in the 80 years since her birth.

Since it was May we passed farms in northern Germany at the height of the asparagus season. Farm stands were everywhere displaying huge bundles of the white asparagus variety. When we stopped at a restaurant, the menu highlighted asparagus-containing items, ranging from asparagus soup to asparagus desert. It reminded me of my aversion to that vegetable before my taste buds had matured as a teenager. Asparagus dominated our conversation until we reached the East German checkpoint on the Autobahn to West Berlin.

Althea and I spent three days visiting my favorite spots in Berlin: museums in the city's center, my house in Wannsee and my favorite restaurant *Nikolskö (Nikoslkoe,* as named by its original

Russian owners to honor their Czar Nicolas) in the forest overlooking the lake near Potsdam, not far from East Germany. We could have spent more time in Berlin, but cut our visit short to have sufficient time to explore Europe on the other side of the Iron Curtain.

***

It took us a couple of hours to reach the Polish border at Frankfurt on the Oder. We were somewhat apprehensive driving through an Eastern European satellite of the Soviet Union at a time when there were signs of potential political unrest. Shipyard workers at the Baltic port of Gdansk (Danzig) led by Lech Walesa had started demonstrations half a year before our visit. How such a potentially explosive situation would be dealt with in a Soviet satellite was uncertain.

Our first stop on our way to Warsaw was Poznan (Posen). My maternal grandmother's ancestors had lived there before moving to Berlin in the 19th century. This part of Poland had been part of Prussia until the First World War. Jews from that mixed ethnic area preferred to be considered German, not Polish. Poznan did not strike us as particularly interesting.

Before reaching Warsaw the next day, we noted that the famous 19th century Polish composer Chopin's birthplace was in the village of Želazowa Wola, a short detour from our route. We stopped in a well-preserved white cottage, looked at the furniture, but heard no music. Concerts were scheduled only on Sunday afternoon. Disappointed, we reached our modern-style hotel near the Warsaw airport and started to explore Poland's capital. Little was left from the past. The revolt in the Ghetto and its ensuing destruction, the Partisan uprising, war damage by the Nazis and the Red Army had left little to preserve. Soviet era massive block structures had taken over the center of the city. What we saw confirmed the impression that I had gained from countless newspaper accounts and pictures: Warsaw had lost its historic character and charm. Of course, we could not have known in May 1981 that this period was the calm before Lech Walesa and his Solidarity union movement would stir up a storm beyond the shipyards in Gdansk and create a new mood of optimism. With help from Karol Wojtila, Cardinal of Krakow, who in 1978 had become

Pope John Paul II, Poland would gradually emerge from its decades of operating in the Soviet orbit.

We spent only one full day in Warsaw, leaving the following morning for Krakow. On our way there, we went on a detour, stopping near the city of Lublin, which Stalin had recognized as the first major city in liberated Poland. The Soviet Union had annexed a considerable part of pre-war eastern Poland. We spent the night in Krakow, a University City and Cardinal Wojtyla's bishopric before his call to Rome. Krakow's market square and medieval-looking buildings had survived the war in a reasonably good condition Krakow impressed us with its well preserved past, in sharp contrast to Warsaw's post-war Soviet style make-over.

We did not come to Krakow only to admire this impressive symbol of Polish history and culture, but also as a stop on our way to Auschwitz (Oswiecim). There could not have been a greater contrast between Krakow, the seat of the University, and the Bishop's see and Auschwitz, the incarnation of hell on earth. What a contrast, only an hour's drive apart!

Arbeit Macht Frei, in big letters, greeted us at the entrance to Auschwitz. Millions of uprooted Jews had to pass under that sarcastic Nazi slogan, *Work Makes One Free*, on what was for most, the final station on the way to the gas chamber. I had seen that sign before in 1960 in Terezín, my grandfather's final stop. At the Visitors Center we were greeted with a recorded lecture explaining to the visitor from outer space what Auschwitz was all about. Althea and I were somewhat amazed that anybody taking the time and trouble to visit this concentration/extermination camp would be welcomed with such trivial information. We were even more shocked by the failure to mention that the millions of victims were Jews. The phrases used in the lecture were "anti-fascists, victims of the Hitler regime, patriotic Polish liberation fighters", etc. This was in part Stalin's legacy: his own version of anti-Semitism that had involved purges in Central and Eastern Europe, culminating in the "Doctors Plot" before his death in 1953 as well as deeply imbedded local anti-Semitism.

The railroad tracks leading to the camp's walled entrance have been preserved and maintained as mute testimony to the fate of millions, ignored by much of the world during the last three years of World War II. For most, passing through those gates after jumping out of the tightly packed filthy freight cars, led to a short stay in equally uncomfortable barracks, while the chemical poison gas chambers were prepared for ”customers” waiting to take the required final “shower”. A little further on, fires burned and flames awaited the dead corpses. The extermination process was completed in a typically efficient and “clean” German manner. The technical details having been worked out at the January 1942 Wannsee Conference.

As we stood there and looked at the railroad tracks, I was reminded of the story that my cousin Arnošt had told me of his experience at this stage of his family’s deportation. After disembarking from the train, the line of “passengers” was directed to a point where the passenger/prisoners were separated. Those judged by the Nazi officials capable of doing slave labor were directed one way, and those who were too young, too old or sick, were sent to barracks, on their way to the gas chamber. As Arnošt approached the key spot where his and his family’s fate was about to be decided, he was shocked to recognize the doctor who answered the Nazi officer’s inquiries about the state of health of victims awaiting their fate. It was the doctor, who had treated him in Prague. Arnošt had the presence of mind not to give any hint of their relationship. The doctor directed him and his sister to join those selected to work for the German war effort. As Arnošt passed by, the doctor whispered, “Take those god damn glasses off, if you want to live!” Arnošt did as demanded. The doctor knew that he was practically blind and could not read without glasses. By warning Arnošt, he had saved him from the line that ultimately led to the gas chamber. His mother, father and sickly younger brother were not so lucky and perished.

Except for the tracks not much else reflected conditions at the camp when it had functioned as the last stop on this earth for so many. Hitler’s victims were there only because of the decision by a maniac who had been permitted to leave his jail cell not quite two decades earlier after writing his so-called Memoir, *Mein Kampf.*

After staring at collections of possessions, including hair, taken from the camp’s victims, we had seen enough and left. We, especially Althea, were emotionally exhausted. We drove south to the Tatra Mountains at the Polish-Slovak border reaching Zakopane in about an hour. We left Poland and entered Czechoslovakia. The mountain resort where we stopped was a welcome relief from that day's earlier depressing tour of Hitler's Extermination Factory.

***

After a short stay in a Tatra mountain hotel accessible only by cable car and some tentative hiking with inadequate shoes and outdoor wear, we drove south, crossing into Hungary. There the highway signs confused and discombobulated me. I complained to Althea that the Hungarian language was impossible to figure out. Those Hungarians are descended from ancestors who migrated here a thousand years ago from Mongolia or some other place in far away Eastern Asia. Hungarian is unlike all the other languages that I can figure out. "What do you mean? German, Polish, Czech, Slovak are just as incomprehensible as Hungarian, as far as I am concerned. Just because German is your mother tongue and you spoke Czech in high school and studied other Slavic languages, you think everybody should be familiar with these alien tongues!" Althea's response made me aware how lost she must have felt when we covered hundreds of kilometers with unfamiliar road signs that I could sort of figure out. For me they were informative and had given me a sense of place and direction.

We stopped in Budapest just long enough to visit interesting museums and be charmed by gypsy musicians serenading us as we ate our meals. We stopped briefly at Lake Balaton, then crossed to Zagreb in Yugoslavia, took a plane to Dubrovnik, the most scenic renaissance port on the Dalmatian coast. On this, my third visit to Yugoslavia, taking the ferry up the Adriatic coast, had lost its magic. It had become just another coastline with island ports catering to visitors.

Our arrival in Venice was different. Althea was overcome by the magic of the Square of San Marco. The colors of the incredibly impressive Palace of the Doges, the Church, restaurants with their musicians and tables competing with their rivals for maximum space and noise on the square, flocks of pigeons descending on tourists who might drop some crumbs, gondoliers attempting to imitate their ancestors depicted in romantic stories, all this transported us to another world. The next morning we celebrated Althea's 57th birthday breakfast on the hotel's restaurant balcony overlooking the Grand Canal while boats passed below us. Althea said that Venice was the perfect location for a birthday celebration.

I promised we would have another one there, a promise I failed to keep.

***

I was anxious to introduce Althea to the Alpine landscapes that had always impressed me. South Tyrol in Italy had been the forbidden land of my youth. My parents had taken me twice to Austria's Tyrolean Alps, on the other side of the mountain passes that separated the two countries. I still remember how I had in the 1930's I looked up at the peaks of the highest mountains, surrounded by glaciers. There on the other side is Italy, governed by that terrible fascist monster, Benito Mussolini. "Why can't we visit there," I asked. "After all, did Mussolini not stop Hitler from taking Austria in 1934?" My father praised Mussolini for that, but added that visiting Italy ruled by Fascists was too dangerous. Our Austrian Tyrolean restaurant served us Italian spaghetti. They tasted so much better than the spaghetti, we ate at home that it made Italy a beckoning and tempting place in my youthful dreams.

I also remembered the postcard my grandfather had sent me when I was five years old, which had him and my grandmother pick grapes from branches in the hotel restaurant garden in Merano. That is where Althea and I stopped on our way north. The grapevine had long since been removed from the restaurant garden, but Merano had not lost its charm. We tried their Pinot Grigeau and had lots of spaghetti. Althea helped me celebrate the memories of my youth.

As we reached the Jaufenpass, a high elevation on our way to the Austrian side, our rented car acted up for the first time on the entire trip. At the point where the two lane serpentine Alpine highway provided a tiny parking area to permit a brief stop so that the incredibly beautiful Alpine vista could be enjoyed, the engine died and the car refused to budge. Althea and I shifted our mindset from contemplating the Alpine crest to the mundane topic of getting a car started with a malfunctioning battery. "Let's just roll down into Austria"."Suppose the engine refuses to cooperate and the brakes do not function?" "Let's try it anyway." Somehow, we pushed the car out of the parking area onto the road where there was a slight decline, jumped back into our seats as the car started to roll slowly at first. I shifted gears and the engine started. We were saved from a mountain rescue operation! We looked at the paperwork the Avis car rental agency had given me in Hamburg for the first time to locate their closest office. It was in Munich where we planned to arrive late that night. Until then, I would always stop the car on a hill so that I could repeat our successful Jaufenpass maneuver. When we arrived the next morning at the Munich Avis office, they did not even look at the battery, gave us an identical substitute car and shooed us out of the office.

On the way to Munich we made a slight detour to stop at Breitbrunn am Ammersee. It was here, not far from Munich by train, that my parents had spent the first two years of their marriage from 1923 to 1925. After I was delivered in a Berlin hospital at the insistence of my grandfather, they brought me back to Breitbrunn from where in my post-embryonic condition. I could admire the beautiful lake and the mountains in the distance. At least that is what I heard my parents say many, many times. We looked for the house that my mother described as my first home. We could not follow her somewhat romantic and vague description. While the contemporary village of Breitbrunn does not exactly measure up to the countless stories I was told, it is a perfect place for relaxation and contemplation of the Bavarian pre-Alpine landscape. Perhaps it is the memory of my staring at the mountains from my crib that led me to admire mountainous landscapes the rest of my life.

We stopped in Munich just long enough for Althea to realize here was a city that required another visit: there was too much to see in a couple of days. We had one unexpected experience. At the square where in November 1923 Adolf Hitler had attempted to seize the Bavarian government [Beer Hall Putsch] and where he was stopped and arrested. Suddenly a half dozen college age kids ran up the steps of the building that dominated the square, took off their clothes and showed us their naked behinds. Beside Althea and me, there were maybe a half dozen spectators. We had just enough time to take in the fully exposed anatomies of a bunch of healthy young men when the sirens of approaching police vehicles warned that a challenge to decent behavior would not be tolerated. The kids put their pants back on, gave the policemen who were racing up the steps some very dirty looks, which the police answered in kind. Peace and order were quickly restored before Althea and I could speculate about the intent of this interesting spectacle.

From Munich we drove to Prague via Plzeň (Pilsen), my father's birthplace. We drove by the apartment house on

Kopernikova 46, my grandparents' home, and stopped at my grandmother Matilda's grave in the Jewish cemetery on the highway leading out of the city. The impressive Jewish synagogue had not yet been restored and was still used by the Communist government as a storage facility.

Althea was overwhelmed by ancient Prague's incredible architectural beauty. The postcard of Charles Bridge with the Presidential castle Hradčany overlooking the Vltava River became alive as we climbed the many steps up to the ancient small houses surrounding the castle. All kinds of memories and tender feelings welled up inside me as I tried to explain the history behind the small and big monuments and structures surrounding us. "So this is the place you had to leave in 1938?" "Yes" I answered. We were both silent for some time. One cannot reminisce forever. We had dinner in a remarkably modern restaurant, a stone throw from the most historic part of the city.

There was one more stop on my pilgrimage to the past: Terezín [Theresienstadt]. This concentration camp, where my grandfather Gustav from Plzeň was taken in late January 1942, was on our route to the German border. I had visited the camp twenty years earlier and located my grandfather's approximate grave a few feet away from the Krematorium. He had spent the last seven months of his life there. He died when he was 86 years old.

When we arrived at the East German border in Cinovec it was 1 pm, a couple of hours later than intended. This mattered because we were going to get only a transit visa permitting us to travel through the German Democratic Republic (DDR). The transit visa required us to be out of the DDR before midnight. The distance from the Czech border to Hamburg was more than 300 miles. When we informed the East German frontier official that our destination was Hamburg, he looked at me, looked again at my passport and noted that I was born in Berlin. Somewhat reassured that a native Berliner wasn't likely to get lost in East Germany, he gave us the transit visa and a strong admonition that I better make sure we get to the frontier near Hamburg in plenty of time before midnight. Instead of speeding our departure, he enjoyed conversing with me. "How come, you got here so late from Prague?" I informed him that we had stopped in Terezín. He gave me a kind, knowing look and told me that he had visited the Terezín camp. It was a terrible thing the Nazis had done, he said.

As he finally bade us good-bye, he gave me conflicting advice: "Watch your speed, drive safely, and make sure you get to Hamburg at least one hour before midnight!" I asked him what would happen if I did not make it by then. He shook his head instead of answering. Althea had difficulty following my conversation in German with the frontier official. When I summarized it, she shook her head and asked, "If we don't make it by midnight we end up in a DDR jail?" I did not answer. I was scared.

After passing Dresden without stopping, we began to relax. After all, it was only 3 o'clock and traffic was light. We were hungry and stopped for half an hour at a restaurant near the Autobahn. We had to take a road circling Berlin to avoid delays at the West Berlin crossing checkpoints. When we reached the Potsdam area, I suggested that we stop there for a half hour. The Potsdam royal palace area was one of my childhood's favorite excursion destinations. I just had to show it to Althea. We were impressed not only by the outward maintenance of the royal garden and palace but the restoration of Potsdam's inner city. We strolled along the downtown streets. It was a perfect summer day, actually the longest day of the year. The sun was still up. Suddenly a clock stared us in the face. It was after 9 pm!! We raced to our car and sped out of town to the Autobahn, direction Hamburg.

This particular section was not one of the better-maintained East German highways. There was only one lane in each direction. Signs limiting speed were prominently displayed. One car overtook me, just as we were about to pass several police officers on motorcycles cleverly camouflaged on a side road. I was surprised that the police did not stop him. About ten minutes later another police posse appeared on the side of the road and the car that had overtaken us was surrounded by men in flashy uniforms. From then on Althea warned me each time I reached normal U.S. cruise speed. I realized we had the choice of spending time in a DDR jail for a traffic violation, or for exceeding our time allotted in East Germany. We reached the border at one minute before midnight. When I looked at my watch, as the official carefully scrutinized us and the contents of the car, he smiled. I asked him whether we were the last ones to meet the deadline. He smirked, implying the deadline was not quite as strictly enforced as we had feared.

It took us another hour to get to Kate and the baby who had grown considerably while we had spent our time exploring Central and Eastern Europe. It had been a wonderful trip.

***

After I introduced Althea to my past, it was Althea's turn to show me hers. We did that one year later in August 1982. We started in Portland, Oregon, where we stopped at Elena's, Althea's high school friend of the late '30's. Elena and her husband, an Oregon state environmental commissioner, had us stay at their house in an incredibly scenic part of the city, way up on a steep hill. It was my first visit to Portland, after attending Ronald's wedding there five years earlier. The city then had made quite an impression with its hills, parks and incredible view on clear days of the Cascade Mountain range, especially Mount Hood towering in the distance. In 1977, however, I had been too preoccupied with the wedding as well as the Meredith's crisis back home, to be in the proper mood to appreciate fully the city near the mouth of the Columbia River, the final destination of the Lewis and Clarke expedition almost 180 years earlier. It gave Althea a great deal of pleasure to prove to me that her Cascade mountain range was just as impressive as the Alps we had crossed a year earlier. "Yes," I responded, "but the mountain trails in the Alps are much easier to climb than the ones in the Cascades, and in the Alps they have got all those restaurants way up above the tree line." Of course, I chose to ignore the fact that we had gotten by car a considerable distance up to a National Park-run mountain resort on Mount Hood. I considered that cheating since we did not have to exhaust ourselves using our legs.

From Portland, we crossed the Columbia River into Althea's native state of Washington. That is where the fun really began. We veered off the Interstate on a side trip to see nature's devastating power: the remnants of Mount St. Helens, which had blown its stack May 18, 1980, two and a half months before our wedding. The eruption and consequent fall out on Washington State and Idaho had worried Althea a great deal at the time. Fortunately, none of her family had suffered any damage. A little more than two years later, this was her first chance to see with her own eyes what the forces of nature had done. Never having seen Mount St. Helens, only pictures of the crater area before and after the eruption were embedded in my mind. I recall especially one picture of a small blue lake surrounded by a glacier and fumes erupting from vents nearby.

As the road wound its way higher up, we expected a panorama to emerge each time we passed another curve. No such luck. Instead, I had to focus my attention on fully loaded lumber trucks which carried trunks singed by the eruption's firestorm, that could be used for profit by lumber interests. Instead of admiring the beauty of nature, Althea and I discussed the damage caused by profit-motivated mega-industries. As the road climbed higher and higher, reality finally hit us: When Mt. St. Helens exploded, it lost its top 1,000 feet and as a result there was not much to see. The new dome and snow-covered glaciers would need some time to form. We thought we could see some fumes coming from vents, but perhaps they were passing clouds. After looking and exploring the areas open to visitors, we called it quits and turned around. I had learned a lesson: a volcano is most interesting when it erupts. At that point, it is safest to watch it from a great distance on television.

It did not take us too much time to approach Mt. Rainier National Park. The massive mountain with its extensive snowcap dominated everything. It is as if Mt. Rainier were gloating about having lost its rival St. Helens, 60 miles to the south. We had dinner and spent the night at Paradise Inn. Trails lead from there to the peak. We were not equipped, nor in the right frame of mind to embark on a strenuous and somewhat risky mountain climbing exercise. I also remembered my father's observation: a mountaintop is most impressive when seen from below. If you have reached the top, it looks flat and it has lost its attraction. We spent about half an hour taking the first one hundred steps up the trail, admired the view, and filled our lungs with a lot of mountain air, turned around, stepped into our rented car and circumnavigated the base of the mountain massif.

After a lot of scenic driving, we arrived at Althea mother's modest house in a Seattle suburb. Hilda had moved there after Althea father's death a few years earlier and had not lived there too long. The home was as new to Althea as it was to me. We spent several very enjoyable and comfortable days there. It served as an excellent base from which to explore Seattle, Puget Sound with its many islands and the Olympic Peninsula.

The first night Althea wanted me to meet Stuart, her kid brother. He was about five years younger. When she had entered college, the age gap was significant enough for it to have left a permanent mark in her thoughts about her brother. We were to meet in a restaurant located in a scenic location on Lake Washington Canal. We were first to arrive and waited for Stuart. Seated at a table, Althea assured me that we would have no trouble locating him. "Why?" I asked. "You'll see". A few minutes later, a tall, impressively large person with a broad grin entered. "Is that your kid brother?" I asked, incredulously. Stuart explained to me that he had a hard time convincing his older sister that kids do not stop growing when they reach the ripe old age of twelve. Stuart introduced us to his wife, a charming person who had grown up on an Indian reservation and gone to college in the Northeast.

I encouraged Althea to take me to her place of birth, Bremerton. The name intrigued me. Had it something to do with the German harbor Bremen? She assured me that there was no connection. Since she never gave me an alternative explanation, I continue to connect the two harbors. Bremerton is a major shipyard and serves the U.S. Pacific fleet. That is what brought her grandfather there from Indiana by way of Idaho at the beginning of the 20th century. To get there we took a Washington State Ferry. Ferries connect all the islands in Puget Sound almost as regularly and quickly as subways in New York. The air is delightful and the view exciting, at least the first couple of times that we crossed the Sound. Hilda had given Althea the address where they had lived when she was a baby. Some memories came back, but she failed to recognize places where she might have spent some time as a young girl. The area bordering the shipyard was not attractive.

Althea had memories living on other islands. Those were memories of going into the Sound when the water was ice cold, washing herself in frigid water, and moving from house to house because her father could not pay the rent. Her father had a job delivering laundry, but lost it when an appendectomy went awry. He had to be hospitalized for several weeks and as a result lost his job in the Great Depression. It became obvious to me that memories of living in an incredibly scenic environment were overwhelmed by memories of constant concern about the family's earning enough to survive.

A tour of the Olympic Peninsula, the San Juan Islands and a short stop in British Columbia's Victoria and Vancouver, helped me understand Althea's pride in her roots in America's "other Washington". Few places that I visited are so full with scenic wonders and possess as interesting a past as the greater Seattle area.

On our way to the plane at the Seattle airport, my impression that we were a continent away from New England was brought home by the automatic voice on the train taking us from the main terminal to our departing airline terminal. The brief announcement of the next stop was first in English and then in Japanese. Yes, we were not that far from Asia!

***

Althea and I managed to take enough time off in the nineteen eighties from our respective administrative and teaching responsibilities to enable us to explore the many places in Europe both of us had always wanted to see with our own eyes, but had until then only read about or passed through too quickly. We managed to cover the continent from Finland in the north to Spain and Greece in the south, from England and Scotland in the west to Georgia in the Caucasus. In planning a particular trip and selecting the itineraries, we chose to revisit places we had explored earlier and loved, but we also wanted to discover places we had only read about or seen in movies.

Looking back at the many diverse places and cultures we explored a definite pattern does emerge. I was attracted to places where important events had occurred that I had covered in my lectures. Perhaps talking to people in such contested areas as Alsace-Lorraine might give me a better understanding of the long-standing Franco-German conflict that had caused World War I. Was Greece really such a marvelous place causing my father to decorate all the walls in our Wannsee house with pictures of ancient Greek sculptures? What was it beside the Channel that separated England from the rest of Europe? How about the Soviet Union: could normal people manage to function effectively in a totalitarian system? We did not plan our trips with these questions in mind, but each trip, without exception, turned out to add some unexpected information that improved our knowledge of the world we live in, hopefully adding spice to my lectures.

Mundane considerations, like cheap airfares, also influenced our itineraries. In the early eighties, *Iceland Air* offered reasonable fares to get to Europe. It took longer, however, because of the required stop at Reykjavik, Iceland's capital. Taking advantage of this detour, we decided to explore a country with a name that advertised its chilly but interesting location. We gingerly ventured into an area with hot rocks where steam escaped from an intermittently active volcano. Of course we had no inkling that a quarter century later Iceland would defy its name and play a leading role in Europe's financial meltdown.

Iceland charmed us with its weird landscape of steep mountains plunging down to rocks at the very edge of the Atlantic. Clouds shroud the peaks that occasionally puff fumes into the sky from hot lava fields. In Reykjavik we were proudly shown a greenhouse where banana plants defied nature's climate range. Even more impressive was an outdoor swimming pool heated by warm water that bubbled up from subterranean cracks caused by a continental fault line. The second time that we stopped in Reykjavik we went on a one-day excursion by plane and bus to a remote area north of the Arctic Circle. Signs warned tourists not to touch rocks heated by a subterranean cauldron. I could not resist testing the validity of the warning and discovered most rocks were warm, but not terribly hot. The scene turned even more romantic when snowflakes, mixed with June raindrops, touched the rocks. Steam rose on both sides of the path. At midnight we returned to the capital while the sun still cast its rays over the mountaintops below.

Flying from Iceland to Luxembourg, Iceland Airline's European destination, also became quite an adventure, not only because of a very early morning departure at odds with our sleeping habits, but also because of a somewhat frightening incident. As the plane accelerated on the runway, the pilot suddenly applied the brakes, and aborted the lift-off. We had to defy the forces that pushed us forward. The calm voice of the pilot over the public address system tried to reassure us, "there was a little problem and we are returning to the terminal." After taxiing several miles, with the terminal coming into view, the pilot spoke to us again over the loudspeaker, "We checked the warning signal, resolved the problem and are ready for take-off. Please check your seat belts." As we exchanged looks with nearby passengers, Althea and I clutched hands that were hot and sweaty, the plane accelerated and this time left the ground. Iceland disappeared behind us in the clouds and normal conversations resumed. Fellow passengers excitedly expressed a variety of opinions about the crisis that we had met successfully. Someone pointed out that the exceptionally long runway that made the plane's maneuver possible had been built by the U.S. in World War II to enable us to supply our wartime allies as well as our own troops. It was only as we landed in Luxembourg that Althea and I looked at each other, relaxed and dared to prepare ourselves for our next phase.

We rented a car with a big **L** on the license plate, identifying us as Luxembourgers. I was delighted to place that Duchy on the list of the European countries that I had visited. The Duchy was however so small that we crossed into France before getting comfortably settled in the car. We stopped in Thionville about a half hour drive from the airport. Not merely did this place us in Lorraine, which together with Alsace, had been contested by France and Germany for more than half a century, but it also happened to be close to the Maginot line of fortifications. In the travel literature in our hotel there was one inviting tourists to visit the Maginot line. As soon as practical Althea and I drove to an impressive looking fortified wall. A gate guarded the entrance to a dark passage. We paid a nominal entrance fee and boarded an open coach that whisked us through the tunnel. It felt like racing through a New York subway tunnel on an open bench. The noise was ear shattering. Flying creatures sought refuge in crevasses as we sped by. We passed empty halls where according to our train conductor and guide there had been social, medical and other facilities for the French soldiers not on duty operating the guns. He added that the soldiers had opportunities to see movies, socialize with ladies from outside, etc. etc. Finally, our "train" stopped below a gun outpost. We climbed the stairs and saw daylight. I do not recall an elevator. At the top, a big gun pointed to Germany in the east. "Can these guns be turned around to shoot in the opposite direction?" I asked. "Of course", he answered.

Our short visit confirmed everything I had told my classes when the Maginot line was the classic example of military thinking that prepares for the next conflict by resolving problems of the last war. The Maginot line would have saved thousands of lives lost in

World War I when continuous battles in open trenches created hell on earth without achieving any strategic success. With fortifications like the Maginot line, my uncle Kurt might have survived his four-year service for the Kaiser. Germans watching the French build the immovable gun positions in the late twenties and thirties required little imagination to plan the obvious strategy of overpowering the impregnable trenches of a *Sitzkrieg* (comfortably seated war) with the speeding tanks of a *Blitzkrieg* (lightning war) . With minimum effort, but great mobility, the tanks encircled the comfortable French facilities and approached the open gate from the West the way tourists do now.

On our way south to Alsace, we experienced a somewhat different aspect of France: the French cuisine. We stopped at a small restaurant overlooking the Moselle River in Liverdun near Nancy for lunch. When we saw that the menu had seven or eight courses Althea assured me we could manage such an extravaganza. She was right! Each course consisted of three or four bites meant to stir ones imagination and tease ones appetite. Just when I was tempted to ask for more, another course arrived, preparing me for a new culinary adventure. There were also tiny glasses containing drops of liqueur to “clear the palate”. The whole dining experience was over too soon. We left the restaurant before I could ask for three or four more courses with a further mélange of tidbits.

In Alsace, the province contested by France and Germany, we stayed at an inn with the name, *A l'ami Fritz.* The very name of that inn in Obernai near Strasbourg illustrated the linguistic Franco-German entanglement, the result of centuries of ethnic interaction. After listening to the desk manager talk to someone on the phone, in what sounded like a German dialect, I asked her whether this was indeed German that I had overheard. She raised her voice several octaves and shouted to me in her best Parisian French, “of course not! We speak only French here. This is France, don't you know that?” Not surprisingly, it is not easy to cast off traditional explanations taught in grammar school.

By chance, we visited a fair in Lorraine where several booths featured literature that illustrated the Franco-German linguistic mixture of dialects in the region that stretched all the way from Switzerland in the south to the Netherlands, butting on the North Sea. It covered the area contested for centuries by French kings and a variety of German speaking dukes. I had to revise my perception of a clear delineation between two old enemies and replace it with a realistic view of naturally intermingled villagers from nearby places interacting, falling in love, stealing each other's cattle, yelling at each other or whispering into each other's ear. They could not have been particularly worried about correct grammar in their attempt of getting the point across to the other guy or girl.

We traveled for more than two weeks in France, northern Italy and western Germany through the heart of Europe. It was the world where everything of importance that I had read about in my youth took place, but which I had never seen with my own eyes. I was able to catch up finally. It was fun to pass through Besançon, a city with the same name as Mademoiselle Besançon, my favorite French teacher when I was eleven years old; the Langue Doc, where so many French romantic novels were centered, and of course the Côte d'Azur, the symbol of sea side romance. Driving up a steep road from the coast near Monaco to the tiny town of Eze, perched tightly in the fold of a mountain, was quite an experience. Finding some place to park the car on a street rising at an angle of more than 35 degrees and stepping out of the car so that Althea and I could look at and perhaps purchase, a locally made piece of art, made the maneuver worthwhile.

Again, I was reminded of a recent conflict. The beautiful scenic area on France's easternmost coast was demanded by Mussolini at the start of World War II in order to keep up with his Axis partner Hitler's rapidly expanding German Reich. He had to let Hitler know that he had not fallen asleep and that Italy was a worthy wartime ally. Driving from Nice to Italy's next-door coastal villages made it obvious that Mussolini's demand for France's Nice region made little strategic or historical sense. It however gave Mussolini something to crow about.

The highway from Menton on the French-Italian border to Genoa is a remarkable engineering feat. There are so many tunnels that we stopped counting. Each tunnel was followed by a narrow window giving us an incredibly beautiful glimpse on the sea far below. Barely able to admire a ship on the horizon, darkness enveloped us again. When Althea and I tried to figure out which port we had just discovered in its scenic setting, an entirely new panorama emerged. For nearly an hour, we sped at a maximum rate of speed that Italian drivers expected everybody to follow. We stopped at scenic Portofino, a place close to paradise. Our fancy hotel gave us a taste of living the life of luxury. Even in this Garden of Eden, I could not avoid thinking about my Foreign Policy lectures. Some twenty minutes from our hotel, there was Rapallo, the city where in 1922 an extremely important international conference had taken place that enabled Germany and Communist Russia to resume normal relations. This undermined the harsh terms of the Treaty of Versailles that had been imposed by the victors on defeated Germany in 1919. "This was very important," I informed Althea. She nodded slightly, barely interrupting her surveillance of the goings on in the harbor below our window. In Parma, we looked at opera composer Verdi's villa, but without the sound of an opera performance, that visit was a disappointment.

Crossing the Alps in the Graubűnden (Grison) province of Switzerland on our way back north, we stopped at the Hotel Margna in Sils Baselgia, my mother's favorite vacation refuge. In her seventies and eighties, she invariably spent at least one week each year there. When Althea and I checked in at the hotel, we realized immediately that my mother had made an excellent choice. Not only was the hotel comfortable and located near a lake surrounded by Alpine peaks and glaciers, but the easy access to well marked Alpine trails enabled us to "climb the Alps" with the greatest of ease. We were fascinated by the variety of rare Alpine flowers most of which Althea managed to identify. Althea also gave me sufficient confidence to help me overcome my fear of heights. Somehow, she convinced me to take a cable car ride up to the Furtschella hut from where we had a fantastic view of the entire Engadin valley below, with its lakes, villages, surrounded by rocky walls reaching the clouds. The hut had of course excellent dining facilities. Coffee, Swiss chocolate and ice cream added just the right flavor to the mountain panorama.

Sils Baselgia had attracted visitors for more than a century before our visit. The 19th century German philosopher Friedrich Nietzsche spent a lot of time there in the 1880's before his mental illness interfered with his writing. We visited the house in which he stayed. Since my father had often talked and written about Nietzsche's philosophy I was interested to note the many facets of his life and work displayed in the several rooms on the two floors that we entered. There was reference to the controversy about his use and misuse of his writings by his sister and the Nazi era philosopher Martin Heidegger. I was transported back to my father's discussions with fellow intellectuals in Berlin and Prague. Trips are meant to open new horizons, but visiting this house forced me to admit that I had missed the opportunity to follow the advice of my father to delve into his writings and those of his fellow philosophers.

Another historical marker surprised me. Strolling on a path near the Hotel Margna, I noticed a small cemetery. Casually surveying the names on the tombstones, I discovered a very familiar name, Arnold Wolfers. A professor at Yale, he wrote *Britain and France between the Wars* that was published in 1940. It was required reading for the inter-war diplomacy section of my international relations course. Professor Wolfers also was my mother's first employer when we moved to New Haven in 1940. She was his assistant in a research project. The project provided background information for our subsequent invasion of North Africa. He died in 1968. My mother told me that they discussed Switzerland and I assume her idea to go to Sils Baselgia for vacation may have originated with Professor Wolfers.

Germany was not half as exciting as France, Italy or Switzerland, except for driving on West Germany's Autobahns. The task was to match the tactics of German drivers. There are no speed limits. Headlights would start blinking from a car in back approaching me from a distance of at least half a mile. That meant I had better get out of the fast lane immediately, or else the headlight covers would open and close incessantly like that of a crocodile ready to devour me. I thought this was funny. Althea did not, and started ordering me to get out of his/her way.

On our return from Germany to the Iceland Air terminal in Luxembourg, we decided to spend our last night in Trier. We learned not only that Trier claims to be Germany's oldest city going back to Roman days, but also that it is the place where Karl Marx was born in 1818. In the house where that event occurred, there is now a museum on the second floor. The house was bought and restored by the German Social Democratic Party in 1928. The Nazis naturally kicked the Social Democrats out and used the house for their own purposes. Marx was their most important symbolic enemy. After the War, the house was returned to the Social Democrats. It took them some time to come to terms with communism's godfather, but shortly before our visit they restored it.

The exhibits proudly describe his life and display copies of all his writings. I had known that his father, a lawyer, considered his Jewish background a hindrance to his career and converted to Protestantism. Karl Marx was baptized at the age of six. He studied at Bonn University, not far from Trier. He spent his thirties publishing articles and editing a newspaper in the Rhineland. He traveled to Paris and Brussels until his *Communist Manifesto* and the 1948 Revolution forced him to leave the continent and spend the rest of his life in England at the British Museum Library. There he wrote his magnum opus, *Das Capital*, while separated from his native land on the continent. It was only after visiting the area where he grew up and lived as a young man that it made sense to me that Marx treated the world as if national and cultural boundaries did not matter. After all, he had crossed religious boundaries, was almost within walking distance of France, Luxembourg and Belgium and could imagine workers of neighboring countries making common cause. In some ways I found it ironic that his greatest admirers were in Russia, a part of Europe with which he was least familiar.

***

Having spent several trips on the continent, we decided to cover the more familiar United Kingdom. After all, England was Althea's mother's country of birth and several centuries ago Manchester was the city where my maternal grandfather spent the last eight years of his life. Althea had spent several months in England with her first husband Charles on his sabbatical. On trips in the past, I had stopped only briefly in London on my way to somewhere else. We were both struck how much we had to learn about that "little island" across the Channel (me) or across the Atlantic (Althea). Skipping London, we fell in love with a village in the Cotswold that transported us back several centuries. We were lucky to stay in a tiny inn where we were treated as guests were in prior centuries. The facilities were of course up-to-date, but the hosts emerged from an earlier century novel.

On the way north, we detoured through Wales. As I drove, I was extremely busy and somewhat unnerved in a futile effort to make sense of the Welsh place names on the road signs. It was difficult to focus on oncoming traffic when my eyes were mesmerized by the incredibly long names with double ll's, dd's, and other double consonants which I attempted to pronounce as we passed them at 50 miles an hour on the British left side of the road. Althea was worried that instead of concentrating on approaching traffic, I preoccupied myself with the impossible task of studying Welch pronunciation. In spite of my battle with the Welsh language, we managed to get to Snowdonia with its relatively high hills (mountains?) and ancient castles. It almost seemed as if we were turning the pages of a medieval storybook.

Reaching the coast in North Wales, I finally understood why my aunt Lise, who cared for my grandfather Willy in Manchester during and after the War, had written so excitedly and enthusiastically about her vacations in resorts along the coast of Wales. Watching the big waves crashing on the rocks, afforded a romantic escape from the humdrum suburban routine without having to travel far from Manchester. Forty years after Grandfather Willy's death, I was finally able to look at the house where he had spent the last years of his life after his just-in-time escape from Nazi Germany.

As we passed through the Lakes District on our way to Scotland I was amazed to discover that England had mountains that were almost as exhausting to climb as those in my more familiar Central Europe. The large highway signs simply saying *North* intrigued us. Can't they indicate we are on our way to Glasgow or Scotland? It almost appeared as if for the British Scotland is a land to be ignored. We persisted nonetheless and after bypassing Glasgow we reached a region of peninsulas along the Scottish southwestern coast that look like fingers poking into the sea opposite Northern Ireland. One of those land slices testing the ocean waves is named Carrick, the name of Althea's younger son. Why Charles, her first husband who had Scottish roots picked Carrick I cannot recall. The panorama of that section of the Scottish coast was certainly romantic.

Driving east to the opposite side of Scotland we stopped at a Visitors Center that commemorates the 1746 Battle of Culloden. Listening to the recorded account of those events two and a half centuries ago we were amazed at the venom with which the British action against the Scots was described. In my youth in Prague we were told how the Czechs were defeated by the Hapsburg Austrians in 1620. The Czech account of a national tragedy was far more forgiving than the story the Scots told about the Brits.

We could not leave Scotland without stopping at Balmoral Castle, the summer home of Queen Elizabeth. Apparently she was there or was expected soon and therefore the grounds were not open to visitors. We were impressed by the large castle and the perfectly kept grounds behind the closed gate.

Driving back to Heathrow airport from Scotland seemed to take forever. The somewhat narrower highway matched our interstates but the trucks we passed caused turbulence that was bothersome. I also had difficulty adjusting myself to driving for hours on the wrong side of the road.

Our tour of the United Kingdom made me aware that "UK" was more of a wish than reality. Before our visit I did not realize that it was not only the Irish who had a very different cultural heritage, but so did the Welsh and Scots. I also was made aware that the island off the coast of the European continent is much bigger than it had been in my imagination. Althea pointed out to me that Scotland was as far north as southern Scandinavia and London paralleled central France. How very true!

***

In the mid-eighties, after retiring from more than thirty years as a Methodist missionary family in South Korea, Shirley and Jeff, Althea's sister and brother-in-law, had settled in San Antonio, Texas. We decided to accept their invitation in 1991 to visit them. Having become reasonably familiar and quite comfortable in the Caribbean Sea we thought we might stop in Texas on our way back from a short winter escape to Cancun, Mexico. I must admit that this was not an easy decision since Texas did not strike me as a particularly friendly state to visit. Its political landscape was not appealing and *Dallas* was a show I preferred to see on TV. Visiting Shirley and Jeff changed all that.

In Austin, we rented a car and drove the longer than expected distance to San Antonio. Stuck behind a van that had a couple of rifles prominently displayed on a rack and a bunch of nasty aggressive slogans on its bumper I was quickly reminded of all my prejudices about the Lone Star state. This rifle displaying truck was one of many and appeared to advertise the spirit of the Old West. Althea and I asked ourselves whether we softies from New England were adequately prepared to spend a week in this Texas cowboy environment. We resolved to keep our prejudices under control, after all as Althea reminded me," my sister chose to retire here, she must have had some good reasons." Having watched *Dallas*, a decade earlier, we prepared ourselves for a week in this unfamiliar environment.

Approaching Shirley's neighborhood, we were relieved that when we finally located her house, we did not see a ranch surrounded by armed cowboys, but entered a modest home in well cared garden not that different from a New England one. Jeff, a retired minister, was busy in his study preparing a sermon that he was to deliver in a local church on Sunday. Shirley was proud to show us her study where she worked on college course assignments to meet her long delayed graduation requirements. More importantly, she practiced her new hobby, portrait painting. She also introduced us to a church-related community center where she helped Mexican immigrants learn English and familiarize themselves with U.S. culture. We had to admit that our preconceived notions about life in Texas were not quite correct.

Althea and I were impressed by Shirley's extensive activities. She combined the lives of a college senior, painter, social worker with that of a still active minister's wife. Althea made it clear to me that our relatively short stay in San Antonio helped her change her view of her sister dramatically. It closed a nearly half century gap in their relationship. The obstacles stemming from Althea's first marriage that had distanced her from Shirley had vanished. It was extremely satisfying for me to witness all this.

We spent one morning on the required pilgrimage to the monument honoring the Alamo. I was much more impressed by the San Antonio River Walk that reminded us a little bit of a Venetian Canal. The best, Shirley kept as a surprise: She took us on a tour of Spanish Missions dating from the 18th century and now maintained in the Missions National Historical Park. The well maintained and lovingly restored San José and Concepción Missions made us recognize the legacy of Spain's role in the Western hemisphere. We expressed our surprise that modern Americans have largely ignored the fact that Spanish missionaries and adventurers had established a foothold in America's South-West and West long before our 19th century adventurers, gold diggers, oil riggers and settlers staked out their holdings. Our encounter with the legacies of Spanish culture in Texas reinforced my misgivings about the virulent anti Hispanic immigration bias in many political circles. After all, our war against Mexico had taken place more than a century and a half ago!

For reasons that I cannot recall, we decided on a further excursion before leaving southern Texas. Perhaps, the name Corpus Christi intrigued us. We drove several hours along a highway where there was absolutely nothing of interest except an occasional farm building on the horizon, until we finally reached our destination on the Gulf of Mexico. There were a few ships anchored and some fishing boats, but Corpus Christi lacked excitement and charm. We quickly proceeded along a causeway to San Padre Island. We could have walked along the beach for hours and reached the Rio Grande and Mexico beyond. That would have taken at least a full day's walk. Instead, we watched the waves, admired the sandy beach, turned around and after another day at Shirley's, we drove back to Austin, got on a plane and ended our surprisingly pleasant Texas venture.

We had met Althea's nephew, Shirley's son Breck, a couple of times earlier on a family visit in Connecticut and in Washington, D.C. He was there in connection with a job he had with the military in Hawaii. I realized then that he seemed to be extremely well informed about what was going on in the world but would not tell me what exactly he was doing. He asked me what I knew about events in Eastern Europe. When Shirley suggested we visit Breck in Hawaii later that summer, we did not think twice about accepting the invitation.

After stopping in Seattle to say hello to Althea's mother, we flew non-stop to Honolulu. I was surprised that instead of flying directly to our destination from Seattle, the plane followed the coast to Los Angeles before finally turning west to cross the ocean. Flying over the Pacific took a lot of time and was rather boring. While the view of the island was not as stunning as that portrayed on TV, it was nevertheless quite impressive to descend on a tropical island with its palm trees surrounded by blue water and foaming white waves hitting sand and rocks. The storybook atmosphere was enhanced by flight attendants greeting us at the gate with leis draped around their neck and offering us a couple of flower petals.

Breck welcomed us and helped us to our hotel, the famous *Royal Hawaiian*. This picturesque hotel with its photogenic beach, while somewhat old fashioned, was very comfortable and gave us a feeling of luxury. After a quick stop on the beach and feeling a couple of drops sprayed by a crushing wave a mile away, we went on a pilgrimage to the Pearl Harbor Memorial of the *Arizona*. Fifty years earlier as a sophomore at Cornell, listening to the newsbreak announcing the attack on Pearl Harbor, I never could have imagined one day visiting the remnants of that disaster. It somehow did not feel real. Everything we looked at was just the way it had been portrayed in pictures we had seen, but never experienced. That was also long before I had ever watched *Hawaii 5-O*. Breck suggested we take his car and visit nearby beaches. I asked him how come soldiers saluted the car whenever we approached one of the many military entrances that we passed in Honolulu. The car had regular license plates, not identifying it as belonging to a military or civilian governmental official. He answered that the car had a small tab near the front bumper that permitted him to travel anywhere in Hawaii because of his job. "Does that mean that when I drive your car I get that same salute?" "Sure", he answered, "you'll be the officer for that afternoon". I told him that I would prefer taking a tourist bus instead of pretending to be a high-ranking officer.

Before leaving next day for our stay in the neighboring island of Kauai, we had a very interesting conversation at dinner where we learned a little bit more about his job and life style. He had a boat anchored in the harbor where he and his wife spent most of their time, even eating and sleeping. He also had a small plane. I gained the impression that he was an expert on potential threats to U.S. security on the Pacific rim of the Asian continent. Sometime later, I received a postcard he had mailed from China in a town not far from the North Korean border. The weather was fine, he reported. He kept in touch, mostly with Christmas family information. That is how I learned that he had shifted his center of activities from Hawaii to Washington, D.C. He flew his small plane single-handedly in short stages all the way across the continent to the east Coast. I like to speculate that it is the greater role that Asia now plays in our strategic global thinking that led to Breck being shifted to the nation's capital where policy decisions are made.

It was Shirley, who had suggested that the main island was far too commercialized to get a real taste of Hawaii, the 19th century idyllic Pacific paradise. She encouraged us to spend several days in Kauai, a name I had difficulty pronouncing, even though only the letters K and u replace H and w. Althea was perplexed that speaking all those crazy Eastern European languages, I complained about this island's simple name. Aside from this linguistic barrier, the short flight was pleasant and the change of scenery remarkable. At Lihue, the airport at the island's eastern end, we rented a car. This enabled us to explore those parts of the island where roads have been built. A very high mountain rises in the center of the island, surrounded by a rain forest. We rented a condo in a resort in the town of Hanalei, at the opposite side of the island from the airport. Hanalei is at the edge of a tropical mountainous wilderness. The combination of a perfect Pacific beach in front and tropical vegetation climbing up on the slope behind us, made us feel that we had finally arrived in our own tropical paradise.

As we settled in our beach chairs around the corner from our building, we realized that there were some guests, who focused their binoculars on the sea beyond a sandbar below us. Althea first saw the seals that were huddled in the areas beyond the crushing waves. We learned from the guest observers that the seals had come from distant areas in the Pacific to carefully nurture their young ones until they were ready to embark on their own solitary sea adventures. While nurturing their young, the seals were very vulnerable to sea predators as well as local hunters from the island and just ornery tourists. The beach had signs requesting tourists not to disturb the seals. Some local residents organized a watch group to protect the seals. We volunteered to spend one afternoon helping the watch group. It took us little time to establish a special relationship with a mother seal and her offspring. We cheered when the mother after an hour's absence appeared with a fish dangling from her mouth and not so gently made her offspring taste the delicacy.

At our resort we noticed a motorboat excursion advertised that followed the western coast of the island where the mountains reach the sea. In the absence of roads, that scenic part of Kauai can best be explored from the ocean. A modern motorboat awaited us and a dozen fellow tourists. The captain turned out to be a friendly smiling female in her late twenties. She read us instructions about properly securing our life jackets and settling safely on the bench below the gunwale. As the boat left the pier and the engine roared the captain disrobed her formal attire revealing her real self as the harbor disappeared from view. The captain gunned the motor, raising the bow of the boat above the foaming waves. We entered the open sea. As we reached cruising speed our captain sucked in the sea air, her face took on the look of ecstasy and a minimal bikini was all that was left to cover a beautiful body that easily fitted into the tropical paradise on the not too distant shore.

I stared at her, my eyes attempting to ask her to slow down because I was scared stiff sitting there right above the foaming spray. She seemed to misinterpret the message from my eyes and cast me a suggestive look. I turned to Althea and told her I was scared. She suggested I drop down to the floor and sit there; it might make me more comfortable. I took her advice and she comforted me by putting her hands on my shoulder. I noticed the captain giving Althea a dirty look. The rest of the boat excursion was anticlimactic. We watched seals cavorting not far from the boat. There were also bigger fish, possibly a whale. We stopped at a beach where our group had the ocean all to ourselves. When the trip was over I thanked the captain, telling her we had a great time. She shook my hand and said “on the floor, I hope you could see the fish!”

Chapter 21
A Brief Family Reconnection

Following Grandfather Willy's death in 1947 and Aunt Lise's in 1958, I had only two close relatives left: Aunt Käte and her daughter Cousin Ruth who lived in Chile. Käte visited us once in the late 60's in Storrs. I had last seen Ruth in Switzerland in 1938 shortly before leaving Europe. My mother had kept in touch with her sister and I exchanged occasional letters with Ruth.

Having ventured as far south as San Lucia in the Caribbean islands, Althea suggested we travel a bit further. "All the way to Chile, at the bottom of the American continent" I asked. "Why not, let's visit Ruth, your only living close relative". Aunt Käte had died in 1981. Time seemed to be running out, if I wanted to maintain any contact. The dictator Pinochet had lost his punch and Chile was gradually rejoining the ranks of reasonably safe countries open to normal tourism.

We picked my Christmas/New Year vacation as a logical timeframe for a trip south of the Equator to celebrate New Year 1986 in mid-summer heat! This was something to look forward to. Our direct Lan Chile flight to Santiago took off from JFK, stopping briefly in Miami. We had to cross only one time zone, turning our watch one hour ahead, even though we crossed from the Atlantic to the Pacific Ocean because the tail of South America swings in an easterly direction. Traveling the enormous distance all the way south of the Equator took the entire evening, night and morning, most of it in the air. A brief stop in Lima, Peru, helped reduce the boredom. We stretched our legs while the plane was refueled, but could not enter the terminal, apparently closed to transients at that hour.

The brief stop in Lima before dawn revealed a darker side of Peru. Outside the terminal, within sight of our plane, there was a ten or eleven-year old boy with tourist trinkets arranged on the ground, trying to sell us some item, so that he could eat and survive. He looked obviously malnourished and disheveled. He must have made a deal earning the "privilege" operating the only "open shop" on the tarmac at 4 a.m. This experience in Peru shook us up.

As the plane rose from Lima on the last lap of the journey, I had to correct my imagination-based impression that all of Peru was high up in the Andes mountains. Lima was not far from the Pacific. The foam from the ocean waves came clearly into view as the rising sun's first rays hit the shore. A couple hours later, we finally approached Santiago, nestled in a valley, surrounded by hills and mountains. It resembled a city in the Swiss Alps.

Ruth, accompanied by her husband Hernán greeted us at the gate. In spite of an absence of 47 years, we had no problem recognizing each other. I had said good-bye to a seven-year old refugee and greeted now a 54-year old Chilean mother, surrounded by her family that spoke Spanish, a language I unfortunately did not speak. We were shocked to be told that Ruth suffered from cancer. It fortunately had been arrested, at least temporarily. After that news as we reacquainted each other, the topic of Ruth's health was not mentioned again during our entire visit.

Hernán drove us from the airport through the very busy metropolis. I had not realized that the city lies in a bowl surrounded by hills in the West and the Andes in the East. After a stretch on Isabel la Catolica Avenue, a name that forced me to recall the 15th century, we reached Ruth and Hernán's house in Los Condes, an upscale part of the city. Behind their comfortable house, there was a cabin. It included a bedroom and bathroom, perfectly suited for guests. That is where we stayed. The cabin was built for my aunt when, during the last years of her life, she could no longer live alone in Viña del Mar, a suburb of Valparaiso on the shore of the Pacific, where she had spent nearly 40 years after arriving in Chile in 1939. When guests were not occupying the cabin, it served as the domicile of their housekeeper, cleaner and performer of all necessary functions. What intrigued me was that this crucial helper was an Indian from Chile's south who in addition to Spanish seemed to be fluent in her native Indian language.

Ruth and Hernán made us feel very comfortable as we enjoyed dinner. We tried to help each other understand the many events in our respective lives that spanned half a century on opposite ends of the American continent. We had some linguistic problems. Ruth and I shifted unintentionally from English to German, when necessary to get a point across, while Hernán needed Ruth to translate our conversation into Spanish, but got lost when Ruth and I lapsed back into German.

Hernán earned his living traveling from Santiago to the southern tip of Chile selling factory-produced men's and women's clothing from his van to customers living in the many small towns that stretch between the coast and the Andes Mountain chain. December to April was his busiest season. We were lucky to find him at home, he told us. We apologized for interfering with his routine.

We quickly learned that our visit was not the only reason why he had postponed his marketing journey. Ruth and Hernán's younger daughter Rebecá was about to get married. We were invited to attend! This was a total surprise. When we scheduled our trip, we had no idea we would witness such an important family event. Romance had interrupted Rebecá's academic career. She was studying law, thus carrying on the tradition of her grandfather, Hans Grűnberg. Hans had been a lawyer in Berlin, but could not pursue his vocation in exile. After a short stay in Belgium, Hans brought his family to Spain, where my grandfather Willy helped him start a candy business. The Spanish Civil War cut that venture short. In Chile, he tried to make a living as a graphologist. He died relatively young. Given this background, I could not help but rejoice that some strands of the past could be traced in the entirely different present and prospective future.

The wedding took place in a small church not far from my cousin's home. The groom Manuel, his family, Rebecá's relatives and friends, filled several rows. Althea and I were the unexpected guests from far away Connecticut. The ceremony was simple and meaningful. After the formal ceremony the fun started. We were all invited to a restaurant in a big park on a hill, overlooking the capital city of Santiago below. From our seats at a long table, we could see the lights of the city and the twinkling stars above. I could not have imagined spending an evening of the brand new year 1986 in a more romantic setting. Air conditioning kept the restaurant comfortable. Outside, in the garden, there was a pleasantly warm summer breeze. If only we could have found a way to bring that warm air back with us to wintry Storrs!

Our tablemates were Hernán's businessmen friends. We got to talking about the rapidly expanding trade between our two countries. I told them that the blueberries I was buying at our Stop and Shop usually came from Chile. There were problems trading with the U.S., they retorted. When they were about to conclude a deal selling Chilean goods to the U.S., the American entrepreneur would ask them to ship a large quantity of the particular item at very short notice. Such a request exceeded the productive capacity of the Chilean manufacturer by a considerable margin. The deal was off. He remarked that such conversations, and there had been many, had forced him to shed his small country's cocoon and think on a new much larger global scale. Althea got very involved in conversations with the wives of my conversation partners. They compared their respective social problems and political concerns. Our evening at the restaurant overlooking the sparkling lights of Santiago, celebrating Rebecá's wedding, was both romantic and extremely informative.

The following afternoon we were invited to a picnic at the home of Rebecá's older sister, Perla [Firelei]. She, her husband Carlos, eight-year old Carlitos and five-year old Denisse spent the afternoon in the backyard of their modest home in a typical suburban environment. Bringing up kids, dominated the discussion. Political issues were carefully avoided. Walking back to the car we heard the same voice emanating from radios in every house that we passed. General Pinochet addressed the nation in the New Year. None of the Chileans we saw preparing their outdoor picnics, seemed to pay the least bit attention to the address of their dictator.

Intent on exploring Santiago and the wider region, we decided to rent a car. It turned out to be a KIA, a model I had never heard of. It gave us no trouble. We ventured to an outdoor artisan market where we purchased a copper carved chicken that still stares at me, suspended from the ceiling in my study, a quarter century later. In a fancy downtown store we ended up with two candlesticks.

We asked Ruth to show us her mother's former apartment in Viña del Mar where Aunt Käte had spent most of her life. Ruth of course grew up there. She was delighted to take us there. She had a key to the apartment and led us to the balcony. When the door opened, a panorama of the Pacific was revealed. Käte had managed to make a living there as a photographer. I believe that living in a pleasant suburb, overlooking the ocean protected her from being swallowed by a country with a culture so different from the one of her birth.

I recall Käte's liberal views dating back to her stay in Barcelona during the Spanish Civil War in the mid-thirties. Generalissimo Franco forced the family to abandon their refuge in Europe from Nazism in 1938. She was happy in Chile and wrote favorably about Salvador Allende's left-wing government in the early seventies. After Augusto Pinochet's violent coup in September 1973, it was no longer safe for Käte to write about politics. Pinochet was still President during our visit, but his authority had been significantly curtailed. Public criticism was however still curtailed. We asked Ruth whether we could meet some independent thinkers. She introduced us to a labor leader who was circumspect in discussing the current political situation. He urged us to be careful. Chile was not yet a real democracy, he warned us.

We felt we could not leave Chile without a closer look at the Andes Mountains. We left early one morning driving north, past Los Andes, to the ski resort Portillo, on the Argentine border. On the winding highway up the mountains, signs intended for winter tourists, warned us of snow avalanches. We were amused since it was in the middle of summer, comfortably warm with hardly any leftover snow in sight. Most resorts on top of the mountain were closed; after all, it was July in January. We had hoped to cross into Argentina, adding it to my collection of countries on whose soil I had stood. It turned out that we were not allowed to take our rented car out of Chile.

At the end of our ten-day visit, we said good-bye to Ruth and all the members of her family that we had met for the first time. In subsequent letters, we learned that Ruth's cancer had returned and restricted her active life. Sadly she passed away less than four years later in November 1989. Her daughter Rebecca whose wedding we were so fortunate to attend died in 2012.Unfortunately, the language barrier has prevented me from staying in touch with Perla who had invited us to a family picnic in their garden.

As we checked in for our return flight, the Chilean officials inspected our passports, exchanged glances, looked at us quizzically. Finally they asked where we lived in the U.S. We confirmed the address in the passport: 11 September Road, Storrs, Ct. Looking at us again, they shook their heads. They exchanged comments and then in English, "they are Americans, let them go".

Only later, did we learn that September 11 was the day in 1973 when Pinochet had staged his coup. The airport officials may have believed that our address was a political message of some sort. Maybe we should have informed U.S. intelligence agencies to watch out for suspicious activities on that day, 15 years later!

***

We interrupted our return flight in Lima. Peru was historically important enough to require more than an hour's stop at the airport runway. We considered visiting the famous Incan Machu Pichu ruins, but were unwilling to spend three or four days on a somewhat complicated trip by small plane, train and then climb a mountain to reach this scenic Indian historical treasure. Instead, we concentrated on the capital, Lima.

We were most impressed by unexpected encounters that shed a great deal of light on Peru's social and economic problems. On the way from the airport, our taxi was stuck behind a slow moving van that had all windows tightly covered. As we finally passed the vehicle, we could peer through the windshield and see an incredibly large number of heads behind the driver, their bodies packed tightly together like sardines in a can. When we expressed our shock at this sight, our driver remarked that such travel was necessary and a common occurrence. After all, workers had to get to their place of employment.

A short time later, on a visit to a major museum, our attention shifted from interesting items in the glass-enclosed showcase to the partially open window that carried the noise of a marching band of protesting workers on the street below, who chanted loudly. Our inquiry as to why was met by a shrug of the shoulder and some comment like, "this happens all the time".

We felt we had to visit the Gold Museum; after all, the search for gold had attracted the Conquistadores to the Americas in the first place. We expected an interesting account of Peru's past. Instead, the museum reminded us of a high school graduate's proud collection of sport trophies. The jewelry and other artifacts made of the precious mineral were impressive, but the showcases were poorly arranged and the gold did not even shine. It was a great disappointment.

Chapter 22
Ronald's Growing Family

While our travels in the 1980s helped Althea and me add some spice to our regular routine, the growing impact of Meredith's mental illness on her ability to conduct a reasonably normal existence had a serious effect on our state of mind. Her problems were always with us. There was fortunately also a bright side in our life: it was watching Ronald's new family grow.

Ronald had met Ariela, his second wife, at ERCO, the Company where Cathy, his first wife also worked. They shared a desire to supplement professional pursuits with a more exciting outdoor life. While Ronald had explored the northern regions of Quebec and Ontario canoeing down the rivers in a sparsely inhabited wilderness, Ariela had spent a year navigating and exploring the islands of the Caribbean. At college in Michigan State, she had learned to ride a horse. Ronald continued to enliven his job routine by playing squash, a sport he loved and excelled. Ariela had to curtail her life style by devoting herself to raising Nathan and, three years later, Elliot. Eventually she resumed her professional life and became a tax analyst and consultant.

Early in their relationship Ronald and Ariela invited Althea and me to meet her Chicago parents, Gideon and Joy Friedlander Goldschmidt, at a restaurant in Cambridge. This was not an ordinary social call: Ariela's parents wanted to make sure that we fitted into their cultural and religious world. Apparently we passed muster. It reminded me of the story my mother often told about my two grandfathers traveling several hours to meet on neutral ground to discuss and approve her marrying my father. While Ronald had told me that Ariela's parents had been in Palestine before and during the Second World War, I did not realize until much later that Ariela's maternal great grandfather Herbert Bentwich was a late 19th century British Zionist who had played a role in Britain's 1917 Balfour Declaration that supported a Jewish homeland in Palestine. Ariela's parents however did not stay in Israel after it gained its independence. They chose the United States instead.

While Ariela was proud of her family's fascinating background it was her positive personality and charm that made her a very pleasant daughter in law. Her intelligence, cheerfulness and determination filled the space left by Ronald's occasional reticence. Together they formed the perfect couple to bring up Nate and Elliot.

When Ronald and Ariela moved to their new home in the Boston suburb of Bedford we were impressed by the charming surroundings in which Nate and Elliot could spend their early childhood. We were excited at our first opportunity watching Nate develop. He was active, cheerful and a pleasure to welcome to our world. Ronald and Ariela provided a very interesting and pleasant environment for him to grow up. There were stories, watching Sesame Street on television, outdoor games, toys galore and very early pre-kindergarten learning experiences.

We soon introduced Nate to his aunt Meredith and to my mother, by then in her mid-eighties. She was thrilled to have a great-grandson and bought a small tree as a symbolic expression of her pleasure that at least some of the seeds of the past had taken roots ensuring continuity. Ronald planted the tree on the lawn not far from the house. He has long since moved to another suburb and Nate lives on the other side of the American continent but the little tree has grown and is still there and survives at least in my memory.

We watched Nate grow in Bedford. There was a five-year detour to Holland. He became a person with whom we could communicate. That was fun. It gave us a great deal of pleasure seeing him observe his fascination with Public Television's programs especially geared for his entertainment. There were birthdays and holiday celebrations, family get-togethers with Nate's grandparents on his mother's side, attending pre-kindergarten parents' day parties. We quickly learned that becoming grandparents is a very pleasant experience.

When Nate was three and a half years old, we were asked to keep him company while Ariela was about to deliver his brother, Elliot. He complicated the Bedford household: keeping track of two young family members more than doubled the effort parents require to maintain fun, law and order. For grandparents on the other hand, there is only joy and pleasure and minimum work. It was fun to watch the family grow.

When Nate was ten and Elliot seven, they both were extremely capable in meeting the challenge of switching from the American school system to the European one in Holland. They had hardly any problem making many friends who spoke only Dutch. Five years later and back in Massachusetts, they readjusted quickly to the entirely different atmosphere that prevailed at the very fancy Andover Phillips prep school. They successfully completed their education at Princeton and Bowdoin respectively where, following in their father's footsteps, they became successful squash players.

Chapter 23
Visits to Gorbachev's Soviet Union

As an alumnus of four universities with sophisticated money raising organizations, I am regularly targeted with requests for contributions. When in the fall of 1987I received the usual request and was about to discard a fat envelop from Johns Hopkins, I noticed an invitation for SAIS (School of Advanced international Studies) alumni to go on a ten-day trip to the Soviet Union during the Christmas/New Year recess. It was advertised as an opportunity to visit Moscow, Leningrad and Tbilisi (Georgia), interview members of the Soviet media, as well as ordinary citizens. It took Althea and me only a brief peek at our calendar to convince us to accept the offer to visit Gorbachev's rapidly changing Soviet Union. It promised to be quite an adventure and an unusual way to greet the New Year 1988.

Our group consisted of about two dozen alumni, husbands and wives, none of whom I had met before. They were all more recent graduates. We met our guide at JFK airport. She was a middle aged émigré who had left the Soviet Union 15 years earlier. The flight to Helsinki on Finn Air went smoothly. In Helsinki, we changed planes for the last lap to Moscow. The Aeroflot plane, unlike all the other planes at the airport, was not parked at the terminal but at a tarmac some distance from the gate. It required a several minute bus ride from the terminal and an awkward climb of stairs. Hand luggage was placed on netting above our seats. Once aboard and seated, the doors were shut quickly, the plane started racing down the runway and off we took.

As soon as the seatbelt signs were turned off, a flight attendant appeared and was intent on placing a tray of Russian delicacies in front of me. I indicated I was not hungry and thanked her for her offer. Her demeanor changed instantly. I was about to receive a lecture in heavily accented English that this Russian food was good for me and I had better try it. I informed her that I had just overcome a stomach bug and my doctor had suggested that I limit my food intake. She rejected my explanation and made it clear that after barely entering the Soviet Union I had already insulted her country. Each time she passed my seat I could clearly detect a dirty look in my direction.

I peeked out the window and tried to catch my first sight of the Soviet Union. On that day in late December, Russia was obscured by dense clouds. A warm weather front from the west, clashing with the stationary cold air from the not-so-distant Siberian region, created a moist blanket that hid everything below us. As the plane started its descent, the clouds became ever denser. Suddenly bright lights pierced the fog. The wheels touched the tarmac. We had landed in Moscow. A member of our group said that as a licensed U.S. pilot, he was certain that an American commercial plane would never have been granted permission to land under conditions with such limited visibility. He gave the Russian pilot credit for having done an outstanding job under these circumstances. As we waited for the doors to open, the pilot and co-pilot emerged from their cabin in front. The passengers applauded. The pilots left the plane before the passengers were given the green light to disembark. In the Soviet Union pilots were always the first to leave the plane after landing at an airport.

After a relatively easy passage through customs and passport checkpoints, we met Tanya, our Intourist guide. She had the responsibility of guiding and protecting us on our entire stay in the Soviet Union. On the way to the Hotel Rossia, our bus passed a monument, not far from the airport that commemorates the location where German tanks on their way to Moscow were finally stopped and forced to retreat in December 1941.

Hotel Rossia, a classic example of Stalin-era architecture, a gigantic artless cement quadrangular structure, was out of character with the nearby vestiges of Czarist Russia: the beautifully colored church onion domes. To enter the hotel one had to pass through air turbulence created by two sets of parallel glass doors intended to keep the frigid street air from entering the excessively heated hotel lobby. Only one set of six or eight outdoor doors is unlocked and the only set of the inner door barrier is unlocked at the opposite end. The intent is to keep hotel guests comfortably warm. Unfortunately, things don't work out as planned. Because of the steady stream of guests who enter and leave, there occur frequent interpersonal collisions that anger the guests and keep the doors open over long intervals. Intense air turbulence kept us alert.

It was easy to get lost in the hotel with its 6,000 rooms. Each floor, however, had its special manager, the Key Lady, who gave us our room key and kept an eye on us to make sure we behaved ourselves. When asked, she was quite helpful and answered all our questions. Althea suggested a short walk around the neighborhood before going to bed. The Kremlin wall loomed above us, a five-minute walk from the hotel. As we approached a stone-paved square, a fairytale picture revealed itself in front of us. On our left was St. Basil's Church with its brightly lit colored onion domes and straight ahead, the dark reddish stone wall of the Kremlin. Gently floating snowflakes gave the scene an even more magic appearance. Such a perspective of the Kremlin was not the picture that I had expected in the capital of the Evil Empire.

At this time, shortly before midnight, we were nearly alone, as we peered at the center of power that had threatened the United States for nearly four decades. In front of us and a dozen other tourists, a change of guards at Lenin's tomb was about to take place. Two soldiers marched in synchronized steps to the guardhouse, shifted their rifles, shouted orders and relieved two other guards who had stood motionless for an hour, The relieved soldiers marched away. Silence enveloped the square. We turned around, admired the brightly colored onion domes and walked back to our hotel.

Breakfast next morning was another adventure. It was scheduled for the dining room where we had our dinner the previous evening. It took a long walk for us to realize that there were four identical hotel entrances, foyers and dining rooms in the gigantic quadrangular hotel. We joined a group that was sitting at what we thought had been our table the previous evening. When they conversed in a language that we did not understand, we realized our mistake. We had to race around the hotel to reach our own group, swallow our breakfast a few minutes before the table had to be cleared. We were picked up by our bus and driven to our first interview with the editorial staff of the *Literaturnaya Gazeta*. Our serious task, informing ourselves about the dramatic changes taking place in the Soviet Union under Gorbachev's direction, was about to begin.

***

I had not expected that our meetings with editorial staffs of a number of different prominent Soviet newspapers and journals would be conducted like graduate school seminars. We were seated around a table, introducing ourselves, heard brief opening remarks, asked questions, got involved in fascinating discussions and usually stayed far longer than planned. It did not take us much time to realize that our Russian hosts were as much interested in what was on our minds, as we were to learn about *glasnost* (publicity, openness), *perestroika* (reorganization, restructuring), the Soviet political scene, etc. Fortunately, most members of our group had studied Soviet affairs and international relations and thus were familiar with current events and refrained from asking embarrassingly stupid questions.

The Russians wanted us to share their enthusiasm for the changes Gorbachev's *perestroika* was accomplishing. It was not just an effort to reconstruct the Soviet economy but it was what one of our hosts called, the Soviet Union's Second Revolution, "a revolution of thinking". I was struck by the sense of excitement that gripped almost everyone with whom we talked. The journalists stressed that there was finally an opportunity to think and write about matters that had been off limits. One reporter, who concentrated on Moscow's local news, told us that he was proud to have been called Moscow's Ralph Nader. He had written about some of the absurd actions of the bureaucrats who ran the Moscow subway system. Not only was he not fired for his criticism of the local establishment, he was publicly praised for speaking out and encouraging policy changes.

It was made quite clear to us that the "revolution of thinking" required judgment and a lot of caution. The need for change had to be handled adroitly. It was necessary to avoid stepping on too many sensitive toes. How was that to be accomplished? Use your common sense, we were told. I reached the conclusion that *perestroika* in essence was a call for Russia to face reality and that those in power had to openly admit that Stalinism was not only past and outdated, but that it had been seriously wrong and had caused a great deal of damage. That observation was confirmed by the popularity in the Soviet Union of the film *Repentance*, caricaturing Stalin. As we were having these discussions, my mind wandered back to my time in the State Department when I had the task of analyzing the infamous Slansky trial ordered by Stalin. I could not have imagined then, that only 35 years later in Moscow, I would hear such critical remarks about Stalin within walking distance of the Kremlin. When we left our sessions with journalists and newspaper editors, Althea and I were excited and overwhelmed by the incredible changes in the Soviet Union that we were privileged to witness. It was exciting to witness intellectual leaders recover from a seven decade long nightmare.

While the meetings with editors and Soviet foreign policy analysts occupied most of our stay in Moscow, we managed also to reconnoiter and see some of the famous sights. Entering the Kremlin, we toured a huge hall that for some reason did not impress me. I guess I had expected something more dramatic inside the historic fortifications that had protected Stalin and his gang. On another day, we were invited to Spasky House, the residence of U.S. Ambassador Matlock. He cautioned us not to be carried away by *perestroika*. While Gorbachev's new approach solved some problems, there were still many obstacles left that prevented better relations between our two countries. Matlock spent an hour with us and answered most of our questions.

After our visit to the U.S. Embassy, with only a couple of bites of a sandwich from a brown bag, we rushed to a performance at the Moscow Circus. I had to divert my eyes when incredibly agile performers sailed through the air straight above our heads. The dramatic antics of the Circus performers pleased everybody. I worried however that a performer might lose his balance. We also visited Gorky Park, where we were served vodka and then taken on a Troika Sleigh Ride. Later, switching transportation, we explored Moscow's impressive subway system.

Given the choice of an additional city tour, we went instead to the Pushkin Museum, where we were amazed to discover on the second floor an incredibly exciting display of modern French paintings, Matisse, Picasso (blue period), Gauguin, etc. They had apparently been only recently taken out of storage. We were stunned as we strolled slowly through the well-lit display of modern art that Stalin for so long had ordered to be kept in storage.

***

Saturday, the second day of the New Year, not much was going on in Moscow. Intourist, our Soviet travel agency, had the bright idea to take us on a 132-mile bus journey to Tolstoy's 19th century home. Not all members of our group chose to join us on this excursion. Perhaps they had not read *War and Peace*. They missed a lot of excitement and a memorable experience!

We left our hotel slightly late, but were soon on a modern highway, headed in a southerly direction. Only two of the four lanes were cleared of snow. Once we left the Moscow region, the highway narrowed and became bumpy. Our driver eventually pulled over to the side, stopped, kept the heater on and proceeded to jack up the bus with all of us inside. After a while, he informed us that the hydraulic pipe was frozen. "What now?" we asked. The driver put on his outdoor winter work outfit, lighted a torch and proceeded to focus the flaming torch on the underbelly of the bus in order to defrost the pipe. We, the passengers inside this big box that was being cooked on a fire below us, looked at each other with ever-growing concern, until someone suggested that it might be safer to watch the flaming torch from outside. We asked for permission to open the door, file out and occupy an outdoor viewing stand.

While safe from a potential accident, we faced the unpleasant prospect of waiting a period of unknown duration on a snow-covered field in below freezing temperature. With no outhouse, restaurant nor gas station in sight, where were we to relieve ourselves? "That is no big deal for you", Althea quipped "you got trees. What am I going to do?" Most of us males found one of the few narrow birch trees that gave us an illusion of privacy. Eventually, Althea and the other ladies created their own protective circles and secured a degree of privacy.

We were impressed that almost every bus and truck driver stopped and offered their help. Our driver thanked them, but stated emphatically that he had the situation under control. Our Intourist guide had one of the passing trucks take her to the nearest police station and tried to call her Moscow office, requesting a substitute bus. She returned, driven by a police officer, complaining that the telephone connection did not work. Eventually our driver completed the repairs and we were able to resume our journey. We had spent two hours outdoors on the vast white Russian wintry plain. It gave me some inkling how German soldiers must have enjoyed Russia's frigid wintry landscape while spending two winters not that far from where our bus was stuck.

Resuming our journey, we stopped at a restaurant for the much-delayed lunch and arrived at our destination partially obscured in twilight. Dim lights outlined a wide path leading from the parking area to Tolstoy's home. Heavy snow covered the trees that lined the walk. Ahead was the spot where Tolstoy wrote his famous books! The approach struck us as incredibly romantic. Through some magic, we had gone back in time and were ready to visit Tolstoy. Our guide knocked at the door and a babushka invited us in.

A local English-speaking guide informed us that Tolstoy's home was about to close for the night, but since we had come from such a long distance, all the way from America, we could take a quick tour. We admired the rooms and furniture that had hardly been changed since Leo Tolstoy's departure in 1910, 78 years before our visit. Each room was guarded by an elderly lady. Althea, wanting to check something that had aroused her curiosity in a room we had left a few minutes earlier, encountered the stare of the guard who was putting on her coat and scarf, turning off the light, ready to go home. For some reason I was fascinated by Tolstoy's wife's work room where she had to make sense of Leo's scribbled notes and dictations and transform them into a workable manuscript. In view of the enormous length of *War and Peace*, this must have been a monumental task. It may have contributed to their strained relationship.

I had not been aware of Tolstoy's concern with the welfare and education of the former serfs on his wife's large estate. Nor had I really digested the events that led to his tragic death and the end of a nearly magical writing career. One day, he just left his home and wife, walked to the train station, took a train going south, slept on benches in train stations and was found dead lying on a bench a few days later. As we left Tolstoy's house, still deeply affected by the tragic account of the end of his life, our guide asked us whether we wanted to see Tolstoy's grave. Of course we said yes. We traipsed through deep layers of snow for about five minutes. The guide stopped. We wondered where the grave was. He pointed to a somewhat higher mound of snow. There, without any marker protruding from Mother Nature's snow cover rests Leo Tolstoy. Our eyes filled with tears as we walked back on the snow-covered path to the bus.

***

After contemplating the difficult life and tragic death of Russia's most illustrious literary pre-revolutionary figure, we flew, as if carried by a fairy, over high mountains into the Caucasus. We landed in Tbilisi, the capital of Georgia, Stalin's original home. In Moscow, we had been dealing with Stalin's legacy. Now we were to explore the environment that produced someone as terrible as Stalin.

We were privileged to interview the producers of *Repentance*, the first Russian movie that openly criticized Stalin. It had swept over Russia and had undoubtedly hastened the transformation of the Soviet Union, a vital part of *Glasnost*. In the museum of Gruzfilm, Georgia's Hollywood, Tengiz Abuladze, described the obstacles that he had to overcome to make a movie that challenged decades of accepted faith in Stalin's objectives and achievements. He singled out the encouragement Shevardnadze had given the producers of *Repentance*. Shevardnadze had been the Communist Party boss in Georgia before moving to Moscow as Foreign Minister in Gorbachev's government.

I asked Abuladze whether there was not some irony or special significance in having a Georgian create the most significant and popular movie attacking Stalin, the ruler of the vast Soviet Union, given Stalin's Georgian roots; a Georgian attacking a fellow Georgian. Abuladze stood still for at least a minute, looked straight at me, took several steps from the lectern and looked at me again. The members of our group started to get nervous. We looked at each other with questioning glances. He continued. "If you were not some American, but someone from the U.S.S.R., I would be very, very angry that you asked such a question, but since I know you are from the U.S. I forgive you and I shall answer."

"Let me start by saying that the Stalin in *Repentance* was intended to symbolize the universal tyrant. He has Hitler's moustache, Mussolini's absurd gesturing manners, and is meant to resemble Peron, Pinochet as well as Stalin. Did you know, or perhaps have you forgotten, that we Georgians suffered more from Stalin's crimes than all the rest of the peoples of the Soviet Union? Did you know that whenever Stalin needed troops to defend a hopeless position in Hitler's drive to take the Crimea, encircle Stalingrad and advance in the Caucasus he had his generals pick depleted reserves of Georgians? Did you know that every third citizen of Georgia perished in the Second World War, a higher percentage than any other ethnic population in the U.S.S.R.? Stalin had absolutely no qualms about sacrificing us, our brothers, fathers, his fellow Georgians. Purges were handled by Beria, another Georgian, who made us suffer." He expanded this initial comment, adding dramatic and hair curling illustrations. He went on for at least ten minutes and left us, his audience, deeply moved. I cried, many of us cried.

***

A three-hour flight took us over the western Soviet republics, all the way to Leningrad, the last stop on our tour. Leningrad's very name symbolized the break with Russia's past that the 1917 October Revolution was intended to achieve. St. Petersburg (*Petrograd* in Russian) its prior name, had honored Czar Peter the Great who, in the early 18th century, had tried to rescue the Russian people from their isolation in their northern European Russian forests and focus their sight on the Baltic Sea and Western Europe. As *Perestroika* revised Soviet history, Czar Peter the Great got his name back. This change of name took place only after our visit.

From our hotel at the outer edge of the city, we traveled by bus to the city's center. We stopped at a tributary to the Neva River where the *Aurora* was moored. That is the cruiser from which on November 7, 1917, sailors fired the shots, a signal to the soldiers at the Winter Palace to overthrow the Kerensky regime and seize control.

The Winter Palace and the Hermitage Museum were the next major projects which we intended to explore. Illustrations in guidebooks had not properly prepared us for the treasures of this palace. The quarters occupied by generations of Czars were impressively decorated, exuding an ancient air of grandeur. I asked a guide whether the fancy circular stairway was the one I had seen on pictures that showed revolutionary soldiers, storming up the stairs to seize control of the Palace. The guide set me straight. "If you think that this stairway is where Kerensky's forces were defeated, you are wrong." When I raised my eyebrows, she smiled and continued, "The stairway makes a good picture, but that is all". "Where did it take place?" I asked. She answered by taking me and other interested members of our group to a door that led to a narrow passageway and a metal stairway, obviously intended to be used by servants whose task it was to clean and polish the palace. "It was this narrow passage that the revolutionaries used to enter in order to take over the seat of power".

The Hermitage Museum, a part of the Winter Palace, mesmerized us with its incredibly impressive collection of modern French paintings. Stalin's regime had kept many modern paintings in storage to protect members of the proletariat from "dangerous aesthetic" influences. We also visited other museums and palaces of the Czars that had recently been restored. Our own guide was amazed to find a gallery in one palace restored and open. It had been closed for most of the century. She almost fainted when she entered. "What a treasure!" she exclaimed. We agreed. We toured city streets, crossed surprisingly many bridges over small canals, and tried to remember places where Dostoyevsky's characters had met their doom. We even visited a modern porcelain factory, attended a concert and ballet performance.

Althea and I were curious about a World War II Memorial across the circle facing our hotel. Why was it not on our itinerary? We decided to find out, crossed the circle and descended into a large marble hall below the Memorial, dedicated to the survivors of the 900-day siege that Leningrad had suffered. The rooms had pictures showing conditions in the city while encircled by German forces in 1941 until liberated in 1944. Only in winter, when the lake that connected the city with Soviet-controlled territory was frozen, was it possible for Stalin's forces to send very limited supplies to the starving inhabitants of the city. I had read some gruesome accounts of conditions in the beleaguered city. Stalin was intent on preventing Leningrad and Stalingrad, two cities named after the leaders of the Soviet Union, from falling into Hitler's lap and becoming his trophies of conquest. As we were about to leave the Memorial, we asked the lady in charge at the counter of the visitor's center, where books, pamphlets and postcards were on sale, whether by chance she had been in Leningrad during the siege. She looked our age and might have been there as a teenager. That question instantly changed her demeanor. Extreme sadness overcame her. "Yes, I was here. I lived through it." We had not expected to meet someone who had experienced this horrendous phase of the Soviet past. We told her that we were very touched to meet a real survivor. She continued, "I do not know whether the siege was worth it."

Then she added, "If the Nazis had taken Leningrad, that would not have helped them win the war. Why did Stalin not let us move a short distance east and wait out the war there? He made us suffer!"

We left the Soviet Union by train from Leningrad to Helsinki. We had to rush to catch the train and could not linger in the Finland Station to get a feel for the place that had acquired a special renown as the spot where Lenin had re-entered Russia in 1917 to lead the revolution. We had visited the Soviet Union at a historic moment, when the structure built by Lenin was in the process of being replaced by something quite different.

***

The School of Advanced International Studies, SAIS, decided that our 1987/88 Soviet adventure called for an encore and scheduled one exactly two years later. Althea and I decided to take advantage of this opportunity to repeat a journey that had been so interesting and had helped me enliven the scenery and background of my international relations courses. While the repeat performance was worthwhile, it lacked the excitement of discovery. The second trip turned out to be a more traditional tour of historic sites, meeting interesting people and comparing tasty delicacies. Not until our arrival in Tbilisi, Georgia, did we encounter a new adventure.

Landing at the Tbilisi airport was very informal: hardly any signs of security measures. The bus took our twenty-five member group to the same hotel where we had stayed in January 1988. When we approached the hotel this time, our bus was stopped and directed to unload us at the back entrance. We were casually informed that there was a demonstration on the thoroughfare in front of the hotel. After going to our room and unpacking, we had some time to spare before our next scheduled activity. Althea welcomed the rest because a cold she had contracted in Moscow temporarily dampened her quest to reconnoiter the Tbilisi neighborhood. I was curious to find out what the fuss on the street in front of the hotel was all about. "Be careful", she admonished me as I left her in the room." Don't forget, we are in a Communist country!" Of course, I was going to be careful, after all, I had spent much of my career studying the history and politics of the Soviet Union and Eastern Europe.

On the street I followed the crowd that moved in one direction and then congregated in a large square in front of a big Stalin-era building that served either as local headquarter of the Communist Party or of the Georgian Government. In Moscow, I had no problem reading signs and overhearing people's conversations. After all, I had studied Russian in college, a Slavic language closely related to Czech. Russia's Cyrillic alphabet required getting used to, but was not particularly difficult to decipher. Georgian, on the other hand, was not related to any language I had ever studied. The Georgian alphabet resembled an artist's effort to design a complicated hanging flower arrangement. In short, I moved in a mass of people as a complete stranger. I had no idea what the commotion was all about. Were people assembling to hear their leader speak? Were they going to overthrow the government? Were they storming the Bastille? What was going on?

I tried to get closer to the front. Maybe near the first row there would be a clue as to what this was all about. I started to look more closely at the people around me. People returned my inquisitive look. It downed on me that my Russian headgear was totally out of place here. How would they know that I was an American, not a Russian? I became a little more circumspect. Maybe they don't like Russians. I was now far enough in front to see the gigantic cement blocks that thwarted any attempt to enter the building. The entrance to the building was entirely obstructed.

Suddenly the crowd around me turned their heads. There was a commotion in the rear. People started shouting. Maybe they were cheering the Georgian way. A big bulldozer slowly made its way to the front. It raised its shovel and banged it against a concrete block that barred the crowd's march to the building's entrance. The voice on the loudspeaker became more intense. I surmised that somebody ordered us to disperse. Other voices used bullhorns egging us on. Maybe it was the other way around. In any case when I saw the bulldozer opening a wedge in the protective wall and armed police revealing themselves on the steps of the suddenly accessible building, it occurred to me that it might be wiser to put some distance between me and a potential battlefield. As I sneaked to the rear, I imagined people looking at me disapprovingly.

I returned to the hotel and told Althea about my exciting experience. She was shocked about me being so close to a bulldozer knocking over the barricade." Do you realize how dangerous this was?" Then she wanted to know what this was all about. I had to confess I did not have the faintest idea, except that, whatever it was, it got them very excited. O.K. I promised to find out before dinner.

In the hotel lobby, I located our Russian travel guide. I asked her. She shook her head, "I am a stranger here". I did not quite believe her. "I'll find you an English speaking Georgian, maybe he knows." A university student introduced himself and we had a half hour conversation over a cup of hot tea. The hotel lobby was freezing. It is all about South Ossetia. I asked him to repeat the name. While I was reasonably familiar with the geography of the Soviet Union, South Ossetia drew a blank. He explained South Ossetians were attacking Georgians and were trying to break away from Georgia. They wanted autonomy. "Why?" I asked. He did not know or did not feel like telling me. "That is what all the fuss was about this afternoon?" "Yes, we Georgians believe South Ossetia is part of Georgia and should remain in our republic". That is how I learned there was a conflict in Georgia.

Later I learned that Gora, not far from Tbilisi, was Josef Stalin's birthplace. Stalin's father, Dzhugashvili, was a Georgian and his mother an Ossetian. And of course Beria and many of the most notorious Party officials responsible for the terror under Stalin's regime, hailed from Georgia. It is somewhat ironic that Stalin, a Georgian, who epitomized the worst aspect of Soviet rule, would more than half a century after his death ignite strong antagonism in his home state Georgia against Russia that had repudiated Stalin back in the 1950ies. After the excitement we witnessed in Tbilisi there was hardly any mention of a conflict involving South Ossetia; instead an Azerbaijan-Armenian dispute in a nearby region got the little attention that we paid in the 90's to the Caucasus.

Chapter 24
The Velvet Revolution: Postscript to my Ph.D. Thesis

45 years after focusing my scholarly pursuit on issues involving the encounter between communism and democracy, particularly as it affected the survival of an independent Czechoslovak Republic, the issue returned to the center of the stage. My concern how a democratic neighboring state could manage to survive Stalin's threats increased as the Cold War intensified. Events in Prague in 1948, 1968 and 1977 demonstrated the continuing struggle between communist and democratic leaders to achieve control. It was both exciting and annoying to pursue a scholarly research project with so many missed opportunities of hoped for conclusions. Finally as Gorbachev shifted Soviet domestic and foreign policy, light appeared at the end of the tunnel.

In Czechoslovakia, the denouement of the Soviet-imposed political system took its own distinct course. No walls were knocked down. A former ruler was not shot after Kangaroo Court proceedings. Instead, there was an outpouring of people on Wenceslaus Square at the center of Prague, protesting harsh police methods. The aroused citizens in huge numbers impressed and overwhelmed the repressive bureaucratic and unimaginative Communist regime. This happened on November 17, 1989. The Kremlin took notice, appeared to be pleased and, unlike 1968, did not intervene. While the change was dramatic, there was minimal violence. That is why the event became known as the Velvet Revolution.

Parliamentary elections were scheduled for June 8 and 9, 1990, to complete the political transformation inaugurated by the Velvet Revolution six months earlier. That date tied in with my academic schedule: I had time to grade final exams and attend commencement exercises before taking off on my way to Prague to watch an important chapter in Czechoslovakia's transition from communism to democracy. Althea's important projects at the Institute for Institutional Research could not be interrupted and therefore I would have to go alone.

From Frankfurt where I landed, it took a five-hour drive to reach Plzeň, my first stop in Czechoslovakia. At the German-Czechoslovak border, formerly an iron curtain crossing, Czech officials waved me on with only a cursory look at my American passport. After locating Hotel Central, a comfortable recently renovated hotel, I went to Plzeň's Square of the Republic. I remembered that square from my youth, when I accompanied my father on visits to his aunts, uncles and cousins. Unhappily, none had survived the Nazi occupation. Posters advertising a museum exhibit featuring the liberation of Plzeň by U.S. forces in May 1945 attracted my attention. American forces had withdrawn after a brief presence, in line with a U.S.-U.S.S.R. military deal. The exhibit symbolized Czechoslovakia's new pro-Western orientation. It showed the arrival of U.S. troops, tanks, waving, welcoming citizens, who had survived the six-year Nazi occupation. Records played American popular music, including the *Yellow Rose of Texas*.

Prague had changed dramatically since my last visit in the early eighties. Václav Havel, the playwright, whose courageous stand in 1977 to uphold the basic freedom of expression had emerged untainted by Czechoslovakia's recent past. Having earned his people's respect and confidence, he was honored to guide Czechs and Slovaks to the peaceful revival of democracy. He reminded everyone that Czechoslovakia's founding first president, Thomas Masaryk, originally a professor of history, sociology and politics, had established democratic guide lines that had served his people well, until they were victimized by Hitler, and then by Stalin. It was time to restore Masaryk's legacy.

A temporary small statue of Masaryk occupied the lower end of Wenceslaus Square. A former heavily traveled thoroughfare, *Na Příkopě [Canal, Ditch]*, now converted to a pedestrian mall, served as an al fresco history-learning center. Twenty- two regularly spaced kiosks featured photographs, newspaper headlines, cartoons and statistics covering the major events between 1918 and 1968. A steady stream of passersby seemed fascinated by the past re-emerging from obscurity and confusion. The fog was finally lifting. As I watched the young and the old, the well dressed and the disheveled, stopping and reading intently the accounts of past events, I could not help wiping away my tears and had to hide in a corner to regain my composure.

The parliamentary election lasted two days. Polls opened on Friday, June 8 at 2 p.m., closed at 10 p.m., reopened on the ninth at

7 a.m., finally closing at 2 p.m. Extending voting over a 24 hour period enabled almost all voters to participate in restoring a parliament that would fairly represent the entire population. 95% of eligible voters participated.

I watched the results on TV in the comfort of my Hotel Splendid (Prague-Bubeneč). Channel 1 had exit polls within minutes of the official closing of the polls. Actual results followed in short order. The Civic Forum, a party Václav Havel had spearheaded, was the clear victor. It was followed by the Communist party and a Catholic party. The elections confirmed the spontaneous change in political direction that began six months earlier.

Two hours after the polls closed, Channel I switched from election results to a national unity concert televised from Prague's Old Town Square. Rafael Kubelik, self-exiled Czech orchestra conductor, returned from abroad to lead members of three orchestras, representing Bohemia, Moravia and Slovakia, the three provinces of Czechoslovakia. The program naturally consisted of selections from Smetana and Dvořak. President Václav Havel sat in the front row. Later he attended a rock concert. The election was truly a turning point in Czech history. When I drove through Moravia and Slovakia on my way to Vienna, I found the same mood celebrating the restoration of democracy.

Chapter 25
Confronting Meredith's Illness

Audrey's tragic suicide in 1983 had a serious impact on Meredith. Having recovered reasonably well from her 1977 psychotic episode in Gambia, West Africa, she had managed to complete her course work at Harvard and graduated with a major in psychology in 1979. Even though she had been able to hold a job in Connecticut's state government, first in the Department of Labor and then as an administrative assistant in the Hartford Regional Center, an agency of the Department of Mental Retardation, she did not enjoy the life that she was leading. She had her own apartment but participated in very few social activities. Audrey's death dealt a fatal blow to her recovery.

Our instant concern about the emotional impact of Audrey's suicide on Meredith was fully justified. When the news of the suicide was broadcast, friends of Audrey picked Meredith up at the Hartford Regional Center and telephoned me that they thought it best for Meredith to be brought immediately to our home so that I could impart the news to her. An hour later, when she appeared at our door, it was clear that she already knew. I have since heard many psychiatrists make the profound suggestion that individuals suffering from a mental illness should avoid exposure to stressful situations because stress aggravates the illness. How in the real world is that to be implemented?

Meredith had located her mother on the Dunham Pond dock on her first suicide attempt and was therefore not entirely unprepared for the shock that Audrey had finally succeeded in her effort to leave this world. Althea and I had the difficult task of reconciling Meredith with the loss of her mother; an enormous challenge when a mind is capable of functioning at its best, but nearly impossible when the mind is seriously impaired by an illness that blurs the line between reality and fantasy. We were fooled to believe that we had partially succeeded when Meredith managed to resume a near normal daily routine. I noticed a growing disorder in her apartment but hoped it was just an aberration, and not an indication of the worsening effects of her illness.

A couple of weeks later, when she was a passenger in our car, I saw her smiling and silently talking to somebody who was not in the car. I realized then that things were perhaps worse than I had been willing to admit. She did not respond when I asked her who she was talking to. The fact that she heard voices, which appeared completely real to her, was something that I had trouble understanding. I rationalized that at least the voices made her happy and that was some comfort. Unfortunately, just at this critical juncture, her psychiatrist who had helped her quite a lot, left town and moved to Texas. Meredith informed us casually about this loss, mainly because she missed having conversations with him that she had enjoyed and that had apparently helped her significantly.

Other disturbing incidents occurred. One evening I received a phone call from one of her friends who felt that I should know that Meredith had called her from East Hartford with the news that she was on her way by foot to South Windsor, having walked all the way through Hartford from Farmington at the edge of the heavily traveled shoulder of I-84. There was nothing wrong with her car that she had left at the entrance of her apartment. When I called a psychiatrist and asked how Meredith could be helped to avoid such a potentially dangerous situation, he answered: "If she is not in mortal danger and does not seek help, there is nothing anyone can do". This was not the first, nor the last, time that I received this legal yet absurd counsel. It became increasingly difficult for Meredith to drive, since she could not keep her eyes from staring upward and away from oncoming traffic. In retrospect, it is amazing that she managed to be involved only in a relatively minor accident, scraping a tree at a bend on North Eagleville Road in Storrs.

Finally, Meredith was referred by a local psychiatrist to Elmcrest, a small private hospital in Portland, across the Connecticut River from Middletown. After a stay of six weeks when her insurance coverage ran out, she was declared "cured" and released. She was referred to a therapist in the Greater Hartford area and left to fend on her own. It took only a few weeks before Meredith went to the UCONN Health Center in Farmington and requested psychiatric care. I was kept informed and we called professionals we knew for advice. She was kept in the hospital's emergency room for nearly 24 hours. It took that long to locate a place for her at Cedarcrest, a state operated mental health facility. Reluctantly I had been convinced that Meredith's illness was extremely serious. It would affect her future to an extent I had not wanted to face.

***

Before Meredith's diagnosis of schizophrenia, my awareness of mental illness had been limited to memories of a building in a nearby suburb of Prague that looked different from others. When I pointed to it and asked my father what it was, he lowered his voice and answered that it was an insane asylum. My curiosity was aroused when my mother added that her aunt, my grandfather's sister, had been confined to such an asylum in England. After telling me about a 19th century Austrian monk and botanic scholar Gregor Mendel who had developed theories about genetic inheritance, my father strongly suggested that to prevent having my offspring carry mental illness genes I should avoid marrying a woman who has mental illness in her ancestry. Of course, I had not considered it possible that forty years later Meredith, my own daughter, could conceivably be suffering from schizophrenia. She had had a brilliant career in high school and college and now relegated to live in an insane asylum?

There was a lot that I had to learn about mental illness. It was a strange coincidence that beginning in the late 1970's the topic of mental illness had emerged from the closet. *One Flew over the Cuckoo's Nest,* a popular film, featured the horrors of a mental asylum. New medications had enabled some severely mentally ill patients to leave mental hospitals and rejoin the rest of society. A psychiatrist, E. Fuller Torrey, published an extremely useful and widely read family manual, *Surviving Schizophrenia*. It was intended to help people like me to deal with the entirely new world that one enters as a close relative is diagnosed with the illness. Unfortunately, as the title suggests, Torrey concentrates on helping individuals who suffer from the illness but says little about measures to help them recover and resume a normal existence. Emphasizing recovery had to wait several decades. Thirty years later the *New York Times* ran a feature story about mental illness issues for several months and the commentator/interviewer Charlie Rose had a series of very informative discussions dealing with illnesses of the brain hosted by the outstanding scholar Eric Kandel on Public Television.

***

We were soon to realize that illnesses of the brain affect far more people than I had ever imagined. A friend, with whom I had discussed local and state politics, asked me casually one day whether Althea and I would be interested in a group discussion that dealt with helping those affected by mental illness. That led us to attend a local NAMI (National Alliance on Mental Illness) meeting. Usually a dozen individuals would have a regularly scheduled meeting where family members discussed the latest incidents and problems encountered by their sick son, daughter, wife, parent or friend. It was clearly understood that information from these discussions would not leave the meeting room. Comments, suggestions flowed freely from those sitting around the table. Those comments often helped a family member cope by realizing that the odd behavior of their relative/friend was behavior typical of the disease. Of course it did not help to learn that there was little hope of recovery from a mental illness.

It became obvious that compared to the stories I heard at these meetings, my concerns about Meredith, while serious, were manageable. There were situations where a parent was relieved when a son or daughter ended up in a prison. That was better than not knowing what their son/daughter was doing spending weeks homeless in nearby woods. There was the parent who had cleaned up the rented son's room, only to be reprimanded by the son for having gotten rid of his favorite treasured rat. When she cleaned up the next time, he protected his rat and she wanted some advice from us around the table what to do. I actually wrote to the Mental Health Department Commissioner and asked him to provide some guidance and help in this situation. The Commissioner told me he was concerned, amused, but did not know how to be of assistance in resolving the dispute involving the fate of the rat.

The issue of available housing for the homeless mentally ill, came up frequently, especially in the Willimantic area. The story most often heard involved examples of inadequate support from the agencies, private and public, that were charged with the responsibility of helping mentally ill patients recover and regain the ability to function as independently as possible. Years of attending meetings of Connecticut's Board of Mental Health and Addiction Services and the NAMI family support groups lowered my confidence in the ability of state agencies to implement their task of providing effective mental health and recovery support. I could not help feel disillusioned.

As a member of NAMI I met many new friends with whom I could share my concerns. Whitney Jacobs, a retired administrator at the UCONN Health Center, active in Connecticut's NAMI chapter, became a leading advocate for having the state of Connecticut fund clozapine for all of the state's schizophrenia patients. More than anybody else, he succeeded in convincing state legislators that it was cheaper for the state to pay for a drug that might help get patients like Meredith out of a state psychiatric hospital, than to pay for that patient's long-term institutional care. I got to know Whitney very well and we worked together for several years pushing state officials to make clozapine available to sufferers from schizophrenia. This helped Connecticut become a national leader in treating schizophrenia patients by adopting legislation that had the state pay for the use of clozapine by patients suffering from schizophrenia. It was a long, but ultimately successful battle that undoubtedly helped Meredith deal with the worst aspects of her illness.

After retiring from my academic career, I could spend more time attending NAMI meetings. One day in 1993, Whitney Jacobs asked me to have lunch at a New Haven restaurant with members of CAMI, the Connecticut chapter of NAMI. Following the discussions at that lunch, I was asked to chair the CAMI Board.

I was pleased and honored to assume the responsibility of chairing an organization that hoped to improve communication between those affected by an illness of the brain and their families and friends. The organization also sought to further a better understanding of mental illness by a wider segment of the population. While CAMI Board members shared very important common objectives, I soon discovered that conflicting personalities split the group. It was not an easy task to preside over Board meetings, where some members were so irritated that they had to leave the room and pace outside until they regained sufficient control to express their opinions in a reasonably calm fashion. I had to face the fact that the heat emanating from conflicts of opinion by CAMI Board members was far more intense than that which I had encountered on the Mansfield political scene or at UCONN faculty meetings.

Althea played a crucial role in helping me transform an informal CAMI organization into one with a permanent headquarter, staff, and budget. I lobbied state legislators, Congressmen and Senators in Washington. We sought support for mental health parity legislation, ending discriminatory medical treatment of the mentally ill. We also sought federal support to finance research that could lead to a more effective method of treating mental illness. In short I behaved like a volunteer lobbyist who had left cloistered intellectual university life and now confronted the turbulence created by steps taken to modernize the mental health system in Connecticut and other states. All these activities not only helped me avoid old age somnolence, but I hoped would benefit Meredith. It did not take long for me to realize that, compared to my new CAMI responsibilities and serving on the State Board of Mental Health, life at the University had been a breeze.

As president of the Connecticut chapter of NAMI, I was expected to attend the national conventions of the organization in Washington, D.C., Miami and Albuquerque, New Mexico. This made me aware of the fact that with all of its shortcomings Connecticut's mental health system was a leader in adopting up-to-date methods of handling patients suffering from a mental illness. While that was encouraging, it was, however, a testimony to the reality that the United States faces an enormous task of having treatment programs catch up with innovations made possible by medical research. I was surprised to learn how many well-known legislators, academicians, authors, executives, had friends or relatives affected by a mental illness. The positive side is that there are a significant number of influential people interested in lobbying for improving our mental health system.

***

With fewer responsibilities at the University approaching retirement, I was able to devote time to meetings of the local, regional and state Boards of the Connecticut Department of Mental Health and Addiction Services (DMHAS) to which I had been appointed several years before my retirement. This also coincided with the period when mental health issues moved from curtained off corners to the main stage, where they caught the attention of a wider public. Efforts were made to develop some form of communication between agencies supervising the operations of mental health institutions and the interested public.

I took seriously the responsibility of letting administrators know how I, as a very concerned member of the public, believed the agencies and institutions handled my daughter's troubled life. Discussions shifted from pleasant generalities to explanations of how concrete situations were handled or frequently mishandled. I have to admit that I enjoyed my role as a reasonably well informed critic. Some of my colleagues on the state, regional and local mental health boards probably thought of me as a troublemaker who made their evenings unnecessarily contentious. I did try to be positive and constructive.

The public's interest and concern with treating the surprisingly large segment of the population suffering severe mental illnesses led to important discussions among experts and even among a broader interested public about implementing new approaches to the treatment of mental illness. Deinstitutionalizing the mentally ill and treating them in the community, became a topic of general interest, encouraged by the widespread expectation that recently developed more effective drugs might make hospitalization unnecessary. The prospect of saving money by closing large mental hospitals gave this idea political momentum. It also immediately affected the families of the patients who would now have to be treated at home or in the community. There was widespread fear that returning individuals suffering from a mental illness to their homes might endanger the general population. Another major issue was expanding health insurance to cover mental illness like any other illness by stopping the traditional exclusion of mental illness from medical insurance policies.

My participation on Mental Health Boards helped me understand that Meredith's debilitating illness was certainly not unique. It also taught me the enormous impact of mental illness on individual families, on society, the state and its finances. There was a glimmer of light at the end of a very long tunnel: new imaging techniques had opened a crucial window on how brain cells sometimes malfunctioned. It was recognized that mental illnesses were biological illnesses and had to be treated like any other illness of the human body. New drugs intended to counteract the debilitating aspects of schizophrenia were being tested. This meant that the practice of isolating those affected by a mental illness in hospitals for the insane could be replaced by treating the affected in a community recovery setting with available medications and effective psychiatric counseling. Significant progress in treating the illness seemed at last possible.

***

Meredith had to spend more than a decade in mental hospitals before benefitting from the newer approaches. After a short stay at Cedarcrest, she was transferred to a Mental Health Clinic in New Haven, a facility jointly operated by Yale University Medical Center and the State of Connecticut, where new treatment methods were tried, with only modest success. The worst phase in her long journey was the time spent at Connecticut Valley Hospital (CVH) in Middletown, to which she was committed in 1985. Its location reflected traditional outdated attitudes of dealing with the mentally ill. Located in the center of the state, it has a panoramic view of a peaceful landscape bisected by the Connecticut River. The towers and other buildings of Middletown, the boats floating around the bend, the meadows and wooded areas and the remnants of forests at the edge of the river, can all be seen from the parking lots near the many old and some newer brick structures housing the patients. It is far better located than Wesleyan University, only a short distance from CVH in Middletown. Unfortunately, the patients at CVH never had the opportunity to admire the panoramic view. They were restricted to their wards and rooms with windows out of reach for security reasons. While the windows let the light in, they were too high to enable those inside to contemplate the outer world from which they have been cut off. In the 19th century when CVH was built, people felt that they had done a good deed placing the mentally ill in a "nice spot" where they were sufficiently isolated, so that they could not bother "normal people"; out of sight, out of mind.

It bothered me that there were so few cars in the parking lot when we visited Meredith at CVH. On most of our visits, we were among the very few relatives and friends who spent any time with a patient in the hospital. This reflected the fact that the average person is uncomfortable in the company of someone who suffers from an illness of the brain. Such an illness is put into an entirely different category from an abnormality affecting any other part of the human body. Unfortunately, this fact became a major issue in the subsequent effort to shift treatment of the mentally ill from state institutions into the community.

As we visited Meredith regularly at Connecticut Valley Hospital, we became increasingly concerned as her condition deteriorated. Not only did it become more difficult to communicate with her, her appearance and demeanor changed significantly. She was transferred from a ward in a building, housing moderately impaired patients, to one resembling a prison. The staff seemed to be more concerned with preventing mayhem, than with efforts to help patients recover. A therapist who treated Meredith spoke to us at one of our visits and suggested that something be done to take Meredith out of CVH. "The environment does not help her recovery", she warned us. Meredith was lucky that there was at least one professional CVH employee, who cared for her patient's welfare enough to jeopardize her relationship with CVH administrators.

Because of my participation on the regional and state Mental Health Boards, I had gotten to know the Director of Norwich hospital. I was impressed by the way he administered that hospital which served Eastern and a part of Central Connecticut. I asked him whether it would be possible to transfer Meredith to his Norwich Hospital. He readily agreed and Meredith moved there in January 1989. Following her transfer, Meredith did indeed show some improvement. While Norwich Hospital on the Thames lacked CVH's panoramic view above the Connecticut River, she benefited almost immediately from less crowded wards, a staff trained to give attention to the needs of individual patients and a much more relaxed atmosphere.. It was also at Norwich that she eventually received the crucial help of the more effective recently introduced drug clozapine. Her mood improved significantly What a relief to watch Meredith improve!

Althea and I were determined to do more than just visit Meredith regularly. We discussed the use of more effective drugs and other measures for her to regain self reliance and finding ways of helping her live a better life. After years watching Meredith's illness getting worse while in the care of state hospitals and her ability to function effectively deteriorate, I reached the conclusion that I not only could, but also had to intervene and stop being a passive bystander.

It did not take us long to understand why schizophrenia was considered the most difficult mental illness to treat. Changes in the way the brain functions are not visible the way a heart attack or a broken leg is. Meredith talked to us, but she saw not only us, but also people from a different world and clearly preferred those other people who understood her better than we did. Her world was sometimes a very disturbing one, affecting her mood and activities. She never lost touch with the world that she knew when her sickness began but assumed it had not changed. Thus, she lived in three orbits: the present, the past and her preferred imaginary one. The professionals who treated her tried to explain to us what was going on, protecting of course her right of privacy. They were unable to help her leave behind that third imaginary world that was so precious and real to her and prevented her from leading a constructive life. I asked a leading research psychiatrist who gave a lecture at a Schizophrenia Conference at the New York Columbia University Presbyterian Hospital what could be done to help Meredith get out of her imaginary world. His response: If those voices that talk to her cheer her up why interfere? His answer failed to cheer me up.

There were rays of hope. One of the new break-through drugs was clozapine. It had been tested in Europe and the U.S. for nearly a decade. Unfortunately, it had a side effect. Slightly more than one percent of those taking the drug died. That "significant detail" kept the U.S. government from approving the drug. Nevertheless, several European countries, were willing to take the risk, and approved it. The positive results in Europe led to a major effort to make clozapine available here. The Swiss drug company [Sandoz] producing Clozapine, devised a system for the U.S., which involved requiring patients to undergo blood tests every other week, before giving them the next pill to further the magic cure. The blood test could detect the loss of white blood cells, a warning sign of possibly disastrous consequences. The bi-weekly blood tests were intended to eliminate any potentially fatal accident. It solved a medical problem, but at a huge cost, raising the serious political question of funding a patient's $10,000 dosage of clozapine for a single year.

The effort to overcome the financial obstacles that slowed down innovative treatment of schizophrenia, shifted attention from medical research to building support for making clozapine available to those patients who needed it. The legislature and the Governor had to be convinced, that public funding of the medical expenses, specifically enabling patients to obtain their weekly doses of clozapine, was as important as funding state mental hospitals.

***

My involvement efforts to reform mental health care on the state level was facilitated by legislation giving the public a greater voice in shaping state policies treating patients with a mental illness. Local, regional and state boards were given the task to recommend treatment improvements to the relevant authorities. Such public involvement was also intended to limit the power of a deeply entrenched bureaucracy. In theory, administrators would lay their problems on the table and seek advice from the public who would help resolve difficult controversial issues. This gave me an opportunity to practice what I had been preaching in my courses: it is crucial to involve the public in vital policy decisions. Equally important was the effort to encourage the bureaucracy to adopt innovative treatment approaches. All this would help Meredith recover.

There was a wide gap that separated reform-minded innovators from tradition-bound defenders of the status quo. Relatives and friends of patients suffering from a severe mental illness, as well as "consumers", i.e. patients receiving treatment, voiced their concerns. Administrators and others involved in running the mental health system, listened politely. Unfortunately, reforms were either too expensive to consider seriously or involved changing long-standing practices and even closing institutions, thus depriving workers of their jobs.

There was an even wider gap. Those of us who represented families and patients, as well as those who provided mental health care services, were on the same side when it came to facing problems of mental illness. We all recognized that mental illness was a serious issue that a modern society had to address. On the other side, those steeped in the past either closed their minds to the problem or wanted to protect "normal citizens" from the "insane" by pushing them behind an impregnable wall, so that they would not bother and worry us. Out of sight, out of mind: putting it more bluntly, warehousing the mentally ill eased the rest of the population's conscience. The mentally ill had a bed and food. That was meant to solve the problem. As long as the emphasis was on warehousing the mentally ill in state institutions, there was minimal emphasis on helping them recover their ability to function.

As patients suffering from a serious mental illness improved due to the availability of clozapine and similar recently developed more effective drugs, the way Meredith did, the possibility of releasing patients from mental institutions became real. The issue of helping patients recover in the community, as against keeping them in institutions, entered the public debate. I had some premonition about the intensity of the developing debate

Discussion about the possibility of closing Norwich Hospital started years before that decision was finally made. It struck me as strange and certainly illogical, that as the hospital moved to closure, major improvements were made that had too long been delayed. A modern comfortable recreation room was added with large windows through which the patients could observe a world from which they had been excluded. A huge modern air conditioning plant was built to help patients survive dangerously hot rooms in the summer. The plant was to serve all the buildings on the large campus, even though many were no longer used and the rest were to be closed in two or three years. I asked state officials why they did not simply install air conditioning units serving wards or entire floors instead of a several million $ plant that was never in full operation and became a white elephant on the soon to be abandoned campus. Their answer was that it was their responsibility to maintain and improve the facilities as long as the buildings were there, regardless of occupancy. The possibility of closure was irrelevant; it was not on their agenda. I even served on a committee in the mid-nineteen-nineties that was asked to explore possible use of the Norwich hospital structures once it stopped serving patients afflicted with mental illness. Interested members of the public and administrators discussed a variety of proposals. We reached no conclusions. Nobody else did either. 15 years later the buildings stand abandoned. They are slowly disintegrating. They command a wonderful view of the Indian Casino across the Thames.

It was fortunate that Connecticut had governors going as far back as Abe Ribicoff whose interest in caring for those afflicted with mental health issues led to the appointment of outstanding commissioners of mental health in the 80's and 90's. Commissioners Michael Hogan and Albert Solnit were appointed respectively by Governors William O'Neill and Lowell Weicker. Their leadership created the appropriate environment for pushing necessary reforms.

The prospect of transferring patients from state hospitals into the community might help Meredith, we hoped. She might manage to return to a more normal life style and possibly full recovery. Indeed, after a dozen wasted years in state hospitals, Meredith was released in 1996 to Plainfield House, a small group home in Eastern Connecticut, the "Quiet Corner" operated by United Services. There she started on the path to recovery. Ten months later, she was able to move into a nearby apartment that she shared with another recuperating patient. I was however somewhat too optimistic in expecting rapid progress in her path to a more normal existence helped by the new medication as well as "talk therapy". As she improved she was able to communicate with her therapists. She informed me that she enjoyed those discussions. It was obvious that she was gradually regaining some of her ability to function. The better her condition however, the less time was allotted to her meetings with "talk therapists" and other mental health specialists who sought to help her on the path to recovery. Treating the mentally ill in the community rather than in state insane institutions was a worthy objective that encountered an enormous obstacle: it was more than the public and the politicians were willing to pay.

In spite of her illness Meredith managed to adjust relatively easily to the world around her. She made friends when she lived in her apartment in Plainfield and later on in a nursing home in Brooklyn, Connecticut. Even in her darkest period she always tried to communicate with me. It did not take me long to figure out that when she repeated the phrase *seeing, seeing black* over and over again she meant to say *I am very, very sick.*

The voices she heard made her smile at many inappropriate occasions. I followed the psychiatrist's suggestion that as long as she liked what her voices told her I had no cause to worry. She often demonstrated compassion for others in need and tried to help them in many different ways.

She got along very well with Althea, even during the most serious phase of her illness. After her release from Norwich Hospital we regularly took her for dinner. Althea's illness and death affected Meredith deeply and she helped me in that dark period. She took to Ina Ruth, her new step mother, as soon as she met her and established a close relationship. Our weekly dinners at restaurants all over the "Quiet Corner" were very pleasant. Our discussions may have been difficult for others to comprehend.

On March 11, 2011 I received a phone call from her nursing home in Brooklyn that she had died that night from a brain aneurism. When I arrived there half an hour later I saw her lying on the floor in her room in the position that the staff had found her. The smile on her face had become a permanent testimony to her positive attitude even under the most adverse conditions imaginable. Many of her friends from the nursing home and elsewhere who had known her in the years of her slow recovery attended the funeral and expressed their sorrow at having lost Meredith who they liked very much and admired greatly. She was only 55 years old.

We laid her to rest next to her mother Audrey. The inscription on her grave stone reads:

Meredith Bright and Very Kind.

Chapter 26
Israel

I recall from my childhood in Berlin and Prague overhearing earnest discussions among my father's friends about Theodor Herzl and Zionism. Was Palestine a safe haven where Jews, threatened by pogroms in Russia and later by Hitler's fury, could pursue normal activities? Were Jews better off assimilating and joining the culture of their non-Jewish neighbors or form a separate state in a land from which they had been driven two millennia ago? This quandary was replaced in the thirties by the immediate issue whether the British would let Jews enter Palestine before the Americans unlocked their door. Courses at the Fletcher School dealing with the Middle East further directed my attention to the fascinating developments in the territories controlled by the pre-World War I Ottoman Empire. That led me to teach seminars on the Middle East at UCONN.

When my son Ronald married Ariela, the topic of Israel arose closer to home. Ariela's father, also born in Berlin, immigrated to Palestine to escape Hitler's wrath. He participated in the British defense of Palestine against the Nazis and then in Israel's quest for independence. Ariela's maternal great-grandfather Herbert Bentwich, a prominent British Zionist played a significant role in Britain's support for a Jewish state in Palestine during World War I. In 1947, Ariela's parents left Palestine, then still a British Mandate, and moved to Chicago where Ariela was born. Ariela however stayed in touch with her many relatives in Israel. She suggested I visit them, if I ever decided to explore that historic part of the world.

I must give Althea credit for helping me overcome any remaining reluctance to visit Israel, a controversial topic in family discussions before World War II. Althea was very interested in my Jewish background and argued that after traveling to Berlin and Prague, the cities of my youth, and to her ancestral England, it was high time to see the land where Moses took his people, including perhaps some of my ancestors.

We chose the German airline *Lufthansa* to fly to Frankfurt, where we had to change planes for the final leg to Tel Aviv. After a long walk to the center of Frankfurt's modern terminal, we failed to find any mention of our flight to Tel Aviv on the big board listing scheduled departure flights. Luckily, we had been given a Frankfurt Boarding Pass at Logan Airport's check-in counter listing Frankfurt's gate number B55. It took us some time and effort to locate B55. It was tacked away on the lower floor of the terminal. The waiting room was enclosed and small. It became obvious that all waiting passengers were being carefully scrutinized to determine whether someone was a security risk. Althea and I stopped our casual conversation and started to think carefully before expressing any profound opinion about the status of the world. Somebody might misinterpret what was on our mind. Fortunately, the wait was short. A bus stopped right outside the waiting room and took us on a relatively long ride to an area where planes headed for dangerous destinations stood ready to load their passengers. The location was close to runways used by planes that gathered speed as they prepared to lift off. Loading was quick and we were ready to depart. The security measures taken to protect our flight impressed us.

After flying over the Balkans, we reached the Mediterranean. It took longer than I had expected to reach Ben Gurion Airport. Entry controls went surprisingly fast. We left the terminal and located our limousine, destination Sheraton Plaza Hotel, Jerusalem. After leaving the coastal plain and ascending the Judean hills we passed the ruins of a Crusader Fortress and the site where a crucial battle of the 1967 Six Day War had been fought. Success in that battle enabled Israel to control the territory of the entire former British mandate of Palestine. I had finished reading an exciting account of that battle in Herman Wouk's book a short time before the trip. I was not comfortable looking out of the window of the limousine and imagining that before my eyes were the locations that had come under intense fire, as Israeli troops were reinforcing their units in Jerusalem.

The Sheraton was a modern 22-story structure, located within walking distance of the Old City. From our room on the 15th floor, we had an excellent view of the newer and less interesting part of the city. If we had paid a little more, we could have had a room overlooking the Old City. We were intrigued that two of the four elevators were designated Sabbath elevators. Since we arrived Friday afternoon, we learned that as the sun disappeared behind the horizon, the Sabbath elevators were programmed to run continuously and stop automatically at every floor. Jewish law was followed to avoid having to push a button; no light switches were to be turned on: The command to rest on the Seventh Day had to be properly observed. Obeying rules from ancient times in a modern very different environment, struck us as odd. We stopped laughing when we realized that the Sabbath elevator made our 15th floor location somewhat inconvenient. It took some time for the elevators to reach us. Then stopping at each floor, giving a chance to every one of the imagined potential guests to enter, slowly closing the door, so none of the imagined passengers might get hurt, all this took a lot of time. We started to look for a stairway with steps. Walking down 15 floors did not appeal to us. Finally, somebody informed us that two regular elevators were also running and available for non-observant hotel guests. What a relief! Observance of Jewish law also closed most restaurants on Friday night. We had little choice but to visit the hotel bar that served previously prepared sandwiches on the Sabbath.

My daughter-in-law Ariela had urged us to get in touch with Simon Agranat, the husband of her mother's older sister Carmel. A retired Chief Justice of Israel's highest court, he is very knowledgeable and interesting, she told us. I dialed the phone number she had given us with considerable trepidation. After all, I was not in the habit of calling up someone of such an exalted status. Aunt Carmel answered the phone and invited us over for lunch the next day. "Will there be transportation problems on Saturday?" I asked. "Take a taxi", she answered. Indeed, we had no problem hailing a taxi. It was probably driven by a Palestinian or a non-observant Jew.

Carmel and Simon received us in their pleasant but not extravagantly furnished two-story home and served us an excellent chicken dinner that Carmel had prepared with the help of one of her daughters. During and after dinner, Simon and I had a very interesting and stimulating discussion for more than four hours. Simon told me about his youth in Kentucky and his law school experience at the University of Chicago. His father, a strong Zionist left the U.S. for Palestine in the 1920's and urged Simon to follow. After passing his bar exam in Illinois, Simon took his father's advice and started practicing law in Palestine, then a British Mandate. Simon obviously excelled in his profession and soon became a judge. After Israel's independence in 1948, Simon advanced in the newly independent country's judicial system. When he became Chief Justice, he had to move from Tel Aviv to Jerusalem. He stressed that the move was one aspect of the job he did not like. He preferred Tel Aviv's secular environment to that of Jerusalem's orthodox atmosphere.

It was clear from our lengthy conversation that Simon was deeply influenced by American judicial thinking. He referred several times to U.S. Supreme Court Justices with whom he had maintained contact. Some had visited him. There was also a note of regret that Israel had failed to establish a judicial system as independent and respected as the one in the United States. When I stated my favorable first impressions of his country, he surprised me by his serious and somewhat grave response that" unfortunately Israel's best times were in the past". It was quite a momentous occasion for me to witness someone as successful as Simon feel so concerned about Israel's future. The lunch and subsequent discussion with Simon Agranat was an event that I had not expected. It was an incredibly thought provoking introduction to Israel. Subsequent Israeli political developments have reminded me of Simon Agranat's pessimistic prediction. .

***

The many stories that I had read about Jerusalem had focused on the ancient inner city where Arabs, Jews, Catholics, Protestants, Russian Orthodox and many other Christian sects co-exist. They are encircled by a wall that shielded those inside for centuries from unwanted outside interference. On our second day, we entered the Old City through the Jaffa Gate, a sort of neutral point of entry that separates the Christian Catholic and Armenian quarters, leading to the point several hundred feet further on, where the Jewish and Moslem quarters meet. At the Jaffa Gate, we noticed an arrow pointing to steps leading to a walkway on top of the wall. Althea and I considered the advantage of first getting an overview from above before entering the cauldron below and decided to try that approach.

Having set aside less than two hours for our initial Old City exploration we used a detailed map to identify the buildings, squares and churches that emerged in the walled in city below us. After proceeding on the wall a considerable distance, we began to wonder how much further we had to go to locate stairs to get back to the ground. There were not that many gates on our map. Suppose some gate is in a location, where they don't like casually dressed strangers? Going all the way around the Old City to get back to the Jaffa Gate was out of the question because we now realized that the Old City was far bigger than we had imagined. As we were about to consider retracing our steps, a gate came into view. It was the Damascus Gate. From the commotion below, we assumed that this gate opened into the Palestinian Moslem section. Guarding the Gate was a small contingent of Israeli soldiers who ate their lunch in an obviously relaxed mood. That reassured us and we descended into the sea of humanity below.

Before Althea and I had time to implement our carefully planned security measures to hide our wallet and pocket book, we became engulfed by Palestinians searching for just the right item in the market stalls that stretched as far as we could see. I led the way, Althea closely following me, watching that nobody would grab the wallet from my pocket. We were told later, that we should have watched for knives and not thieving fingers. The aromatic smells from spices, exotic vegetables, fruit, baked goods, chicken and freshly slaughtered meat overwhelmed us. The sheer task of finding sufficient space to navigate around the stalls, boxes, people, made us forget our initial concern for our safety.

Suddenly, all the tumult and confusion ceased. The noise level dropped and we could hear each other's voice again. We had reached an intersection where the Jewish quarter started. It being Sabbath, the store fronts were shuttered. Some merchants sat in their chairs, conversing with their neighbors. On our way back to the Jaffa Gate, we detoured through the Christian Quarter. No longer alert we were not prepared when a bunch of 11 to 14-year old kids approached us on their way from school and intentionally struck the brim of Althea's sun hat. Startled, we could not tell, whether this was done in jest or anger.

The next day, we again entered the Old City through the Jaffa Gate, but went directly to the Jewish Quarter. It struck us immediately how much the atmosphere differed from that in the Moslem market area. In the Jewish area, there were Mediterranean plazas with laid back outdoor restaurants. The stone wall was whitewashed. Nearby steps led to recently renovated apartments and a small museum. A huge empty square came into view and the famous Wailing Wall appeared straight ahead. Women and men with access to different sections of the Wall prayed in separate groups and placed little slips of paper with their special wishes into crevices in the ancient Wall.

The Wailing Wall appeared very tranquil on the day of our visit. Raising our sight above the Wall, there was a path to the Dome of the Rock, El Aqsa Mosque and the Islamic Museum. Once there was a Jewish Temple on that plateau. It is amazing, but also disturbing, that happenings nearly two thousand years ago continue to galvanize real and would-be descendants of those who built, conquered, destroyed, suffered, built again, lost and regained a place where they worshipped one God, who supposedly guides them to a better destiny.

We paid for a ticket that enabled us to enter the Moslem area above the Wall. To enter El Aqsa Mosque, we had to remove our shoes and arrange them so that we would find them on our way out. That was not an easy task, since there were several hundred pairs of shoes arranged in some sort of order unbeknown to us. We found the Mosque more impressive from the outside than the inside where darkness reigned. The absence of benches was more than compensated by beautifully designed rugs on which the pious kneeled to pray.

After our short exploration of the Wailing Wall and the Mosque above, we joined a group viewing passages below the ground that archaeologists had dug in their search for the foundation of the Second Temple. To put a positive spin on this, I suppose one can thank current conflicts between Palestinians and Israelis for motivating intensive archaeological explorations of all possible sites that can prove their conflicting claims.

After the Wailing Wall and the Aqsa Mosque, the Church of the Holy Sepulcher attracted our attention. A visit there would complete our pilgrimage to the major sites of the ancient Holy Land. As we approached the Church from the east it was hidden behind a warren of lesser buildings. We thought we were lost because we could not find any steeple towering over the roofs. We located an open door that led into a small chapel. It appeared to be empty, except for one lonely individual, half asleep. The person was dark and unkempt. Opening his eyes, he motioned me to take off my sun hat. When we asked him, apparently a priest, whether this was a

Coptic Church, he repeated a word several times, until we understood his answer: an Ethiopian Church. Its appearance was certainly very quaint. Exiting on the opposite side, we finally found ourselves facing the main entrance leading to the Church of the Holy Sepulcher.

We were impressed by the extent to which this Church illustrates through its architectural layout the diverse nature of Christianity; its countless schisms, ethnic conflicts, historical and geographical separations. I recalled my Fletcher School Professor Helmreich's referring to the many sects of the Eastern Orthodox Church in his lectures on the Ottoman Turkish Empire. How I wished he were here now and repeat the interesting stories he had told us then. Too many significant parts of his stories had faded from my memory. At the lowest level of the Church, we joined a line of visitors to the Holy Tomb.

***

After our four-day exploration of ancient Jerusalem, we decided to rent a car and explore present day Israel. But first there were several museums, restaurants, the Hebrew University and the *Knesset* (Parliament) to visit in the modern sections of Jerusalem. There is however little I can add to the many excellent descriptions in books and guides.

Visiting the Mount of Olives we had an unexpected experience. From Hebrew University on Mount Scopus, we passed a military checkpoint at a junction leading to the Church of the Ascension on the Mount of Olives. We did not attach any significance to the fact that a small contingent of Israeli soldiers guarded the access. After all, they waved us tourists on, apparently not worrying about us. We parked on the road, near the path, lined with olive trees leading to the Church entrance. We were the only visitors to this small size church. It is located where Jesus was said to have risen to heaven 40 days after his resurrection. A Palestinian caretaker sold us for a couple of shekels a ticket for admission to the Church and a picture of the panoramic view of Jerusalem as seen from the Mount of Olives. We were soon to learn that spending that many shekels marked us as "wealthy tourists".

Almost immediately a kid appeared, offering an olive branch held in one hand and stretched out his other, waiting for a shekel. As soon as I had met his plea, other kids appeared from nowhere, all offering us olive branches while begging for more shekels. While somewhat worried that I might become responsible for denuding the Mount of Olives of its precious historic trees, my more immediate concern was that there was no way in which I could produce enough shekels to satisfy the local gang's hunger for shekels. The Arab caretaker tried to chase the kids away and help me, as well keep his business going. He failed, the kids stayed and the situation was clearly getting out of hand. Althea pretended looking at some small nearby building diverting the gang's attention, while I unobtrusively, got my car key, opened the door, stopped to let Althea jump into her seat and we sped away from this "potentially dangerous situation".

Next day, we left Jerusalem on our way to the Dead Sea. Road signs pointed to place names that we recalled from bible stories we had read in our youth. However we could not find one that simply pointed to the Dead Sea. That did not matter, since it turned out the main highway we were on, led straight to it. At first, we were somewhat nervous driving through the Palestinian inhabited West Bank. We watched intently for any suspicious acting characters that might lurk behind a rock on the side of the road. We also concentrated on their ammunition of choice: rocks. Those were available in unlimited quantities. Soon we put our fears aside and marveled at the incredibly well engineered highway that skillfully wound its way down the mountains through dry riverbeds, deep crevasses, while offering us stunning views of a totally eroded, but colorful land. We were mesmerized by a landscape that had a beauty, defying all conventional criteria. With minimal vegetation, each clump of grass or barren bush was visible from a great distance. The rocks and gravel were reddish or orange. Haze softened the colors. The heat was bearable in our air- conditioned car. The highway descended continuously the entire way to the Dead Sea. We passed a sign informing us that we had sunk down to sea level. Our descent did not stop. Three miles from the Jordan River and the Jordanian frontier, we turned south. After reaching the Dead Sea, we drove along the Sea's western shore until we reached a hotel with access to the beach, not far from Mount Masada. The two-hour ride had taken us to an entirely different world.

Our plan the next day was to climb Mount Masada, 1,300 feet above the Dead Sea. Lazy old people could reach the top via cable car in ten minutes. We decided to use our feet and take the Snake Path up the mountain. Young people can do that in 45 minutes. We were warned not to try the climb when the sun was high in the sky. 6 A.M. was the preferred time to start. We however refused to skip an excellent hotel breakfast and started two hours late, at 8 A.M. Temperature was around 90 degrees. Equipped with excellent walking shoes and carrying a water bottle, we managed to reach our destination in one hour. We felt fine, though I was slightly worried that Althea kept on forgetting to take the required sips of water. That was somewhat unusual because it was she, who normally reminded me, to have a drink of water.

We assumed there would be shade on top of the mountain. However there was little. We toured the remnants of the fortress built by King Herod in 36 BC. A Jewish rebellion held off its enemy on Mount Masada for three years until 73 AD. That is why contemporary Israel considers Masada a venerated symbol of ancient Jewish history. The broiling sun above us kept us from properly appreciating the fascinating rediscovered site dating back two millennia. A small partially shaded area was jammed with tourists.

We started our descent, assuming that going down a mountain would present no difficulties. After our first half mile, we realized our mistake. Althea started feeling dizzy and we had to stop in the hot sun. We should have taken the cable car down. I also started feeling a little bit strange. We realized that we were both dehydrated and suffered from heat exhaustion. I was only slightly affected, but Althea collapsed when we reached our hotel. She had to skip dinner. After a good night's rest, she recovered rapidly and we were able to resume our normal activities next morning.

Alone at dinner, I was joined by a couple of Germans. I learned that a week's vacation at the Dead Sea beach in Israel was a very popular cheap get-away in "the tropics" for younger German tourists. Apparently, they did not mind that the beach on the Dead Sea had hardly any white sand and a limited supply of water, nor that the water was so salty that it required a great deal of effort to lower one's body below the surface. None of that mattered. The northern Europeans just wanted a clear blue sky and a hot sun to tan their snow-white skin. They had been driven to the Dead Sea hotel straight from the Tel Aviv airport. German tourists coming to Israel for their vacation! One could not have imagined that in the nineteen thirties.

Having climbed Mount Masada, we were ready for our next adventure: a drive from the Dead Sea in the south, all the way to Mount Carmel in the north. We averted our eyes from Sodom and then stopped briefly in Beersheba to look at Israel's desert-located university. At some intersection on the desert plateau, we were stopped by Israeli police who informed us that it would not be safe to travel to Gaza. When we told them that we were headed way up north to the Haifa region, they wished us good speed and a safe ride. As we kept driving, we became aware that apparently the same lonely fast flying jet plane reappeared at regular intervals, flying always in the same direction as our car. We concluded that it was probably an Israeli air force jet, constantly checking and securing the entire country, while we were slowly progressing below. We waived at the pilot who obviously had more important matters to care about than us tourists.

Our destination was Zichron Ya'akov, a small community, situated not far from the hills surrounding Mount Carmel further north. We had been invited by Didi, Ariela's cousin and daughter of retired Supreme Court Judge Simon and Carmel, to stay in Beit Daniel, a music camp set up to honor Daniel, a musician with a fascinating, but tragic life. Daniel was the son of Israel Friedlander, Ariela mother's uncle, who was killed in the Ukraine July 5, 1920, when Daniel was an infant. Israel Friedlander had been on a humanitarian mission sent to the Ukraine to help victims of the early Lenin-led revolutionary battles. The mission was sponsored and supported by an American Jewish organization, the Joint Distribution Committee. Friedlander became a victim of the conflict, just as he arrived to help Jews caught in the Civil War. Ariela's grandmother, Liliana Friedlander, member of a prominent British Zionist family, an accomplished musician, brought up Daniel who also turned out to be an excellent musician. When Daniel was in his early twenties, he himself met a tragic death. To honor his memory, a camp had been set up on land owned by Daniel's mother (Ariela's grandmother). Grandmother's house serves now as a guesthouse for overnight visitors who attend lectures and musical performances by distinguished musicians. It is part of a concerted effort to further the appreciation for music among younger Israelis. Beit Daniel struck me as a miniature version of Tanglewood. [*Margery Bentwich, Lillian Ruth Friedlander, a Biography.* Rubin Maas, publisher, Jerusalem, 1957. Foreword by Leonard Bernstein]

We were treated to an excellently prepared dinner and then listened to compositions by Mahler and Debussy. What a perfect ending for a day that had started on the shore of the Dead Sea, continued as we passed through Sodom and the Negev desert, and now brought us to a small chamber in Beit Daniel, where we were greatly moved by a perfectly performed music recital. This demonstrated the incredible variety of moods, cultures and scenery that characterizes modern Israel.

Next morning, our host Didi insisted that we cool off in the comfortable waves of the Mediterranean Sea. The beach at Dori, was Israel's best beach, our host claimed. It certainly was a relief not to have to wade a mile, before water reaches one's knees, and then not to have to splash intently in order to push the body below the sea's surface, as we had learned to do in the steaming salty Dead Sea. Before leaving Zichron Ya'akov, we visited a beautifully landscaped park where a mausoleum preserves the remains of Baron Edmond de Rothschild, a cultivator of grapes used in the production of famous wines and an early financial supporter of Jews seeking a home in Palestine.

On our way to Israel's border with Lebanon, we stopped briefly in Haifa, not far from Israel's northern border which, compared with the other places we had explored, failed to make much of an impression. By contrast, Rosh Hanikra, above the sea at the Lebanese border, fascinated us. From the parking lot on a steep cliff, one takes a cable car to a grotto deep below. The path from the edge of the sea to the adjoining caves is spooky. There is contrast of colors, peeks at white cliffs, blue sea and the green water of the caves, all of which gives the area a special spell. That this should be on one of Israel's frontier flashpoints is especially remarkable. The remains of an abandoned railroad connecting Beirut and Cairo before 1948 are still visible: rusting rails, a blocked tunnel, and a roadbed. Back on top of the cliff there is a restaurant where we had some refreshing watermelon slices and perfect views of the shore, the sea, the cultivated fields of a kibbutz and the comings and goings of U.N. peace keeping soldiers overseeing the frontier crossing through which no normal traffic passed. Our waitress was from Great Britain, spending several weeks at the nearby kibbutz. On the day of our visit there appeared to be no visible tension at Israel's border with Lebanon.

Our next destination was the Sea of Galilee. After all, we could not skip it because of the role it played in both Jewish and Christian history. How to get there was a tricky question. The quickest way was to follow a highway that parallels the Lebanese border most of the way. This area had a history of occasional violence, when shots and other acts had disturbed the peace. After discussing this briefly, Althea suggested we 0have some fun and follow this potentially dangerous short cut. It turned out to be a quite relaxing drive with very little traffic. What struck us was the entirely different landscape on the Lebanese side that we could see occasionally as we passed through hilly terrain. While Israel had trees and green meadows, Lebanon looked barren. Since the climate was the same, Israel's greenery reflected its long-standing policy of planting trees and introducing measures that stress the latest agricultural techniques.

In the more idealistic phase of my adolescence, I had followed with some interest the stories of Central European Jews who had immigrated to Israel and formed a kibbutz (community settlement organized along collectivist principles), in an effort to establish and live in a community based on equality. Former urban residents would work in the fields, cultivate crops and jointly reap the rewards of their labor. Erstwhile housewives would operate group dining facilities and teach their children and adolescents in work-related schools. Living accommodations resembled dormitory facilities. The kibbutz was the Jewish version of ideals pushed by the Soviets in the twenties. Kibbutzim flourished in the thirties, but declined in popularity after Israel achieved its independence in 1948. There was a kibbutz on the shore of the Sea of Galilee which ran an inn. We stopped there, not only to rest, but also to learn what had happened to the idealistic dreams of pre-World War II pioneers. It soon became obvious that the kibbutz had not been a particularly successful agricultural enterprise. Its main success, however, was its location: a beach on the Sea of Galilee. That is why they built a modern inn with comfortable facilities. Our expectation of spending a night roughing it on a collective farm came to naught.

Next day we passed Capernaum with its Franciscan monastery and archaeological sites associated with Jesus telling the parable of feeding the multitude loaves and fish. In this environment of fertile fields and a teeming sea, it was easy to see the relevance of such biblical stories.

After crossing the Jordan River inlet with its sparse flow of precious water, we ascended the Golan Heights. Our attention shifted from biblical times to current Israeli strategic concerns. Our initial surprise about the peaceful nature of the countryside ended when cannon fire broke the silence. A short time later, we encountered Israeli soldiers who guarded a barricade blocking the road we were about to take. After a brief friendly conversation, we learned that in half an hour the barricade would be lifted. By then, the tanks firing the salvos would have finished their exercise. We noticed a soldier very active on his communication device and, after only a few minutes, he informed us we could go ahead, but warned us to be careful because we would encounter big tanks that would take up most of the highway. We would have to go to the very edge of the pavement. He also assured us, that while the guns would be facing us, they were not aimed at us. Althea and I exchanged one of our very meaningful glances and off we went. After driving for about two or three miles, we saw a pair of tanks approaching us. We had plenty of space and our car was not touched. By the time that we were back down on the shore of the Sea of Galilee, our adrenalin flow returned to normal. We stopped at our kibbutz hotel for a relaxing swim and dinner.

The final phase of our tour brought us back to the present: touristy Tel Aviv. We had a room on the tenth floor of the Carlton Hotel that would have given us an incredible view of the Mediterranean, if we had been willing to pay more. Instead, we were privileged to look at a cityscape, not very different from one back home.

When we left Israel, I had some final thoughts. We were impressed by how much Israel had achieved in its 41 years of existence. Reforestation, irrigation, creating modern cities, a warm ambience for its Jewish population, incredibly interesting museums and archaeological sites, the plethora of major universities in such a small country, a system of modern highways, a very friendly citizen army, all these are obvious assets. However, we were concerned by the loss of the pioneer spirit of Zionism. The willingness to depend on Palestinian Arab and foreign labor for menial tasks, the divisions among Jews relating to diverse cultural and historical backgrounds, the fanaticism of Jewish religious fundamentalists and the absence of real political leadership, all worried us. On the other side of the ledger: when push comes to shove, there does appear a willingness to reach agreement. One cannot help being impressed by the openness of society and the tolerance of diversity. Events since the 1980'ies unfortunately altered my optimistic perspective.

Chapter 27
My Mother: The Wandering Scholar in East Africa

I do not recall when my mother first became interested in how British and German colonial administrations tried to introduce modern medical practices in their East African colonies in the early 20th century. Her interest in medicine started around her parents' dinner table when her mother and aunt talked about her maternal grandfather who had served as a doctor in the Prussian army in the Franco-Prussian War (1870-71). Since he was Jewish, it was remarkable for him to have been appointed to a professional position with considerable authority. Then in the turbulence at the end of the First World War careers completely dominated by men suddenly opened to women. This was due in part to fill the void created by the vast number of male wartime casualties and in part to the early 20th century growing feminist movement for equal voting rights. Universities opened their doors to women just at the time when my mother, after graduating from her gymnasium (high school), was ready to continue her education and postpone marriage. She pursued the study of medicine first at the University in Berlin, then Heidelberg and finally Munich. She told me that she liked her courses until she had to watch corpses being cut open. Like *Doc Martin*, she could not stand the sight of blood. At that moment in her studies, she met my father who conveniently diverted her attention from the study of medicine and married her. Two decades later in America, in her mid-forties, she resumed her academic pursuit, ultimately getting a Ph.D. in the history of science at the University of Illinois. The title of her thesis, *The Beginning of Public Health Control in England, 1870-1890,* is highly relevant even now. She was proud to tell me that she got her Ph.D. one year before I got mine.

After my father's death and the start of her academic career she spent several summers in Great Britain in the early 1960's doing research in university archives expanding the topic she had explored in her Ph.D. thesis. She was intrigued by the fact that students from Britain's East African colonies had done considerable work at British colleges on topics in which she was interested. Some of these former students led the Kenyan anti-colonial movement that created independent Kenya in December 1963.

Following with considerable interest my 1963 visit to the newly independent former French and British West African colonies, she applied for a grant to travel to Kenya to continue her research on the legacy left by the British colonial administrators in the field of public health. Not only did she receive her grant, she was so successful, that she had her book *A History of the British Medical Administration of East Africa, 1900-1950*, published by the Harvard Press. This was followed by many articles in professional journals. When she applied for grants in the following years to do research in Kenya, Uganda and Tanzania, her requests were granted. It became almost automatic that, at the end of the spring semester, having finished teaching her courses at the University of Hartford, she would start packing and get ready for her annual pilgrimage to Nairobi.

On her return, she would regale us with accounts of her stay at the well-known Hotel Norfolk in Nairobi. Dating back to colonial times, it was featured in many British films. She would visit national parks and tell us stories about wildebeests, tigers and other animals that she had observed from a very safe distance, she assured us. She would also describe impressive waterfalls and fascinating landscapes. I learned to refrain asking her whether she had plans to visit exotic islands in the area, because the moment I mentioned the Seychelles in the Indian Ocean or Madagascar, she would devise a strategy to include a side trip to those islands and elsewhere. We were impressed by the vast new areas of the world that had become part of her ever-widening horizon the older she got.

She considered her African adventures a part of her life as a scholar and continued her academic career for many years past her retirement as a History Professor at the University of Hartford. After finishing her specific research project in Kenya or Tanzania she deserved a short vacation. Since *Swiss Air* was the only airline she trusted, a detour to the Alps was obviously logical. She stopped briefly in Zürich at the *Hotel Zum Storchen*. A comfortable train ride would take her to St. Moritz in the Engadin and a short ride on a bus to Sils Baselgia dropped her off at the entrance to the *Hotel Margna*.

Her love for a vacation in the Alps can be traced to her childhood when my grandfather Willy took his family on vacations in the Alps. I have a photograph of my seven-year old mother standing next to her sisters, brother and parents, dressed ready to climb an alpine

trail. In her seventies and eighties, she managed to walk on a path from the *Hotel Margna* all the way to a point from which she could not only see a glacier but touch it.

One spring day, on the way to our regular Sunday visit at my mother's home in South Windsor, Althea asked me whether it was safe for my 87-year-old mother to go on her usual African journey. "Is it not dangerous for her to travel alone to Nairobi and Dar es Salaam?" O.K., I thought, let us raise the question at dinner. As we ate the food my mother had prepared for us, we could not help notice that several dishes had been left too long on the kitchen stove and were overcooked and slightly burned. My mother refused to accept the fact that age might possibly affect her ability to function as effectively as in the past. When we brought up our concern about her safety traveling alone in Africa, she pointed out that she had traveled for two decades in all the East African countries and knew her way around in all major towns. Did we not remember how she had handled the situation when somebody had tried to steal her handbag?

That incident had taken place on her last day in Dar es Salaam. She had finished her tasks and relaxed on a bench overlooking a sandy beach that circled an inlet of the Indian Ocean. Her plane was scheduled to leave in the evening. As she was dozing, a young man grabbed her handbag that contained her passport, airplane ticket and essential travel documents, but no cash. The thief did not stop when my mother yelled that there was no money in the handbag. The thief fled on the beach, a trail of sand following him. My mother decided to pursue him on the paved road at the edge of the beach, figuring that she might catch him since the pavement would give her better traction. All this took place not far from a government building. A guard could not avoid watching in disbelief as this scene developed before his eyes. An old woman running after a nimble young thief? He decided to join the fray. As the guard and my mother reached the thief from opposite ends, the thief threw my mother's precious handbag into a foaming wave. The guard handcuffed the thief and went into the water to retrieve my mother's handbag. My mother got her feet wet, following the guard into the water. When my mother tried to take possession of her bag, the guard informed her that she would have to accompany him to the nearby government office, where my mother was to tell the official in the presence of the thief, all that had occurred on the beach. As soon as that was done, she could get her bag back. The thief would immediately be sent to prison and my mother would witness how Tanzania followed rules of law and order. My mother was much more concerned with the task of drying her passport and her Swiss Airline ticket. In this matter, her hotel manager was very helpful.

When my mother reached the age of ninety, an incident occurred that finally convinced her that the days of traveling were coming to an end. It was in Zűrich, not in East Africa. It was the day we were to pick her up at Logan airport in Boston. Just before we were to drive to Boston, we got a call from her at the ticket counter at the Zűrich airport. The plane had taken off without her. Why, I asked. “The taxi driver got lost on his way.” When we met her the next day, I realized that my mother finally recognized the fact that maybe she had gotten confused and that the taxi driver had done nothing wrong. There was no more talk about trips to Africa or Switzerland, Her world had begun to shrink and close in on her.

When my daughter-in-law Ariela arranged a special birthday party for my mother’s 90th birthday at the Trapp Family Resort in Vermont, I expected this to be like any previous special occasion celebrating my mother’s accomplishments. On our drive to Vermont, my mother, a world traveler, repeatedly asked where we were and where we were going. Althea and I raised our eyebrows, looked at each other, tried to cheer up my mother and started to worry. Later that day, Althea had to help my mother find the switch to turn on the light in the bathroom of her hotel room. It took me a couple of years before I finally faced the fact that my mother’s ability to function normally required assistance.

***

A phone call from the South Windsor police forced me to confront reality. “I want you to know that I had to deprive your mother of her driver’s license and drive her back to her house. If you have any questions about this, you may reach me at the South Windsor Police Department.” My mother had driven to a store one block from her house where she always purchased the *New York Times*, orange juice and her favorite rolls. She claimed that she had “encountered obstacles” as she tried to enter the parking lot from the heavily traveled road. As she backed up into the road and tried various maneuvers to enter properly, rush hour traffic on the road came to a stop. At first, the waiting drivers must have been amused. After several minutes, the waiting drivers lost their patience watching my mother's maneuvers. One of the waiting drivers was an off-duty police officer who politely asked to see my mother's driver license. When he looked at her year of birth and realized she was 93 years old, he asked her to move over so that he could drive her to her house around the corner. That is when he called me up. My mother explained that the sun had interfered with her locating the entrance to the parking lot. This explanation did not satisfy the police officer who pointed out that the sun came from a different direction. In his report, he termed my mother's actions at the entrance of the parking lot, "weird maneuvers that interfered with traffic."

It was obvious that without a car my mother would no longer be able to live in the house that she had bought three decades earlier, greatly improved and hated to abandon. Althea, always the practical type, immediately started the process of locating an apartment in the Juniper Hill senior housing community in Storrs. It took however, a considerable effort to persuade my mother that living closer to us would make her life easier. After we had helped her move to Storrs she kept plotting a return to South Windsor.

Eventually she managed to accept her new living arrangement, but new problems arose. In her apartment's small kitchen pots turned black because "vegetables just cooked too fast" and smoke came out of her kitchen window. This alarmed the management of Juniper Hill. They disconnected the power connection to her kitchen stove. My mother had to eat in the common dining room. The dining room staff noticed that her chair had to be wiped dry after the meal was over. When informed of this frequent occurrence, my mother responded that she had just come from her porch and had sat in a chair still wet from the rain. That explanation did not work very well since it had not rained in Storrs for a week. All efforts to help my mother deal with the problem of incontinence led nowhere. Her increasing age only strengthened my mother's stubbornness.

In the beginning the Senior Housing Management had been delighted to welcome my mother who appeared to be still quite active in her nineties. As they became aware of my mother's refusal to accept any help or advice, they began to hint that maybe she needed more intensive care than they were able to provide. The manager smiled kindly and casually pointed out that Althea and I met the age requirement to reside at Juniper Hill, but that my mother was somewhat too old with too many problems. That approach aroused my own stubborn temperament that I had obviously inherited from my mother. I managed to keep her there for five years until I had to transfer her to an Alzheimer facility in Farmington where she stayed only a few weeks because she injured her hip one night, walking at night in an unfamiliar place. From her 98th to her 102nd year she had to get used to a confined life style in a nursing home in Avon. She made it clear to me that this was not a life style she would have chosen. As I watched my mother deteriorate in the last decade of her extremely active and eventful life, I had to face the prospect of less pleasant aspects of old age that might lie ahead even for me. My mother died in 2002, less than a week after celebrating her 102nd birthday.

Chapter 28
Governor Weicker's Golden Handshake

In the early 1990's, a disturbing thought entered my mind. I might have to give up lecturing and abandon my daily discussions with interested students several years before the start of the new millennium. While the age of the students who attended my lectures remained the same over nearly half a century, there was the indisputable fact that I had only two more years before reaching seventy, when one is supposed to think about shifting gears and retire. With my ninety year old mother, still active in her scholarly pursuits, I was in no rush to reach the exit. Special circumstances, however, led me to face reality.

In 1991 Connecticut confronted one of its periodic fiscal crises. Lowell Weicker, our outspoken independent Governor, rising above conventional party politics, chose to push for a state income tax in an honest attempt to resolve the crisis. To do this, he had to reduce the number of state employees, offering long-serving ones "golden handshakes". My retirement compensation would be based on three extra years, a total of 48 years, instead of the 45 that I had actually taught. When it dawned on me, that staying home, I would earn almost as much as I would by continuing to correct hundreds of examination papers and appearing punctually at 10 a.m. in a large lecture hall, I shook the Governor's hand and retired on March 1, 1992, in time to meet the deadline.

Having accepted Governor Weicker's offer and helped him balance the State budget, I anticipated a major change in life style. Very little did change. I continued to teach my course on World Diplomacy for several years as a special lecturer. I had to clear my desk of decades of "unfinished stuff" and make my 1950s era office available to a forty years younger instructor. There were some changes in my daily routine, but none that would permit me to relax and contemplate the world from a veranda overlooking the gently waving sea. I did feel less guilty spending more than an hour every morning deeply involved in events all over the world, thanks to the *New York Times.* I did not have to worry about handing back exams on time.

In my new status as a professor emeritus I reflected on what I had sought to accomplish and what had influenced my academic pursuits. At the start of my teaching career I had been preoccupied with developments in Soviet dominated post-war Eastern Europe that related to my Ph.D. thesis and led to articles dealing with Czechoslovak politics and history. That also led to my serving as an intelligence analyst in the State Department. McCarthyism, a reaction to the ideological tension that accompanied the Cold War in the early 50's made a scholarly examination of events behind the Iron Curtain difficult. I became involved in politics on the local and state level in an attempt to do my bit to encourage political leaders to emerge on the national scene that could be trusted with issues on a rational basis. Political involvement in Mansfield and Connecticut helped me divert concentrating exclusively on Eastern Europe.

In the 1960's and 70's, the Cuban Missile Crisis and the War in Vietnam kept my research and lectures focused on the Cold War. Students and some faculty had noisily asserted their dissatisfaction with the status quo. Richard Nixon had forced us to re-examine the proper exercise of presidential power. Academic, social and political issues moved to the center of the stage. Often we were diverted from our primary tasks of teaching and seeking answers to crucial problems affecting our current society and the recent past. It was disconcerting to witness some of my best students use tidbits from my lectures at public forums to issue irrelevant and, from my perspective, inappropriate statements on what our foreign policy should be. Fortunately in the 1980's the mood began to improve. While I completely disagreed with President Reagan's philosophy, I welcomed the comments and smile of the professional actor that calmed things down. Of course, there were escalating conflicts in Central America highlighted by the Iran Contra affair, but those controversies failed to match the excitement that had surrounded our involvement in Viet Nam.

I was able to redirect my attention to my primary academic responsibilities: teaching and research. This led to my taking responsibility for the Political Science Department's growing program of supervising student internships. For many students assisting a Public Defender Counsel, a state legislator, a local or state government official and others who had public responsibilities, added reality to abstract theories. It may also have helped my students reach decisions about what career to pursue. The papers student interns were required to write to meet the internship requirement were often extremely valuable and interesting. From those papers, I learned how the state really operated. I was impressed to see one of my students a decade later play a prominent role as the key defense lawyer in a news-making trial. I was impressed with the performance and demonstration of mature judgment by many of my students and was prepared to continue to enjoy the stimulation of an active academic career for the indefinite future.

Looking back at my 45 years at UCONN I was happy to have had an opportunity to help many students gain some insight in why nations behave aggressively and at other times had leaders who managed to resolve previously hopeless conflicts. I hope to have encouraged them to keep up with developments close to home and those far away so that they would support policies that help our and other countries avoid dangerous conflicts. I regretted however that I had not spent more time and effort to make significant scholarly contributions. Why? Perhaps I was more interested in influencing the course of events than in critically analyzing past failures.

The extraordinary times in which I grew up in Berlin and Prague had a decisive impact on my intellectual development. Having a somewhat idyllic routine interrupted just as I became interested in the world beyond our garden gate in Berlin created my incurable desire to understand what external factors cause interference and destruction of a "normal existence". It also taught me to pay attention to what is going on beyond one's immediate neighborhood. I never forgot overhearing guests arguing about the Nazis and Communists at our home in Berlin and then in Prague, unable to influence the course of events. I had to listen to Adolf Hitler ranting and raving over the shortwave radio and waiting in vain for Chamberlain and Daladier to respond effectively. After crossing the Atlantic things got even worse. I had to watch isolationists argue that what Hitler was doing in Europe was none of America's business. America even would not permit a ship carrying Jewish refugees unload its passengers who therefore were forced to land back in Europe, frustrating their plans to avoid annihilation. While Franklin D. Roosevelt had warned America in his Chicago speech in 1937 about the threat Hitler posed to Western civilization he had to wait until December 7, 1941 when Hitler's ally Japan attacked Pearl Harbor, thereby helping him convince

America's isolationists that we had to become involved in the war to stop Adolf Hitler. The Fletcher School of Law and Diplomacy and the School of Advanced International Studies were created in the thirties and early forties in response to America's belated recognition that knowledge about what is going on far from our shore would ultimately affect us.

While the Cold War helped keep America's interest in events beyond our shore alive, it was soon interpreted as a contest between us, the good guy and devils like Stalin, Khrushchev, Brezhnev and Mao Tse Tung. That fitted the traditional Cowboy pattern of us, the heroes killing the Bad Guys. This oversimplified picture of global diplomacy led to our renewed lack of interest and information about details, including important developments in Eastern Europe, the Middle East, East Asia and Africa.

My deeply felt commitment to exert some influence, even on a very limited scale, led me to get to know and support candidates for Congress from Eastern Connecticut. It started in my first year in Storrs when my chairman invited Chase Going Woodhouse, one of the very early women elected to Congress on their own merit, to explain to our Government Department students how Congress really operates. I got to know almost every one of her successors, one of whom, Sam Gejdenson, was even my student. Following closely and involving myself in discussions of important national and foreign policy issues protected me from having a sense of guilt if events were to take a dangerous wrong turn. At least I had not been a silent bystander at a critical turn of events, a path that so many of my parents' friends had traveled in the twenties and thirties. Placing priority on real world developments limited my scholarly contributions. In retrospect this is something I regret.

***

When my son Ronald informed us in the Fall of 1992 that his computer company had asked him to spend several years in Holland to market its product in Western Europe, I considered this an interesting turn of events: Ronald was about to reconnect my family's ties with Europe in the very country where those ties had been cut in 1938. A few weeks after arriving in The Hague, Ronald invited us to visit him and his family. Althea and I jumped at the opportunity.

Holland had never lost its special place in my life: After all it was in Rotterdam where we had embarked on the Veendam to leave Europe on September 3, 1938. It was not only a break with the life of my youth, but a change of continents, language, culture, not to mention the break with all my past friends and acquaintances. Even after more than five decades on the other side of the Atlantic, I still had a special feeling for the land where I had spent my last two weeks before crossing the Atlantic. While I had visited Europe many times in the sixties, seventies and eighties, I had touched down in London, Paris, Luxemburg, Brussels, Frankfurt, Helsinki and Zűrich but never in Amsterdam.

So much had changed. In 1938 Holland was the symbol of neutrality in the century-long Franco-German conflict. It had granted asylum to Kaiser Wilhelm following Germany's defeat in 1918. After Hitler became the Chancellor of Germany in 1933, many German refugees chose Holland to await Hitler's demise, convinced that they were safe in neutral Holland. No such luck! Hitler invaded Holland in May 1940 and occupied it ruthlessly for five-years. Not just the celebrated Ann Frank, who shared my mother's maiden name, suffered terribly because of her parents' poor judgment, but almost all refugees stuck in Holland, suffered a terrible fate. Holland's wartime experience had left a deep mark on its traditional confident national character.

In 1938, we had flown non-stop in a small propeller driven plane over Hitler's Germany from Prague to Rotterdam's airport. This time, a big jet plane took only seven hours to cross the wide North Atlantic Ocean and deposited us in the huge modern Amsterdam airport. In 1938 we had stayed in a bed-and breakfast house in Katwijk aan Zee (Katwijk on the Sea), only a few hundred feet from the North Sea. In 1992, we chose the Parkhotel Den Haag, a restored old hotel in the center of the city of The Hague, not far from the International Court of Justice.

Spending many hours on the beach with my mother and father in Katwijk in 1938 quickly lost its appeal since I was 14 and there were no teen-age girls speaking German, French or Czech on the beach. I was awed by the ocean waves lapping the sand and leaving shells behind as the wave receded. It was my very first encounter with the open sea. Watching a seagull dive into the sea and miss its prey for the third or fourth time, tested my patience. I needed a change of scenery. Taking advantage of my mother's frequent admonition that exercise and physical activity would keep me healthy, I suggested we explore the shore and take a several mile walk to Scheveningen, located not far from The Hague. I set out with my mother in a southwesterly direction, walking where the low tide had created solid ground. With dunes on the left, waves on the right and the endless beach ahead, it was exciting when finally an impressive looking pier became visible in the haze on the horizon. It had taken us almost two hours to reach our destination. We climbed the steps of the pier structure and realized that fishing from the pier was not its main function. There were all kinds of stalls where things were for sale. Even with a very limited knowledge of Dutch, I quickly figured out that interesting things were advertised for people older than me. Facing a long walk back kept us from exploring The Hague, a short distance from Scheveningen by public transportation. On one other occasion, we all went to The Hague and an acquaintance of my father asked me to join him on an exploration of the capital by bike. The flat terrain and the specially developed bike paths made such an exploration not only interesting but also pleasant. Stopping in front of the gate leading to the International Court of Justice was the highlight of the bike adventure. The building was impressive and the lawn immaculately kept. When I studied international law half a decade later, the image of the Court Palace had reappeared clearly in my mind.

Returning 54 years later to the city I had explored by bicycle as a teenager, was not as much of a contrast as I had thought. There were still bicycles waiting for our car to pass. While there were some modern buildings, the old ones dominated the city. The apartment that Ronald and Ariela had chosen for their stay in Europe struck me as comfortably modern. They were in the midst of getting settled and just barely prepared to entertain visitors like Althea and me. I suggested to Ariela that we visit Scheveningen with its pier so clearly etched in my mind. Ariela had a market area that she wanted to show us. There was a store with interesting items. I pushed us in the direction of my treasured pier. When the present clashed with the past, I had to protect my memories. A kerfluffle ensued, interfering with our planned activities. We did get the chance to see the school and kindergarten that Nathan and Elliot attended and were impressed by the almost instantaneous acquisition of the Dutch language by my grandsons. A planned Thanksgiving dinner got lost in the kerfluffle.

Althea and I spent the rest of our visit exploring as much of modern Holland as possible. Amsterdam was our prime destination. The Rijksmuseum with its incredible collection of paintings by Dutch and other world-renowned painters was impossible to appreciate fully in the limited time at our disposal. Next door, there was the Museum of Modern Art. What an embarrassment of riches! Walking along downtown canals, we passed through the world famous Red Light district where not much seemed to be going on in the middle of the day. We even stopped at a huge covered flower and agricultural goods fair where each day, early in the morning, fresh flowers, fruits, vegetables and other goods from all parts of the globe are bought, sold and shipped that same morning from the airport next door to other parts of the world. We were fascinated to learn how the tradition of Dutch trading had gained speed and efficiency incorporating the latest technology.

We could not leave Holland before admiring Dutch expertise in controlling water levels near the estuaries of the countless bays at the confluence of the rivers and the North Sea. We drove on a highway southwest of Rotterdam that passed over endless bridges and dams. Finally, we reached a huge dam where visitors were shown how the flow of water was controlled so that inland low-level cultivated areas could be protected from flooding. It was obvious that without Dutch expertise in controlling water levels the Lowlands could not exist. Growing up in Holland led my grandson Nathan to write a scholarly criticism of the U.S. Corps of Engineers handling the Mississippi flood control crisis following Katrina in the New Orleans area, based on more sophisticated Dutch engineering techniques. That was his senior thesis at Princeton.

Chapter 29
A Sad Prognosis

Early in the spring of 1996, Althea and I made plans to attend our grandson Nathan's Bar Mitzvah in The Hague scheduled for May. We decided to expand that visit and explore neighboring Belgium and north-west coastal France. I made detailed plans, bought tickets for a flight to Paris and arranged car rentals and hotel reservations. Sadly these plans had to be altered.

A month before our scheduled departure, Althea went for her regular medical checkup. She complained about feeling uncomfortable in her stomach area and her doctor ordered x-ray pictures. She then referred her to the Yale-New Haven gyn/oncology clinic for a further examination. After the doctor at Yale examined Althea, we did not have to wait long before he called us both to his office and said "this is the situation…" His voice and demeanor prepared us for very bad news. He traced Althea's discomfort to a cancerous growth on her uterus, which if diagnosed earlier, could have been removed. Unfortunately, it had enough time to spread to her liver. It was too late for an operation and/or radiation treatment. While we were waiting, he had consulted a foremost cancer expert at Cornell Medical Hospital in New York who was one of his professional colleagues with whom he regularly conferred. They had reached the conclusion that chemotherapy was the only remedy left. Althea's cancer had metastasized, reaching stage four, a term unfamiliar to us until that day. We learned that on a scale from one to five, four gave Althea the prospect of living less than a year. This was unexpected terrible news. My other question, whether this uterine cancer could have been diagnosed in time for remedial action, his answer was not only an unqualified yes, but also an only barely disguised criticism of Althea's regular doctor who had failed to do so. Her regular doctor also continued to insist on calling Althea's cancer ovarian, instead of uterine, in an apparent effort to justify her failure to make a correct diagnosis. At the Yale clinic, they also asked Althea to stop immediately any hormone estrogen medication prescribed by her Willimantic doctor.

The Yale doctor quickly shifted to the more positive topic of ameliorating Althea's condition. He explained what chemotherapy involved: a full day spent at the gyn/oncology clinic while slowly dripping chemicals were injected into Althea's bloodstream. The effects on her body would be carefully monitored. That would be followed by a week of minimum activity at home; two weeks of more or less normal activity and then the procedure would be repeated. There also was a week when Althea should have minimal contact with people who might expose her to colds, the flu or other contagious infections, because her system would offer less resistance due to her chemical treatment. "Incidentally" he added "of course you know that you are going to lose your hair, so if that bothers you, you had better get a wig". "When will Althea's chemotherapy start" I asked. The doctor called in the nurse in charge of the clinic and after looking at the list of scheduled appointments, the nurse told the doctor that a chair was available the next morning. "O.K. we'll start then". On the hour and a quarter-long drive back to Storrs, we tried to come to terms with the new reality that our life would change dramatically.

The visit traumatized me. I could not believe that my so energetic and healthy Althea was at death's door. In Althea's own suddenly totally different world, the top priority was to get a wig, her immediate concern. Althea refused to be drawn into speculation about "the distant future", after all, according to her Yale doctor there was a 28% chance that all of this might turn out to be only a bump in the road on our exciting highway of happiness that might lead to further adventures.

After several trips to Hartford, Althea located the perfect wig to replace her gray-white hair that she had cultivated so diligently and carefully over the last several years. She also managed to go to the Motor Vehicle Department to pose for a picture on her driver's license that had to be renewed. These two tasks were completed just before the first bundle of hair fell out. It took very little time for Althea to become completely bald. Fortunately, the wig was ready and Althea could pretend that nothing had changed.

We had to re-think our plan to attend Nathan's Bar Mitzvah in Holland. Althea's chemotherapy schedule did not allow for a three or four day interruption of her tight schedule. We decided that I would go alone for an abbreviated trip and skip most of the planned French northern coast detour. My solo trip to The Hague in May 1996 to celebrate my grandson Nathan's transition to adulthood was a brief pause from watching the approach to the end of Althea's life.

What a contrast! The impressive ceremony took place on May 18 in The Hague's ancient Spanish synagogue.

The accompanying festivities were extremely pleasant. I was amazed how much Nathan had grown and how he had matured. Meanwhile 10 year-old Elliot acted as a very experienced museum guide who helped me and other relatives admire a crowded Vermeer exhibit in the cozy Mauritius House Museum. His not yet fully-grown size enabled him to find holes in the densely packed small rooms and point out hidden passageways for me and the other members of his family to bypass congested areas and locate treasures the mob had overlooked. This special exhibit happened to coincide with his brother's day of celebration. Ariela had become the perfect hostess. The visit was more than a celebration of Nathan reaching maturity; it was a very successful conclusion of Ronald's five-year European venture.

Meanwhile back in the United States, Althea had to face an additional calamity, the death of her ninety one year old mother in Seattle. Kate, Althea's daughter, accompanied her on a quick trip to the West coast to attend the funeral services. Fortunately, the strain of flying across the country did not affect the delicate condition of Althea's health and she managed to resume an almost normal life style upon my return from The Hague.

Althea had to make arrangements with the Director of the Bureau of Institutional Research at UCONN on how to complete the regular reports that she had continued to prepare, even five years after officially retiring. In the nearly two decades in which she had become extremely familiar with all the proper and not so proper operations in almost all academic departments, her summary reports had acquired sufficient importance for her to have been asked to continue preparing them on a more limited time schedule. Chemotherapy did not change the pattern too significantly at first. "Use your computer at home and the telephone!" Althea did not mind continuing her normal tasks on a more *ad hoc* basis in her "office" at home.

What I liked least about Althea's changed condition was, of all things, the extremely boring task of driving several times a month to New Haven. The forty-minute segment from Storrs to Hartford was O.K. because I could have driven it with my eyes closed, but I-91 to New Haven was so completely tedious that even noting which mile indicators on the right side of the highway were missing, ceased to divert me. After accompanying Althea to the Clinic, I was free to amuse myself on the nearby Yale campus. Decades earlier, I would have ended up at the Yale Library, even though it was no match for my Harvard Widener Library. Instead, I explored several museums, bookstores and restaurants. I even ran into one of my colleagues who, in his retirement had moved to an apartment only a couple of blocks from the Clinic. However none of these activities could shake my sense of gloom.

At the Clinic, I inquired whether chemotherapy had helped Althea's recovery so far. Yes, I was told, the cancer cell count had dropped significantly. After a three or four chemotherapy sessions the count was way down. When I asked the doctor whether he might possibly cheer me up by raising the prospect of her survival from 28 % to something over 50%, he looked at me and was about to give me a lecture on probability statistics, when I quickly added, that occasionally I believe in miracles. Not sufficiently amused, he added, only a total absence of cancer cells raises the prospect of recovery.

In December, the cancer cell count resumed its upward path. The doctor informed us that he would try a new experimental chemical drug after skipping the January session in order to prepare Althea's body for the change in treatment. I asked the doctor immediately whether it might be possible for us to take advantage of the hiatus and take a short vacation. His enthusiastic response surprised me. I guess he recognized that an escape from reality was the only remedy available for some of his patients.

We chose a beach club in Providenciales, an island in the Turks and Caicos, a former British colony south of the Bahamas, that I had never heard of before. It turned out to be an idyllic spot for Althea to spend her final vacation. Even in the middle of January, the water was warm enough to enjoy swimming in comfort. While the plugs covering the entry points where tubes used for chemotherapy were clearly visible, Althea did not mind being seen in her swimsuit. She swam as if nothing unusual had happened. She even dove some distance below the surface to show me the exotically colored fish that swam above the shells on the ocean floor. The resort had a French restaurant where the gourmet dishes were genuine. The island had a special meaning for us as former members of the Dunham Pond residential neighborhood association in Storrs, because a daughter of one of our neighbors, had sailed with a friend all the way from Stonington to the Caribbean, landing on Providenciales where they sought to relocate. We visited the conch farm that they had established. We were shown the sea basin where conches developed, increased their size and were packaged to be shipped to Florida and elsewhere to satisfy the quaint demand for conch soups and conch shells. We talked with the owner of the conch farm. His sailing partner, fellow adventurer and companion had left him several years ago. Apparently, our Dunham Pond member's daughter was now living happily in Hawaii.

Back at the gyn/oncology clinic, Althea was being prepared for her revised set of chemotherapy treatments. A small operation was required to insert a permanent entry point into the abdominal area so that a tube could be attached whenever necessary to extract excessive liquids that accumulated because of the metastasizing cancer. The excessive liquid had given Althea the appearance of pregnancy. She started looking for appropriate clothing to fit her new condition.

As Althea recovered from the operation at the Yale New Haven hospital, her doctor asked to speak with us and discuss future arrangements. We asked him how much time we had left. He answered that Althea was doing better than he had expected, but… He refused to be more specific. "Enjoy the time that you do have, he admonished us. Then he asked us about any special wishes we had when medical intervention would cease to be of any use. Both of us made it very clear that we did not want any unnecessary measures taken prolonging life when such measures would hurt and not help Althea. We also informed him that we did not want any special religious intervention when the end was approaching. The doctor thanked us profusely for stating our views so clearly. He was greatly relieved. Most of his patients refuse to deal with this end of life discussion, making his task much more difficult. We could not help noticing his happy countenance each time Althea or I encountered him in the following weeks and months.

Half a year later in July, the gyn/oncology clinic informed us that no further treatment sessions would be scheduled. The July session was the last. The entire staff, including the doctor assembled and said goodbye to Althea. Tears were in everybody's eyes. They would miss her, not only because she was such a good patient. They kept on shaking my hand. It was probably the most meaningful and sad departure anybody could possibly wish,

We went on a final trip to Bethesda, Maryland, to visit Kate, Althea's daughter. Even though it had become increasingly strenuous for Althea to climb the stairs to the guest bedroom on the second floor, Althea appreciated the opportunity to spend a couple of days going over the past. She had a difficult time staying awake on the way back on the New Jersey Turnpike, barely managing to open her eyes when I pointed to the Manhattan skyline. We stopped briefly at her son Malcolm's house in Ardsley, near the Tappan Zee Bridge in New York. Althea had lost most of her customary energy but was happy to have been able to say good bye.

August 1st was our 17th wedding anniversary. We celebrated quietly at home, knowing that this would be our last. Ronald, Ariela, Nathan and Elliot, back in Concord Mass, from their five-year stint in Holland, visited us on August 5, my mother's 97th birthday. Meredith, now settled in Plainfield, joined us also. This turned out to be Althea's last family gathering. Even in her weakened condition, she enjoyed this special occasion. Everybody sensed that this would be her last good bye.

Next morning when Althea woke up, she realized that the plug to her abdomen entry point had popped out and a mess resulted giving her considerable pain. I called the Visiting Nurse Association (VNA EAST) to whom the Gyn/Oncology had turned over the responsibility for caring for Althea. The nurse who arrived in about half an hour appeared overwhelmed by the task handling the situation. She telephoned Althea's doctor at Yale/New Haven. He not only directed her how to restore the plug into the open abdominal entry, but also gave her a very loud lecture on what steps she was supposed to have taken. It was so loud that we could hear the doctor's voice on the telephone at the other end of the room. He ordered a morphine pump to be delivered immediately to us to relieve Althea's pain. After waiting until late in the morning, a pump finally arrived and an expert connected it to Althea. Her pain was quickly relieved and she was able to resume her regular routine, mostly relaxing in bed.

Everything appeared to be normal. I had no premonition that I would have to face Althea's ultimate crisis a few minutes after going to the TV room to watch the 11 o'clock late night news. I thought I heard Althea cough and went to her bed. She did not respond when I asked whether she was O.K. I looked at her open eyes. I checked her breathing and realized that she did not move. I could not hear a heartbeat. I called the Visiting Nurse Association and told them I needed help immediately since I feared Althea was no longer breathing. As I waited for help, I discovered a little booklet that somebody had left on the dining room table. The booklet was left open at the page, which described how one can tell whether somebody is dead. Unfortunately, Althea had all the symptoms.

The nurse explained why it took her more than half an hour to get to our house from Ashford. She had to get out of bed and get dressed. She confirmed Althea's death, did a lot of paper work and dated the time of death early morning on August 7; even though I told her, the last heartbeat must have occurred at the time of the 11 o'clock news on the 6th. She corrected me pointing out that she was the official who examined Althea's final status and, according to the law, a person lives until she, or another official, has determined the definitive status of the deceased. Funeral Home staff came shortly after the nurse completed her forms and we were told to leave the bedroom. They wrapped Althea in bed sheets and carried her to the waiting funeral limousine.

It was 2 A.M. when I was left all alone in the house. Not until then did I realize that the morphine pump had a lot to do with the timing of Althea's death. While the narcotic eased Althea's pain, the dosage was probably set at that point in the range where body functions were gradually terminated in a painless manner, just as we had hoped in our January discussion with Althea's doctor. I only wish I had been informed of that so that I could have spent the last few minutes talking about everything with Althea, instead of watching the 11 o'clock news.

Part VII - Getting Old Can Be Fun

Chapter 30
Path to Recovery

After spending a year and a half in trepidation of Althea's expected final departure I had to face the reality of a solitary life. When the funeral was over and the many guests who had tried to console me parted, it finally sank in that I would be all alone at home. Althea had taken unusual steps to prepare me for that moment. In her last year, she had insisted that I make all kinds of house repairs to insure that everything would function properly. She even had me resurface the driveway so that it would last another decade. "But you won't be able to enjoy it," I told her. "So what," she answered, "I feel better this way when I know that you are less likely to get stuck after I am gone". She was also not at all reluctant to suggest that I find someone to take her place. I told her to stop joking. She insisted she meant it.

The bantering and Althea's premonitions and advice notwithstanding, the reality of living alone for the first time in 46 years, hit me hard. There were many of Althea's friends and some of my own old friends from decades ago, who tried to cheer me up by asking me for lunch at the Mansfield Depot before that very convenient and pleasant railway restaurant went up in smoke. Someone even attempted to reconnect me with the distant past by having me reacquaint myself with Minerva Neiditz, the widow of one of Audrey's fellow Senators who had committed suicide leaving the world the way Audrey had. It did not take me long to recognize the obvious: regurgitating the past was not a very helpful way of dealing with the loss of Althea, the perfect partner in my life.

I also felt badgered by the Visiting Nurse Association which kept on inviting me to attend sessions for the grief stricken. I got so annoyed by their sugary voices of concern for my well being that I ended up claiming that I was too busy dating X, Y, and Z to attend the VNA's sessions. While the calls did not cease they became less frequent.

One day, while driving and listening to Connecticut Public Radio, I heard the announcer mention a ten-day trip to Germany and Austria, sponsored as a fundraiser. Normally this would not have interested me since Althea and I traveled as a pair without joining a group. In my new status without a travel companion, the advertised Public Radio group tour struck me as a plausible diversion. I stayed in the car until the trip was mentioned again so that I could take down the phone number to ask for more details. A few weeks later, in the middle of October, I joined twenty fellow travelers, none that I had ever met before, and we landed in Frankfurt on our way to Dresden.

On the way from the airport to Dresden, I finally managed to get out of my funk, shift gears and ready my mind to observe the restoration of a treasured past in the recently unified Germany. The center of the city, totally destroyed in the waning months of World War II, was being rebuilt as close to its pre-war appearance as possible.

Dresden was a city I had passed through many times, without ever stopping and exploring it. I recalled the huge railway station on my Prague to Berlin train journey when I was ten years old. In 1966, driving by car from Berlin to Prague through what then was the Communist German Democratic Republic (DDR), I hesitated at a key intersection leading into the city when a policeman stuck his head in my window asking me what the hell I was waiting for. I pretended not to understand his Saxon-German accent. After looking at my Danish car license plate, he made an unmistakable motion directing me away from the center of the city. This time the bus, on the way to the heart of the city, passed not far from the ruins of what had been until February 1945 a monumental church. The blocks saved from the ruins lay carefully assembled by size and location in the destroyed structure. One could clearly see the church rising from the ruins after a half-century snooze. The bus then crossed the Elbe and deposited us in front of our modern Westin Hotel Bellevue. From my room I had a spectacular view of the river and the old city.

That evening we went to the famous Semper Opera House to watch Puccini's *La Boheme*. With our last minute tickets, we were sent to a front seat on the balcony near the ceiling of the opera house. I felt I could almost touch the ceiling. Scared of heights I did not dare at first look down at the stage right below. It took me a little while to screw up my courage and admire the scene on the stage. When the opera reached its dramatic tense climax and the heroine described her fears and sorrows, I tensed up and missed Althea's reassuring touch.

The next day, I was able to regain some confidence and admire the efforts made to restore the city to its pre-war architectural beauty. We visited the Zwinger Palace Complex, as well as modern commercial and residential areas. Not far from the city, we admired Moritzburg castle, in a picturesque setting surrounded by a lake. There was a UCONN connection: The Benton museum had, when I first arrived in 1949, quite a collection of drawings by Käte Kollwitz, a German painter of the Weimar period. Within walking distance of Moritzburg Castle, we visited a museum honoring her and giving her political and artistic history. The tour group had dinner at the Waldschänke, a charming rustic restaurant hidden in a forest not far from the castle. We were told this restaurant had been a favorite of Nazi leaders. Fortunately, we had finished our excellent meal before learning that we shared the Nazis' taste for excellent food in a romantic setting.

It was just the right kind of trip to rekindle my interest in music and the recent past. We inspected Wagner's lair in Bayreuth, Mozart's birthplace in Salzburg, but unfortunately attended hardly any concert performances. That was somewhat strange since the trip was sponsored by the Hartford's Connecticut Public Radio music station. In Salzburg, I rented a car to take a side trip to Berchtesgaden, across the German border, to look at Adolf Hitler's headquarters. It was too late in the season to drive up to Hitler's command post on top of the mountain; snow had already fallen at the higher elevation. That was not a location where I wanted to get stuck.

***

My grandson Elliot also helped me recover from my loss. It occurred to me that I might invite him to cheer me up on another trip, just like the one that had started my recovery. Elliot enthusiastically accepted the offer. Ronald and Ariela pretended not to be worried about entrusting Elliot to his grandfather's care. In record time, I arranged a two-week trip to Germany, Czechoslovakia and Austria on what had become my pilgrimage to the lost world of my youth.

Crossing the Atlantic was no big deal for Elliot; after all, he had done it in the opposite direction on his return from Holland only a year earlier. I soon realized that he was a seasoned traveler, more concerned with my state of comfort than his own. He had brought several books to read and quickly was completely absorbed, occasionally asking me, whether I was comfortable. If I had answered that I was not, he probably would have tucked me in. While waiting at Heathrow airport for the plane that was to take us to Berlin, Elliot discovered an exciting video game of racing cars that he activated with British coins.

Unable to catch on to Elliot's video game skills, I tried to make up by renting a German car at the Berlin-Tegel airport and driving it carefully to our small hotel in the heart of the city. In the next few days, I managed to show Elliot many different attractions in Berlin. Sixty-five years had passed since my departure in June 1933! When I tried to explain events of the nineteen thirties, Elliot must have thought that grandpa was reminiscing about pre-historic times. None the less he was very polite and made every effort to show some interest in the treasured memories of my past.

I took him to KaDeWe (*Kaufhaus des Westen*: Department Store of the West), the favorite department store of my youth, which had enough interesting things so that I had not minded the boredom of trying on the clothing my mother had carefully selected for me. As I marveled at that surviving landmark, we discovered something quite interesting: one entire floor featuring exotic fresh food from all parts of the globe, picked yesterday in Australia and shown today on the counters on the fifth floor of KaDeWe. On the top floor, there was even a cafeteria where some of the food met Elliot's pizza-centered taste buds. I have to admit, there was one issue where Elliot and I had distinctly different opinions: Elliot did not share my enthusiasm for the many gastronomic delicacies that we were offered. He did not care for *Königsberger Klops,* nor for *Wiener Schnitzel*. All he wanted was pizza or cheeseburgers. That made me wonder: what did I like when I was his age? I could not remember.

In my effort to connect Elliot to some of his ancestors, we drove to 73 Sächsische Strasse. My grandfather Willy had lived there until 1939, departing for Manchester, England, just before the War. The apartment house that I remember was not there anymore. It probably was destroyed in the War. Then we drove to Wannsee to check on my old house on *Robertstrasse* 9. That treasured place of my childhood had been replaced by a new one. Even the street name had been changed. The sign read *Scabell Strasse*. However, at the end of the street there was still the same old Wannsee, with a lot of row boats and sailboats attached to the pier, the same view that I recall from my distant past.

We stopped at the infamous villa where the "Wannsee Conference" had taken place. There the plan for the "Final Solution" was worked out by Reinhard Heydrich and other top Nazi leaders on January 20, 1942. Following this required lesson of history, I tried to evoke the more cheerful memory of *Nikolskö*, a restaurant in the woods overlooking the Havel River not far from Potsdam. That restaurant had been a favorite destination going back to my earliest childhood. *Nikolskö* was named after Czar Nicholas by White Russian emigrants, a fact that I learned only in college a decade later. I think Elliot enjoyed the place and the dessert, perhaps not its ambience the way I did. After a quick peek at the Prussian King's *Sans Souci* Palace in Potsdam, we returned to Berlin.

Next on my agenda, a genealogical task: a visit to the Weissensee Jewish Cemetery, to show Elliot his great grandmother's grave. She had died in December 1937. Only my mother had attended the burial with Lise, her oldest sister, and her father. A few years earlier, I had visited the Weissensee Cemetery with the intent of locating Grandma Clara Hirsch Frank's grave. I had no success then because the cemetery office was closed, it being a Jewish holiday. This time, I was given a map marking the location of the grave. A map is essential in a cemetery where a huge number of Berlin Jews going back to the 19th century are buried, excluding of course those who died in the Holocaust. It required Elliot's size and skills of observation to discover my grandmother's tombstone hidden under the low-hanging branches of a huge rhododendron bush. We spent some time making the tomb more visible. We also discovered nearby tombstones marking the final resting places of grandmother's sisters and other relatives. Near the entrance of the cemetery, we passed the Ehen Reihe (honor row) where my grandmother's relative, Dr. Hermann Munk, a medical researcher and professor at the University of Berlin in the late 19th century, was honored for his contribution to society. I never understood why the Weissensee Cemetery escaped unscathed the horrors of the Nazi regime. I am grateful to Elliot for helping me reconnect with an important link to my past.

After leaving Berlin we drove a considerable distance south to Dresden. There we stopped at the same hotel where I had stayed eight months earlier. Approaching the mountainous region of the Czech frontier, Elliot corrected me, informing me that we were looking at hills, not mountains. After all, he had seen the real thing, the Alps. I tried to share with Elliot my excitement in entering the Czech Republic at Cinovec, with barely a glance at our passports from the Czech frontier official. What a change from the past, when long waits and extensive interrogations were the norm! Elliot tried to share my excitement, but when he quickly resumed reading his book it was clear to me that it was difficult for him to imagine why crossing this particular frontier could excite anybody, even grandpa. It was raining, there was an open field, trees at a distance of a hundred feet, no houses, no armored vehicles, no soldiers, how boring!

On the Czech side of the border, the road descended through a dense forest on the way to the meadows and villages of the pre-war Sudeten German minority inhabited area. Not far from the border, I noticed a young woman walking on the side of the road without any protection against the rain. A little further, there was another one. This one was missing not only a raincoat but wore an extremely short skirt. The third one, dressed in what might be described a bikini for a non-tropical climate, finally made me realize I was not passing though a landscape of impoverished people down to their last garment, but that I had entered a red light district. All doubt disappeared when a "hotel" appeared advertising heavenly comfort in several languages. This was clear evidence that communism had been replaced with a flourishing free enterprise. The inclement weather did not seem to dampen roadside attractions. Suddenly aware of my responsibility as the guardian of a twelve-year old grandson, I turned my head to look at Elliot in the backseat and was immensely relieved to note his being absorbed reading his novel. A little later, I commented on the beautiful forest we had just passed through. From his reaction, I realized I was in luck. I did not have to discuss a seamier aspect of society marring the landscape.

We stopped in Terezín, a relatively short distance from the border. I explained to Elliot that Terezín, Theresienstadt in German, got its name from the1 8th century Austrian Empress Maria Theresa. I showed Elliot the Krematorium next to which my paternal grandfather Gustav's remains were buried in a mass grave at the end of August 1942. The location had been shown to me in1960 on my first visit by an old guard who had records going back to the War. Elliot's seriousness expressed his understanding of the macabre events of the Holocaust, but unfortunately, there was no way, in which I could resurrect the kind and friendly feeling that Grandpa Gustav still evokes in my mind.

In Prague, we happened to stay in a hotel located in a suburb only a couple of blocks from the French Gymnase Réal (high school) that I had attended before coming to America. It was hard to convince Elliot how beautiful and brand new that high school remained in my memory 60 years later after it had survived the Nazis, the War and the Communists. I also showed him the apartment house in Dejvice, #1681, Na Černém Vrchu #10, where we had lived on the second floor for five years. From my window, I had always enjoyed looking at the open fields, the valley further on and the village on the horizon. Now the apartment house overlooked blocks of recently built apartment houses that reached to the horizon. I quickly stopped trying to explain to him the visions of the past that were indelibly etched in my memory.

I was delighted to show Elliot the ancient tower at the center of the Old Prague City Square where figures emerge when the clock strikes and then march in a circle only to retire and rest for their next appearance. I remember watching that spectacle when I was his age, and now my own grandson stood there! Walking over the Charles Bridge to cross the Moldau (Vltava) turned out to be a challenge. Crossing this bridge, one is entrapped by merchants who focus on their target with hard to resist determination. One merchant advertised little musical instruments. Elliot succumbed and I surrendered, buying him a ceramic flute. The merchants and their ware almost obscured the famous panoramic view of Hradčany Castle, the presidential residence, rising above the city, the symbol of Prague. Elliot counted the steps as we climbed the hill to the square facing Hradčany in the west and the ancient cathedral in the east; his count confirmed the number of steps cited in our guidebook. Our usual argument about finding a restaurant with a menu acceptable to American taste buds was quickly resolved in his favor and we left Prague in an excellent mood.

On our way to Bavaria, we stopped at the Jewish cemetery in Plzeň, where I showed Elliot my paternal grandmother Matilda Kantor Beck's grave. As usual, it took Elliot less time than me to locate it. Like my maternal grandmother, she too had died in 1937. She also was lucky to have escaped the Holocaust. The apartment house on 46 Kopernikova Street appeared to have been untouched by the events of the six decades since my last visit with my grandparents.

Near the city center, we passed a tall big building that before the German occupation had served as a synagogue. I recognized it as the one to which my grandfather had taken me in order to introduce his grandson to his friends. During the Communist era, the synagogue had been used mainly as storage shed. I had read that in the post-Communist era, it was being restored, but in a previous visit, its doors were locked. This time I parked our car nearby and, accompanied by Elliot, we walked to the building and tried the door. I was amazed that it opened and that we could enter into the restored and well-maintained synagogue. Near the entrance, there was an original tablet listing the names of those who had helped support the construction of the synagogue in the late 19th century. There were several Becks on that list, including the name of my great-grandfather Jacob Beck. I had never seen or been shown that tablet before. The synagogue has the distinction of being one of the tallest in Europe. Hardly any of the pre-war Jewish community survived or returned to Plzeň, leaving a monument with too few to honor those who had built, socialized and worshiped in it.

We spent the last several days of the trip on a lakeshore in Bavaria, close to the Austrian border and in the Austrian Alps. We went on a mountain road that took us through one-lane tunnels over serpentine turns past a huge dam to the foot of a glacier. We pretended to do some mountain hiking, but cows that obstructed our narrow path gave us the excuse to turn around and enjoy delicious desserts in a mountain restaurant.

The pleasure of traveling with Elliot had enabled me to face a new phase in my life and helped me deal with the loss of Althea.

Energized by my travels I managed to get re-involved in political and mental health Board activities. That was also the time, when Meredith, after spending more than a decade in state mental institutions, moved into an apartment in Plainfield. She tried to resume a near normal life style and welcomed my weekly visits. I also visited my mother, now 97 years old, who still did not feel comfortable in her senior apartment complex at Juniper Hill.

In the following winter warmer Florida attracted me. Mary, a former student and very successful State Department and Foreign Aid official, who had retired after rising to a top position and who had kept in touch with me, invited me to stop by her retirement home in northern Florida. She tried to demonstrate how relaxing a life of retirement in the near tropics can be and introduced me to places off the beaten path, but in spite of her best efforts, I found Florida not very interesting, especially since I was all alone on most of the trip.

Chapter 31
Romance of two Septuagenarians

An interest in my Jewish heritage had been rekindled by my son's marriage to Ariela, whose family included many members with distinguished Zionist and Israeli connections. Althea's desire to know more about Judaism and our1989 exploration of Israel furthered this interest. Half a year after I had lost Althea, this interest was reignited by an article announcing an introductory course on Judaism conducted by Rabbi Fuchs at the Beth Israel Synagogue in West Hartford. I decided to learn more about the religion and culture of my ancestors.

Discussions led by Rabbi Fuchs held my interest but he shied away from my efforts to have him relate important pearls of wisdom to aspects of our current lives that called for guidance in a world that followed few moral principles. He kept on raising controversial issues, but gave few answers. His audience was diverse and his main objective was to encourage those who had weak ties with their Jewish heritage to reexamine and strengthen them. There was also an opportunity to learn Hebrew. At the age of seven in Berlin, I had some lessons intended to enable me to decipher the words printed in the Torah. I guess I was now too old to resume that task and the ancient Hebrew language remained indecipherable. The lectures and discussions also reminded me of the deep cultural and political differences that make up the diverse elements of contemporary Jewish people.

Meanwhile in Storrs at a meeting of the World Federalist Mansfield chapter Ina Ruth whom I did not know too well, expressed her condolences for my loss of Althea. She casually mentioned traveling to Israel. I told her about my trip there a decade earlier and my attending a course on Judaism in West Hartford. This led to a lengthy conversation that only ended when others sitting around the table interrupted us. A few months later, at another meeting of the Mansfield World Federalists we resumed the conversation and we both realized that we shared many interests.

Ina Ruth told me how a trip to Israel organized by her now deceased older brother, had widened her horizon and led her to pursue research in areas she could not have imagined years earlier. In Israel she had met Jews who had recently left Ethiopia and had found a safe haven among Jews in Israel with whom they shared a distant religious past but little else. For centuries, they had lived in isolation, a lost tribe of the Diaspora. Ina Ruth listened to the stories the Ethiopian Jews told. As a retired schoolteacher, she had developed an interest in folk tales and decided to get a graduate degree in folklore, collect, analyze, interpret and possibly publish the stories she had heard her Ethiopian friends tell her. With that in mind, she had actually traveled to Ethiopia to get to know the place her storytellers had left. I found all of this fascinating and wanted to hear more, but as always at such meetings in Storrs, others break in the conversation and we said good-bye, hope to meet again to hear more.

Time passed. I missed meeting Ina Ruth at subsequent world affairs meetings. A year later, in April 1999, I got a postcard from Israel addressed to me at my former home on Dunham Pond Road. I had left that house almost two decades earlier. Fortunately, the Storrs Post Office knows me well and delivers me my mail wherever I live. The postcard featured a Bird's eye view of a sailboat occupied by tourists on the Red Sea. The intense blue color of the sea, called Red, struck me as ironic. Eilat, the Israel harbor not far from Egypt and Jordan, was printed in large letters on top of the seascape. Ina Ruth wrote on that card that she had visited Eilat, adding that she was mailing it from Ben Gurion airport and would be back in Storrs by the time I saw the card. She wrote that she had remembered my telling her about my daughter-in-law's relatives in Israel and my renewed interest in Judaism. I found her name in the phone book, called her and set a date for lunch two days later, on Monday April 26. This was the start of a new phase in my life.

We had a lot to talk about since we had not finished our World Federalist meetings discussion months earlier. We both enjoyed traveling to places we had not seen before, compared our different past experiences in Storrs and learned interesting stories about her three daughters and my son and daughter. While the food at the Indian restaurant in Glastonbury was somewhat short of our expectation, we quickly realized that there was more to this encounter than food and travel stories. We both were somewhat lonely and our common interests created just the right atmosphere for romantic thoughts. We continued our encounter in Ina Ruth's home and were brought back to the real world, when several hours later, Janet, Ina Ruth's daughter who shared her mother's house, laughed and apologized for interrupting our séance on the couch in the living room as she returned from her job.

That spring with visits to the beach at Watch Hill, restaurants in Pomfret, Mystic and Manchester, movies in Hartford and plays at the Hartford Stage, saw our relationship develop into one of a couple of long standing. Ina Ruth had a commitment to do some volunteer English teaching at Hebrew University in Jerusalem in the ensuing summer. Why not join her in Jerusalem for ten days in July, I wondered. Ina Ruth loved the idea. It would give her an opportunity to share her excitement about Israel with me.

Ten years had passed since my first visit to Israel in 1989. I looked forward to seeing what had changed and whether the impressions gained on that visit had stood the test of time. The last time I had taken Lufthansa, the German airline, this time I chose the more neutral Swissair with a stop in Zűrich. Flying alone, made the twelve hours spent in the air feel interminable. At the Tel Aviv airport, I rented a car and drove all alone to Jerusalem. I enjoyed leaving the coastal lowland and rising to the plateau dominated by the city that played key roles in Judaism, Christianity and Islam. I had a room in a modern hotel not far from the Old City. It took only five minutes to walk from the hotel to the apartment Ina Ruth had rented for the summer. Even though I was somewhat exhausted from the flight and drive, dinner with Ina Ruth reenergized me.

***

After spending a few days reacquainting myself and exploring Jerusalem, I joined Ina Ruth on a short trip to Jordan. She had managed to arrange what turned out to be quite an adventure with a local travel agent. Ina Ruth was aware of my interest in the Near East beyond Israel that went back to courses at the Fletcher School. We started early in the morning on a long bus ride from Jerusalem all the way to the Red Sea through occupied West Bank Palestinian areas, finally reaching Eilat in the afternoon. We had no time for Ina Ruth showing me Eilat, the town featured on the postcard that had started our romance because the travel agent had arranged for us to meet a Jordanian guide within minutes of our arrival in Eilat. That proved to be not so simple. First, we had to get a taxi to take us from the bus stop to the border. Conversations in the taxi added at least fifteen minutes to the ride. Then there was the task of crossing the only recently opened Arava border. After leaving Israel, we had to walk what seemed to be at least a mile before reaching the first of several Jordanian officials who examined our passports, asked us many questions about the purpose of our entering their land. That took plenty of time because we were two among very few others crossing the border at that time. I sought some Jordanian currency and that precipitated a lengthy discussion. They wanted my American dollars and not Israeli shekels. They would not believe me that I had exchanged my Dollars for shekels in Jerusalem. Their eyes indicated that it was stupid for me to have done that thereby cheating them of valuable dollars.

While we were engaged in all these formalities, we could see beyond a barrier a man waving at us: our Jordanian guide and taxi driver. He greeted us and loaded us into his modern taxi. He not only drove us for three days from the southern end of his country to the center, but also acted as a very knowledgeable guide and helped when we needed his support. Aqaba, where we started is near Eilat on the Red Sea. It was the lowest point on our trip. We were amazed that a modern highway rose almost effortlessly in serpentine curves from the sea to the ever-rising plateau. What struck me as even more interesting was the nearly constant flow of large trucks carrying heavy loads from Aqaba north. When I asked our taxi driver-guide whether the trucks carried all this heavy stuff to Amman, his uncertain response made me realize that this highway was a back way for equipment to reach Saddam Hussein's Iraq without having to pass under U.S. and Iranian eyes through the Persian Gulf. Gradually the road leveled off and our guide took a detour to Wadi Rum, a charming narrow valley in which a small Arab settlement was located. There was also a small eatery and trinkets were for sale. On the way to this valley, we had crossed railway tracks. When I asked our guide whether these tracks dated from before World War I when they were to provide modern transportation for pilgrims to reach Mecca from Constantinople, and incidentally, help the Kaiser cut Britain's route to India, he nodded uncertainly. It was then that I realized that we were not far from where Britain's Lawrence of Arabia and his Hashemite allies had led the Arab revolt against the Turks. Neither Ina Ruth nor the guide shared my excitement as we crossed those tracks in what struck us as a very lonely desert landscape.

Back on the modern highway that went in a nearly straight northern direction, our driver increased our speed until a bell started ringing. I enquired what this meant, "Were we perhaps out of gas?" "No," he responded, "my boss installed this in the taxi to warn me when I go too fast". The bell kept ringing because he did not slow down and the noise started to interfere with our otherwise very comfortable and enjoyable ride. After suffering for about ten minutes, I asked him why he did not follow the orders of his boss. "I often argue with him, but we get along" he answered. Then he asked me whether we minded the bell ringing. I told him that it interfered with our enjoying the charm of Jordan, his country. He immediately slowed down and the noise stopped.

We passed many trucks, but when one, and then a few more, had camels visible in the back of the truck, we asked the driver why the camels needed a ride. When we grew up we believed that camels were the preferred providers of transportation in the desert. He informed us that the camels were too slow to cover distances and had to be given a ride so that they get to the destination where they are useful. Thus, I learned that even camels benefit from our modern super highway system.

Just in time for dinner, we reached a modern hotel outside the ancient city of Petra. After an excellent buffet dinner with a selection of Jordanian and European dishes, we were invited to a lecture on Petra delivered by an American scholar who happened to be from Rhode Island. We learned that Petra, an ancient Nabataea town, had been rediscovered by a Swiss adventurer and archaeologist early in the 19th century. Excavation and restoration of extremely well preserved structures began only in 1929. UNESCO, a United Nations agency is involved in Petra's restoration and maintenance.

The next day, our driver/guide took the day off while we ventured into Petra's past and explored an incredibly impressive and interesting monument that had been protected from inquisitive predators. It survived because it was hidden behind a mountain range. Even now, access is not so easy. There is a narrow opening serving as a passageway for pedestrians and donkey as well as horse drawn carriages. What we expected to be a ten-minute Spaziergang to cover the one-mile distance, took us half an hour because we had to admire all the interesting rock formations stumbling over greeting cards left by donkeys and other animals. When we finally emerged, a massive building, known as the Treasury, dominated the scene. While one can enter it, it is its very presence in this obviously long hidden spot, which makes it a truly hidden gem. It was carved out of sandstone some two thousand years ago. Whether it served the Nabateans as the center of government or, as some suggest, tombs for kings, may be argued by politically minded historians. Either explanation appeared credible.

Emerging from the Treasury there was a wide-open space, the amphitheater with mausoleums, and other structures in the process of restoration. We decided to relax on a bench and take in the panoramic view. Visiting all the tombs was too much for my limited mental historical storage bin. Our preoccupation with the unexpected peek into this fascinating chapter of ancient history was however soon interrupted. Two local girls, carrying a small basket on one arm, who appeared to be not even twelve years old, had noticed us as obvious targets. Zeroing in on Ina Ruth, they had located their prey. The younger girl had little shells, coins and other "local recently discovered treasures" for sale. The older girl had more substantial items in her basket, and let her cohort do most of the talking. While I whispered "watch out for fakes" into Ina Ruth's ear, the younger one offered Ina Ruth two tiny coins as a gift, to get the process moving. Ina Ruth did take a liking to a couple of small items and uttered the dangerous question, "what is their price?" The instant response was a dollar amount appropriate for an item in a jewelry store. Ina Ruth is not usually shocked, but this was something else and she said decisively "no". Realizing this was not to become the customary oriental bargaining negotiation, the younger girl seized Ina Ruth's hand and took from her the coins she had given her as a "gift". They left and we tried to get back to our window into the ancient past, only to realize the present had cast a shadow over it for us to be able to enjoy it fully.

We returned to the square facing the Treasury, on our way to the narrow passageway separating the protective mountain range. An assembly of donkey-taxi carriage drivers offered to ease our painstaking trip back to the outer world and its hotels on the other side. We accepted one driver's offer. Once seated and isolated in the narrow passageway, the driver mentioned the price in dollars. When my face showed somewhat of a shock, he quickly added,

"You can get out now and walk". We paid his price. That was a very expensive short donkey taxi ride!

We had an excellent dinner in our hotel and then capped our stay in Petra at a lecture/discussion where we learned a great deal of valuable information about the history and archaeological findings of a site so recently professionally explored.

Next morning our regular driver/guide reappeared, ready to take us on the last stage of our journey, to the Allenby Bridge. It would be a three to four hour ride, he informed us. On the other side of the Jordan River, a taxi driver would be waiting for us to drive us back to Jerusalem. "How would that taxi driver know when we would be there," we asked. "Not to worry, my office in Amman is in touch with his office in Jerusalem. Then our driver/guide wanted to know whether we wanted to be driven on the main highway to the outskirts of Amman where we would take the road that leads directly to the Allenby Bridge, or get off the main drag, take a short cut and visit Mt Nebo. Since we would not have enough time to see anything in Amman, the answer was obvious: Mt. Nebo.

While still on the highway going north, we wondered whether we might stop at one of the interesting looking roadside shops and get a bite to eat. Soon we found ourselves in a social club/restaurant/general merchant store. The food was O.K. The atmosphere straight out of an exotic travel book: young and old men relaxing in comfortable chairs occasionally exchanging a couple of sentences with others in the area, while taking long puffs from their extended winding pipes that touched the floor, each one covering considerable space. We, however, were pressed for time and could not afford to slow down and relax in a super comfortable easy chair. On our way out, there was an obstacle. We saw some beautifully hand-decorated plates. Ina Ruth and I bought a few.

Eventually we turned onto the road leading to Mt. Nebo. It did not take very long to reach our destination. A parking lot led to the entrance to a Franciscan Monastery, which owned and maintained the park near the top of the mountain, from which Moses is supposed to have seen the Promised Land on the other side of the Jordan River below. When we stood there and looked at the river and then at the hills reaching to Jerusalem on the horizon, we could easily understand the ecstasy felt by anybody of any century who reaches this outpost whether by car, by foot or by camel. Modern reality returned when I saw a nearby outpost where a lonely Jordanian soldier playing with his heavy rifle, relaxed while presumably protecting his country's strategic outpost from an opponent on the other side.

It had never occurred to me that Moses had led his people from the Nile, through the Red Sea, the Sinai desert and then up to the Jordan plateau to Mt. Nebo before looking at Jerusalem. Here I was, not a religious type, going on a religious pilgrimage! I could see my grandfather Gustav smiling!

Back to the real world; our driver/guide was waiting for us impatiently in the parking lot. He probably had been told by his boss, to get us to the Allenby Bridge quickly, time was running out. As we started downhill on an unpaved very curvy road, he explained this was a brand new shortcut. There may be very tight curves and he might have to back up occasionally, but it would do. For somebody like me who is not particularly happy looking down over steep cliffs, I settled back into my comfortable seat and only occasionally looked at the countryside far below us. There were occasions where we had to back up several feet so that a car going in the opposite direction could climb the steep slope.

Maybe a quarter hour had passed and I noticed some unusual movements from Ina Ruth. Her hands started to grope under the seat, touched the floor, explored the inside of her jacket. "What is the matter", I asked. "Did you see my pocket book?" she whispered in my ears. Our driver, always alert, slowed the car to a crawl and turned his head "Is there something wrong?" "I am missing my pocket book; I may have left it in the ladies room up there in the Monastery" Ina Ruth responded. "Does it contain anything really important?" "Yes, my passport, driver's license, etc. " Without any further ado, the driver started the extremely exciting maneuver of going back and forth sideways until he had turned the car completely around. It seemed that it was faster to climb back up than to carefully descend.

When we returned to the Monastery entrance hut where I was about to ask whether I had to pay admission to retrieve what we had lost, we saw a group of tourists on their way out and a lady noticing the obviously agitated Ina Ruth, ran toward her and asked her what her name was. When Ina Ruth responded, the lady pulled Ina Ruth's pocketbook from her coat and they embraced. Ina Ruth was suddenly in seventh heaven. The group identified itself as Canadian tourists exploring Jordan the way we were. The one who had returned Ina Ruth's treasure had noticed the handbag in the Ladies Room, looked for some identity and decided it would be wiser to get in touch with U.S. authorities than to leave for a local cleaning crew to return it intact to the owner. After lots more embraces and goodbye's, we complied with our driver's request to get into the car. On the one hand, he seemed to be happy that everything turned out to be O.K., on the other, he became increasingly worried about the dressing down he expected to receive from his boss for not meeting his deadline.

We were so happy that I did not even mind the sharp curves that made the car seem to hang over the cliffs. After reaching the main road to the border, we thought we could relax. Such hopes were premature. We still had to face inevitable delays at the Allenby Bridge, now renamed after a Jordanian King. It used to be, and still is, the main crossing point between Jordan and Israel. Formalities are more complicated, time consuming and thorough. Before getting out of our Jordanian taxi, we expressed our enormous appreciation to our driver/guide who had made our visit to his country an experience we would never forget. We gave him a tip that seemed to satisfy him. He smiled and waved at us before he raced the car back home.

Officials directed us to a vehicle where we had to wait our turn to have our passports stamped to prove we were properly exiting from Jordan. After some more formalities, we crossed the bridge to the Palestinian side of the Jordan River and were welcomed by Israeli officials. As we reached the parking lot, it was obvious that an impatient taxi driver had identified us as the culprits who had ruined his afternoon. "Are you Ina Ruth and Curt?" As soon as we nodded yes, the doors were open and we were almost pushed in. The car started moving instantly, we were barely settled in our seats when the driver, not slowing down, turned his head and gave Ina Ruth the cell phone. "My boss wants to talk with you". The boss told Ina that we were several hours late and her taxi employee had to waste his afternoon at the Allenby Bridge. She was not in the least bit interested that the delay had been caused by Ina Ruth having to retrieve her precious bag from the toilet room on Mt Nebo. She ordered us to give the driver a tip that would make up for the hours he could have earned a pile of money. She named the amount. Fortunately, I had enough dollars in my wallet. In record time, we reached the Judean hill plateau and Jerusalem.

Our Jordanian trip turned out to exceed all my expectations. It was a real adventure. We explored history, including the history of ancient religions, we met interesting people and most important, it widened my horizon. The remainder of my stay with Ina Ruth in Israel was spent revisiting many of the sights I had explored in my previous 1988 visit with Althea. We enjoyed again a music performance at Beit Daniel in northern Israel, cooled off at Dori Beach in the Mediterranean and visited the Rothschild vineyard.

***

While Ina Ruth and I were both interested in Jewish issues, those were only a few of our common interests. Among those was travel. A few months after Ina Ruth returned from Jerusalem we went on a Connecticut Public Radio-sponsored tour of Scandinavia. The combination of modern life within a romantic northern forest environment in Finland and the lively activity on the pedestrian malls in Copenhagen and Stockholm charmed us. What impressed us the most in Stockholm was our visit to a maritime museum a couple of hours before our scheduled overnight ferry crossing to Helsinki. We admired the restored 17th century Wasa, a gigantic tall warship equipped with heavy canons on its upper deck that were intended to destroy the enemy from a great distance and permit the Swedish king to land and overcome any opponent daring to fight the Swedes. The canons were so heavy that the ship had barely left the shipyard when it lost its balance and tipped over, never giving the Swedes a chance to fire a single shot at the enemy. A few hours later on our way to Helsinki on the tenth floor of a modern gigantic ferry, we discussed the sea worthiness of this modern giant. We hoped it would not tip over like the Wasa in the museum.

We attended performances of classical and modern plays regularly at the Hartford Stage. They supplemented the many of shows and concert performances at UCONN's Jorgensen Hall. Movies were also on our agenda. No longer having to prepare lectures nor reading lengthy term papers gave me the luxury of enough time to relax and enjoy aspects of our culture that I had skipped in my earlier too busy scheduled life. Ina Ruth also shared my deep involvement in Democratic politics. She participated in the

Mansfield Democratic Town Committee and helped voters appear at the polls. Her enthusiasm for Obama had no limits.

Very early in our relationship Ina Ruth joined me in my weekend dinners with Meredith. As she got to know her better, Ina Ruth developed a strong bond with her and tried to help her recovery. Meredith enjoyed the attention and love that Ina Ruth expressed for her. It must have given her a sense of hope. Our regular weekend meetings were an essential aspect of Meredith's slowly improving condition.

In October 2002, three and a half years after I received the postcard from Eilat, we decided to formalize our relationship and get married. Neither our kids nor our close friends were surprised. Perhaps some of them wondered why a couple in their late seventies chose to proceed with a ceremony usually reserved for much younger couples. I suppose we were a little old fashioned. We even asked Rabbi Ullman to perform the ceremony on the lawn surrounded by trees in front of our living room. The festive occasion was witnessed by our children, their wives, husbands and many friends. This almost traditional Jewish ceremony differed not that much from my first marriage ceremony with Audrey, performed by a Congregational Minister, or from my second with Althea witnessed by a Justice of the Peace on my mother's porch. While these ceremonies reflect the wide range of backgrounds of my three spouses, each one led to a very happy marriage.

Ina Ruth introduced me to her extensive family spread out in the Northeast and Middle West. Judy, her oldest daughter, a psychiatric counselor, lives with her husband George, a jewelry company executive, and their two sons and daughter in a pleasant suburb of Cleveland. While George's father and grandfather were both U.S. navy officers, his grandfather was also the naval commander at the signing of Japan's surrender in August 1945. Our conversations however rarely dealt with military matters. Janet, Ina Ruth's second daughter, had the challenging task of keeping a company run by a group of university scientists in line with the provisions of the grants that had created the outfit. She is now married to a financial management expert and lives in Simsbury, Connecticut. Jessica, the youngest, is a professor of music and is married to a professor also teaching music at Boston's Berklee College of Music. They had been living several years in Salem, the town in Massachusetts where witches were tried a couple of centuries ago. They recently moved to their own house in Swampscott. The diversity of occupations and interests of Ina Ruth's immediate family served to further expand my knowledge about America.

Ina Ruth often reminisces about her early childhood in Far Rockaway, Queens, on the shore of the Atlantic at a considerable distance from Manhattan. We drove there for her to show me the first house she remembers living in and climbing up the stairs. She also retraced the path to her grammar school. She had to abandon this idyllic location at the age of ten when her father died of heart failure. We were lucky to see this important chapter in her past before hurricanes caused a great deal of damage to the shore areas of Far Rockaway. Was it significant that I married wives from Bremerton on the northern Pacific coast and Far Rockaway on the North Atlantic Coast on the opposite sides of the America? I could not have imagined meeting anyone living on the Atlantic and Pacific Oceans when I cultivated chestnut trees in my garden near the lake in Wannsee.

Very early in our relationship Ina Ruth introduced me to her brother Joel who had played a very important role in her life, replacing her father after his premature death. Being five years older, he was a caring and helpful counselor and protector in his little sister's adolescent and even adult life. Escaping New York's metropolitan environment he settled as a veterinarian in Brockport, New York, not far from Rochester. Visiting him and his family reacquainted me with the upstate New York of my time at Cornell. It made me realize the vast expanse of the "Empire State" we had to cover to reach him at the far end of the New York Thruway. Counting the miles on that Thruway was more than made up by enjoying Joel's subtle sense of humor, his family and his location. His house was a two-minute walk from the Erie Canal along which Joel did his daily walking exercise. Watching boats float by on the Canal brought the Canal from my high school history book into the real world. Joel was the down-to-earth practical man who not merely treated animals, but was skilled in making beautiful wooden bowls. His Lazy Susan sits on our breakfast table reminding us daily of that skill. He also loved to sail a boat on Lake Erie and off the Florida coast in his retirement. There he had me join him on his boat and like Audrey half a century earlier tried to teach me a sailing lesson. Ina Ruth talked a great deal about her brother: He was extremely helpful and kind. Keeping animals fit was the source of his income but cheering up his relatives and friends was his more important role. His passing at the age of 87 was a loss which Ina Ruth has had a hard time accepting.

***

Several years have gone by since I had to replace my heart valve. Ina Ruth celebrated her 85th birthday and I my 88th in 2012. I started to worry about how much longer I could keep my driver's license, and more importantly, would I continue to be able to convince Avis, Hertz or some other car rental agency to entrust their vehicle to me to drive at 120 km an hour on the Autobahn? After Ina Ruth challenged my reluctance for us to travel any distance from Storrs and have fun to which old people like us are entitled, I agreed and started making plans for a trip.

As the question shifted from whether to where, Ina Ruth asked me to make specific proposals. My mind wandered from Hawaii: too long confined in a plane; the Caribbean: a hurricane may mar the visit; southern Europe along the Mediterranean: the fiscal crisis and resulting popular protests might stir things up too much. Why not go back to my old haunts and travel in Germany, the Czech Republic and Austria? This proposal pleased Ina Ruth who proposed adding Venice to the journey. I objected. After all, we had been there several times and I had gotten tired of telling the gondoliers that I preferred looking at the canals without their crooning. When confronted with the prospect of my taking her over an Alpine mountain pass with her terrified expression as she stares at the valley a thousand feet below shrouded in a fog and the road disappearing behind the sharp curve a few feet ahead, Venice and a trip in the Alps vanished from consideration.

We decided to start our adventure in Munich where my father had spent the happiest years of his life a hundred years earlier. He had talked a lot about it when I was too young to appreciate the role it had played in his youth. It was there that his mind was opened to a much larger world than his provincial Bohemian Plzeň and where he had met my mother. For some reason his mentioning the Pinakothek, stuck in my memory. In past visits, there never was enough time to explore that famous museum. It is huge and consists of three separate palace-resembling structures that exhibit paintings ranging from the Renaissance to contemporary avant-garde. Ina Ruth and I explored the New Old Pinakothek, so named because the original building that my father had visited had been destroyed by our bombs in 1944. A new one was opened in 1981and the paintings that had been protected from destruction during the War could again entrance viewers. As I focused on several prominently displayed pictures, my mind began to wander back to our staircase in the Wannsee house where my father had hung up copies of these paintings above each step for my mother and me to admire. He must be chuckling now in his grave that it took me so long to appreciate his effort to instill at least some appreciation for the art that he loved.

We followed our day at the Pinakothek with a visit to the Starnberger and Ammersee lakes, a short distance south of Munich. Breitbrunn on the Ammersee was the village where I spent the first year of my life. While I have absolutely no memory of my stay there, I do however recall my parents telling me far too often how much they had enjoyed their stay there in spite of the constant attention they had to give to their newborn baby. Why not visit the place my parents enjoyed? Frankly, Breitbrunn had nothing that might have made it a special tourist attraction. It has to remain simply a special name in my memory. We had lunch in a lakeside town with an even more interesting name that I recall from my father's stories: Tutzing. This village on the Starnberger Lake had some real charm. Our restaurant also served as a YachtClub social center and served excellent food. The view across the lake to the mountains was memorable. Lunch there brought me closer to the time my father had talked about so often.

In Berlin we went to KaDeWe, the seven-story world famous department store located only a few blocks from the street where my grandparents had lived for the first three decades of the last century and where my mother had grown up. I remembered it well, because that is where my mother had taken me to buy my shoes and everything else that I wore. When Ina Ruth complained about her shoes, we went to the fourth floor and Ina Ruth got the same professional attention, service and care that I remember getting when I was five years old.

On the way to Potsdam, we went off the beaten path when I saw a sign pointing to *Pfauen Insel,* Peacock Island, a path on which my parents had taken me on special occasions in the summer to eat delicious deserts in the log house restaurant, *Nikolskö*. It still served Königsberger Klops, Rote Grűtze and other excellent menu choices that I recall eating 80 years ago. It was too cold for Ina Ruth and me to sit on the veranda overlooking a lake and the tiny island inhabited by the peacocks. We went indoors and sat next to the Russian style fireplace. In the nineteen thirties, I had not known that my favorite restaurant was built by White Russian exiles who wanted to honor their former emperor Nicholas by giving his name, Nikolskoe, to their new home.

Crossing the border from Bavaria to the Czech Republic in Eisenstein used to involve extensive delays and interrogations by the guardians of the Iron Curtain. This time I was shocked not to find any frontier officials. There was no warning that we were crossing into another country except for a small sign stating Czech Republic, in Czech of course. The extensive buildings that two decades ago housed an armada of officials were either razed or vacant. A day later, driving on an interstate-type highway to Prague I learned that Communist style officials had not disappeared into the dustbin of history. As I was merrily driving my Avis rented Ford with German license plates through the familiar central Bohemian landscape, I noticed a police car among the batch of cars in the lane next to me. After looking me over for at least a mile, the police officer turned on his flashing lights. Why did he stop me, I wondered. He stepped out of the car. I pretended not to understand his Czech, saying in German that I was from the U.S. After I gave him my passport, driver license and the Avis car registration, he informed me that I did not have on my windshield a small sticker entitling me to drive on the expressway. I told him I was a foreigner and had no idea that I needed such a sticker. "You broke the Czech law and have to pay a fine of five thousand Czech Crowns." We got into a 15-minute long argument about how I could have known about this requirement for a permit to drive on highways that have no tollbooths. His persistent answer: "This is the Czech law. You are in the Czech Republic!!!" Meanwhile, his trainee assistant was working the computer. He apparently discovered nothing about me that might cause me further trouble. The policeman lowered his voice a little and told me he would charge me only 3,000 crowns. O.K. I agreed to pay the fine. “How do I pay?” “Credit card, of course”. I gave his assistant my visa card. That ended the kerfluffle. He also told me to stop at the next gas station and get this crucial sticker for my windshield. The sticker fee was minimal.

The charm of walking in Prague’s Old Town; watching the puppets perform their dance on the Town Hall’s clock tower every hour; attending the closing half hour of the Jewish New year celebration in Prague’s New-Old Synagogue; hearing an incredibly impressive concert performance by an organist and chamber orchestra masters in the Klementinum, a famous church in the Old Town; more than made up for the police stop.

Chapter 32
My Postmillennial Family

While we octogenarians enjoyed our relaxed lifestyle, traveling, reading interesting novels, attending concerts and stage performances Ronald, Ariela and my grandsons Nate and Elliot were creating their own lifestyles and building their 21st century careers. After returning from their stay in Holland in the nineties they spent a few years in Concord overlooking the Sudbury River not far from Walden Pond thus reconnecting with America's history. A few years later they moved to the neighboring town of Acton where a more comfortable large house with an immaculately kept lawn and three little dogs created the classic backdrop for Nate's and Elliot's attendance at the Philips Andover prep school, less than an hour away.

Ronald adjusted his intellectual orientation to take advantage of the rapidly changing developments in the energy software field. He worked in several companies until he became Marketing Director of Aspen Technology, a company producing software that enables oil producing companies improve their refining process. He wrote articles published in German, Russian and some languages he may not have been able to read. They were intended for his extremely diverse clients in distant parts of this shrinking globe. He frequently travels not only to all parts of Europe but also to the Middle and Far East. He does not share my worry about dangers lurking in unstable regions; after all, I had set an example of traveling to Africa and behind the Iron Curtain when he was a kid. As fathers do…

Meanwhile Ariela with a degree in accounting created tax return computer programs for a number of states in the U.S. In the months leading to the federal income tax return deadline she helps prepare tax returns at an H & R Block office. Ronald's and Ariela's professional responsibilities however have never detracted from their many family responsibilities, especially their support for their kids and their parents.

Nate reminds me of the constantly shrinking distances. When I attended Elliot's graduation at Bowdoin College a few years ago in Brunswick, Maine Nate joined us taking a Memorial Day Weekend leave from his job overseeing an oil rig in Alaska. Nate's girl friend, Sarah, also joined us. She flew in from Houston, Texas. Elliot's girl friend Monika a Bowdoin student was about to fly home for the summer to Buffalo, N.Y. to enjoy jumping her horse over artificial barriers. I did not even ask my son Ronald which trade convention in Europe, the Middle or Far East was next on his calendar. What a difference from my father's first train ride a century earlier where he threw up and my first air plane flight when I was 14 and refused the flight attendant's offer of a bag to vomit in case I got sick. But my grandson's crossing the North American continent from Alaska to Maine with a side trip to Texas and returning to his job in four days made me feel that the globe was shrinking too fast.

A few years ago I e-mailed Nate wishes for his birthday and in less than 24 hours I received his answer from his home in Alaska where he works for Schlumberger, an international company that provides technical scientific advice to oil drilling teams. He got that job a couple of years ago after graduating from Princeton with a degree in environmental engineering. I had asked him not quite seriously, "If you had been giving scientific advice to those working on the BP oil rig off New Orleans, could you have prevented whatever led to that disaster?" He apparently took my question quite seriously and answered, "in the Gulf of Mexico incident, not all the details are clear, but it does not quite seem like something that I would have been able to help with, but it is CLOSE to the type of incident I am trained to help prevent. It seems like a big part of the issue was them not thinking this was an option, because they thought they had covered the sensitive areas with cement and [there were] also mechanical problems in the system they use to fight this type 'of well-control' incident".

With travel so easy the danger of rootlessness increases. It was therefore quite appropriate that the speakers at Elliot's commencement stressed the connection between Bowdoin's Ivy College character and the local community in the state of Maine. For our family the connection was made real by gorging on stuffed lobsters caught off the coast of Maine. They were served by the College in a huge tent, and later supplemented by us at a strangely named outstanding restaurant, the Muddy Rudder. Some of us were fussier than the rest, but we all managed to crack the huge red shells.

While listening to the commencement speakers my thoughts turned to earlier visits to Maine: Camp Androscoggin when I was 15 and Pemaquid in 1951 when Audrey, Elliot's grandmother, and I spent our honeymoon in a small ideally located house overlooking the rocks at Pemaquid Point that give the Maine coast its wild distinct character.

It gave me a great deal of joy and pleasure to attend my grandsons' commencements at Princeton and Bowdoin. I had planned to hear more about their college experiences. Elliot introduced me to his favorite teachers in the German department. The German professors had wonderful things to say about Elliot, but the opportunities for discussion were all too few. I was also quick to realize that grandfathers have to take a secondary role behind the much more important developing relations between grandson and his girl friend Monika. Following his graduation, Elliot started his career as a teacher of math, German and a coach of squash and other sports at Loomis Chaffee, a prep school in Windsor, less than an hour from Storrs.

***

Nate and Elliot had weddings a year and five months apart, Nate in Louisiana and Elliot in Connecticut. They were quite different but equally impressive and remain permanently imbedded in my mind.

When we reached Lafayette Square in New Orleans on Saturday March 15, 2014, about an hour before Nate's scheduled wedding, a small crew unloaded folding chairs and set them up to prepare the park for the planned festivities. As the first guests trickled in I surveyed the area and was fascinated by a prominent statue of Henry Clay. What was he doing here? I thought he was from Kentucky and spent his time more than a century and a half ago seeking the presidency in Washington, D.C. There was also an impressive Federal Reserve Building facing the Square. It was Lafayette Square in the Central Business District, a few blocks from the French Quarter, that my 31 year old grandson Nate and his fiancée Sarah had chosen as the location to tie their wedding knot. Quite some distance from Anchorage, Alaska.

The seats soon filled with people, young and old, formal and informal, conversing in accents covering all sections of the United States. Ina Ruth and I had been told that we were to lead the procession of the wedding participants. After all, I was the oldest grandfather, my 90th birthday having occurred six weeks earlier. A bagpiper properly dressed in his Scottish outfit led the procession. We followed at a respectable distance. Behind us were Sarah's paternal and maternal grandparents, the couple's parents and brothers. Finally with much excitement Nate stepped on the platform to await his bride. Dressed in a beautiful long white wedding dress, Sarah smiled and joined Nate, facing him. She was flanked by six exceptionally well dressed bridesmaids, while Nate had his brother Elliot and six groom mates wearing fancy vests on his side.

The night before, the fancy restaurant *Galatoire's* on Bourbon Street in the French Quarter was the location for a Rehearsal Dinner that had given us an opportunity to meet and talk with some of the relatives and friends who had traveled from all over the U.S. to attend the wedding. We had been seated at a table reserved for the six grandparents. Sarah's paternal grandfather, sitting next to me, gave me a fascinating account of his rise from a laborer fixing gas pipes in the streets of Pittsburgh to ultimately managing that city's gas company until retiring to enjoy the climate and citrus fruit of Florida. He traced his ancestry to the "Boot of Italy". Sarah's maternal grandfather and mother were descendants of Cajuns living in Louisiana. Donna Colosimo, Sarah's mother, had been involved in a serious car accident a couple of years ago and was confined to a wheelchair at the dinner but managed to walk supported by her brothers at the wedding procession.

My son, Ronald, and Robert, Sarah's father, painted humorous vignettes of key events that had shaped the bride and bride groom's personalities. Nate had spent five critical years as a teenager in Holland, shifting from English to Dutch almost overnight. Back in Boston's suburbs, he had no trouble adjusting to the somewhat fancy Andover Phillips prep school atmosphere. Environmental engineering at Princeton prepared him for a career providing technical advice to oil companies that help monitor their drilling operations. Off the northern coast of Alaska he practiced his newly acquired skill. On a visit to his company's headquarters in Houston, Texas, he met Sarah. They connected immediately, but Sarah, unlike many in a similar situation, was not one to make a hasty decision. She continued her career of genetic counseling in

Houston. After a couple of years she decided to join Nate in Anchorage and shifted the location of her genetic counseling practice to be closer to him, not far from the Arctic Circle. In 2013 Nate introduced her to his friends on the East Coast. They visited us in Storrs and Nate showed her the town where his father had grown up. Having completed their preparations, Nate and Sarah were ready to embark on a joint permanent venture. Plans for the wedding followed.

At the tables of the *Galatoire's*, laughter, noisy jokes and reminiscences enhanced the festive atmosphere of the evening There were a lot of friends Nate and Sarah had made since their adolescence, in Nate's case from his years as a wilderness canoe camp counselor in a northern Ontario, to his college years at Princeton. There was so much talk and laughter that the extremely well prepared Cajun food was almost ignored. We hoped the chef was not insulted. On our way to catch a taxi to take us to our hotel, we could not help but notice that Bourbon Street at night seemed to attract tourists looking for pleasures of a less sophisticated sort than we had enjoyed at our restaurant.

On Lafayette Square with the bride and groom waiting for the moment when their six year long preparation would finally help them start a new venture, a friendly looking man who had been standing unobtrusively on the platform, stepped up and assumed his role to officiate at the ceremony. Was he a clergyman, justice of the peace or some other official? The program, distributed by a very young boy from a basket that made him look even smaller, only stated that John Zimmer would officiate at the ceremony. He explained in some detail the purpose of the occasion and the outstanding qualities the bride and groom possessed and how this ceremony would enhance their happiness and, most importantly, the value and significance of their joint undertaking. Then suddenly one of the groom mates flanking Nate fell over, like a piece on a chessboard. Mr. Zimmer stopped in the middle of a sentence. Those closest to the fallen groom mate gently moved him a few feet off the platform and surrounded him protectively. We heard a voice say that a doctor up front was on the scene. Then someone else assured us this was not serious. The individual had a condition that had him keel over frequently with no serious consequences. Indeed he resumed his upright position, a few feet further away from the groom. Mr. Zimmer, the bride and groom returned to their respective positions and the ceremony resumed.

This was the moment. Nate and Sarah exchanged wedding vows. Elliot gave the ring to his brother who placed it on Sarah's finger. The couple was officially declared husband and wife. Mr. Zimmer stepped back looking for something. He found the egg-shaped glass container which he handed ceremoniously to Nate who following the Jewish tradition stepped on it. That symbolized the prospect of another generation of Becks.

My grandson and Sarah were now married: the celebrations could begin. We were scheduled to walk several blocks to reach the Foundry where we would have cocktails, light refreshments, a live jazz band and a chance to dance and celebrate in a Cajun atmosphere. As we prepared to start our walk, a brass band assembled on the street facing Lafayette Square. It is only then that I realized that the "walk" was really a parade. Ina Ruth and other guests, not happy to walk an unspecified distance were given a chance to ride in two-seat vehicles driven by smiling pedaling chauffeurs. White cloth pieces were distributed with the motto: *Laissez Les Bons Temps Rouler! New Orleans, Louisiana* (Let the Good Times Roll! New Orleans Louisiana) The brass band aroused everybody's attention and slowly led the nearly two hundred celebrants along St. Charles Avenue and St Joseph Street to the Foundry. Two city policemen on motorcycles with blinking red lights stopped all traffic at each intersection to let our parade proceed uninterruptedly. As we passed shops and apartment buildings, people came to their windows, opened their doors, sat on their front steps and took our picture. We waved our white cloth slogan, *Laissez Les Bons Temps Rouler!* We were in Cajun territory. This was the very first parade in my ninety years that I ever participated in. I truly enjoyed the experience. Not too many blocks separated us from St. Patrick Day parades that same day. Nate's maternal great grandfather Reilly would have been in that parade.

The jazz band at the Foundry encouraged couples of all ages to dance. Nate and Sarah led the way, followed by Ronald and Ariela. The music, laughter and shouts made normal conversations difficult. There was again excellent Cajun food to violate my dietary rules. It was fun to talk with many old and new friends. After thanking Nate and Sarah for giving us this wonderful opportunity to break our routine and have some unusual experiences and fun we left the celebrating crowd at 9 o'clock to recover at our hotel.

Before leaving New Orleans, Ina Ruth and I explored the Board Walk along the Mississippi. We watched large container ships; oil tankers and barges navigate the river that flows from the Midwest to the Gulf of Mexico. How far my family has traveled: from Berlin and Plzeň to the heart of America! The teachers in my French high school in Prague had stressed France's important role in North America's history, something that came back to my memory in full force at the wedding of my grandson!

In January 2017, less than three years after the wedding, Nate and Sarah became the parents of twins, a girl Piper and a boy Portland. While born prematurely their parents took them to the mountains in the Wild West in their first year and to a Thanksgiving dinner in Connecticut where I had the wonderful opportunity to meet a new generation of Becks whose connection with their European ancestors is already somewhat remote. Time passes too quickly!

***

Seventeen months later Elliot, three years younger than his brother, got married in Portland, Connecticut, less than an hour's drive from our home. Elliot and his bride Monica chose Saint Clements Castle as the setting for the formal start of their joint lives. The castle was built at the end of the 19th century by a wealthy entrepreneur who modeled his architectural design on a European castle. Saint Clements location is impressive. It is near the edge of a forest clad hill dropping more than a hundred feet to the Connecticut River below. Looking at the river winding its way peacefully around a curve along the green forested slopes with nary house in sight, creates a sense of privacy. A true oasis in an otherwise densely populated region. The carefully manicured lawns that surround Saint Clements enhance its resemblance to a European castle, except for the inevitable large parking areas that could not be tucked away behind some trees.

When it was time for the ceremony to start the many guests began a five minute walk from the air conditioned hall of the castle to rows of chairs that filled a quadrangular lawn several steps below the level of the surrounding park. Neither trees nor clouds protected us from the scorching rays of the August sun. Three string players created the perfect musical background for the occasion as we chose our seats. Ina Ruth and I picked the second row enabling us to hear everything that was said a few feet in front of us. We were handed a small fan which helped me reduce the temperature of my face by perhaps a degree or two. It took a little while for me to realize that the fan also was intended to serve as a guide to the program of the festivities. Its tiny script listed the names of the principal wedding participants and their relatives.

When the musicians gave us the clue to pay attention, we turned our heads to the castle where the bridesmaids, groomsmen, Best Man, Maid of Honor and finally Elliot and elegantly dressed Monica began the procession. They walked slowly to the raised platform. Jake Smith, ready to officiate at the ceremony, awaited their arrival. The introductory readings created a very appropriate mood for the occasion. I was impressed how the brief accounts of episodes in the lives of bride and groom not only set the stage for the main event but also had me reflect and put me in a quasi-religious mood seated in a meadow under a cloudless sky, a far cry from the confined space of a cathedral or synagogue.

There was an unusual step in the program leading up to the exchange of vows. Monica and Elliot ceremoniously shared a drink from the *German Wedding Cup.* As explained on the fan/program this Wedding Cup, according a centuries old German legend, was created by a young goldsmith (Elliot's maternal grandfather's name: Goldschmidt!) who, in order to be permitted to wed his bride, had to create a cup out of which both could drink simultaneously. Monica and Elliot had indeed an odd looking cup-like contraption out of which they extracted some liquid at almost the same time, Elliot from the top and Monica from an opening at the bottom of the cup. This act struck me as a very appropriately humorous introduction to the main event.

Elliot had met Monica at Bowdoin in Maine when he was an upper class student and she a freshman. They both played squash and Monica also rode a horse, a skill she had acquired at her home near Buffalo, New York. Elliot and Monica were great communicators leading Elliot into a very successful teaching career at Loomis Chaffee, a prep school in Windsor, Connecticut and Monica into insurance industry public relations. Their college romance continued in spite of several years of geographical separation while Elliot started his teaching career and Monica completed her graduation requirements at Bowdoin. They had waited a long time to reach this opportunity to exchange their vows, rings and kisses on the lawn at Saint Clemens Castle and seal their relationship starting a new chapter.

To the accompaniment of the string players' music the newly-wedded pair led the procession back to the Castle. Cocktails and Dinner in the air-conditioned Great Ballroom followed. Ina Ruth and I shared a table with friends and relatives of the groom and bride as we also did the previous evening at the couple's wedding rehearsal dinner. A Polish ancestry can easily be deduced from Monica's last name Wlodarczyk. It was her grandfather who had immigrated to the United States. Her father who is involved in steel industry related operations in the New York's Buffalo region gave us an amusing account of Monica's youth. I assume that it is from her mother's Irish ancestry that Monica derives her communicative skills.

There were no embarrassing silences around the dinner table. Quite the contrary, it was difficult to get in a word in the sometime serious and more often funny conversation with Elliot's fellow teachers at Loomis Chaffee, Monica's younger sister and the many other family members and friends.

As the dinner progressed the music from a modern dance band gathered intensity and rose by several decibels encouraging the guests to join Monica and Elliot on the dance floor. Ronald dancing with Ariela expressed his excitement and good mood about the wedding by dancing as intensely as he played squash. As a nonagenarian married to an octogenarian I was impressed by the intense activities on the dance floor but not prepared to join the fray. The music reverberated in my eardrums and interfered with any attempt to understand anything that Ina Ruth sitting next to me was trying to say. Suddenly a lady not quite my age came to my chair and requested that I dance with her. She rejected my statement that I am not a dancer. She said something about knowing me for a long time. She also rejected my statement that my memory was not so good any more. Somehow she got me to the dance floor, grabbed me and we started to follow the beat. I managed to flow with the music and crowd. She tried to convince me that I was a great dancer. Finally I managed to excuse myself and return to my seat. I was somewhat surprised and even flattered that at this late stage in my life I would be asked to dance, an activity that I was reluctant to engage in when decades younger.

The dancing continued as the music sound level rose several decibels. We were surprised when the waiters suddenly reappeared and served us cake and coffee. It was getting late and I convinced Ina Ruth that we had to go home. We said good bye to the newly-weds and wished them a wonderful honeymoon on the island of St Lucia in the Caribbean. It took some time to thank everybody for making the occasion such a wonderful event before we managed to start on our way back home.

The atmosphere at Saint Clements Castle could not have been more different from

The one in Lafayette Square in New Orleans, yet both weddings were equally impressive. Surrounded by excitement, fun, music, dance and relatives, friends young and old, eating delicious food and drinking wine and other alcoholic beverages the solemn nature of the occasion was not lost: My two very bright grandsons joined partners to help them navigate the challenging obstacles of an ever more complicated world. They both chose partners from diverse backgrounds improving their understanding of society and broadening their outlook on the world. In the increasingly global community it is important not to be confined to narrow ethnic or religious groupings.

Chapter 33
Concerns at the Journey's End

More than eighty years have passed since Hindenburg appointed Hitler chancellor of Germany forcing us to leave Berlin, my Wannsee garden and the chestnut trees I was so proud to have planted. Now in my nineties I am getting rid of branches that a storm has torn from tall oak and pine trees and dumped within sight of my study in Storrs at the edge of a mostly undisturbed old forest. There are no chestnut trees here and my Wannsee giant poplar tree has no comparable solitary tall oak tree inviting a lightning strike. Digging up the weeds among the irises, roses and carnations in front of the stone wall that I built some three decades ago, keeps me in touch with the earth. When I turn over the soil, mow the lawn, rake the leaves, rearrange the flowers and replace stone markers along the driveway, I feel the strong pull that "working in the garden" has played in my entire life in Berlin, Prague and Storrs. Aware of the distinct features of each location, there is something that encourages me to shovel the earth, move rocks and plant flowers wherever I happen to be. Growing deep roots in Storrs has helped keeping my confidence in a turbulent world.

While garden tasks have changed little, other aspects of my life have been altered significantly. My favorite house maid and childhood companion Trudi and her successors have long been replaced by electrically driven dishwashers, laundry machines and cloth driers. Ina Ruth and I enjoy preparing our meals with no assistance. Our main task is to remember that half an hour ago we put our dinner into the microwave oven for an intended four and a half minutes. Stand up showers have replaced sleep inducing bath tubs. My mother who spent most of her life typing laboriously my father's manuscripts as well as her own articles and books on a portable pre World War II Swiss typewriter, could not have imagined my using a keyboard to transmit my thoughts directly to a computer and laser jet printer. Although I can and occasionally do get the latest news on my computer screen I have not abandoned the habit of reading *The New York Times* every day, a pattern that started with the *Vossische Zeitung* in Berlin, continued with the *Prager Tagblatt* in Prague, *The New York Herald Tribune* when we first arrived in New York. My love affair with the woodstove next to my study may be a vestige of my romantic attachment to the coal stoves in our Wannsee house.

Beyond our home the world has changed even more dramatically. Horse-drawn vehicles were nearing their last run when I began paying attention to traffic in our Berlin neighborhood. My first grade teacher had taken us to a blacksmith who repaired and attached horse shoes. This, the teacher told us, was an important job even though the blacksmith was one of the few horse shoe repairers left. I also remember watching horses suffer as drivers hit them hard to keep them pulling the wagons loaded with bricks up the highway rising steeply below our house in Prague. Now giant trucks fitted with engines that produce enormous horse power and speed frequently tail me on Interstate 84. They frighten me, which the horses on the highway in Prague never did. Another big change: movies I watched on a screen in a theater not far from my school in Prague on special occasions are now on our own TV where I can follow them much better because pictures are clearer, in color; the action more realistic.

Perhaps the greatest change is the shrinkage of distance. The question no longer is how many time zones separate Prague from New York, but whether I want to get in touch with X instantly via internet or spend an hour waiting to pass the airport security checkpoint to fly and see him/her in a several hours. It is difficult for me to recall that it took ten days in 1938 for the Veendam to cross the Atlantic. In the second decade of the 21st century I watch events as they occur around the globe on the evening television news in my living room. The world has shrunk so that the term globalism no longer refers to countries beyond the horizon on the other side of our planet. Instead globalism now suggests that we are interconnected and reachable wherever we are. Shrinkage of distances enables me to eat fresh blueberries picked in Chile when snow covers the bushes here in New England. I wear clothing stitched in Bangladesh because their garment industry workers do a good job fast and cheap. Obvious problems such as insuring that product quality standards and worker safety and living standards are maintained require attention and can be dealt with through international agreements. These enormous improvements in living conditions and global cohesiveness encourage my optimistic approach to life.

An optimist, when after leaving Czechoslovakia, I reached a new continent where life turned out to be quite interesting and exciting. Optimism served me well when I had to learn to adjust to constantly changing circumstances. It also helped me in the crises confronting me in my academic, political and family life. My optimistic perspective was useful in dealing with the doomsday predictions by politicians and Neo-con Cold War foreign policy ideologues. It is only after Brexit and the election of Donald Trump that I am reminded of the world I thought I had left behind when I boarded the Veendam. I fear that some of the horrors of the past are waiting to pounce on us again because we have failed to learn from our mistakes and, more importantly, some of the fundamental obstacles to a better functioning global society pose increasingly difficult challenges.

There is the challenge posed by not being prepared for our tightening global coexistence. Instant global communication, especially visual exposure to events anywhere on the globe, places us all in one stadium where we can watch the same play while realizing that our neighbors look and act quite differently from us. We do not like the way they look, act or speak and so we attack them. Instant global intercommunication facilitates conflicts in the Middle East, Africa, the Ukraine and elsewhere. Global communication enables people in less developed areas to observe big contrasts in standards of living. Inequality is now not only an intellectual topic of conversation but an observable reality disturbing the many on the wrong side of the divide. It is inevitable that viewers in the less developed countries of Africa, Asia and Central America look at their apps and envy the much greater opportunities that Europeans and we in America, in the more fortunate parts of the globe enjoy. It should not come as a surprise that the less advantaged pull up stakes and migrate to seek the Golden Grail or at least something resembling the pictures they saw on their apps. They are joined by citizens of countries torn apart by domestic and foreign conflicts. Why should anybody be surprised that "progress" has destabilized our shrinking global community?

While idealists see in global proximity an opportunity for international harmony, they should have foreseen that proximity also intensifies conflicts among ethnically, religiously and culturally diverse people. As they look at their new neighbors they cannot help become aware that not everybody shares their values and forms of behavior. Most groups prefer to further their own interests over those of others. The existing state system often does not reflect the boundaries of those only recently made aware of their linguistic, religious and historic identity. Existing internationally recognized boundaries resulted from decisions made in the past by powers that no longer dominate the globe. Will Iraq disintegrate into Sunni, Shiite and Kurdish independent units? Will Turkey hold on to Kurdistan; Spain to Catalonia; The United Kingdom to Scotland and Wales; Nigeria to its northern Moslem provinces?

In the interwar era Czechoslovakia had emerged from the Habsburg Empire only six years before my birth. I believed it would last a long time. I certainly did not expect it to be dismembered in 1938 shortly after I left. Nor that it would be occupied and reduced to the status of a Soviet satellite before finally regaining its pre-war status in 1989. Three years later by its own will, it split into two states, the Czech Republic and Slovakia. Many new countries were born in the last century. The United Nations quadrupled its membership since its creation in 1945. In spite of such frequent changes in the global community we assume that current independent states will remain permanent members of the community of sovereign states. This has raised serious doubts about our ability to transition from the international order antedating the birth of the global society to our current collection of newly assertive cultural, religious entities. It seems unlikely that continued progress in our capacity to increase our knowledge and raise our standard of living can take place in an environment free of often violent intercultural turbulence.

I am also very concerned that we are and will continue to be unable to narrow our economic divide. A century and a half ago Karl Marx based his ideology on the wide gap between the wealthy and the poor. In his day it was just a theory and a gap that pales by comparison with the present one. Attempted solutions such as Stalin's agricultural collectivization and state operated industries; Franklin Delano Roosevelt's resort to a progressive income tax employed by most democratic countries; President Reagan's admonition that helping the wealthy will raise the tide for all; Pope Francis admonition to concern ourselves with the fate of the poor, all have failed to create a fairer distribution of wealth. Periodic economic hick-ups force us to pay attention to potentially explosive reactions to this ever present existential problem.

I am also disappointed that we have made only very limited progress in treating people as equals, regardless of their racial and religious background. Racism is not driven by the existence of human diversity but by the assertion that my racial background is better than yours and that therefore I am entitled to be treated better than you. Racism and the concept that we are all equal are incompatible. I recall vividly that my father, who had written articles repudiating the Nazi doctrine of Aryan racial superiority while still in Czechoslovakia, was shocked that the America that welcomed us tolerated extremely serious practices of racial inequality, not only below the Mason-Dixon Line but in the rest of the U.S. The consequences of slavery are still with us. The fact that advocates of the superiority of people of white European racial background have re-emerged from the bin of history in the 2016 presidential election campaign terrifies me. They even are reported to have raised their arms and shouted something that reminds me of the Nazi salute to Adolf Hitler. Apparently I cannot escape the nightmares of the past.

When I was six in Berlin I had witnessed the collapse of democracy. It was not only the excited conversations between my parents and guests that I overheard when I was supposed to fall asleep, but swastikas and hammer and sickle advertisements posted outdoors wherever there was space. There were noisy crowds even in our upscale suburban neighborhood. I shall never forget the comment by our Physical Education teacher who compared the name of the head of the government, Schleicher (one who slithers), to that of a snake. The economy had collapsed and construction that I had watched on our trips to my grandfather's house in Berlin had come to a complete standstill with trees growing on the unfinished balconies. At my early age I sensed that the normal world around me was collapsing. One must remember that Hitler was appointed chancellor to restore the economy. The lesson that a breakdown of a democratic government and the resulting chaos and misery may encourage otherwise sensible people to turn over leadership to untried potentially dangerous extremists has always stayed with me.

I fear that the revolution in communication has created nearly insurmountable difficulties for democracies to achieve the objective of reaching consensus on the critical issues that affect powerful interest groups. Modern advertising techniques easily overpower the search for rational solutions that benefit a majority of the population. Given the fact that nearly unlimited funds are available for special interests which can control the media to frame the popular discourse, the prospects for sound objective decision making in contemporary democracies are dim. Shrinkage of distances enables almost anybody to watch activities in what used to be distant lands and facilitates greater popular interaction. At the same time it makes individuals more aware of differences that often lead to a defensive attitude of wanting to protect one's own group, i.e. excessive patriotism and nationalism. I hope that my great-grandchildren Piper and Portland will not have to cope with some resurrected ghost of the "leaders" who precipitated World War II.

Brexit, Alt-right, European right wing nationalist parties all have risen in response to large scale populist fears about economic security. They challenge a peaceful transition to an integrated global community. They are the nightmares of the past. I hope that they are only hiccups on the path to a better future.

International relations is a field that always interested me and to which I devoted my academic life. It is a discipline with relatively few basic changes since the 1930's. Some of the main actors have departed, new ones have taken their place, the scenery has shifted, but serious conflicts remain unresolved and the ideal of a peaceful secure world free from threats of nuclear annihilation is still beyond our grasp.

I am especially concerned that we have not benefitted from advances in communication enabling us to be better informed about conflicts anywhere on the globe. We spend too little energy familiarizing ourselves with areas affecting our national interest. In the State Department Research Division on Eastern Europe, most of my colleagues came from the country they were assigned to cover. Why were there so few U.S. born experts? Our current involvement in the Middle East suggests that this has not changed. We continue to be uninformed and surprised about political developments in almost every country in which we have gotten ourselves involved.

I often ask myself whether I aroused enough interest in world affairs in the minds of the students who were enrolled in my courses in international diplomacy. My hope had been to encourage them to become foreign policy experts and advisers to those who conduct our foreign policy. Having spent most of my life following events in lands far beyond our borders I failed to realize how few shared my interest. I continue to be disappointed that public discussion of major world problems often lack depth, understanding and familiarity with underlying issues. Causes of past policy failures are ignored and lessons not learned.

To cheer me up and help me regain some optimism I shall go outside, water the plants and split some wood so that my woodstove can keep me comfortable. Nature is so relaxing and I hope will keep me from having to worry about politicians making serious mistakes that might force Piper and Portland relive the horrors of their ancestors.

Chapter 34
Final Destination

I have spent most of my life in Storrs, on what used to be the safer side of the Atlantic. It was a chosen destination, not just a residence of chance. It will likely be my final stop and the Storrs Cemetery my resting place. That thought led me on a tour of nostalgia to the well kept grounds marked with gravestones large and small.

When our kids were young, Audrey and I took them often on a ride to cemetery hill to admire the view of the campus from the turnaround circle at the top. A panorama of red brick structures amidst green lawns stretched below us far into the distance. Ronald and Meredith were excited by the smokestacks of the heating plants dwarfing the neighboring modest campus buildings. Opposite the cemetery entrance, were the temporary "Oil Can Row Apartments" where Audrey and I spent the first year of our marriage. As UCONN grew these temporary World War II modest faculty apartment buildings were replaced by tall modern science and engineering structures. The panorama that attracted us in the 1950's has been transformed into an array of rooftops capped by exhaust pipes of laboratory buildings meeting the requirements for safe and sophisticated scientific research experiments.

At the outer edge of the campus, the New Storrs Cemetery was originally the burial ground of the Storrs family who had given their land to the state for a college, the seed of UCONN. Their tombs, at the top of the hill, are marked by a tall monument erected by Charles Storrs in 1864, twenty years before his death in Brooklyn, New York. Having made his living in the big city he chose to rest in peace in the rural paradise where he had grown up. The cemetery hill was a perfect location for Charles and his family from which to view the college in its infancy and early development.

The contrast between the past and the present is most apparent at the very top of the hill. The latest up-to-date telecommunication towers dwarf the monuments honoring the Founding family. Their steadily blinking eyes warn errant planes not to come too close. Dormitories, dating back to the 1950's, have encroached upon the peaceful land, pulling the cemetery closer to the campus. Its darkness at night enables students to conduct their intimate social relationships undisturbed. Unfortunately nighttime darkness has enabled some individuals to vent their frustrations by overturning tombstones.

Impressive headstones have the names of my colleagues, deans and provosts who may or may not have given me my expected pay raises and shaped my academic career. The size of the stones reflecting their ambitions and pride matter little to me now; they are all buried underground. Well known names of town residents have joined them. I am amazed how many names I recognize. I suppose that happens if one lives in one town for more than 65 years. Not very far from the upper section there is now a headstone marking the final resting place of Audrey buried there in 1983. Her parents and Meredith are resting next to her.

Closer to the Storrs family, near the top of the hill, I noticed the other day the easily overlooked headstone marking the graves of George McReynolds and his wife Miriam. I regret that I do not recall noticing them in the past. It was after all McReynolds who had played such a very important role at a crucial stage in my life when I had passed my PhD oral and chosen the topic of my dissertation. I had reached the threshold leading to a teaching career. At this critical juncture I met George McReynolds who led me to Storrs and opened the door to the rest of my life's ventures.

From McReynolds grave stone viewing the campus dramatizes the transformation that UCONN has undergone this past century. When in 1949 I proudly drove Arthur, my long-term family friend, to Storrs to show him the campus where I was about to teach, he asked, after we had crossed the entire campus, "Where is Storrs, are we there yet?" I had a difficult time convincing him, the typical wise guy Berliner, that Storrs was not some lost village in Connecticut's Quiet Corner, but a growing university community. If Arthur were still alive I would proudly show him that my confidence in the potential growth and development of an incipient academic institution was justified, in fact more than I could possibly have imagined.

What about the challenge to reorient American attitudes to foreign affairs so that the failures of early 20th century U.S. foreign policy would not be repeated? Has enough been done to raise the public's understanding of crucial issues essential for peacefully coexisting in a shrinking global community? Are George

McReynolds and my hopes for mutual respect regardless of a person's skin color or religious beliefs closer to fulfillment? Judging from statements made by prominent public officials that are met with applause, the level of understanding crucial issues affecting our future has changed little over the last 75 years.

We thought we had learned to handle international conflicts through diplomacy

Unfortunately we have not bridged the gap between doing what is logical and what the instinct of the masses in a democracy desires. We have not resolved the problem of educating the people (vast majority) so that they have enough information to use judgment in making critical decisions to avoid catastrophes.

I had better stop before losing all my optimism. I can probably deliver much better lectures on world affairs from my future residence in Storrs Cemetery. I hope some earthworms and grasshoppers will restore my optimism.

www.ingramcontent.com/pod-product-compliance
Lightning Source LLC
Chambersburg PA
CBHW031229090426
42742CB00007B/131
* 9 7 8 0 9 8 9 1 9 9 4 6 9 *